noah's
three sons

VOLUME I: THE DOORWAY PAPERS

noah's three sons

Human History in Three Dimensions

ARTHUR C. CUSTANCE

ZONDERVAN
PUBLISHING HOUSE   OF THE ZONDERVAN CORPORATION
GRAND RAPIDS, MICHIGAN 49506

NOAH'S THREE SONS

The Doorway Papers, Volume One

PREFACE

This volume contains five papers selected from a series of sixty published by the author under the general title DOORWAY PAPERS, over a period of some fifteen years from 1957 to 1973.

The first paper sets forth the basic concept that from the three sons of Noah have arisen three divisions of the human race which, even at this time, can still be sorted out and identified with a measure of certainty. Furthermore, each branch has made a unique contribution in the course of human history, a contribution for which each seems to have been divinely prepared. The second paper is a somewhat detailed analysis of the Table of Nations in Genesis 10, to establish the validity of this three-fold division. The third paper is a very short treatment of a problem passage in Genesis 9 which has a direct bearing on the theme of this volume. The fourth paper is a very fully documented validation of a particular claim made for one branch of the race which, at first sight, must seem to be totally without foundation, but upon more careful analysis turns out to be the most easily established of all. And the final paper is an exploration of the broader implications of the thesis, with some thought given to the underlying causes (linguistic, cultural, etc.) that have led each branch to *continue* making its unique contribution throughout history.

It should be borne in mind by the reader that each of these papers was originally published separately and therefore there is some repetition.

It is tempting to ignore the notes except to establish a source of information for a particularly interesting piece of information. But the notes in this volume, totaling more than seven hundred, are something more than merely a bibliography. They are a reservoir of further ideas which bear upon the papers, but which — had they been introduced into the text itself — would have disrupted the immediate flow of thought. If the papers are read through without referring to the call numbers, I believe it will still pay the reader to glance at the notes at the foot of each page.

ACKNOWLEDGMENTS

To two tremendous people.

To Dr. John R. Howitt of Toronto, a kind and generous friend of over forty years, I owe an enormous debt for constant encouragement and unending generosity in supplying so much of the material upon which this research has been based.

And to Evelyn M. White, who has for twenty years been an unfailing co-worker, taking all my dictation, doing most of the typing, handling much of a worldwide correspondence, and serving as the gentlest but most faithful critic any author ever had.

Many others have helped in countless ways for which I am indeed grateful. To these I can only say thank you, in the name of the Lord Jesus Christ, who is not unmindful of all your labors of love in His name.

CONTENTS

PART I

THE PART PLAYED BY SHEM, HAM, AND JAPHETH IN SUBSEQUENT WORLD HISTORY

PART II

A STUDY OF THE NAMES IN GENESIS 10

PART III

WHY NOAH CURSED CANAAN INSTEAD OF HAM: A NEW APPROACH TO AN OLD PROBLEM

PART IV

THE TECHNOLOGY OF HAMITIC PEOPLE

PART V

A CHRISTIAN WORLD VIEW: THE FRAMEWORK OF HISTORY

PART I

The Part Played by Shem, Ham, and Japheth in Subsequent World History

GENERAL INTRODUCTION

THIS STUDY was begun in 1938. It started with one of those incidental observations that occasionally end up proving exceptionally fruitful. Some fifteen years later the material had more or less become organized into a tentative philosophy of history. Shortly afterwards it was presented as a paper to a Scientific Affiliation in the United States. Its fate was swift and terrible to behold.

Probably it deserved it at the time. But it was not the basic idea that was faulty. It was the presentation which suffered because the author lacked formal training in certain fields that figure prominently in the thesis. This I believe has now been corrected, and a fresh attempt to communicate the central idea seems justified. One of the main stumbling blocks to early acceptance has been thoroughly swept away by subsequent research. In fact, the Canadian Government was sufficiently impressed by the evidence to undertake to publish for internal use a 250-page report on the matter,[1] which was then supplied to a number of their research laboratories.

The thesis contains a simple concept, the kind of concept which is either beautifully true and correspondingly useful, or is bound to become self-evidently false and will simply die a natural death. Every year supplies new evidence for the essential truthfulness of it. Yet even if it should, after all, prove to be mistaken, it can still be of real value as a working hypothesis. It is not so much false theory as mistaken observation of fact that is dangerous. Dr. A. Lewis[2] observed that history is filled

---

[1] Custance, A. C., printed by the Government under the title, "Does Science Transcend Culture?", 1958.

[2] Lewis, Aubrey, Prof. of Psychiatry, Univ. of London, in *The Lancet,* Jan. 25, 1958, p. 171. He even quotes De Morgan as saying, "Wrong hypotheses, rightly worked, have produced more useful results than unguided observations." E. R. Leach, "Primitive Time Reckoning," Vol. 1 of *A History of Technology,* Oxford, 1954, p. 111, gives an excellent illustration.

with instances where false theories proved fruitful because they stimulated the imagination of competent people, who were then led to undertake further research and purify the concept.

Now, it is obvious that in such a wide ranging thesis as this turns out to be, there are bound to be some errors in basic information, and personal bias is almost certain to have colored the selection of data, as well as their interpretation. Nevertheless, while personal factors are unavoidable, a very serious effort has been made to keep close to the facts. Yet certain problems presented themselves from the start, especially in the matter of terminology. For example, it seems logical to call the descendants of Ham *Hamites*, as the descendants of Shem are called *Shemites*. But the term *Hamitic* has come to be applied by anthropologists and ethnologists in a rather restricted way to a group of people which it seems evident from Genesis 10 by no means now represents all the nations that can with some justification be traced back to Ham. So I have to remind the reader that I am reverting, in my use of the terms Hamite and Hamitic, to their older and strictly biblical meaning.

A second problem arises from the current confusion of technology with science, a confusion which I feel has been very detrimental to our understanding of the nature of each. James B. Conant has dealt excellently with this in his little book *On Understanding Science*,[3] and many other writers have underscored the fundamental distinction between the two areas of human endeavor. Technology is directed towards the solution of specific problems: what has been aptly termed "mission oriented." Science, by contrast, is ideally concerned only with understanding the laws of nature, understanding for its own sake rather than to make use of nature. Technology is often a spin-off from scientific endeavor, but technology existed for centuries and became highly developed in some countries where science in the pure sense was not only of no interest, but was essentially unknown at all. The Hamitic people have all been, virtually without exception, technologically oriented and extremely adept, whether highly civilized or very primitive. Japhethites, or Indo-Europeans, have essentially carried the torch of pure science.

The reader is urged to keep this distinction between technology, which is applied to practical ends, and science, which is

---

[3] Conant, James B., *On Understanding Science*, Mentor Books, New American Library, 1955, 144 pp.

directed toward intellectual satisfaction, constantly in mind throughout the following five papers.

This is a study of the contribution to civilization made by the descendants of the three sons of Noah: Shem, Ham, and Japheth. My basic thesis is that the tenth chapter of Genesis, the oldest Table of Nations in existence, is a completely authentic statement of how the present world population originated and spread after the Flood in the three families headed respectively by Shem, Ham, and Japheth. I further propose that a kind of division of responsibilities to care for the specific needs of man at three fundamental levels — the spiritual, the physical, and the intellectual — was divinely appointed to each of these three branches of Noah's family. History subsequently bears out this thesis in a remarkable way. Scripture itself clearly takes this into account and makes consistent allowance for it, even in respect to one notable exception which will be considered in due course. The interaction of these contributions has at times wholly obliterated their specific nature, but a discerning view of history permits us to identify each stream, so that although the currents mingle quite freely, careful analysis can often still separate them, allowing each to be traced back to its individual source. Rightly understood, the thesis is a key that proves to be an exciting tool of research into the spiritual, the technological, and the intellectual history of mankind since the Flood.

Whether this thesis receives a favorable hearing or not will depend to a large extent on the attitude of the reader towards Scripture. This is particularly true, for example, on whether one takes the genealogy of Nations, given in Genesis 10, at its face value. If this Table is a historically trustworthy document and its generalized conclusions are valid (particularly the universality of v. 32), then it is clear that the present population of the world has been derived from the eight souls who survived the Flood, and can be grouped together under three family headings: Shemites or Semites, Japhethites or Indo-Europeans, and Hamites. No people exist or have existed anywhere in the world since the Flood who are not members of one of these three family groupings. The second paper examines this point.

With this settled, the Semites are not difficult to identify. The Indo-Europeans, or Japhethites, also seem clearly to be a related family of people. The balance of mankind, in short what might comprehensively be referred to as "the colored races," must then be members of the third family group, the Hamites. And by *colored* races I have in mind simply all those who would not in common parlance list themselves under the heading, "The White Man."

It is at this point, probably, that the most violent exception to the thesis of these papers will be taken, since it is not customary to lump together such peoples as the Mongoloids and the Negroids. It is more usual to set forth the racial divisions of mankind as being Caucasian, Mongoloid, and Negroid. The Semitic people are seldom singled out as a race (or stock). There are good reasons for this reluctance since racial mixture, especially in Europe, has proceeded so far that an attempt to classify a segment of the population such as the Jewish people, along racial lines is not considered possible.

It sometimes helps however, to stand back from a situation and view it oversimply. Almost all philosophies of history do this, and for many people some kind of philosophy of history seems essential. Such people create patterns because their minds work that way, and thus they satisfy a need to assure themselves that there is some meaning to life as a whole. These imposed, or discovered, patterns can be highly stimulating, and as long as it is recognized that a particular view is to some extent a mental creation which inevitably reflects the bias of the originator, not too much harm will be done. Those who are horrified at such ethnological oversimplification as we are proposing may find some comfort in the knowledge that the author is keenly aware of the extent to which this thesis cuts across pretty well-established orthodoxies of modern anthropological opinion.

An extensive study of the identification of all the names listed in Genesis 10 will be found as the second paper in this volume. It may be said in anticipation that the Semites would include such people as the Jews, the Arabs, certain people in Asia Minor, and the ancient Babylonians and Assyrians. The Japhethites would include the Indo-Europeans who, although now strictly denominated by their languages, seem for the most part to have preserved a certain racial character in spite of considerable mixture with Semites and Hamites. The Hamites, according to my thesis, include virtually all the people who in ancient times were the originators and creators of civilization in both the Old and the New World. It is this fact, for which we now have massive evidence, that comes as such a surprise to most Indo-European readers, and which, in the words of one high

Canadian Government authority, came almost as a "revelation." Out of Ham have been derived all the so-called colored races — the "yellow," "red," "brown," and "black" — the Mongoloid and the Negroid. Their contribution to human civilization in so far as it has to do with technology has been absolutely unsurpassed. The contribution of Japheth has, by contrast, been essentially in the realm of thought. The contribution of Shem, in terms both of true and false religious conceptions, has been in the realm of the spirit. Where Japheth has applied his philosophical genius to the technological genius of Ham, *science* has emerged. Where Japheth has applied his philosophical genius to the spiritual insights of Shem, *theology* has emerged. The interaction of these three contributions is the theme of history. Human potential reaches its climax when all three brothers (in their descendants) jointly make their common contribution with maximum effectiveness.

These are brash statements as they stand, but the remarkable thing is that they can be substantiated to a degree quite unsuspected by most students of history up to the present time.

Let us turn, then, to Scripture itself in order to examine to what extent the continuance of the threefold division of mankind, which originated with Shem, Ham, and Japheth, was subsequently preserved throughout the historical period covered by the biblical record.

Chapter 1

THE THREEFOLD FRAMEWORK AS REFLECTED IN SCRIPTURE

THE ESSENTIAL burden of Scripture is the redemption of man. It is not surprising, therefore, that the threefold framework of which we have been speaking becomes more apparent in those portions of Scripture which relate most specifically to this theme of redemption. This will be evident at once from the five illustrations from Scripture given below. This threefold framework is a key that wonderfully opens up in an entirely new way the meaning of these familiar passages. Moreover, it will be clear also that the order of introduction of the leading characters in each example follows the same sequence: first Shem, then Ham, and finally Japheth. As one studies these little cameos one further point is worth noting. It seems as though God was determined to preserve the trilogy, by introducing characters at the appropriate place who otherwise seem almost entirely incidental to the main thread of the biblical narrative at the time. I have in mind, for example, the "certain Greeks" who would see Jesus (Illustration No. 3), or the Ethiopian riding in his chariot (Illustration No. 4), or Simon of Cyrene who was suddenly called upon to share the burden of the Cross (Illustration No. 5). Here, then, are five such trilogies:

1. *Abraham's Three Wives.* Abraham had three wives: The first was Sarah, a daughter of Shem (Gen. 11:29). The second was Hagar, the Egyptian — a daughter of Ham (Gen. 16:3). The third was Keturah (Gen. 25:1). According to Hebrew tradition, presumably based upon genealogical records preserved in the Temple prior to their destruction by fire in A.D. 70, records which were priceless to the Jewish people, particularly where

15

Abraham was concerned, Keturah was descended in the line of Japheth.[4] It may be pointed out that in Genesis 10 the sons of Noah when grouped together are habitually put in the same order — Shem, Ham, and Japheth — although it is not absolutely certain that this is the order in which they were born. As will be seen with reference to Abraham's wives, this order is preserved. The implication of Scripture seems to be that in Abraham, the father of the faithful and the father of many nations, the whole race was in a unique way united into a single family. The subsequent events of Hagar's life in no way alter the fact that she had become a wife to Abraham.

In the New Testament recognition of this threefold division is consistently accorded.

2. *The Three Synoptic Gospels.* The Gospels of Matthew, Mark, and Luke are termed synoptic because they deal with the events of our Lord's life in a way quite distinct from the Gospel of John, yet it has always been recognized that three Gospels form a mosaic.

It has been observed from the time of the earliest commentaries that Matthew presents a picture of the Lord Jesus Christ as King, and wrote his Gospel primarily with the Jewish people in mind. The opening genealogy traces this King, appropriately, back to David and to Abraham. His Gospel is full of references to the Old Testament and continually points out how this or that event was a fulfillment of prophecy. This was a message directed primarily to the children of Shem.

Remembering the order in which the sons of Noah are always given, one might logically expect that the second Gospel, Mark's, was directed to the children of Ham. We believe that it is. In considering this aspect of the subject, it is very easy to introduce the idea of racial superiority. For Mark wrote his Gospel with the clear intent of portraying our Lord as a Servant of mankind. In doing this he may either be thought to have degraded the Lord to the level of a servant, or elevated the servant to the position of God's Anointed. The former view which seems the most obvious, is most false. One is reminded of Luther's hymn, which points out that he who sweeps a floor as unto the Lord makes both the floor and the action "fine." This is a wonderful truth. That the children of Ham have been servants

---

[4] Keturah. This is referred to in *Hebraic Literature: the Talmud,* Universal Classics Library, Dunne, London, 1901, p. 241.

par excellence to mankind[5] — have in fact habitually served mankind better than they served themselves — is not to degrade them but to acknowledge a debt which we with our ethnocentric pride have been slow to admit. As we have already said, this is a point to be considered more fully.

That Mark wrote from this point of view seems clear. There is no genealogy of the Lord. A servant is known by his service, not by his pedigree. Mark is full of such phrases as *immediately, straightway, forthwith,* etc. This Man commanded power. It is a striking thing that the gods of Hamitic people on the whole were gods of power, whereas the God of Shem was preeminently moral, and the gods of Japheth were gods of illumination. Mark's Gospel is a Gospel of doing, ceaseless activity; and there are some references to the sublime position of a servant which are not found in the other Gospels.[6] Here and there Mark refers to people as servants where the other Gospels omit the fact, and Mark himself is singled out elsewhere as of particular service to Paul.

Luke's Gospel was clearly written for the Gentiles. It appears traditionally that the term Gentile was reserved for the children of Japheth. This is reflected in Genesis 10:5. It is further probably reflected in a passage which we shall examine a little more fully subsequently. In Genesis 9:27 the text reads, "God shall enlarge Japheth, and he shall dwell in the tents of Shem." This seems to be a reference to the fact that in due course the position held in a unique way by Shem would be taken over as a second area of responsibility by Japheth, i.e., by the Gentiles. This occurred when the Jewish people committed national suicide by rejecting their King. The Kingdom was taken from them (Matt. 21:43) and the responsibility for its administration was given to Japheth. But this is a temporary arrangement, and when "the times of the Gentiles" (Luke 21:24) are fulfilled, the original division of responsibilities will be restored.

Luke wrote for these people. Being himself a Greek, this was an appropriate divine appointment. In his Gospel, the genealogy of the Lord quite properly goes back to Adam; and the characteristic delineation of the Lord is as the "Son of Man."

---

[5] Servant of Servants. For evidence that this phrase is not one of degradation as commonly assumed, see Part III, "Why Noah Cursed Canaan Instead of Ham."

[6] Mark's unique reference to the place of "Service," is found in Mark 10:44. He is referred to as a particularly valuable minister, by Paul in II Timothy 4:11.

It is also worthy of note that the name Japheth means "fair" or "light," as the word Ham means "dark" (not necessarily black). The word Luke also means "fair" or "light."

So we have three synoptic Gospels which, by many internal evidences far too numerous to enter into here, seem clearly to have been written under divine direction specifically for Shem, Ham, and Japheth, in this order. It is not certain of course that the actual text of each Gospel was completed in this chronological order, but the fact remains that God has seen to it that they should be preserved for us from the earliest times in the order in which we find them today. There is no direct evidence, as far as I know, that the writers or the receivers were conscious of this association, but the association surely is clear.

3. *Those Seeking the Lord Jesus Christ.* Three groups of people came with the express purpose of seeking the Lord.

In the New Testament there were numerous instances of men being sought and found by the Lord. There are cases also of men who went in search of others to bring them to the Lord, such as when Andrew first found his brother Peter. These cases seem to be the result of the ordinary processes of daily association, though the results were always extraordinary. We can say this because we are given further information about what happened to these individuals.

But there were three delegations of people who came deliberately looking for the Lord and who, having found Him, disappear from view entirely and are never mentioned again. The first of these delegations was composed of shepherds, the second was of the Wise Men, and the third was of "certain Greeks." It is quite obvious from the record that the first delegation represented the family of Shem, for they were Israelites. It is also quite clear that the third delegation represented Japheth, for they were Greeks.[7] The question remains as to the identity of the Magi.

We might be accused at once of bending the facts to suit the theory in this instance. However, these Wise Men have always been a subject of peculiar interest, partly because of the uncertainty surrounding their origin; and consequently very determined efforts have been made to identify them. Needless to say, imagination has supplied all kinds of fanciful details with respect to their subsequent fortunes. We can discount these and confine

---

[7] Certain Greeks, John 12:21.

ourselves to what may reasonably be deduced from details of the record, particularly the gifts they brought.

These gifts were gold, frankincense, and myrrh. It is almost certain that they came from Southern Arabia or even possibly the adjacent portions of Africa, namely, Ethiopia and Somaliland. That these areas were sources of supply and stimulated considerable trade via Southern Arabia up into Palestine and from there to the Mediterranean world is well known, constantly referred to by early historians and by the early Church Fathers. This led to the almost universal opinion that the Magi had come from Southern Arabia. Although it is commonly assumed that Arabs are Semites, this is only part of the truth; Southern Arabia was populated by people who were largely Hamitic in origin. This was particularly true of Hadramaut and Yemen. Elliot Smith pointed out that the peoples of Arabia conformed in all essentials to the so-called Mediterranean race. The earliest inhabitants of Mesopotamia, the Sumerians, are believed to have been members of this Mediterranean race.[8]

A few years ago the Rev. Eric F. Bishop from the Newman School of Missions (Mount Tabor, Jerusalem) remarked regarding the Wise Men:[9]

> Very few people seem to have given much thought of Arabia as the home of the Magi. The Jewish magician met with in Cyprus (Acts 13:6-8) was actually blessed with an Arabic name — Elymas. . . . The world's supply of incense comes from Southern Arabia and it is generally admitted that the best frankincense is now obtainable from Somaliland.
>
> People coming from Arabia could not be described as coming "from the East," some will argue. There are certain things that may be said in reply. First, several commentators take the phrase "from the East" with the noun rather than the verb. It was "Wise Men from the East" who came to Jerusalem, i.e., Oriental astrologers.

The point here is that the term "Wise Men from the East" had come by usage to stand for a certain type of astrologer whether he came literally from the East or not. To the Chinese, America is eastward, yet the educated Chinese would refer to its culture as Western Culture. The Chinese to us are still Orientals, i.e.,

---

[8] Smith, Grafton Elliot, as quoted by Henry Field in *The Am. Jour. of Arch.*, Oct.-Dec., 1932, p. 429, referring both to Southern Arabia and to the Sumerians.

[9] Bishop, Eric F., *The Palestinian Background of Christmas*, Royal Army Chaplains' Dept., M.E.F., Jerusalem, 1943, p. 18.

"Men from the East," though they almost certainly arrived in this country from the West! Bishop points out that when Clement of Rome wrote to the Corinthians sometime before the end of the first century and discussed with them the fable of the Phoenix, he happened to use two interesting phrases that bear upon this subject. He spoke of "the marvellous sign which is seen in the region of the East, that is, in the parts about Arabia" and then observes that "when the time of its disillusion approaches, the Phoenix makes for itself a coffin of frankincense, myrrh, and other spices." Justin Martyr, who lived only 40 miles from Bethlehem, three times in his Dialogue with Trypho the Jew mentions that the Magi came from Arabia.[10] *Murray's Bible Dictionary* says in this connection,

> The Magi of Matt. 2 probably came from Yemen in South Arabia. The inhabitants of this region were brought much into contact with the Jews by trade, and were considerably influenced by Judaism. They seem in fact to ultimately have abandoned their original heathen religion for Judaism: for while Yemen inscriptions of 270 A.D. speak of the heathen deities of the land, those of 458 and 467 A.D. speak of One Rahman, a name which seems to be connected with the Hebrew Rahman, "the Compassionate One."

The old heathen religion of Yemen included the worship of the sun and of the moon, a matter of some significance in the light of Matt. 2:2, 9, 10. The district was then rich in gold, frankincense, and myrrh (16 Strabo 4, 4). An inscription of Tiglath Pileser II (733 B.C.) mentions Saba, the Seba of Genesis 10:7 who was one of the sons of Cush, a Hamite. This district was part of Yemen and is listed by the King as paying tribute in gold, silver, and incense. In the Annals of Sargon (715 B.C.) Saba is again mentioned as paying tribute in the form of gold and spices.

It was the queen of this land, the Queen of Sheba, who visited Solomon bringing gifts of gold and spices (I Kings 10:2, 10). Himyaric Inscriptions in Southern Arabia show that the early inhabitants of the region were not Semites and their language is said to have affinities with certain Abyssinian tribes. This accords well with the traditions which associate the Ethiopian monarchy with Solomon via the Queen of Sheba who herself may have been black and very comely (S. of Sol. 1:5).

---

[10] Justin Martyr, "Dialogue with Trypho," Chapters 77 and 78, "Ante-Nicene Fathers," Vol. 1, N.Y., Scribners, 1913, p. 237.

In a recent quarterly journal there is a note regarding the Queen of Sheba which bears on this:[11]

> The latest American Archaeological Expedition in South Arabia has proved that King Solomon's empire and the empire of the Queen of Sheba were co-existent, contrary to the theory held at present. According to Prof. W. F. Albright, the Expedition was the first to carry out a proper archaeological excavation in South Arabia, and established contrary to the hitherto accepted view that the rule of the Kingdom of Sheba preceded that of other countries by many centuries. . . .
>
> The Shebean Empire was a military and commercial one which extended not only to the coastal cities of Arabia but also to Ethiopia.

Hormuzd Rassam, writing in a paper presented before the Transactions of the Victoria Institute in London, remarked:[12]

> There is one noticeable fact in the history of the Queen of Sheba which proves more than anything else that her sway extended to Ethiopia, and that is the possession of such a quantity of gold and spices (fragrant and aromatic), which could only be obtained in tropical climates (cf. Herodotus VI. 20).

Putting these fragments together, it seems not unreasonable to argue that the Wise Men were representatives of the family of Ham who brought their gifts from Southern Arabia and came to Jerusalem and Bethlehem along the so-called northern route, up from Jericho. They could return via Hebron and the southern end of the Dead Sea, thus going home by another way.

It should also be pointed out that they "saw His star in the East," a fact which indicates that for at least part of the journey they came from the west. It may also be noted in passing, though the point contributes little to the argument, that there are church windows in Europe which portray the Wise Men as Negroes. It may be conceded then, whether as a coincidence or by divine providence that three delegations did come to seek the Lord representing Shem, Ham, and Japheth in this order, and having come and established the record of their visit, are not again referred to in the New Testament. Yet this was not the end of the matter, for the Gospel was preached specifically to representatives of these three branches of the race in the same order after the Resurrection.

---

[11] In the quarterly journal, *The Fundamentals,* July-Aug., 1954, p. 88.

[12] Rassam, Hormuzd, "On Biblical Lands: their Topography, Races, Religions, Languages, Customs," *Trans. Vic. Instit.,* 30 (1896): 33.

4. *The First Preaching of the Gospel.* The Gospel was preached first to Shem, then to Ham, and finally to Japheth.

Once again there is no doubt about the first and the last of the two branches to receive the Gospel. The message was first to "ye men of Israel" (Acts 2:22) and subsequently to the Centurion Cornelius of the Italian Band, a Roman and a child of Japheth (Acts 10:34). Between these two we have that incident of Philip telling the Gospel to an Ethiopian who gladly heard the message and believed (Acts 8:35).

Although a casual reading of Acts 2:9-11 might suggest that people of many races heard the Gospel at the time of Pentecost — Parthians, Medes, Elamites, and so forth — it is clear from verse 5 that these were Jewish people of the Dispersion. Yet proselytes are mentioned in verse 10. This might be taken to mean that when Peter preached his first sermon he preached to representatives of the whole race of mankind. However, Scripture seems to make it clear that when Cornelius received the Gospel, the Gentiles were for the first time brought under the Covenant. It may be, therefore, that Acts 2:9-11 does refer only to Jewish people from these countries, who are distinguished in much the same way as German Jews from Canadian Jews. It must be admitted that the issue is not absolutely clear. There may have been converts to Judaism who were not Jews in the congregation who heard Peter proclaim the Gospel.

The case of the Ethiopian followed by the Italian Centurion seems to stand in a different context. These were individuals singled out, who were searching for the truth but were not in any sense proselytes.

5. *Those Playing an Official Role in the Crucifixion.* Each branch of the race took a specific part in the Crucifixion.

The moral responsibility was accepted by Israel (Matt. 27:25); the physical burden of carrying the Cross was placed upon a Cyrenian, a child of Ham (Luke 23:26); the responsibility for execution was assumed by Japheth, who in the soldiers completed the sentence which only the Roman authorities could perform (Matt. 27:26). As far as Semitic responsibility is concerned, the issue was clear. They said, "His blood be upon us and our children," though afterwards they sought to unburden themselves of this responsibility (Acts 5:28). It should be stated here that Japheth also shared in this moral responsibility, though it seems that Pilate would have released Jesus if he could have found a way to do it without endangering his own position. Washing his hands did not relieve him of the moral responsibility, yet there is a sense in which he did not have the same kind of moral responsibility as that borne by the Jewish authorities. They set the stage and engineered the course of events, and Pilate found himself trapped. However, in Acts 4:27 Shem and Japheth are both held responsible. Ham is omitted, and what Scripture omits to say is as important as what it takes care to say. Simon of Cyrene was forced to do what he did, and his share in this ghastly undertaking was an involuntary one — one might almost say a merciful one.

Who was Simon of Cyrene? F. F. Bruce points out that one of the leaders at the church at Antioch was a man named Simeon who bore the Latin name Niger meaning "Black man," identified by some with Simon the Cyrenian who carried the Cross of Jesus.[13] In Acts 13:1 two people are mentioned together, Lucius of Cyrene and a man named Simeon Niger. Some commentators have suggested that the words "of Cyrene" in this verse are intended to be applied to both names, i.e., both to Lucius and to Simeon. The name Simeon is simply another form of Simon. In II Peter 1:1 Simon Peter refers to himself as "Simeon." An article appearing in *His Magazine* by Steven Trapnell dealing with Simeon of Cyrene makes the following observations:[14]

> Cyrene was a colony founded by the Greeks on the coast of North Africa. It is possible that Simeon might have been a Jew who had come to Jerusalem for the Passover; but it seems more probable that . . . this Cyrenian who carried the Cross of Christ was a Negro, coming as he did from North Africa. . . . Such an honour and privilege, initially granted to only one man, was given not to a Jew but to a Gentile; not to a Judean but to a Cyrenian; not to a white man but to a Negro.

Steven Trapnell applies the term Gentile here where we think it should perhaps be reserved for the children of Japheth. But the point is not important. What is important is that the order is preserved in all these instances — first Shem, then Ham, and finally Japheth.

There are one or two brief observations that it seems desirable to make at this juncture. First, when a new theory like this is proposed, the elaboration of it at first appears to be stilted and artificial. But once the idea has been mulled over for awhile, it begins to appear to be a little more reasonable, and in the end

---

[13] Bruce, F. F., *The Spreading Flame*, Eerdmans, 1953, p. 102.
[14] Trapnell, Steven, "Simon of Cyrene," *His*, April, 1956, p. 2.

may seem plain and obvious. My own impression is that Scripture is designed to teach this important truth, that God has never lost sight of Shem, Ham, and Japheth, nor ceased to work out His purposes using certain unique qualities which can be shown have, by and large, characterized their descendants. We shall return to this subsequently.

Secondly, it will be noted that in each of these last three trilogies, the part taken by a representative of one of the three branches of the race (not always the same branch) is often of an apparently incidental nature. The incident of the Greeks (Japheth) who desired to see Jesus, of Simeon of Cyrene who happened to be passing, and of the Ethiopian who seemed quite by chance to have met Philip, all these are incidental to the main course of the narrative as a whole. They might, in fact, have been omitted entirely from the New Testament without greatly affecting the story as a whole. However, "might" should perhaps have been emphasized, because if our interpretation is correct, each of these incidents is an essential part of a theme emphasizing the real existence of three distinct groups of people, Semites, Hamites, and Japhethites, each of whom singly, and all of whom together, play a fundamental part in fulfilling the purpose of God.

We turn now to the specific contribution of each of these families.

Chapter 2

GENESIS 9:24-27: HISTORY IN CAMEO

> And Noah woke from his wine, and learned what his younger son had done unto him.
> And he said, Cursed be Canaan; a servant of servants shall he be unto his brethren.
> And he said, Blessed be the Lord God of Shem; and Canaan shall be his servant.
> God shall enlarge Japheth, and he shall dwell in the tents of Shem; and Canaan shall be his servant.

THIS PROPHETIC statement is the climax of an incident which really begins in verse 20. Noah cultivated grapes for the first time and drank himself into a drunken stupor. In this condition he exposed his nakedness as he slept and was seen by Ham as he lay uncovered. The young man for some reason omitted to cover his father's nakedness as he should have done, but went and reported it to his two brothers, Shem and Japheth. The latter discreetly averting their gaze, respectfully covered the old man's nakedness. When Noah awoke, he soon found out what had taken place, and undoubtedly under inspiration — yet inspiration which did not ignore Noah's own mental attitudes — pronounced judgment upon the offender and blessing upon the others.

It has always been a matter of controversy as to why Canaan rather than Ham should have been cursed. Canaan was Ham's son, and was therefore grandson to Noah. Some people have supposed that the name Canaan was substituted for Ham by Jewish scribes who had particularly strong feelings against this branch of Ham's family. Evidence for this is believed to be provided by some manuscripts of the Septuagint version and the Arabic versions, which have the words "Ham, the father of Canaan" instead of the word "Canaan" alone.

25

There is another explanation which seems to me more probable, and which if it is true, means that Noah really was cursing Ham. It is a common social custom among many primitive people to attribute the greatness of a son to the father, who then receives the honor for having raised such a worthy child. This is clearly reflected in Scripture where Saul seeks to honor David after the slaying of Goliath. He asks his general whose son the lad is (I Sam. 17:55). This has always seemed to mean that he did not recognize David, which would seem very strange in view of David's close associations with him. Undoubtedly Saul knew David well enough, but evidently he did not know who his father was. It was his father he was seeking to honor according to social custom. Also, a woman could not bless a worthy son's father, but she could bless his mother thereby giving personal witness to his worthiness. This seems to be the background of the woman's observation in Luke 11:27.

A man in blessing his own son was in fact blessing himself. This was true when Noah blessed Shem and Japheth. By the same token, however, if he had cursed Ham, the real offender, he would at the same time have been cursing himself. Quite logically, he could only pass judgment upon Ham by cursing Ham's own son, which is what he therefore did.

Nevertheless, the curse which he pronounced for what seems really so mild an offense, was not perhaps as severe as we have made it out to be. It may be less honorable to be a servant than to be a master, though the Lord Jesus suggested that the opposite may really be the case. Yet it is true that the servant is not above his master, and in this sense may find himself in a less desirable position. In the case of Ham and his descendants history shows that they have rendered an extraordinary service to mankind from the point of view of the physical developments of civilization. All the earliest civilizations of note were founded and carried to their highest technical proficiency by Hamitic people. There is scarcely a *basic* technological invention which must not be attributed to them. As we shall show later, neither Shem nor Japheth made any significant contribution to the fundamental technology of civilization, in spite of all appearances to the contrary. This is a bold statement but it is not made in ignorance of the facts.

The phrase "servant of servants" does not normally (if ever) mean basest of servants but servant par excellence. The form of the phrase is common in Hebrew literature and always means that which is highest: Lord of Lords, Song of Songs, Holy of Holies, and so forth. I think the judgment was not so much that they were to render such outstanding service to their brethren, but rather that they were to profit so little by it themselves. Japheth has been enlarged and most of this enlargement has been not only at the expense of Ham but because of a technical superiority which has resulted directly from building upon the basic foundation provided by the latter. There is historically little or no indication that Japheth would have achieved the technical superiority which he has if he had been left to his own devices.

The blessing of Shem was tied in a peculiar way to a covenant relationship with God, as indicated by the use of the extended term "Lord God," which is a covenant title. However, by inspiration Noah was able to foretell that this covenant relationship would in some way be interrupted — so that Japheth would one day assume the responsibility which had been divinely appointed to Shem, adding this responsibility to one already apportioned.

Thus it has come about that the pioneering task of opening up the world, subduing it, and rendering it habitable, was first undertaken by the descendants of Ham. This seems to have been done under divine pressure,[15] for in a remarkably short time the children of Ham had established beachheads of settlement in every part of the world.

Centuries later, spreading at a more leisurely rate, Japheth settled slowly into the areas already opened up by Ham, in almost every case adopting the solutions, suited to local survival, which the predecessors had already worked out. Yet in all cases Japheth took with him a certain philosophizing tendency which acted to modify the somewhat materialistic culture which he was inheriting. In a few cases, as in the Indus Valley, Japheth almost obliterated the high civilization which Ham had established.

In the providence of God the Semitic people, represented

---

[15] The Hebrew of Gen. 11:9 is very forceful. The word "scattered" has almost the meaning of "splattered." It implies violence. Hebrew tradition has it that it was only the family of Ham which was involved in the tower incident and the judgment which followed. This concords well with history, for neither Shem nor Japheth were scattered at this time, nor did either of them even have a word for "city" of their own. They were not disposed to city-building. On this point see Robert Eisler, "Loan Words in Semitic Languages Meaning 'Town'," *Antiquity*, Dec., 1939, No. 52, p. 449. In spite of the title of his paper, he is concerned with the Indo-Europeans also.

in Israel, remained at the center until their spiritual education had reached a certain point. They were then scattered among the nations and carried with them their pure monotheistic faith. But when they should have received their King, they failed to recognize Him, and their particular Kingdom was taken from them and the responsibility of its administration given to Japheth instead.

The enlargement of Japheth has continued to this day, an enlargement greatly accelerated geographically in the last few centuries — frequently at the expense of the Hamites who first possessed the land. To a great extent this power of expansion at the expense of others has resulted from a far superior technology. However, this was not the consequence of any superior inventive genius on Japheth's part. It is rather that Japhethites have looked upon man's relationship to Nature as a "Me-it" relationship rather than an "I-Thou" relationship. This has permitted — indeed encouraged — experiment and exploitation in a way that never seems to have occurred to the Hamites. It has brought an unbelievable enlargement of man's power and control over the forces of Nature.

This "enlargement" has also brought its own undesirable consequences. Perhaps this is because the spiritual responsibility taken over from Shem has never been completely undertaken by Japheth who received the commission. If Shem should be restored once more to the spiritual leadership of the nations, it may be that the service rendered by the family of Ham and its extension by Japheth will usher in a golden age of unbelievable promise.

This is all gross oversimplification. But it presents the picture in readily conceivable form. It remains to fill in sufficient detail to demonstrate that this view of history does have some concordance with the facts.

Chapter 3

THE CHARACTERISTICS OF
SHEM, HAM, AND JAPHETH

I T IS FORTUNATE for us that Shem comes first in the list. Certainly as far as Western Civilization is concerned the three most important religions are Judaism, Islam (Mohammedanism), and Christianity. The picture is more confused toward the Far East because in those countries it is difficult to know where "philosophy" ends and religious belief begins. Many authorities, for example, point out that Confucianism is not in any sense a religion and only in a limited sense a philosophy. Its founder did not concern himself with God at all nor was he vitally interested in pure philosophy — only in a kind of practical wisdom. It seems desirable to make some effort at this point to distinguish between philosophy and religion. There is plenty of room for disagreement here, but I think that certain points of vital distinction can be noted to which there will be general assent.

In the first place revelation is essential for religion, but for philosophy it must be rejected, human reason being the only justifiable tool. Religion is concerned with morals, philosophy with ethics: the difference between the two being essentially this, that morals have to do with man's relationship to God and ethics with man's relationship to man. Morals are absolute, ethics are relative. If we may substitute metanature for metaphysics, we may say that the subject matter of philosophy is metanature (the subject matter of science is Nature), but the subject matter of religion is supernature. In religion, miracle is in a sense an essential adjunct, but in philosophy miracle is simply of no concern. The end object of all religion is to find God, but the end object of philosophy is to find the truth. This does not mean that religion does not have the discovery of truth as an object, but only that it is a secondary one.

29

With this very brief explanation of how we are using the terms we can go one step further and observe that while Semitic people have tended to lay the emphasis on the search for righteousness, the Japhetic or Indo-European peoples have laid the emphasis on the search for understanding, and the Hamitic people have searched for power. All men are religious to some extent and the nature of their gods tends to reflect something of their own personal goals. The gods of the Semites, and preeminently the God of Israel, rewarded conduct that was righteous. This is true of Judaism, Islam, and, of course, Christianity. But to a large extent it is also true of that form of paganism which, deriving its source of inspiration from the Babylonians and Assyrians (both of whom were Semites), subsequently spread in modified forms far beyond the confines of its original home in Mesopotamia. The extent to which this pagan religion underlies the religious beliefs of many non-Christian people is remarkably revealed by A. Hislop in his well-known book "The Two Babylons."[16] The gods of the early Indo-Europeans were gods of light, but this light was not moral light but rather the illumination of the mind or understanding. The gods of the Hamites were gods of power, in fact — in the absence of the moral component — were gods of ruthlessness, demanding appropriate sacrifices.

To sum up thus far, it seems clear that from the Semites have come all the religions, rightly so-called, both false and the true. The contribution of Shem has been fundamentally to the spiritual life of man.

To preserve the characteristic order of these three names, it would be proper to deal next with Ham. But there are reasons for considering Japheth first. One feels somewhat at a disadvantage here because to avoid misunderstanding the ideal approach would be to state the whole case at once. Of course this is impossible, so we have to take it a step at a time and trust that the reader will be patient until he has heard the end of the matter.

First, we should state the proposition. If philosophy is defined as strictly rational speculation, concerned with the ultimate nature and meaning of reality, apart from revelation, to satisfy a purely intellectual need — then the family of Japheth has been responsible for the world's philosophies. Older peoples have produced works dealing with "successful behavior." Such men as Solomon, Ptah-Hotep, Pachacutec, Confucius, etc., have written

---

[16] Hislop, Alexander, *The Two Babylons*, Loiseaux, New York, 1953.

their books of Wisdom. These are not philosophy as philosophers understand the term, because they had a purely practical purpose.

Only Indo-Europeans have continually returned to the fundamental problems of metaphysics, the Aryans in India (giving rise to Hindu Philosophy), the Greeks in Greece, and much later European and New World Philosophers. This does not mean that non-Indo-Europeans have never produced philosophers, though this observation is so nearly true that it could be argued very forcibly. Popular opinion is contrary to this view, but informed and authoritative opinion supports it almost unanimously. A few notable exceptions such as Paul Radin, for example, can be quoted as holding the opposite view. But for every authority who would support the latter, one can find dozens who will agree that philosophy has been the unique contribution of Indo-Europeans.

Jacques Maritain made this observation:[17]

> All the great Indo-European civilizations on the other hand, manifest an impulse which no doubt took widely different forms, towards rational and in the strict sense philosophical speculation.

In this quotation the words, "on the other hand," are used by the author because he has just made a broad sweep of all other civilizations of non-Indo-European origin, ancient and modern, and shown that they were not characterized by any particular interest in this kind of speculative thought. As we shall see, it was not until the philosophizing aptitude of Japheth was brought to bear upon the pabulum of technology provided by the Hamitic peoples that science became possible.

Before we turn to the positive contribution which the Hamites have made to world civilization, we should perhaps give a few authoritative statements to bear out the observation made previously that they have not produced philosophers. The Chinese are Mongols and therefore derived from Ham, so Confucius seems a good man to begin with, because almost everyone thinks of him as a philosopher. Epiphanius Wilson, an authority in this field, put the matter this way:[18]

> The strangest figure we meet in the annals of Oriental thought, is that of Confucius. To the popular mind he is the

---

[17] Maritain, Jacques, *An Introduction to Philosophy*, Sheed and Ward, New York, 1955, p. 26.

[18] Wilson, Epiphanius, *The Literature of China*, The World's Great Classics, Vol. 39, Colonial Press, New York, 1900, p. 3.

founder of a religion, and yet he has nothing in common with the great religious teachers of the East. The present life they despised, the future was to them everything in its promised satisfaction. The teachings of Confucius were of a very different sort. Throughout his whole writings he has not even mentioned the name of God. He declined to discuss the question of immortality. When asked about spiritual beings he remarked, "If we cannot even know men, how can we know spirits?"

The influence of Confucius springs, first of all, from the narrowness and definiteness of his doctrine. He was no transcendentalist. His teaching was of the earth, earthy.... He died almost without warning in dreary hopelessness. For Confucius in his teaching treated only of man's life on earth, and seems to have had no ideas with regard to the human lot after death.

Even as a moralist he seems to have sacrificed the ideal to the practical — the slight emphasis he places on the virtue of truth (of which indeed he does not seem himself to have been particularly studious in his historic writings) places him low down in the ranks of moralists.

In view of the fact that philosophy must be added to technology if science is to emerge, it is striking to find A. L. Kroeber, no mean authority on patterns of cultural interactions, making the following remarks:[19]

It is significant that the Chinese have made many important inventions, but not one major scientific discovery. They have sought a way of life but neither an understanding nor a control of nature beyond what was immediately useful.

They are of course not abnormal in their attitude: most cultures have done the same. It is, with minor exceptions, only the few civilizational growths that have at one time or another been under the influence of Greek example which really tried to develop Science.

It may be argued that these are prejudiced views. We may, however, quote a Chinese scholar, Liu Wu-Chi, writing specifically on this question.[20]

The distinguishing features of Confucianism are many. First of all it is a moral system which is both practical and practicable. Without any trace of the metaphysical (philosophy) and the supernatural (religion), its contents are readily understood by the man in the street; and its ethical teachings, replete with wisdom and common sense, can be applied in daily life.

In view of the concept that Buddhism in China created a

19 Kroeber, A. L., *Configurations of Culture Growth,* Univ. of Calif., 1944, p. 184.

20 Wu-Chi, Liu, *A Short History of Confucian Philosophy,* Pelican Books, 1955, p. 9.

genuine system of philosophy, the following observations made by Alan Watts are important.[21]

> Although Buddhism was originally an Indian religion, emerging from the traditions of Hindu philosophy, it did not attain its full vitality until the T'ang Dynasty in China — about the eighth century A.D. Philosophy, Buddhas, Bodhisattvas, and religious rites are far less significant in China. Chinese Buddhism ceased to be a matter of other worldly mysticism. . . .
>
> When Buddhism first came to China the method used for attaining spiritual illumination followed the lines of Indian Yoga: it was concerned with the practice of Dhyana — a profound state of consciousness obtained by sitting for hours, days, months, or even years in solitary meditation. But this did not really appeal to the practical spirit of the Chinese, who wanted a Dhyana that could be applied to every day life.

We may thus speak of the wisdom of China but scarcely of their philosophy, though this is in no way intended to challenge their intellectual capacity. The Chinese who adopts to some extent Western modes of thought and forms of speech is every bit as capable as we of philosophical abstraction of the purest kind. It should be noted that the same is true of Semitic people. But as Jessie Bernard has pointed out,[22] it is not Jewish people who remain true to their religion who make this contribution. The great Semitic philosophers were unorthodox Jews, and culturally speaking had turned their backs upon their unique Semitic heritage.

Another Hamitic people who are commonly supposed to have been great philosophers were the Egyptians. This, too, is a false impression. Martin Engberg says,[23] "Nowhere is there any indication that Egyptians were interested in theoretical problems." Sir Alan Gardiner, an authority on the Egyptian language, puts it even more strongly:[24] "No people has ever shown itself more averse from philosophical speculation, or more wholeheartedly devoted to material interests."

William Hayes, another authority, remarked in the same connection:[25]

---

[21] Watts, Alan, "How Buddhism Came to Life," *Asia*, Oct., 1939, p. 581.

[22] Bernard, Jessie, "Can Science Transcend Culture?" *Sci. Monthly*, Oct., 1950, pp. 268ff.

[23] Engberg, Martin, *The Dawn of Civilization*, University of Knowledge Series, Chicago, 1938, p. 153.

[24] Gardiner, Sir Alan, *Egyptian Grammar*, Oxford, 1950, Sec. 3, p. 4.

[25] Hayes, William, "Daily Life in Ancient Egypt," *Nat. Geog. Magazine*, Oct., 1941, pp. 425, 428.

Though intensely devout, the ancient Egyptian had neither the mental nor the spiritual equipment necessary to the creation or even the adaptation of a great religion. . . .

Though intelligent and quick to learn, he had a mind of the practical unimaginative type. He was a materialist and not given to deep speculative thought and seems to have been unable either to evolve or to express a purely abstract idea.

In spite of the great contribution they rendered in the field of medicine, James Newman,[26] speaking of one of their best known medical texts, remarked:

The Egyptians were practical men, not much given to speculative or abstract enquiries. Dreamers were rare among them. . . .

The Rhind Papyrus, though it demonstrates the inability of the Egyptian to generalize and their penchant for clinging to cumbersome calculating processes, proves that they were remarkably pertinacious in solving everyday problems. . . .

Frequent reference is made by various authorities to the fact that the science of mathematics was not developed by these highly practical people. Their methods of calculation were clumsy in the extreme, their tables were empirically derived, and though they achieved considerable practical skill in the manipulation of figures yet there is no evidence of the discovery or even the search for connective theories.

But the moment we come to a consideration of Hindu philosophy originated by that branch of the Indo-European (Japhetic) family which penetrated into India in the second millennium B.C., we are in a new atmosphere altogether. Robert Lowie points out that "the Hindus made their contribution in the field of *pure* mathematics, to which they added the concept of negative numbers."[27] Kroeber[28] observed that "Hindu civili-

---

[26] Newman, James R., "The Rhind Papyrus," in *The World of Mathematics,* Simon and Schuster, New York, 1956, pp. 170, 171. Reference should have been made to a notable collection of papers in a volume edited by H. and H. A. Frankfort, and published by the University of Chicago, in 1946 and 1948. The original title was *The Intellectual Adventure of Ancient Man,* with the subtitle "An Essay on Speculative Thought in the Ancient Near East." It is significant perhaps that this volume appeared subsequently as a reprint in the Pelican Series, under the new title *Before Philosophy.* This later title is an exact description of the subject matter of the papers. The conclusion reached by all the contributors to this volume is that philosophy did not exist prior to the time of the Hindu philosophers in India, or the Greek philosophers who were very nearly their contemporaries.

[27] Lowie, Robert, *Introduction to Cultural Anthropology,* Farrar and Rinehart, New York, 1940, p. 340.

[28] *Everyman's Encyclopedia,* Dent, London, 1913.

zation is not only otherworldly, but mystical, rationalizing and extravagant in its ethos." An earlier edition of *Everyman's Encyclopedia* under "Philosophy" had this to say:[29]

> It was not until man sought wisdom *for its own sake* (their emphasis) and with no religious or other motives, that he philosophized in the true sense, and the previous theogonies, cosmogonies, etc., cannot strictly claim the title of philosophy....
>
> The beginnings of Philosophy are as a rule attributed to the Greeks, but the Indian ideas of the sixth century B.C. and later, form an interesting parallel philosophic development.

On the other hand these same Japhetic people, until comparatively recently, have shown a remarkable indifference to technology. As Ralph Linton pointed out:[30]

> The Hindus have always been highly receptive to new cults and new philosophic ideas as long as these did not come into too direct conflict with their existing patterns, but have shown an almost complete indifference to improved technique of manufacture. The material world was felt to be of so little importance that minor advances in its control were not considered worth the trouble of changing established habit.

Those who are acquainted with the views of the Greek philosophers in this matter will recognize the close kinship of sentiment, for to the Greeks it was almost a sin even to be tempted to seek any practical application of their ideas. In passing, it may be noted that both the Greeks and Aryans claimed Japheth as their ancestor. Sir Charles Marston[31] points out that in the "Clouds," Aristophanes claims Japetos as the ancestor of the Greeks and in the "Institutes of Menu" dated about 1280 B.C., one of the ancient Aryan histories, it is said that a certain individual named Satyaurata had three sons, the eldest of whom was named Jyapeti. The others were named Sharma (Shem?) and C'harma (Ham?).

To conclude this brief discussion of the descendants of Japheth, we may say that their scientific enthusiasm has strangely proved most fruitful where the objective has been pure understanding without regard to subsequent practical usefulness. This is Japheth at home. It may also be said, though the statement

---

[29] Kroeber, A. L., *Anthropology*, Harcourt Brace, New York, 1948, p. 294.

[30] Linton, Ralph, *The Study of Man*, Student's Edition, Appleton Century, New York, 1936, p. 343.

[31] Marston, Sir Charles, *New Bible Evidence*, Revell, 1935, p. 87; and in the "Clouds," at line 998.

will undoubtedly be challenged at once, that Indo-Europeans have scarcely a basic invention to their credit. W. J. Perry says,[32] "The Celts, like the Teutons, never invented anything." Lord Raglan said,[33] "The old Roman religious ritual gave little encouragement to inventiveness, and the later cults were imported ready-made from the East. As a result the Romans invented almost nothing." Joseph Needham, speaking of another branch of Japheth, said,[34] "The only Persian invention of first rank was the windmill.... Unless the rotary quern be attributed to them, the ancient Europeans of the Mediterranean Basin launched only one valuable mechanical technique, namely, the pot chain pump." Carleton Coon[35] reminds us that "the linguists tell us that the Indo-European speakers did not initially domesticate one useful animal or one cultivated plant." Grahame Clark, speaking of "New World Origins" and referring to the inventiveness of the American Indian in developing his natural resources, says,[36] "during the four centuries since the Discovery (of the New World) the white man has failed to make a single contribution of importance."

The Sumerians (Hamitic by our definition) were highly inventive, but when the Babylonians (Semitic) succeeded them, V. Gordon Childe says,[37] "in the next 2000 years one can scarcely point to a first class invention or discovery...." Similarly speaking of the Semites, St. Chad Boscawen says,[38] "There is a powerful element in the Semitic character which has been, and still is, a most important factor in their national life: it is that of adaptability. Inventors they have never shown themselves to be."

At the risk of boring the reader, one more statement regarding another segment of the family of Shem may be in order. Lord Raglan says,[39]

> Much the same can be said for the Moslems. There was a period of mild inventiveness while their religion was settling

---

[32] Perry, W. J., *The Growth of Civilization*, Pelican, 1937, p. 157.

[33] Raglan, Lord, *How Came Civilization*, Methuen, 1939, p. 179.

[34] Needham, Joseph, *Science and Civilization in China*, Vol. 1, Cambridge, 1954, p. 240.

[35] Coon, Carleton S., *The Races of Europe*, Macmillan, 1939, p. 178.

[36] Clark, Grahame, "New World Origins," *Antiquity*, June, 1940, p. 118.

[37] Childe, V. Gordon, *New Light on the Most Ancient East*, Kegan Paul, London, 1935, p. 203.

[38] Boscawen, St. Chad., *The Bible and the Monuments*, Eyre and Spottiswoode, London, 1896, p. 18.

[39] Raglan, Lord, *How Came Civilization*, Methuen, 1939, p. 179.

down into its various sects but since that process was completed, about 900 years ago, no Moslem has invented anything.

This is concurred in by Rene Albrecht-Carrie who points out that the Arabs were not so much innovators as collectors and carriers of the contributions of other times and other peoples.[40] He adds, "This is not to deny or minimize the crucial importance of their role or ignore the fact that they made some valuable contributions of their own." Finally, to quote Prof. R. F. Grau,[41] speaking of the pure Arabs,

> No science was developed; no new industry or even trades sprang up; the political unity, which religious enthusiasm and the Prophet had created crumbled away....
> The Arabian Empires became the medium for the communication to the West of the knowledge of ancient philosophy and natural science, without making any independent progress in them.

Again and again in the history of Indo-European civilization men have been on the verge of great practical discoveries but have failed to clinch them because they failed to recognize them — because they were not interested. The contribution of Japheth has been in the application of philosophy to technology and the consequent development of the Scientific Method.

As the application of Japheth's philosophy to the technology of Ham produced science, so the application of his philosophy to the religious insights of Shem produced theology. The Hamitic people never developed science and the Semitic people did not develop theology, until the influence of Japhetic philosophy was brought to bear. In keeping with this thought, and the remark made previously by Jessie Bernard, it is striking to realize that the theology of Paul was addressed to the Gentiles by a man who had deliberately turned his back upon contemporary orthodox Judaism.

Most of us have been brought up to believe that we, Indo-Europeans, are the most inventive people in the world. It is exceedingly difficult to escape from this culturally conditioned prejudice and take a fresh objective look at the origins of our technological achievements. One may take almost any essential element of our highly complex civilization — aircraft, paper, weaving, metallurgy, propulsion of various kinds, painting, ex-

---

[40] Albrecht-Carrie, Rene, "Of Science, Its History and the Teaching Thereof," *Sci. Monthly,* July, 1951, p. 19.

[41] Grau, R. F., *The Goal of the Human Race,* Simpkin and Marshall, London, 1892, p. 88.

plosives, medical techniques, mechanical principles, food, the use of electricity, virtually anything technological in nature — and an examination of the history of its development leads us surely and certainly back to a Hamitic people and exceedingly rarely to Japheth or Shem. The basic inventions which have been contributed by Shem or Japheth can, it seems, be numbered on the fingers of one hand. This seems so contrary to popular opinion, yet it is a thesis which can be supported — and has been documented — from close to 1000 authoritative sources. Almost every new book dealing with the history of science (frequently confused with technology) adds its own confirmatory evidence in support of this thesis.

It is quite impossible within the compass of this paper to attempt to do justice to the contribution made by the children of Ham towards the development of civilization in its more material aspects. It may serve as some indication of this contribution to simply list under rather obvious but convenient headings things the invention of which or the first application of which, or the development of which, must be credited to Ham.

A mere list without comment can be most uninteresting. But in this case it seems the only way to put the idea across. In this list, for the sake of brevity, we have not discriminated between principles of operation (Gimbal suspension, for example) and actual products or techniques (like rubber or the electroplating of metals, for example). Documentation for each entry is available but obviously could not possibly be given here. It will be, however, provided in Part IV.[42]

Mechanical Principles and Applications

Block and tackle	Gimbal suspension	Domes and arches
Whiffletrees	Suspension bridges	Lock gates and lifts
Windlass	Cantilever principle	Fire pistons
Gears	Chain drives	Lathes
Pulleys	Catapults	Clockwork mechanism
Steam engine principle		

Materials

Copper	Bellows systems of all types
Bronze	Glass (including possibly a malleable glass)
Iron	Pottery, china and porcelain
Cast Iron	Lenses of several types

---

[42] Part IV, "The Technology of Hamitic People."

Steel   Charcoal and Carbon Black
Cement   Glues and Preservatives
Dyes and inks   Shellacs, Varnishes and Enamels
Rubber   Casting methods of all kinds including
                   hollow casting
Case hardening
Gold and silver working including beading, repoussee, sheet, wire
  and the plating of metals

Building Techniques, Tools and Materials

Nails   Window materials, including glass
Saws   Door hinges and locks
Hammers   Protective coatings
Brace and Bit   Street drainage systems
Sandpaper   Sewage disposal on a wide scale
Rope saws   Running water in piped systems
Carborundum   Piped gas for heating
Stoves   Central heating systems
Plans and Maps   Surveying instruments
Drills (including diamond drills)
Buildings of all types, including genuine skyscrapers and earth-
  quakeproof construction

Fabrics and Weaving, etc.

Linen   Voile   Ikat or tie-dyeing
Cotton   Tapestry   Feather and fur garments
Silk   Batique   Tailored clothing
Wool   Needles   Double-faced cloth
Felt   Thimbles   Knitted and Crocheted materials
Lace   Parchment   All types of thread
Netting   Gauze   Dyes of all kinds
Mechanical looms   Silk screen methods of decoration
Invisible mending   Ropes up to 12 inches in diameter
Flying shuttles   Paper of all kinds including coated stock
Netting shuttles

Writing, Printing, etc.

Inks   Textbooks
Chalks   Encyclopedias
Pencils and crayons Libraries and Cataloguing systems
Block printing   Literary forms (fables, etc.)
Movable type   Envelopes and postal systems
All kinds of paper

Scripts (Sumerian, Cuneiform and its successors, Egyptian, Hittite, Minoan, Chinese, Easter Island, Indus Valley, and Maya Scripts)

Foodstuffs

Aloes	Chickle gum	Tomato
Pears	Cascara	Sweet potato
Kidney beans	Pineapple	Prickly pear
Cereals	Chili pepper	Squash
Cocoa	Cashew and peanut	Corn
Coffee	Manioc	Beans
Tea	Artichoke	Strawberries
Tobacco	Potato	Arrowroot

Animals Domesticated

Pigs	Dogs	Llama
Horses	Cats	Alpaca
Fowl	Camels	Cows, sheep, etc.

And in agriculture, the use of multiculture, fertilizers, mechanical seeders, and other such equipment

Foodgathering Methods

The use of countless fish poisons and animal intoxicants
The use of other tamed animals to catch "game":
— dogs and cormorants for fishing,
— cats for hunting,
— various birds of prey such as eagles, falcons, etc.
Elephants for labor and land clearance
Traps and nets of all kinds

Travel Conveyances, etc.

Compass	Canals and Locks	Road Rollers
Skis	Sternpost rudder	Wheelbarrows
Toboggans	All types of water craft	Stirrups
Snowshoes	Cement paving	Wheeled Vehicles
Travois	Surfaced Roads	

Wheels: solid, spoked, and rimmed and tired
Watertight-compartment construction for boats
Harness for domestic animals
Use of birds for navigation
Bridges of all types: suspension, cantilever, arch, etc.

"Aircraft"

Balloons	Gliders	Helicopters

Kites	Parachutes	Jet propulsion

Weather-signalling, and forecasting

Cosmetics, etc.

Mirrors	Nail polishes	Toothbrushes
Wigs	Scissors	Shaving equipment
Combs	Powders and ointments	Jewelry of all kinds

Mathematics

Geometry	A kind of logarithms
Trigonometry	Concept of Zero
Algebra	Use of place System

Trade and Commerce

Paper money and coinage	Systems of Inspection
Banking Houses	Trade regulations and price-fixing
Postal systems	Wage regulation and compensation systems
Loans with interest	Accounting systems and use of formal contracts
Weights and measures	

Medical and Surgical Practices and Instruments

Gargles	Anaesthetics	Lotions
Snuffs	Soaps	Ointments
Inhalators	Splints	Plasters
Enemas	Quinine	Adhesive tapes
Fumigators	Poultices	Tourniquet
Suppositories	Decoctions	Surgical stitching
Insecticides	Infusions	Bandages
Truth serums	Pills	Curare
Cocaine	Troches	Trephination

Caesarian operations	Vaccine for smallpox
Cascara and other emetics	Tranquillizing drugs
Animal stupefying drugs	Surgical instruments of all kinds; knives, forceps, tweezers, etc.

Identification of, and treatment of, hundreds of common diseases and injuries including brain and eye operations and surgery in general

Household Furnishing

Hammocks	Gas cookers	Fans
Rocking stools	Rotary querns	Clocks
Folding beds	Lamps	Running water

Oil stoves   Space heaters   A form of "telephone"
Whistling pots and kettles   Go-carts for children, and other toys

Games

Wrestling   Revolving stages for theatres
Rubber ball games   Lacrosse
Numerous board games (chess, checkers, etc.)

Warfare

All types of piercing and striking
   weapons   Bolas
Gun powder   Rifled weapons
Guided Missiles   Body armor
Aerial bombardment   Poison gases and toxic agents
Flame throwers
Bows and Crossbows   A repeating bow, a form of machine gun
Heavy artillery (catapults of several kinds)

Musical Instruments

Wind instruments (organ, pipes, horns, flutes, etc.)
String instruments (various modifications of the harp)
Percussion instruments (tubes, bars, stones, bells, and dia-
   phragms)
Tuning forks of various kinds

Miscellaneous

Umbrellas   Safety pins   Straws for drinking
Spectacles   Calendars   Telescopes (?)
Snow goggles Cigar holders   Finger printing for identification

For many readers this list will be entirely unsatisfactory. However, a word of further explanation about it may help to clarify things. Many of the items, in fact the majority of them, could be called Hamitic "firsts." Some of them bear no relationship historically to their western counterparts as far as we can ascertain from a study of the transmission of culture traits. Still, they had the idea before we did. The ingenuity of many of these devices and techniques is truly extraordinary, particularly in view of the paucity of natural resources. It is no exaggeration to state that primitive people have done marvels with their natural resources *as they found them.* The difficulty for us is that we are deceived by their very simplicity. Whether highly civilized or of primitive culture, the Hamitic people have shown an amazing ability to exploit the immediate resources of their environment to the limit. It is only recently that we in our culture have become aware of our indebtedness to non-Indo-European people for practically all the basic elements, simple and complex, of our own technological civilization. The only purpose of this list here is to draw attention to the fact that in each of these elements of culture Hamitic peoples got there first and independently, and in most cases were our instructors. As we have already said this aspect of the subject is elaborated with documentation in Part IV of this volume.

We may sum up what has been said thus far by setting forth the following propositions. First, the Table of Nations in Genesis 10 is a historic document indicating how the present population of the world has been derived from Shem, Ham, and Japheth. Secondly, this threefold division is more than merely a genetic variation of certain "racial" types: there is evidence that it is intended to indicate that the three branches of the race were divinely apportioned a characteristic capacity which has been reflected in the unique contribution each branch has rendered in the service of mankind as a whole. And thirdly, the contribution of Shem has been a spiritual one, of Ham a technological one, and of Japheth an intellectual one: in the process of history, these contributions were made effective in this order.

Chapter 4

THE THREEFOLD NATURE
OF MAN'S BASIC NEEDS

MAN'S LIFE as an individual is lived in three worlds, which, while they can be mapped discretely for the purposes of study, are not usually consciously distinguished in everyday experience. There is the world of feeling, the world of thought, and the world of things. In these worlds, man is aware of three kinds of need: spiritual, intellectual, and physical. For these, man has three capacities which are not shared by animals as far as we know. He has the capacity of worship, the capacity to reason, and the capacity to create. As a result of these capacities, man has developed and elaborated three kinds of activities: religion, philosophy, and technology. Hugh Dryden, writing on "The Scientist in Contemporary Life," remarked:[43]

> Man's life at its fullest is a trinity of activity — physical, mental, and spiritual. Man must cultivate all these if he is not to be imperfectly developed.

And Viktor E. Frankl of Vienna has written:[44]

> Man lives in three dimensions: the somatic (physical, i.e., bodily), the mental, and the spiritual.

Psychology shows that whenever these three personal needs are equally cultivated a full personality develops. It is only when one of these capacities has been denied or neglected that the development of the personality is unbalanced. The man who is entirely spiritual, who has cultivated his religious life to the exclusion of his mental life and his ability to deal with physical

---

[43] Dryden, Hugh, "The Scientist in Contemporary Life," *Science*, 120 (1954): 1054.

[44] Frankl, Viktor E., *Digest of Neurology and Psychiatry* (Inst. of Living, Hartford, Conn.), Feb., 1955, p. 74.

things with reasonable success, is found to be an "odd" person —
though the reasons for this are not always perceived. To the
Christian, it is much more apparent that an incomplete personality has resulted when the individual has concentrated on
skill and knowledge and entirely neglected his spiritual life.
Then, of course, there are those who seem equally abnormal
because they have concentrated on the mental life and neglected
to develop either technical competence or worship.

What is true psychologically of the individual, history shows
to have been true of whole cultures. Nations also have personalities. Whether this is genetically determined or not, is a matter
of considerable debate. There are those who argue strongly for
a hereditary basis, and there are those who argue strongly against
it because the concept could be the subject of national pride and
corresponding abuse. But the existence of Modal Personality —
the idea that there is a recognizable English, French, or Chinese
stereotype — can be very forcibly argued. It is our contention
that something of this nature has providentially been allowed to
characterize the three branches of the family of man. Whenever
the contribution of Shem, Ham, and Japheth has been blended
into a single organized way of life, a high civilization has resulted. But as soon as such civilizations have become unbalanced
and either the spiritual life, the intellectual life, or the technology of the culture has received overemphasis to the detriment
of the other two, that civilization has momentarily appeared to
burst ahead with new vitality only to collapse — frequently with
frightening suddenness. It does not require a vast acquaintance
with the details of history to be able to see illustrations of this
sequence of events. At the present time one has to bear in mind
that the original contribution of Shem has for a time been taken
over by Japheth who has thus assumed responsibility for both
the spiritual and the intellectual life of man. Thus western culture has reached its present heights because it inherited, as a
result of overrunning and to some extent taking possession of
the rest of the world, the accumulated cultural wealth and
technology of Shem and Ham. There is no guarantee that this
high civilization will maintain the proper balance of emphasis
on man's spiritual, intellectual, and physical needs. Indeed,
many people feel that the first of these has already been neglected
too long. And unfortunately there has been a tendency for those
who have insisted on the importance of cultivating the human

spirit to be themselves without a realistic understanding of man's intellectual and physical needs.

The Church has the responsibility of maintaining the duties originally appointed to Shem. If she fails in this, the result must be disastrous. The disaster will be all the more serious as the achievements of Japheth and Ham are all the more extended and powerful; for the greater the potential of civilization, the greater the potential for evil unless it is continually purified and preserved from corruption. As Noah predicted, the responsibility which belonged to Shem was allocated to Japheth when the "times of the Gentiles" began. But it will be restored to Shem once more when the times of the Gentiles are fulfilled and the Kingdom is restored to Israel. This event will usher in a higher civilization than the world has ever seen because the specific contribution of Japheth and Ham will be perfectly balanced by the contribution of Shem.

It might be thought, and indeed is fondly imagined by some less realistic folk, that a highly spiritual culture which attaches little or no importance to material things or to the exercise of human reason, and lays almost all the emphasis on man's spiritual needs, would have the best chance of producing a lasting era of peace and prosperity. But history shows that this has not been so. The early Church within a few centuries of its inception had created the hope of such a spiritual order. But the European world which was most influenced by it, collapsed almost completely in the face of barbarian invasion — and the Dark Ages resulted.

This has seemed a surprising thing to many people, but the reasons for this collapse are perhaps not too hard to see. The Lord pointed out that the children of this world are wiser in their own generation (i.e., in the contemporary situation) than the children of light (Luke 16:8). I think this means that the idealistic dreams of a spiritual society which have prompted the establishment of numerous religious communities in the past overlook the fact that such communities are only a part of the scene and in their contacts with the world at large they lack an essential ground of common understanding. They consequently become an easy prey to any society which does not accept the same standard of morality. In amateur sports, both teams accept the same set of rules. This makes it possible to play a meaningful game. But the moment you have opposing teams, one of which accepts the honorable rules of the game and the other rejecting them without any qualms, the first team finds itself at a great disadvantage because it has no way of knowing how to deal realistically with the tactics of the enemy. Sir Alfred Zimmern has pointed out that the breakdown of international relationships has resulted from the fact that the original ideals governing these relationships were formulated by men largely influenced and willing to accept Christian standards of morality.[45] But today many of the parties involved are in no sense Christian. The consequence is that they have no qualms in ignoring these laws when it suits their purpose, whereas the so-called Christian nations find it an embarrassment to do so. In such a situation it is difficult for the latter to deal realistically with the former.

There is another contributing factor. It has been observed that virtue can be more dangerous than vice, because its excesses are no longer modified by the activity of the conscience. Consequently the over-spiritual community (like the over-spiritual individual) makes demands of others which are not consistent with real life situations and these demands lead in time to a general reaction, which views them as unreasonable. All too frequently it is found that spiritual communities become grossly material within a generation or two. But it is not merely a reaction to the strong emphasis on the spiritual nature of man; it is the neglect or denial of his rational nature and physical needs. God intended that the latter should be balanced and governed by the proper exercise of the former.

In the family of Noah, Shem is given priority, Ham comes second, and Japheth is last. This order may well be intended to underline an important truth. Man's spiritual needs are preeminent, and his physical needs are next. His intellectual needs are last. History indicates that this was the order of development. And historically, as Lord Raglan has pointed out, the expression of man's religious nature came first and led in due course to technological development. Philosophy, the contribution of Japheth, came relatively very late in history.

The demands of the body cannot be neglected. Since the time of the Flood, the major contribution towards meeting these demands has been rendered by the family of Ham. Virtually no people have managed to survive without finding some way of satisfying their spiritual and physical needs. Many societies have survived without philosophy — which indicates that in a sense

[45] Zimmern, Sir Alfred, *The Prospects of Civilization*, Oxford Pamphlets on World Affairs, No. 1, 1940, p. 22.

the contribution of the family of Japheth is least important of all. Nevertheless, this contribution is directly responsible for the extension of the first two into other categories of experience, religious belief into theology, and technology into science.

It seems, therefore, that overemphasis on man's spiritual life will not lead to a high civilization but tends rather in the opposite direction. The corollary is also true. Overemphasis on man's intellectual life or overemphasis on his physical needs have the same detrimental effects. The dominant social classes in India for centuries concentrated on the intellectual life of man to the neglect of the spiritual and physical components, with the consequent impoverishment of the whole man. In the New World we are in danger of allowing the material to dominate the spiritual — and even the intellectual — by too great an insistence on the value of technical education to the exclusion of philosophy and theology.

Such, then, according to our thesis is the biblical view of the stream of history insofar as the rise and fall of civilization is concerned. It is not, as some great historians have suggested, that cultures have a "life" and pass by nature through a process of birth, growth, maturity, senescence and death — or, as others have suggested, always come to an end because of spiritual decay. It is rather that one of these three aspects of man's basic needs has been neglected or overemphasized. It was God's intention that these needs should be taken care of specifically by an appointed branch of the family of man. To Shem, the responsibility of maintaining man's spiritual life; to Ham, the duty of guaranteeing man's physical survival and dominion over the earth; and to Japheth, the enlargement of man's thoughts and the elaboration of the contributions of Shem and of Ham.

The biblical record shows how the experience of these three families was suited to prepare them for their tasks. Ham was scattered far and wide at a very early time in history, reaching the most distant parts of the habitable world far in advance of Shem or Japheth. This experience forced them to bend every energy to the stupendous task of pioneering and achieving mastery over every kind of environment which would allow man to establish a permanent settlement. Necessity quite literally became the mother of invention and the Hamites became the world's foremost technologists. Later in history, when the way had already been opened up, Japheth spread slowly into many of these areas where, becoming heirs to the solutions of their predecessors the Hamites, they had leisure enough to spend more time in reflection and in due course developed their philosophies. Ham excelled in "know-how"; Japheth began to ask "why?"

Meanwhile, the spiritual life of man was in grave danger and the Truth was almost eclipsed. But God called out one man from the family of Shem, and renewed in him the purity of the original revelation. This man became a family, and this family became a nation. This nation by persecution and bondage was knit together into a self-conscious unit, and then by a series of miraculous experiences strongly confirmatory of their mission, was planted in a small country which stood at the crossroads of those great world powers which were the carriers of the world's basic civilization. Through prophets and teachers this small nation was prepared for the task of being spread throughout the whole world as spiritual leaders, drawing their inspiration from a divine King whose throne would be set at the crossroads. From time to time fragments of Shem were scattered among the nations to bring an appropriate spiritual light wherever they went, but, by and large, the family remained a compact unit at the center of things, that the source of Light might be one, and not many. As we know, they failed to recognize their King and Japheth inherited their right.

When the King returns, Shem will become the spiritual head of the nations and under perfect administration the contribution of Ham and Japheth will lead to the appearance of a civilization so much higher and more remarkable than anything the world has known, that we can have little conception of the possibilities of it — the Millennium.

A Note to the Reader

There may very well be differences between races, some being gifted in one way and some in another. Whether such national characters are the result of cultural conditioning or are genetically determined is not at present clear. But differences there do seem to be and I, for one, believe that, however this has come about, it has been by God's providential oversight of history and to serve His own purposes.

The really important thing is that we must never make the mistake of identifying differences with superiorities. To my mind, a great injury is done to the study of Scripture when the fear of being accused of promoting superiorities, merely because one is attempting to assess differences, has the effect of denying one the right even to explore the possibility that differences might exist as part of the economy of God. The question is not one of levels of worth but of uniqueness of contribution, each race making a contribution of immeasurable benefit both to itself and to mankind as a whole.

If this paper encourages the belief that differences exist, it is NOT intended to encourage the belief that any one race is superior or inferior.

PART II

A Study of the Names in Genesis 10

God who made the World
And all things therein ...
Hath made of one blood all nations of men
For to dwell on all the face of the earth.
And He hath determined the appropriate times
And the bounds
Of their settlement,
That they should seek the Lord
If haply they might feel after Him
And find Him.
Although
He be not far from any one of us:
For in Him we live,
And move,
And have our being. ...

Acts 17:24-28.

INTRODUCTION

THE DIFFICULTIES of elucidating, at this late date in human history, the origins and relationships of the various races of mankind, are so great that many would doubt if it is even worthwhile to attempt it at all. Even a cursory examination of such a volume as Coon's "Races of Europe"[1] will quickly reveal that racial mixture has already proceeded so far that in almost any part of the world one may find individuals or groups of people representative of all the currently recognized racial stocks or sub-races indiscriminately intermingled. To propose in the face of such evidence that from the Table of Nations in Genesis one can show the origins, relationships, and patterns of dispersion of these racial stocks would seem at first rather absurd.

Undoubtedly we shall be accused of oversimplification. Yet there is a sense in which this may be an advantage here, since it allows one to ignore certain complicating factors and to avoid being completely overwhelmed by detail: thus permitting the setting forth of an intelligible alternative to current ethnological theories which I believe better explains the distinction both of fossil remains of prehistoric man as well as of present racial groups. There is, therefore, some justification for presenting the grossly simplified picture which appears in this paper.

A second point which I should like to underscore is that what constitutes evidence in favor of, or virtual proof of a thesis, depends, in this kind of research, very much upon the bias of the reader. To demonstrate that the earth is flat would require an enormous amount of evidence! Indeed, most people would feel that *no* amount of evidence was sufficient. But to confirm that the earth is round would require very little. Thus, whether a piece of evidence is considered as strong or weak often hinges

---

[1] Coon, C. S., *Races of Europe,* Macmillan, N.Y., 1939, 739 pp., index.

not so much upon its intrinsic weight as it does upon whether it supports accepted opinion.

I believe that for anyone who accepts Scripture as a touch-stone of Truth, even when its plain statements appear to be contradicted by the reasonably assured findings of secular re-search, it will not require the same kind of evidence to carry weight. If the children of Japheth are, as we shall propose, the people of Europe (and part of Northern India, etc.) as Genesis 10 implies, then slight evidence in confirmation will tend to clinch the matter for those who already believe it, whereas no amount of evidence will clinch the matter for those who simply don't. Similarly, for those who are persuaded that this Table of Nations is truly comprehensive, the colored races must, logically, be included, and somewhere here we shall find the ancestors of the so-called black, brown, and yellow peoples. The question is whether this kind of comprehensiveness is implied in the words (v. 32) "by these were the nations divided in the earth after the flood." In the interpretation of passages such as this, there tends to be a parting of the ways between those who attach great im-portance to the actual words of Scripture and their implications, and those who attach much less importance to the words them-selves and do not therefore examine the implications very seri-ously. The latter tend to be suspicious whenever the former allow implications to play a large part in their interpretation. The question is, more broadly, Does God intend us to look for implications and logically work them out when the kind of con-crete statements which are much to be preferred and which would then clinch the matter are actually lacking?

On this issue some words of Dr. Blunt in his quite famous book, *Undesigned Coincidences in the Old and New Testament,* are very much to the point. After observing, rightly, with what alacrity imagination enters where implications are in view and how readily it breaks all bounds and becomes highly visionary, he nevertheless argues strongly in favor of the wide and active investigation of implications in Scripture. He says:[2]

> The principle is good, for it is sanctioned by our Lord Himself, Who reproaches the Sadducees with *not knowing* (his emphasis) those Scriptures which they received, because they had not *deduced* (his emphasis) the doctrine of the future state from the words of Moses, "I am the God of Abraham, the God

---

[2] Blunt, J. J., *Undesigned Coincidences in the Old and New Testament,* Murray, London, 1869, p. 6.

of Isaac and the God of Jacob," though the doctrine was there if they would have but sought it out.

The point is well taken and, as he adds in the next paragraph, "the proofs of this are numberless." He then proceeds to illustrate his point in some detail. But his opening illustration is particularly apt because while it is perfectly true that the implication of Moses' words was in this instance clearly of profound importance, the learned men of our Lord's time — who incidently were not lacking in devoutness — very probably took the same rather sceptical attitude that is current today in such matters and would have flouted the idea as quite absurd if anyone else than the Lord Himself had proposed it. They did not believe in the resurrection and would not, therefore, have accepted such an inference from Moses' words. And I suspect that in our determination to discourage the over-use of imagination in interpreting Scripture (a determination which is quite proper, I believe), we have nevertheless robbed ourselves of many insights.

This paper is, therefore, an attempt to show:

(1) that the geographical distribution of fossil remains is such that they are most logically explained by treating them as marginal representatives of a widespread, and in part forced, dispersion of peoples from a single multiplying population established at one point more or less central to them all, sending forth successive waves of migrants, each wave driving the previous one further towards the periphery;

(2) that the most degraded specimens are those representatives of this general movement who were driven into the least hospitable areas, where they suffered physical degeneration as a consequence of the circumstances in which they were forced to live;

(3) that the extraordinary physical variability of their remains results from the fact that they were members of small isolated strongly inbred bands: whereas the cultural similarities which link together even the most widely dispersed of them indicate a common origin for them all;

(4) that what is true of fossil man is equally true of extinct and living primitive societies;

(5) that all these initially dispersed populations are of one basic stock — the Hamitic family of Genesis 10;

(6) that they were subsequently displaced or overwhelmed by Indo-Europeans (i.e., Japhethites), who nevertheless inher-

ited or adopted and extensively built upon their technology and so gained an advantage in each geographical area where they spread;

(7) that throughout this movement, in both prehistoric and historic times, there were *never* any human beings who did not belong within the family of Noah and its descendants;

(8) and finally, that this thesis is strengthened by the evidence of history, which shows that migration has always tended to follow this pattern, has frequently been accompanied by instances of degeneration both of individuals or whole tribes, and usually results in the establishment of a general pattern of culture relationships which are parallel to those archaeology has since revealed from antiquity.

With respect to Genesis 10, modern ethnology has to my mind tended rather steadily towards its confirmation. Nevertheless, I see no reason at all to hope that ethnology will ever seek to advance itself by building it upon this Table as a working basis. But I see every reason to believe that once we know enough, we shall find there was never any need to be ashamed of our confidence in it as a guide of the past. We have only to bide our time.

GENEALOGICAL TABLE OF THE DESCENDANTS OF NOAH

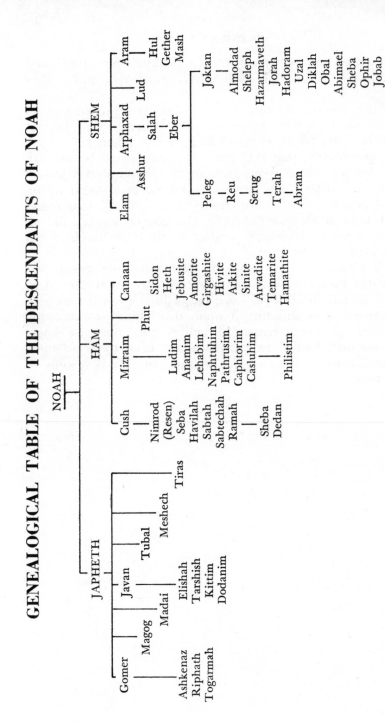

Chapter 1

THE TABLE OF NATIONS:
A UNIQUE DOCUMENT

FOR SOME people genealogies are fascinating things. For anyone who has roamed widely and deeply in history, they serve
somewhat the same purpose as maps do for those who have
roamed widely and deeply over a country. The historian pours
over the genealogy as the traveler pours over his map. Both
provide insights into relationships and a kind of skeletal framework about which to hang much else that has stirred the imagination. As Kalisch observed,[3] "The earliest historiography consists
almost entirely of genealogies: they are most frequently the medium of explaining the connection and descent of tribes and
nations," and inserting where appropriate brief historical notes
such as those relating to Nimrod and Peleg in Genesis 10. Maps,
too, have such little "notes."

Although the genealogies of the Bible are apt to be treated
with less respect than the more strictly narrative portions, they
are nevertheless worthy of careful study and will be found to
provide unexpected "clues to Holy Writ." Genesis 10, "The
Table of Nations," is certainly no exception.

But opinions have differed very widely as to its value as a
historical document. Its value in other respects, for example, as
an indication of how strongly its author was aware of the true
brotherhood of man — a most exceptional circumstance in his
own day — is admitted universally. By contrast, disagreement
about its historical worth is not limited to liberal versus evan-
gelical writers but exists equally sharply between writers within
these opposing camps. To take two representative opinions from

---

[3] Kalisch, M. M., *A Historical and Critical Commentary on the Old Testament,* Longmans, Brown, Green, London, 1858, p. 235.

the ranks of very liberal scholars of half a century ago, we may quote Driver who wrote:[4]

> It is thus evident that the Table of Nations contains no scientific classification of the races of mankind. Not only this, however, it also offers no historically true account of the origin of the races of mankind.

And over against this, we have the opinion of the very famous Prof. Kautzsch of Halle who wrote:[5]

> The so-called Table of Nations remains, according to all results of monumental explorations, an ethnographic original document of the first rank which nothing can replace.

Among Evangelicals, however, the divergence of opinion tends to be not over the historicity of this ancient Table, but rather over its comprehensiveness. The question raised is whether we are really to understand that Scripture intends to signify that this genealogy supplies us with the names of the progenitors of the *whole* of the world's present population, including the Negroid and Mongoloid racial groups: or whether it provides only a summary statement of the relationships of those people who were known to the writer personally or by hearsay. At the same time, there is little disagreement among Evangelicals as to the basic fact that all men, none excepted, are to be traced back ultimately to Adam.

In this chapter, it is proposed to consider the Table as a whole with respect to its value, importance, and uniqueness among similar ancient records; and to examine its structure and its date.

This will be followed in the second chapter by a careful survey of one branch of the race, the Japhethites, the object being to show how reasonable the record is where we have sufficient information to assess it in detail. The assumption one might properly make on the basis of this study is that the rest of the Table would prove equally authentic and illuminating of ethnological history, if we had available the same amount of detailed information regarding the identity of the names recorded as we have of the family of Japheth.

In the third chapter, we shall explore the evidence from contemporary literature that unintentionally supports the im-

---

4 Driver, S. R., *The Book of Genesis*, Westminister Commentaries, 3rd. ed., Methuen, London, 1904, p. 114.

5 Kautzsch, Prof., quoted by James Orr, "The Early Narratives of Genesis," in *The Fundamentals*, Vol. 1, Biola Press, 1917, p. 234.

plication of Scripture: that, all peoples of the world having been derived from the family of Noah, wherever people are found in the world they must ultimately have migrated from the place where the Ark is said to have grounded; and that this assumption must apply equally to historic as well as to prehistoric man. In other words, here is the Cradle of Mankind, and here is the focal point of all subsequent dispersion of all who belong within the species Homo sapiens.

Our conclusion is that this Table of Nations is a unique and priceless document which makes a justifiable claim of comprehensiveness for the whole human race, and supplies us with insights into the relationships of the earliest people known to us, which would be quite lost to us but for Genesis 10.

Intrinsic Value and Underlying Concept of the Table.

Opinions regarding the value of this Table vary enormously. In 1906, James Thomas,[6] in what he is pleased to call a critical inquiry, says simply, "It is certain that the entire list is valueless"!

The famous S. R. Driver is not quite so devastating in his pronouncements, yet the final effect of his words is much the same. In his commentary on Genesis, he says,[7]

> The object of this Table is partly to show how the Hebrews supposed the principle nations known to them to be related to each other, partly to assign Israel, in particular, its place among them. . . .
>
> The names are in no case to be taken as those of real individuals. . . .
>
> The real origin of the nations enumerated here, belonging in many cases to entirely different racial types — Semites, Aryans, Hittites, Egyptians — must have reached back into remote prehistoric ages from which we may be sure not even the dimmest recollections could have been preserved at the time when the chapter was written. The nations and tribes existed: and imaginary ancestors were afterwards postulated for the purpose of exhibiting pictorially the relationship in which they were supposed to stand towards one another.
>
> An exactly parallel instance, though not so fully worked out, is afforded by the ancient Greeks. The general name of the Greeks was Hellenes, the principle sub-divisions were the Dorians, the Aeolians, the Ionians, and the Achaeans; and accordingly the Greeks traced their descent from a supposed eponymous ancester Helen, who had three sons, Dorus and

---

[6] Thomas, James, *Genesis and Exodus as History*, Swan Sonnenschein, 1906, p. 144.

[7] Driver, S. R., op. cit., p. 112.

Aeolus, the supposed ancestors of the Dorians and Aeolians, and Xuthus, from whose two sons, Ion and Achaeus, the Ionians and Achaeans were respectively supposed to be descended.

This excerpt from the work of Driver opens up a number of questions. To begin with, in view of the steadily increasing respect which is being accorded to ancient traditions, it may very well be that the parallel which this learned author has rather cynically proposed, far from being a testimony against the Table, may in fact be a witness in its favor. The Greek counterpart may not be an invention of some early historian at all, but may be a statement of fact. After all, people do not ordinarily invent ancestors for themselves. Names of progenitors are of very great importance to any people who have little or no written history, for such names are the pegs upon which they hang the great events of their past.

A further assumption is made by Driver which is equally unjustified: this is to the effect that the compiler of this Table was writing a kind of fictional history with the deliberate intent of giving his own people, the Israelites, an antiquity equal to that of the great nations around them. Since, as we shall see, the Table certainly does not on its face bear any evidence of being written for propaganda purposes, Driver appears to be reading more into the record than is justified. It is rather like setting up a straw man in order to be able to demolish him with scholarly verbosity.

A third point is — and this is a very important issue — that Driver supposes the only source of information which the writer had was his own fertile imagination and the traditions current in his time — ignoring entirely the possibility that God had providentially taken care to ensure that all the information necessary for compiling this Table should be preserved by one means or another. One only has to make what is, after all, a reasonable assumption for a Christian, namely, that God had a specific purpose for the inclusion of such a Table of Nations at this point in the writing of Holy Scripture. Part, at least, of this purpose is clear enough and will be examined subsequently.

But Driver's opinion about the value and importance of the document has not been shared by later writers who lived long enough to witness the enormous expansion of our knowledge of early Middle East history resulting partly from linguistic studies, partly from archaeology, and more recently still from the findings of physical anthropologists, who are recovering some important lines of migration in "prehistoric" times.

Before giving consideration to these findings, it may be worthwhile pointing out that the value of a document may change with time, so that it does not become more valuable or less valuable, but rather valuable in an entirely new way. There is a sense in which Genesis 10 retains its unique worth as the first document to proclaim the unity of Man, just as the Magna Charta was the first document to proclaim the equality of Man. To say, as Thomas did, that the document is valueless, is to betray an extraordinary narrowness of vision, by making the assumption that the only value a document can have is its use as a source of information for the historian. Historical veracity is one kind of value, but there are other values.

It should not for one moment, however, be supposed by this statement that we are relinquishing the historicity of this chapter in order to establish its value on another footing. The fact is, as we shall try to show, that wherever its statements can be sufficiently tested, Genesis 10 has been found completely accurate — often where, at one time, it seemed most certainly to be in error. This process of steady vindication has served to establish for it a second kind of value, namely, that like every other part of Scripture which has similarly been challenged and vindicated by research, it now contributes its testimony to the dependability of these earlier portions of Genesis, upon the truth of which hangs so much else of our faith.

Moreover, it is very difficult to conceive of the record of Genesis, which carries the thread of history from Adam until well into those ages supplied with monumental documents, without some kind of Table to set forth what happened to Noah's family and how the rest of the world, apart from the Middle East, came to be peopled after the Flood. The Table thus becomes an essential part of Scripture in its earliest portions, not merely for the satisfying of our natural curiosity, but to establish the fact that all men are of one blood, the offspring of the first Adam, and redeemable by the blood of one Man, the Second Adam.

The Table thus serves three purposes. It supplies an essential chapter in the early record of Genesis, rounding out what happened as the world's population expanded. It joined the whole human race in a single family without giving the least suggestion that any one particular branch of this family had preeminence over another — a notable achievement. Finally, as a purely historical document, it has provided insights into the relationships between peoples that are only now becoming obtainable by other means, thereby adding its testimony to the dependability of the Genesis record.

Of the first of these achievements, Dillmann had this to say:[8]

> Egyptians and Phoenecians, Assyrians and Babylonians, even Indians and Persians, had a certain measure of geographical and ethnological knowledge, before more strictly scientific investigation had been begun among the classical peoples. From several of these, such as the Egyptians, Assyrians, Babylonians, and Persians, surveys or enumerations of the peoples known to them and attempts at maps have come down to us in the written memorials they have left behind. But not much attention was paid, as a rule, to foreigners unless national and trade interests were at stake. Often enough they were despised as mere barbarians, and in no case were they included with the more cultured nations in a higher unity.
>
> It is otherwise in our text. Here many with whom the Israelites had no sort of actual relationship are taken into consideration. . . .

We are apt to be so familiar with the idea of the brotherhood of man, that we assume it to be a concept accepted by all races at all times throughout history. Occasionally we observe in our own selves a certain hesitancy in according other nations who do not share our cultural values the full measure of humanness which we accord to members of our own society. Such feelings, however, are apt to be as much concealed as possible, since the proper thing nowadays is to support the heroic assumption that "all men are equal." But there are times when we can give vent to our true feelings in the matter, as for example when we are at war. If the writer of the tenth chapter of Genesis was a Hebrew, it is likely that, for him, the Canaanites were a particularly despised and degraded subsection of the human race, whose status would tend to be put very low in the scale. We have an analogy in the status accorded to the Jewish people by the Nazis. To many Germans at that time, the Jews were not really human beings at all. It is all the more remarkable, therefore, that in this Table of Nations the Canaanites are given equal standing in the pedigree of man with the descendants of Eber, among whom the Jewish people are numbered.

---

[8] Dillmann, A., *Genesis: Critically and Exegetically Expounded*, Vol. 1, T. and T. Clark, Edinburgh, 1897, p. 314.

In his commentary, Kalisch[9] points out that even the curse of Canaan seems to have been forgotten, and no slightest hint of it appears in the record to remind the reader. On the contrary, no other tribe is enumerated with such complete detail as that of Canaan (vv. 15-19). As this learned writer says, "Nothing disturbs the harmony of this grand genealogy."

In the face of this, it is really rather extraordinary that Driver should consider the document as, in one way, a piece of Jewish propaganda.

One further point is worth mentioning. When a civilization reaches a very high level of development, there may come a clearer recognition that all men are blood brothers. However, in a very small, closely knit community struggling to establish itself, there may tend to be a very different attitude. Among most primitive people the habit is to refer to themselves (in their own language, of course) as "true men," referring to all others by some term which clearly denies to them the right to manhood at all. Thus the Naskapi call themselves "Neneot," which means "real people." The Chukchee say that their name means "real men." The Hottentots refer to themselves as "Khoi-Khoi" which means "men of men." The Yahgan of Tierra del Fuego (of all places) say that their name means "men par excellence." The Andamanese, a people who appear to lack even the rudiments of law, refer to themselves as "Ong," meaning "Men." All these people reserve these terms only for themselves. It is a sign of a low cultural state when this attitude is taken, but then, when a people hold the opposite attitude, it is likely a sign of a high cultural state. Thus when any people achieve a stage of intellectual development at which they clearly conceive that all men are related in a way which assures them equality as human beings, they are then highly cultured, even though the mechanics of their civilization may appear at a low stage of development. From this we ought logically to gather that the writer of Genesis was a highly cultured individual. Indeed, it seems to me that only with a high conception of God would such a conception of man be possible, and therefore Genesis 10 would seem to bear testimony to a very high order of religious faith. In the final analysis, one might ask whether it is possible at all to sustain a true conception of the equality of man without also a true conception of the nature of God. The former stems directly from the latter. The only ground for attaching to all men an equal

[9] Kalisch, op. cit., p. 234.

level of worth is the tremendous fact that all souls have equal value to God. Assuredly they do not have equal value to society.

Unless the ultimate standard of reference is the value which God attaches to persons, it is quite unrealistic to talk about all men being equal. Consider the drunken sot, wallowing in the gutter, poisoning the air with his foul language, utterly confusing his children, destroying his family life, disgusting his friends, disturbing his whole society — how can such a man possibly be of equal value with, for example, a pillar of the community who is full of neighborly goodness? Clearly, there is no equality here if the basis of evaluation is man with man, or man with his society.

Any society which evaluates its members by their worth to itself is not attaching value to the individual person at all, but only to his functions. When these functions no longer serve a useful purpose, the man ceases to have any value. This was Nietzsche's philosophy — and Hitler's. It is the logical philosophy of anyone who views man apart from God. It is our modern philosophy of education, emphasizing skill and technology, encouraging men to do rather than be well. Against this tendency of natural man to "de-valuate" himself while supposing he is exalting himself, the Bible could not do anything else than set forth in clear terms these two complementary facts: that God is concerned equally with all men and that all men belong to one family, uniquely related through Adam to God Himself. The argument, so stated, is an argument also for the comprehensiveness of the Table of Genesis 10. Unless it is comprehensive, unless ultimately all mankind is in view here, and not just those nations which Israel happened to have cognizance of, it is a chapter out of keeping with its context. Unless the whole race is intended, the chapter's purpose is in doubt and the message of the Bible is incomplete. We are left only with Acts 17:26 which, at this point while assuring our hearts, does not enlighten our minds as to the fact that it gives.

There is a negative side also to the matter of the authenticity of this historical document. Had this Table been designed for propaganda purposes (to establish Israel's position as of equal dignity though not sharing some of the glories of the surrounding peoples) or had it been merely the work of some early historian creating his own data with a comparatively free hand, then almost certainly some device would have been adopted for deliberately setting forth not only the high status of his own ancestors, but the very low status of that of his enemies. With respect to the first tendency, one has only to read modern history books to discern how very easily individuals of little real significance can be presented to us in such a way as to make us take enormous pride in our heritage. There is, in fact, very little written history which is not in part propaganda, although the author himself is often unaware of it. The number of "firsts" claimed by some national historians for their countrymen is quite amazing, and it is usually clear what the nationality of the author himself is. In complete contrast, it would be difficult to prove with certainty of what nationality the author of Genesis 10 was. We assume he was a Hebrew, but if the amount of attention given to any particular line that is traced were used as a clue to his identity, he might have been a Japhethite, a Canaanite, or even an Arab. This is remarkable and shows enormous restraint on the author's part, the kind of restraint which suggests the hand of God upon him.

With respect to the second tendency, the belittling of one's enemies, this chapter most assuredly would have been a wonderful one in which to put the hated Amalekites in their proper place. But the Amalekites are not even mentioned. Of course, it might be argued that the Amalekites did not even exist at the time he wrote, a supposition which I consider highly probable. If this is the case, this is a very early document, not a later one as Driver would have had us believe. In any case, the author could have treated the Canaanites similarly.

One further aspect of the tone of the Table is the modesty of its chronological claims. Whereas the Babylonians and Egyptians in the "parallels" which they have preserved for us extend their genealogies to absolutely incredible lengths — in some instances occupying hundreds of thousands of years — there are no such claims made or implied in Genesis 10. The feeling which one has in reading this chapter is that the expansion of population was quite rapid. Certainly, all is most reasonable. This feature of the Table is ably summed up by Taylor Lewis who remarked:[10]

> How came this Hebrew chronology to present such an example of modesty as compared with the extravagant claims to antiquity made by all other nations? The Jews, doubtless, had, as men, similar national pride, leading them to magnify

---

[10] Lewis, Taylor, in J. P. Lange, *Commentary on Genesis*, Zondervan, Grand Rapids, Michigan, n.d., p. 357.

their age upon the earth, and run it up to thousands and myriads of years. How is it, that the people whose actual records go back the farthest have the briefest reckoning of all?

The only answer to this is, that while others were left to their unrestrained fancies, this strange nation of Israel was under a providential guide in the matter. A divine check held them back from this folly. A holy reserve, coming from a constant sense of the divine pupilage, made them feel that "we are but of yesterday," while the inspiration that controlled their historians directly taught them that man had but a short time upon the earth.

They had the same motive as others to swell out their national years; that they have not done so, is one of the strongest evidences of the divine authority of their Scriptures.

As a matter of fact, those "parallels" that do exist elsewhere in the literature of antiquity not only completely lack the sobriety of Genesis 10, but owe their existence rather more to the desire to record notable conquests than to any philanthropic philosophy. As Leupold has aptly said,[11]

> No nation of antiquity has anything to offer that presents an actual parallel to this Table of Nations. Babylonian and Egyptian lists that seem to parallel this are merely a record of nations conquered in war. Consequently, the spirit that prompted the making of such lists is the very opposite of the spirit that the Biblical list breathes.

Such records cannot in fact properly be classed as "parallels" at all. As Marcus Dods observed,[12] "This ethnographic Table is not only the most ancient and reliable description of the various nations and peoples, but it has no parallel in its attempt to exhibit all the races of the earth as related to one another."

The Structure and Purpose of the Table.

The structure of things is normally related to the purpose they are intended to serve. This applies in engineering design, and it applies in physiology. It also applies in literature, whether as novel, poetry, legal document, or history. It applies also to Genesis 10. This document has more than one purpose but is so constructed that all its purposes are served equally well because of the simplicity of its conception.

The method of course, is to present a series of names, whether of individuals, whole tribes, or even places, as though

---

[11] Leupold, H. C., *Exposition of Genesis,* Wartburg Press, Columbus, Ohio, 1942, p. 358.
[12] Dods, Marcus, *Genesis,* Clark, Edinburgh, n.d., p. 45.

they were "persons" related by birth. This is done in a simple straightforward manner, several lines being traced for several generations, here and there a comment supplying additional information. As a consequence of the particular form in which our sense of "precision" has developed in Western Culture, we find it difficult to accept the idea that if a man founded a city or a tribe, such an aggregate of people could still be summed up in the person of the founder, so that they could with equal propriety be referred to as his offspring. Thus, in verse 15, Sidon is spoken of initially as the firstborn of Canaan: whereas by verse 19, Sidon is now clearly the city of that name. Similarly, Canaan is mentioned in verse 6 as a son of Ham and subsequently in verse 16 as father of several tribes who indeed, in verse 18, are referred to as his families. In the following verses the name refers to the territory he occupied, which is geographically defined. We think of this as a rather loose employment of the term "son," but it is simplicity itself when it comes to establishing origins. As Dillmann put it:[13]

> In the representation given of this fundamental idea of the relationship of all peoples and men, each particular people is conceived of as a unity summed up in and permeated by the influence of its ancestor.

Although Dillmann does not elaborate the implication of his observation regarding the persistence of the character of an individual in his descendants, so that the observation appears almost as a chance remark, it will be well in discussing the *purpose* of the genealogy (in its bearing on its structure) to pursue this implication a little further, before returning to a more detailed examination of the structure per se.

The point of interest here is that there *is* a sense in which the character of an ancestor may for a short while, and occasionally for a very long time, permeate the characters of his descendants. Sir Francis Galton,[14] and others, first applied statistical analysis for sociological data in an attempt to demonstrate that there is such a thing as hereditary genius. It is not clear today whether such traits are genetically linked or are the result of circumstances: for example, a famous lawyer may bias his children to follow in his footsteps and give them a headstart by his association with them, by his influence in the world, and by his accumulated means and technical aids. The same may happen

---

[13] Dillmann, A., op. cit., Vol. 1, p. 315.
[14] Galton, Sir Francis, *Hereditary Genius*, Watts, London, 1950, 379 pp.

in the practice of medicine. Similarly, circumstances may sometimes result in a long line of great actors. Possibly in the realm of artistic ability we have a larger measure of genetic influence.

The idea that a "father" determines to a significant extent the character of his descendants for several generations underlies a certain class of statements that appear both in the Old and the New Testaments. Jesus spoke of his bitterest critics as "Children of Satan," or "Sons of Belial," denying emphatically their claim to be "Children of Abraham." The very term "the Children of Israel," came to mean something more than the mere descendants of Jacob. The Lord spoke of Nathaniel as "an Israelite indeed," having reference to his character, not his lineage. It is important in this context to guard against the assumption that the "children" of an ancestor will only perpetuate the undesirable elements in his character. I believe history shows that there is such a thing as "national character,"[15] which appears distinctly at first in a single individual and reappears in his children and grandchildren with sufficient force to result in the formation of a widespread behavior pattern that thereafter tends to reinforce and perpetuate itself as the family grows from a tribe into a nation. Where differences in national character do seem to exist, no implication is intended that there is any intrinsic superiority of one kind over another. We are arguing for the existence of differences, not superiorities. In the sum, we are all much alike. This is of fundamental importance.

The possibility that this idea is not foreign to Scripture was noted by Dr. R. F. Grau, who, over 80 years ago, commented:[15]

> The object of the document which we are considering is not so much to call attention by these names to three individuals (Shem, Ham, Japheth) and to distinguish them from one another, as to point out the characteristics of the three races and their respective natural tendencies.

It is customary now to divide the world's present population into three racial stocks, Caucasians (essentially, the White Man), Negroids, and Mongoloids. It is exceedingly difficult to define successfully the distinguishing characteristics of any one of these

---

15 National Character: Compare, for example, Hamilton Fyfe, *The Illusion of National Character,* Watts, London, 1946, 157 pp. with many anthropological studies of native peoples (by Margaret Mead, for example) and modern nations (e.g., Ruth Benedict on the Japanese).

19 Grau, R. F., *The Goal of the Human Race,* Simpkin, Marshall, etc., London, 1892, p. 115.

three, although it might seem quite otherwise. Negroids are presumably black but the Australian aborigines are not Negroid, though quite as black. The straight, black hair, the brown "slant" eyes, the epicanthic fold, and other features commonly accepted as characteristically Mongoloid, can be observed frequently among people who are classed as Caucasians. To repeat, although everyone thinks it is a simple matter to distinguish the three groups — and in most cases they can — it is virtually impossible to *write down* a foolproof description which will clearly mark out what tribe or nation belongs within which group. There is, however, one way in which it could be done — especially if we limit our view to a much earlier period in history when racial mixture had not proceeded very far — and this is to trace the earliest true representatives of each tribe to their known ancestors and set forth in some kind of genealogical tree the relationships of these ancestors. Viewed in this light, the method of Genesis 10 is probably the *only* valid way to go about it.

In this Table, we again meet with three groups of people, the descendants of Shem, Ham, and Japheth. But these three groups do not correspond with the current classification of races, for in this Table it is apparent that Negroid and Mongoloid are classed as one family, and the trilogy is reconstituted by setting the Semitic peoples in a distinct class by themselves. So then, we have the Japhethites who can be conveniently equated for our purposes with the Caucasians, Indo-Europeans, or White Man; the Hamites who are held to encompass the Negroid and Mongoloid branches, i.e., the so-called colored races; and the Shemites who comprise both the Hebrew people (ancient and modern), the Arabs, and a few once powerful nations, such as the Assyrians and Babylonians. This is a very sketchy outline, but it will serve for the moment until the details of the Table can be examined more specifically.

Now, it is my firm belief that God has endowed these three groups — which we shall henceforth refer to normally as Japhetites, Hamites, and Shemites — with certain capacities and aptitudes which, when properly exercised, have made a unique contribution in the total historical development of mankind and which, when allowed to find full cooperative expression during a single epoch, have invariably led to the emergence of a high civilization.

This subject has been explored at some length by the author

and was the basis of an accepted Ph.D. thesis.[17] It is presented in simple outline in Part I, "Shem, Ham, and Japheth in Subsequent World History," and one critical aspect of it is examined in some detail in Part IV, "The Technology of Hamitic People."

In a nutshell my thesis is this: that mankind, considered both in individuals and as a species Homo sapiens, has a constitution which seeks satisfaction in three directions:[18] physically, intellectually, and spiritually. There are people who live almost entirely for the physical; we often speak of them as "living to eat." There are people who live almost entirely in the intellectual, who gladly surrender a meal to buy a book. There are people to whom the things of the spirit are completely paramount. Such people often go into permanent "retreat," and for a large part of Christian history they formed a class. Most of us probably live in these three realms with approximately equal emphasis, depending upon circumstances at the time.

A survey of history with this thought in mind, applied to nations or races rather than to individuals, reveals that Japhethites have originated the great philosophical systems; the Shemitic peoples, the great religious systems whether true or false; and, surprising as it may seem to one not familiar with the evidence, the Hamitic people have supplied the world with the basis of almost every technological advance. This is not the time or place to attempt a demonstration of this thesis, since it has been undertaken in the two papers mentioned above. The extent of the evidence is remarkable indeed, although all the more so in that only in recent years has the debt of the white man to the colored man been recognized to any extent. New discoveries are constantly being made as the result of a continuing research into the origin of inventions, and these bear out the above observation in quite unexpected ways.

When the philosophical bent, which originated with the Greeks and the Aryans and was successively elaborated by Western Man, was finally wedded to the technical genius of Hamitic

---

[17] Custance, A. C., "Does Science Transcend Culture?" Ph.D. thesis, presented to Ottawa University, 1958, 253 pp., ill.

[18] Hugh Dryden wrote, "Man's life at its fullest is a trinity of activity — physical, mental and spiritual. Man must cultivate all these if he is not to be imperfectly developed": "The Scientist in Contemporary Life," *Science* 120 (1954): 1054. Similarly, Viktor E. Frankl of Vienna wrote, "Man lives in three dimensions: the somatic (physical or bodily), the mental, and the spiritual," *Digest of Neurol. and Psych.*, (Instit. of Living, Hartford, Conn.) 1 (1940): 22.

peoples in Africa, Asia, and the New World, there arose the modern phenomenon of Science, enormously enlarging the fruits of this marriage. But the tendency when the union of these two is most fruitful, has always been for a kind of dehumanized civilization to appear. The true and necessary spiritual component was supplied initially through the Shemites and later by their direct spiritual descendant, the Christian Church. Without this spiritual component, civilization is in danger of annihilating man as an individual of worth. Without the Hamitic contribution, the contribution of Japheth led nowhere—as in Greece. Without the contribution of Japheth, the contribution of Ham stagnated as soon as the immediate practical problems of survival had been sufficiently solved. This kind of stagnation can be illustrated by the history of some of the great nations of antiquity, the Egyptians, for example. These interactions are examined elsewhere, but the important point to underscore at this juncture is that the various contributions of the various nations and peoples do not appear as contributions made by any one "family" unless one has the clue of these family relationships, which Genesis 10 supplies. Given this clue, and allowing that it is a true historical record, these three components for a high civilization—the technological, intellectual, and spiritual—suddenly appear in a new light when it is realized which particular group of people made the most fundamental contribution in each area. The dwelling of Japheth in the tents of Shem, that is, the occupation by Japheth of a position originally possessed by Shem; the taking away of a kingdom from the latter to give it to the former, all these biblical phrases assume a new significance. In short, Genesis 10, by dividing the whole race into three families in a way which does not concord with modern concepts of racial groupings, is not thereby discredited but shown to be based upon a much clearer insight into the framework of history. To my mind, there is no question that when we see history as God sees it in its totality and at the end of time, we shall discover that this Table was a fundamental clue to the meaning of it: and, we would repeat, it serves this purpose because it has a structure which does not agree with modern attempts to redefine the interrelationships of the world's peoples.

Now a few thoughts may be in order with respect to the more mechanical aspects of its structure. First of all, it may be noted that the division of mankind into three basic families was not derived from traditions maintained by nations living around Israel or within their ken, because these nations did not have any such traditions. The Egyptians distinguished themselves from other peoples on the basis of color, classing the Asiatics as yellow, the Libyians as white, and the Negroes as black.[19] But in this Table of Nations the so-called colored peoples are not distinguished from one another (for instance, the blacks from the yellows) but are classed, if my understanding of the text is correct, within a single family group. And although it is true that the name "Ham," meaning "dark," may have reference to the skin color — as the word "Japheth" may have reference to fair-skinned people — the principle does not hold entirely, for some, at least, of Ham's descendants were fair. Indeed, according to Dillmann, there were in ancient times fair-skinned as well as the more familiar black-skinned Ethiopians.[20] There is no indication that the Hittites were black-skinned, and the same is probably true of the descendants of Sidon, etc. On the other hand, the Canaanites and the Sumerians (both descendants of Ham) refer to themselves as "blackheaded" people[21] — a designation which seems more likely to have reference to skin color rather than color of hair, since almost all people in this area have black hair anyway; a hair-color distinction would be meaningless.

I'm quite aware, however, that it is customary in reconstructions based upon skeletal remains to picture the Sumerians as anything but negroid. But this is not fatal to our theory for, as we have already noted with respect to the Australian Aborigines, not all black-skinned people are negroids, and were we dependent only upon skeletal remains of these Aborigines with no living representatives to guide us, we should have no way of knowing that they were black-skinned at all. The same may apply to the Sumerians and Canaanites. There is little doubt that the people of Sumer and of the Indus Valley culture were akin.[22] The descriptions of the Indus Valley people in early Aryan literature indicate that they were negroid in type.[23] The

---

[19] Dillmann, op. cit., p. 318.

[20] Dillmann, op. cit., p. 319.

[21] The Canaanites: in the Prism of Sennacherib the Sumerians, according to Samuel Kramer, *From the Tablets of Sumer*, Falcon's Wing Press, 1956, p. 60. Hammurabi's Code (Deimel transcript, R. 24, line 11) also refers to them as "Blackheaded ones."

[22] See, for example, V. G. Childe, "India and the West Before Darius," *Antiquity*, 13 (1939): 5ff.

[23] Piggott, S., *Prehistoric India*, Pelican Books, 1950, p. 261.

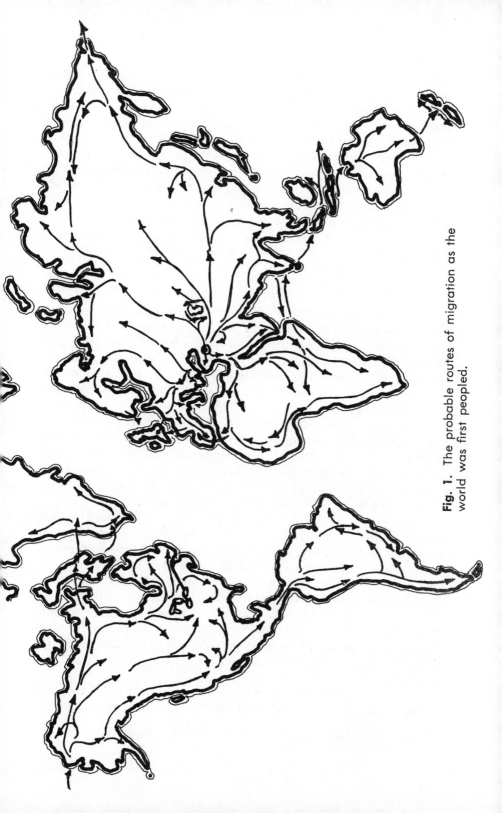

Fig. 1. The probable routes of migration as the world was first peopled.

famous little "Dancing Girl" from the Indus Valley is certainly negroid, and it is equally evident that genes for black skin still form a large component in the gene pool of the present Indian population. In his "Races of Europe,"[24] Coon has a section with descriptive materials devoted entirely to the many racial types which have contributed to the present population of Europe. In speaking of gypsies and dark-skinned Mediterraneans, he includes two photographs of one young man of clearly "negroid" appearance, and comments as follows:

> Of much greater antiquity outside of India is a dark-skinned [in the photo, almost black], black-eyed, and straight-haired Mediterranean type which appears with some frequency in southern Iran and along the coasts of the Persian Gulf. This young sailor from Kuwait will serve as an example. The origin and affiliations of this type have not as yet been fully explained.

Interestingly enough, a further illustration from southern Arabia shows a young man who, as Coon puts it, "except for his light unexposed skin colour . . . could pass for an Australian aborigine." The use of the word "unexposed" inevitably made me think of Ham's reaction to his exposed father. For if Ham was dark all over, he may have expected his father was also, and his surprise at discovering otherwise might have so disturbed him as to cause him to be forgetful of his filial duty. At any rate, it is clear that in this area of the world, once occupied by the Sumerians, there still remain "unaccountable" evidences of a very dark-skinned component in the population. All these lines of evidence lend support to the contention that the Sumerians may have themselves been a black-skinned people.

The three families are not predicated on the basis of language, either. Again it is perfectly true that the children of Japheth, in so far as they have given rise to the Indo-Europeans, would seem to be a single linguistic family. The same may be said of the Shemites. But when we come to the descendants of Ham we run into difficulties for it appears that in historic times the Canaanites, Philistines, and many Cushites spoke Semitic languages, while the Hittites (also Hamites, from Heth) may have spoken an Indo-European language. The trouble with linguistic evidence in this instance is that it really appears too late in history to be decisive.

· It has been suggested that the arrangement of the Table was dictated upon geographical grounds: for example, that the chil-

---

[24] Coon, C. S., *Races of Europe,* Macmillan, 1939, 739 pp., ill.

dren of Japheth spread in one direction — more or less to the north and west, whereas the children of Ham tended towards the south and east, while the children of Shem stayed more nearly at the center. This, however, would make the document something of a prophetic statement for such a dispersion did not occur until sometime later — unless, of course, one gives the document a late date, a point to be considered later. There is evidence that the writer knew only that some of Ham's descendants had entered Africa, that a large part of Shem's descendants had settled in Arabia, and that Japheth was still not very far to the north, though spreading along the shorelines of the Black Sea and the Mediterranean. In fact, the picture presented indicates a Cush quite close at hand which was not the same as the Cush later to be found in Ethiopia. Thus, although the Table recognizes, as indeed it had to do, that some dispersion had already taken place in which the members of each family had migrated in more or less the same general direction, this knowledge was not the basis of the threefold division, but rather stemmed from it.

While the writer admits that his genealogy employs not merely the names of persons but also of places and families, even making use at times of language as a guide, it seems pretty clear that the structure of his Table is dependent ultimately upon a true understanding of the original relationships of the founding fathers of each line to their more notable descendants and to one another. To my mind, the very structure of the Table predicates this kind of knowledge of the facts. On no other basis can one account for the circumstance that for centuries certain statements have seemed to be clearly contrary to the evidence, and that only as more light has appeared has the Table proved itself to be perfectly correct where properly tested.

The use of a genealogical tree which does not slavishly demand that individuals only are to be listed, but which allows the inclusion of cities they founded, tribes which they grew into, and districts which they occupied, provides a simple, straightforward, and concise method of setting forth the Origin of Nations.

The Date of the Table.

We come, finally, to the question of the date of this document. It will already be clear that, in our view, it is by no means "late" in the sense in which Higher Critics have understood the term. If it was composed many centuries after the events described, it has avoided anachronisms and certain errors, which would make it a masterpiece of forgery. So carefully has the supposed forger avoided these kinds of errors that it would seem far simpler and more reasonable to assume he was a contemporary of the terminal events which he describes in the chapter.

Among the lines of evidence which strongly support an early date for this document, the following carry great weight: (1) the small development of Japhetic peoples, (2) the position of Cush at the head of the Hamitic family, (3) the mention of Sidon but not of Tyre, (4) the reference to Sodom and Gomorrah as still existing, (5) the great amount of space given to Joktanites, (6) the discontinuance of the Hebrew line at Peleg, and (7) the absence of any reference to Jerusalem by name.

Let us consider these seriatim.

(1) *The small development of Japhetic peoples.* The descendants of Japheth were great colonizers and explorers spreading around the Mediterranean and up into Europe, and toward the east into Persia and the Indus Valley at a quite early date. Yet this Table views them as settling only in Asia Minor and along the immediate Mediterranean coast line.

Furthermore, Javan receives notice, from whom undoubtedly the Ionians are to be traced, but we find no mention of Achaeans or Dorians associated with him, nor of Phrygians with Ashkenaz. Yet one would only have to shift the time setting by a few centuries to make such omissions inconceivable. Indeed, according to Sir William Ramsay,[25] Homer, who wrote somewhere about 820 B.C. or even earlier (Sayce says 1000 B.C.), evolved a jumble of old and new when he produced Askanios as an ally of Priam and Troy, and an enemy of the Achaeans. Either the writer was quite ignorant of subsequent events because he lived before them, or he was extraordinarily careful to avoid the slightest taint of anachronism. For example, he implies that Javan, a son of Japheth, inhabited Asia Minor and the neighboring Greek coastlands in very early times. Yet there is, I believe, no trace of these old Ionians during the "historical" times of Greece and Israel, but only the survival of the name in one of the Greek states.

(2) *The position of Cush at the head of the Hamitic family.* It has been customary to date this Table as late as the sixth century B.C. But no writer at such a time would have referred to any part of Babylonia as the land of Cush, since by then Cush

---

[25] Ramsay, Sir William, *Asianic Elements in Greek Civilization*, Murray, London, 1927.

was used exclusively for a quite different region, i.e., Ethiopia. If the writer had been attempting a piece of historic fiction, he would surely have added parenthetically that he was not referring to Ethiopia in the present context. As it was, he evidently foresaw not the slightest confusion in the reader's mind since the Ethiopian Cush did not exist.

(3) *The mention of Sidon but not of Tyre.* The omission of Tyre among the states of Palestine is very significant, for similar communities such as Gerar and Gaza, among others, are carefully noted.

Tyre had a quite dramatic history. Founded somewhere about the 13th century B.C., by the 10th century she was mistress of commerce under Hiram. In the 8th century she fell under Assyrian domination, was beseiged by the Babylonians early in the 6th century, and finally came under the Persians in 588 B.C. In 332 B.C. she was once more utterly subdued by Alexander in a classic campaign which forms part of the subject of a separate Doorway Paper.[26]

In other words, from the 13th century on, this city-state made a considerable noise in the world, whereas Sidon made comparatively little. Indeed, those who were anywhere near contemporary with her, among the prophets, spent much time denouncing her (cf. Ezek. 27, for example). The two cities, Tyre and Sidon, were constantly referred to together, and in that order — and Arvad (also mentioned in the Table) faded into insignificance before the splendor of Tyre.

The omission of Tyre in this early Hebrew ethnography clearly implies that she had not yet risen to a position of importance — if she existed at all. This surely indicates that at least this section of the Table was written prior to the exploits of Hiram in the 10th century B.C.

(4) *The reference to Sodom and Gomorrah as still existing.* In view of the dramatic destruction of these two cities of the plain of Jordan, it is inconceivable that a late writer would mention them as in existence at that time and not make some attempt to inform the reader of what happened to them subsequently. It is surely simpler to believe that he was writing prior to their complete disappearance, an event which long antedates Hiram of Tyrian fame and must be set probably somewhere around the 17th century B.C.

---

[26] "Archaeological Confirmations of Genesis" (Part IV in Doorway Papers Vol. VII).

(5) *The great amount of space given to the Joktanites.* If one were to pick up earlier history books dealing with the settlement of North America by the White Man and his constant exchanges in trade and in war with American Indian tribes, one would continually meet with such tribal names as Ojibway, Huron, Seneca, Cree, Mohawk, and Cherokee. But to readers of the present day only a few of these would strike a chord of recognition. One suspects that the Joktanites were analogously both numerous and important in early Middle East history, particularly the history of Arabia. But within a few centuries, at the most, some circumstances had either reduced many of them to insignificant status as tribes, or so united them as to wash out their individual tribal existences. If a Jewish writer of the 6th century had strung off a list of names like this (even if he could have recovered them with any certainty), it is likely his words would have had very little impact or meaning for his readers. On the other hand, at a much earlier time, it might have been analogous to the earliest writings in America, of the Jesuits, for example, or of Catlin. That they have a genuine base in history is borne out by the names of districts or cities in Arabia which seem clearly to be recollections of much earlier settlements. When one contrasts the detail in this portion (vv. 6-20) with the sparse information given about the line of Shem through Peleg, it is difficult to argue with any force that the Table was a piece of Jewish propaganda favoring their own antecedents.

(6) *The discontinuance of the Hebrew line at Peleg.* In view of the great importance attached to the person of Abraham as the father of the Jewish people, it is certainly extraordinary that a writer purporting to present an account of the origin of nations, a writer remember, who is assumed to be himself a Jew, should have neglected entirely to indicate where Abraham originated. Considering that Abraham by almost any reckoning must have been a figure of some importance and well known before the destruction of Sodom and Gomorrah, the only conclusion one can draw from this is that the writer did not know of his existence because he was not yet alive or had as yet achieved no prominence.

The impression is reinforced further by consideration of the fact that although Palestine is treated in some detail, cities and territories being clearly delineated, there is a total absence of any mention of the Hebrews. If the object of the Table was to supply the Jewish people with proof of an equally impressive antiquity with the more prominent nations around them like the Egyptians (Mizriam, v. 6) and Assyria (Asshur, v. 22), would there not have been some mention of the glories of their own nation under Solomon?

(7) And this brings us to one final observation, namely, the reference to the Jebusites without any mention to the city under the more familiar name Jerusalem. This Table occupies itself with the names of individuals, the cities they founded, the tribes they gave rise to, and the territories they settled in. Of these categories the names of cities form a very prominent part. Yet, while the Jebusites are mentioned, their capital city is not singled out specifically, and the circumstance surrounding its change of name to become Jerusalem receives no mention whatever. This would be analogous to a history of early England in which the author, while listing many settlements of importance, makes no mention of London or Winchester. A Canadian historian, living before the formation of Upper Canada, if he should refer to a settlement at the mouth of the Humber River in Ontario but make no mention to "Muddy York," would be dated very early by Canadian standards. If he had casually mentioned that the people of this settlement were called "Muddy Yorkers," one would be more tempted to place him somewhere around A.D. 1800. However, if he made no mention by way of parenthesis that the town of York later became the city of Toronto, one would still assume that he was ignorant of the fact and died before the change was made. This would be particularly the case if he had in the meantime made careful reference to other towns and cities of prominence in early Canadian history.

It seems to me that the total absence of any direct reference here to a city specifically known as Jebus, and even more importantly to the same city as Jerusalem, is a clear indication that the writer lived only long enough to complete a record of events exactly as we have them in this ancient Table. At the very latest, if the above arguments carry weight, he cannot have survived very much beyond the 20th or 19th century B.C.

We turn in the next chapter to a study of certain representative portions of this ethnographic Table in order to show how far it can serve as a guide to ancient history, since it supplies information and vital links that are not otherwise available in our present state of knowledge.

Chapter 2

THE FAMILY OF JAPHETH[27]

THE GREAT majority of those who read this chapter will belong within the Indo-European family of nations, of whom it can be shown that the "father" was Japheth. It is our intention, therefore, to spend more time tracing the descendants of Japheth

[27] General bibliography: the following biblical encyclopedias contain valuable information on the Table as a whole or the individuals mentioned:

International Standard Biblical Encyclopedia, ed. James Orr, in 5 vols., Howard-Severance, Chicago, 1915, under Table of Nations.

Imperial Bible Dictionary, ed. P. Fairbairn, in 2 vols., Blackie and Sons, London, 1866, under individual names, i.e., Japheth, etc.

Popular and Critical Bible Dictionary, ed. S. Fallows, in 3 vols., Howard-Severance, Chicago, 1912, under individual names.

Murray's Illustrated Bible Dictionary, ed. W. C. Piercy, in 1 vol., Murray, London, 1908, under individual names.

A Dictionary of the Bible, ed. J. D. Davis, Westminster Press, Phila., 1934, under individual names.

Bible Cyclopedia, A. R. Fausset, Funk and Wagnalls, London, n.d., under individual names.

Cyclopedia of Biblical Literature, John Kitto, in 2 vols., Black, Edinburgh, 1845, under individual names.

Works dealing specifically with the Table:

Josephus, *Antiquities of the Jews,* Bk. 1, Chap. 6.

Rawlinson, George, *The Origin of Nations,* Scribners, N.Y., 1878, 272 pp.

Rouse, Martin L., "The Bible Pedigree of the Nations of the World," Pt. 1, *Trans. Vict. Instit.,* 38 (1906): 123-153.

————. "The Pedigree of the Nations," Pt. 2, *Trans. Vict. Instit.,* 39 (1907): 83-101.

Sayce, A. H., *The Races of the Old Testament,* Rel. Tract Soc., London, 1893, 180 pp.

Useful information will be found at the appropriate places in commentaries and editions of the Hebrew text by Bullinger, Cook, Dillmann, Dods, Driver, Ellicott, Gray and Adams, Greenwood, Jamieson, Kalisch, Lange, Leupold, Lloyd, Schrader, Skinner, Snaith, Spurrel, Whitelaw.

Archaeological works such as those by George Barton, J. P. Free, M. R. Unger, T. G. Pinches, R. D. Wilson, and A. H. Sayce.

than of Ham or Shem, partly because, as a result of labors by others in the past, we have considerably more information about this particular line, and partly because what can be said about Hamites and Shemites is not only less in quantity, but has perhaps less intrinsic interest for most of us. Nevertheless, there are certain portions of the Hamitic line which we shall study a little more closely because they contribute light upon the issue of whether this Table of Nations is truly comprehensive or merely selective, encompassing all mankind, or only a representative portion.

To begin with, it is well known that Japheth's name has been preserved in both branches of the Aryan family, which very early split into two major divisions and settled in Europe and India. The Greeks, for example, trace themselves back to Japetos, a name which without doubt is the same, and significantly, according to Skinner, has no meaning in Greek.[28] It does have a meaning, however, in Hebrew. In Aristophanes' "The Clouds,"[29] Iapetos is referred to as one of the Titans and the father of Atlas. He was considered by the Greeks not merely as their own ancestor but the father of the human race. According to their tradition, Ouranos and Gaia (i.e., Heaven and Earth) had 6 sons and 6 daughters, but of this family only one — Iapetos by name — had a human progeny. Marrying Clymene, a daughter of Okeanos, he had by her Prometheus and 3 other sons. Prometheus begat Deukalion who is, in effect, the "Noah" of the Greeks, and Deukalion begat Hellen who was the reputed father of the Hellenes or Greeks. If we proceed a little further, we find that Hellen himself had a grandson named Ion; and in Homer's poetry the rank and file of the Greeks were known as Ionians.

Meanwhile, the Indian branch of this Aryan family also traced themselves back to the same man. In the Indian account of the Flood,[30] "Noah" is known as "Satyaurata," who had 3 sons, the eldest of whom was named Iyapeti. The other 2 were called Sharma and C'harma (Shem and Ham?). To the first he allotted all the regions north of the Himalayas and to Sharma he gave the country of the South. But he cursed C'harma, because when the old monarch was accidently inebriated with strong liquor made from a fermented rice, C'harma had laughed at him.

---

[28] Skinner, John, *A Critical and Exegetical Commentary on Genesis,* T. and T. Clark, Edinburgh, 1930, p. 196.

[29] Aristophanes, "The Clouds," Roger's Trans., line 998.

[30] See J. H. Titcomb, "Ethnic Testimonies to the Pentateuch," *Trans. Vict. Instit.,* 6 (1872): 249-253.

Two further brief observations may be made at this point. The first is that the Greeks recollected 3 brothers, for Homer makes Neptune say:[31]

> There are three of us, Brothers, all sons of Cronos and Rhea: Zeus, Myself, and Hades, the King of the Dead. Each of us was given a domain when the World was divided into three parts.

The second is that in primitive Aryan speech the title "Djapatischta"[32] means "chief of the race," a title which looks suspiciously like a corruption of the original form of the name "Japheth." Apart from these few notices, we know little else about Japheth except that, in Hebrew, his name probably means "fair." Of his sons, we know much more. They are given in Genesis 10 as Gomer, Magog, Madai, Javan, Tubal, Meshech and Tiras.

Gomer. Considered ethnologically, it appears that Gomer was by far the most important of the sons. To judge from the ancient historians, as Herodotus, Strabo, and Plutarch, Gomer's family settled first to the north of the Black Sea, giving their name in slightly modified form to that district known as Cimmeria, later shortened to Crimea,[33] (the Arabs, by a transposition of letters, having given it the name Krim). These people appear to have multiplied rapidly towards the west, but a considerable portion of this ancient family were driven out by the Scythians and took refuge in Asia Minor during the 7th century B.C. Their subsequent history is known in some detail from Assyrian records where they appear as the Kimirraa, by which they were already known in the time of Homer.

In concert with the Minni, the Medes, the people of Sepharad, and other populations whose territory they had already overrun, they attacked the northern frontier of the Assyrian Empire. But in 677 B.C. their leader, Teupsa, was defeated by Esarhaddon and some were driven eastwards where they overthrew the old Kingdom of the Elippi, and according to some built Ecbatana, and some westward into Asia Minor again. Here they sacked Sinope and Antandros (which they held for a hun-

---

[31] Homer, *Iliad,* trans. E. V. Rieu, Penguin, Classics ed., 1953, Book xv, p. 276.

[32] Dods, M., *The Book of Genesis,* Clark, Edinburgh, n.d., p. 43.

[33] Wright, Charles, *The Book of Genesis in Hebrew,* Williams and Norgate, London, 1859, p. 35.

dred years), and finally invaded Lydia. The Lydian king, the famous Gyges (687-653 B.C.),[34] sent to Nineveh for help but was slain in battle before help arrived and his capital city, Sardis, was captured by the invading army. Gyges' successor, Ardys, was able to exterminate or drive most of them out of the country. A recollection of their brief ascendency in the area seems to be borne out by the fact that the Armenians referred to Cappadocia as Gamir,[35] although it is not certain whether they intended by this the name of the land or merely the inhabitants. Eusebius in referring to Gomer says, "whence the Cappadocians."[36]

Some of the tribe of Gomer either remained in the country or subsequently returned, and others went west as far as France and Spain — and later still into the British Isles, as we shall see. According to Josephus,[37] the branch which returned to Asia Minor came to be known as the Galatians. It may be pointed out that although the form "Galatia" seems far removed from "Gomer," it is possible etymologically to derive it from the more ancient form of the name. The middle consonant of the word GoMeR can readily be replaced by a W or a U, so that G-M-R can become G-W-R or G-U-R. It is possible that the ancient site known as Tepe Gawra is a recollection of one of these forms. A further change may take place in the substitution of L for the terminal R. This substitution is very common and may be observed, for example, where castrum in Latin becomes "castle" in English. We thus have the following series: G-M-R becoming G-U-R, becoming G-U-L. The final form is to be observed as the more familiar Gaul, where it will be remembered some of the descendants of Gomer had settled. And the connection between the Gauls, the Galatians, and the Celts are all well established historically. Indeed, according to Haydn,[38] the Gauls were called Galati by the Greeks and Galli or Celtae by the Romans. Furthermore, Roman historians claim that these people came originally from Asia Minor and settled throughout Europe — in Spain (Galicia), in France (Gaul), and in Briton (Celts).

---

[34] Herodotus, Book 1, chap. 8, gives an interesting story (with a moral) on how Gyges became King of Lydia.

[35] Skinner, John, op. cit., p. 196.

[36] Eusebius, *Chronicon* (Armenian), ed. by Aucher, Vol. 1, p. 95 (Gimmeri —Cappadocians) and Vol. 2, p. 12 (Gomer, "out of whom the Cappadocians").

[37] Josephus, F., *Antiquities of the Jews,* Bk. 1, Chap. 6.

[38] Vincent, B., *Haydn's Dictionary of Dates,* Ward, Lock, and Bowden, London, 21st ed., 1895, p. 455.

It appears further that many of the Gomerites who formed the restless "barbarians," against whom the Assyrians had to defend themselves, later hired themselves out as mercenaries who, when they had been paid off, were settled as farmers in that part of Asia Minor known as Galatia.

In discussing Paul's Epistle to the Galatians, Dean Farrar observes that:[39]

> It must be regarded as certain that the Galatae were Celts, and not only Celts but Cymric Celts. . . .
> Every trait of their character, every certain phenomenon of their language, every proved fact of their history, shows beyond the shadow of a doubt that the Galatae or Gauls were . . . Celts; and it is most probable that the names Galatae and Celtae are etymologically identical.

Kalisch identifies them with the Chomari, a nation in Bactriana near the Oxus mentioned by Ptolemy.[40]

That these people should be referred to not merely as Celts but Cymric Celts is a beautiful illustration of how a very ancient name may persist, for the word "Cymric" — or without its patronymic termination, C-M-R — is nothing less than the more ancient form "Gomer," very slightly modified. This modified form is still with us in the district of England known as Cumberland. Once more we have a slightly variant rendering of the original name by the introduction of the consonant B, so that Gomer-land becomes Cumber-land. To one not familiar with etymological changes, the introduction of the B may seem strange, but it is by no means uncommon and is to be observed, for example, where the Latin form *"numerus"* becomes "number" in English.

It would appear that the descendants of Gomer were a restless bunch, much of the time on the move and extremely warlike. Where they settled, they tended to form a kind of military aristocracy and when they moved there was scarcely any stopping them. In 390 B.C. it was these same nomads who appeared outside Rome and sacked the city. Meanwhile, in Italy they came to be known as the Umbrians, in which we once more may discern the original form "Gomer" but with the initial guttural presumably replaced by a hard H and then dropped entirely, while the B was inserted in exactly the same way as we have observed in the word "Cumberland."

---

[39] Farrar, F. W., *Life and Work of St. Paul*, Vol. 1, Cassell, London, p. 466.
[40] Kalisch, op. cit., p. 236.

The record is not complete yet, however, for Ireland was in ancient times known as Ivernia and the Irish Sea as Hibernicus. Ivernia has lost the initial gutteral and the M has become a V; Hibernicus replaces the gutteral with an H and the M with a B. All these changes are commonly observed within the Indo-European family of languages. For another example, the simple form "Paul" in Spanish may appear as Pablo. Also the Septuagint of Genesis 10:28 replaces the Ebal of the Hebrew with Eual. Again, Nicholaus appears in the Hebrew prayer book (Aboda Zara) as Nicholabus.

Thus Gomer's children and his children's children went far up into Europe, where, despite their separation both in time and distance, the name of their ancient forebear was preserved among them. Indeed, there is even the possibility that the very name of Germany preserves for us Gomer in slightly inverted form, although the claim made by certain German historians that the Teutons represent the pure Gomer-ic line (a claim which they held accounted for the warlike nature of the German people) is highly improbable and is challenged by virtually every ethnologist of modern times.

Just to complete the record, it may be further observed that the Welsh people refer to themselves as Cymri, and in Denmark we find a port originally called Cimbrishavn which in our speech would be Cimbri's Haven. Jutland also was known as Chersonesus Cimbrica. It would appear that scarcely any part of Europe was not at one time or another settled by the descendants of Gomer, and some areas — notably France and the British Isles — were once inhabited by a homogeneous people speaking a language akin to modern Kumric.

Ashkenaz. Numerous and varied have been identifications of the people descended from Ashkenaz, son of Gomer. Sayce,[41] for example, was inclined to believe that because the name was coupled with Ararat and Minni (Jer. 51:27) they should be identified with the Asguza of the Assyrian monuments. Maspero maintained that they were to be equated with the classical Scythians.[42] Almost without exception, commentators agree that they are to be placed to the north of the Fertile Crescent which encompasses

---

[41] Sayce, A. H., *The Races of the Old Testament,* Rel. Tract Soc., London, 1893, 180 pp.

[42] Maspero, Sir. G.C.C., *History of the Ancient Peoples of the Classic East,* Vol. 3 in The Passing of the Empires, SPCK, 1900, p. 343.

Palestine and Mesopotamia. They point out that there still exist recollections of the name Ashkenaz in Lake Ascanius and a neighboring people who came to be known as the Askaeni.[43] These people lived in the province of Phrygia and seem to be mentioned by Homer in the Iliad (II, 2, 863 and 13, 793). Peake mentions two lakes and a river in the district which bear the old name in modified forms and notes that Ashken still appears today as an Armenian proper name.[44] One of these two lakes in the eastern part of Bithynia near Nicea is mentioned by Strabo (cf. 7, 389) and is now known as Lake Iznik — a broken-down form of Ashkenaz, in which an inversion has taken place. In Bithynia on the borders of the Sea of Marmora there was a Lake Ascenia; in southwestern Phrygia there is another lake similarly named; and midway between them lay Troas, in whose royal family we find, in the time of the Trojan war, a Prince named Ascenius. It is possible that these also may reflect the name Ashkenaz.

As the descendants of Ashkenaz moved northward they found descendants of Tiras (Thracians, as Josephus affirms) already occupying the Plains of Thrace, with a kind of rearguard body in Bithynia, if we are to judge by allusions in Herodotus and Strabo. This circumstance probably contributed to their taking a more northerly route into west central Russia, instead of following Gomer westwards into Europe, arriving in due time in what is now Germany. The Jewish commentators have customarily associated Ashkenaz and the Germans, and probably with justification.[45] From there as they multiplied, they moved further north into Ascania which, along with the islands of Denmark, came to be known to later Latin writers as the "Islands of Scandia"[46] — Scandinavia. The introduction of an epenthetic D crept into the form Ascania in much the same way the Latin *tenere* appears in French as *tendre*.

It is curious how some form of the name Ashkenaz has been preserved in this area throughout history. The inhabitants of the ancient state of Dessau have long claimed descendants from Ashkenaz, and one of their rulers in the 12th century, who for a while held the Saxon estates of Henry the Lion (founder of the

---

[43] Sayce, A. H., under Askenaz in *Murray's Illustrated Bible Dictionary*, Murray, London, 1908.

[44] Rawlinson, G., *The Origin of Nations*, Scribner, N.Y., 1878, p. 181.

[45] Hertz, J. H., *The Pentateuch and Haftorahs: Genesis*, Oxford, 1929, p. 88, n. 3.

[46] Rawlinson, G., op. cit., p. 182.

House of Brunswick), added to his baptismal name Bernard that of Ascenius. For he declared that his ancestors had come from Lake Ascenius in Bithynia.

Meanwhile, far away on the northern borders of Media, a rearguard of the same family remained behind. These people were allies of their neighbors, the Medes, and caused much trouble to Esarhaddon of Assyria. In classical times they dwelt near Rhagae, according to Josephus,[47] a city of some size, which lay near the center of the southern shore of the Caspian Sea. At that point a chain of mountains begins that runs eastward along the shore and beyond it, forming a natural boundary to the territory of the Bactrians and the Saki. This chain of mountains was referred to by Ammianus Mercellinus, the Emperor Julian's librarian and historian who was writing about A.D. 350, as the Ascanimian Mountains.[48] These wild tribes, referred to by Strabo as the Saki,[49] gained possession of Bactriana on the one side of the Caspian and occupied the best districts of Armenia on the other side. These occupied territories "took from them the name of Sakasene," so Strabo tells us.

Thus we know of a range of mountains called in classic times the Ascanimians, around which we know dwelt descendants of Ashkenaz. At the outset of the Christian era, a little to the north of them, cut out of the neighboring kingdom of Armenia and just south of the Caucasus Mountains, there was a country called "Sakasene." It is almost certain that these people, the Sakasenoi, were also descendants of Ashkenaz. And it appears that some time after the Christian era began, a wave of this family of Ashkenaz, calling themselves Sakasenoi, or more briefly Sachsen, marched northward through the Caspian Gates into European Scythia and thence onward with the tide of their German kinsmen, the Goths, into northern Europe where the country they occupied has borne the simple title "Sachsen."

When Tacitus, writing about A.D. 100, lists the peoples of Germany in his own day, although he included in his account Denmark and Sweden where he says dwelt the Cymbri, and also included the Angli, he made no mention whatever of the Sachsens, or as we more familiarly know them, the Saxons. These people appear first in history when Caransius was appointed,

---

[47] Josephus, F., *Antiquities of the Jews*, Bk. 1, Chap. 6, section 1.

[48] On this see M. L. Rouse, "Bible Pedigree of the Nations of the World," *Trans. Vict. Instit.*, London, 38 (1906): 149.

[49] Strabo, I:i:10, and I:iii:21 and XI:viii:4.

about A.D. 280, to guard the eastern British coasts against pirates, at which time he was given the title "Count of the Saxon Shore."[50]

We may believe, then, that Japheth's grandson, Ashkenaz, gave rise to a large component of the earliest settlers in Germany and Scandinavia, and left en route many memorials of the ancestral name, besides providing for us a tribe of people who played an exciting part in English history.

Riphath, another son of Gomer: Little seems to have been discovered that could be related to this name. Several proposals have been made for some districts in Asia Minor. Dr. J. Pye Smith[51] suggests, for example, Rifou east of the Black Sea and the Riphaean Mountains mentioned in ancient geographies by Strabo, Virgil, Pliny, and others. C. R. Conder[52] mentions a people living eastward of the Black Sea named the Rhibii. He also suggests the Riphaeans who were later known as Raphlagonians, whom Josephus identifies as the descendants of Riphath. In the *Popular and Critical Biblical Encyclopedia,* the first map at the end of Vol. III shows the ancient world and the supposed position of the descendants of Noah. There is no authority behind this map other than certain suppositions based upon an intelligent examination of the biblical evidence, but it may be noted that the center of Europe is occupied by Riphath. The conjunction of the word "Europe" on the map with the name Riphath prompted the question whether there could have been some connection between the two. The name "Europe" is generally derived from the legend of Europa, but since dictionaries of classical mythology acknowledge that the etymology of Europus is uncertain, the possibility still remains that if we could reach far enough back in history we would find that the name was originally Riphath. Another suggestion has also been made, that the name reappears in the name "Carpathians." There are also the Carpates, called Alpes Bastarnicae, which separate Dacia from Sarmatia.

Togarmah: The people named after Togarmah, a son of Gomer,

---

50 On this whole aspect of the problem, see also Martin L. Rouse, op. cit., pp. 149, 150.

51 Smith, J. Pye, "Dispersion of Nations," *Popular and Critical Bible Commentary,* Vol. 2, ed. by S. Fallows, Howard-Severance, Chicago, 1912, p. 1213.

52 Conder, C. R., "Riphath," *Murray's Illustrated Bible Dictionary,* p. 749.

are mentioned twice by Ezekiel (27:14 and 38:6), at first trading at the fairs held in Tyre with horses and mules, and later about to come down with Gomer out of the north against Palestine. Neither passage does much towards fixing their homeland, but both agree with the hypothesis that the people intended are the ancient inhabitants of Armenia. And this has some support from national tradition and etymological theory. The Armenian traditions assign as their own ancestor a man named Hiak, who they claim was the "Son of Targom, a grandson of Noah."[53]

By an inversion of letters, the Armenians came to be referred to as the House of Targom, and Jewish writers often refer to the Turks as Togarmah. It should be noted also that the Black Sea, which is northwest of Armenia, was also sometimes referred to as Togarmah. Strabo[54] seems to have taken it for granted that the Armenians were intended, and Herodotus[55] mentions their connection with horse breeding. Josephus says[56] that Togarmah is the father of the people known as Thrugrammeans, whom the Greeks identified with the Phrygians. Prof. F. W. Schultz[57] points out that according to the Jewish Targums Togarmah was the father of Germany. And there are some who believe that the word Germania itself is formed out of the older name Togarmah with the first syllable lost in the process. If this is so, then there can be no connection between "Gomer" and "Germany," as proposed previously.

Magog: Very little is known about the identity of the people descended from Magog. It is not even clear whether the name is the original form or compounded of two elements, "ma" and "Gog." The prefix *ma* was often added in antiquity to a personal name, meaning "the place of." Magog would then mean the "place of Gog," i.e., the territory of Gog.

According to Chamberlain,[58] the prefix *ma* means "earth" in Magyar and Estonia and in the form *maa* it bears the same significance in Finnic. In Cuneiform the sign for *ma* could be understood as an enclosure or an area of ploughed ground, two

---

[53] Armenian tradition: Moses Chorenensis, 1.4, section 9-11.
[54] Strabo, XI:xvii:9.
[55] Herodotus, VII. 40.
[56] Josephus, F., *Antiquities of the Jews,* Book 1, Chap. 6, section 1.
[57] Schultz, F. W., "Gomer," *Religious Encyclopedia,* Vol. 2, ed. by Philip Schaff, Funk and Wagnalls, N.Y., 1883, p. 889.
[58] Chamberlain, A. F., "The Eskimo Race and Language," *Canad. Jour.,* 6, 3rd series, p. 326.

different ideograms being used at different times. A number of ancient names appear with and without the prefix *ma*. According to Lloyd,[59] the two forms Chin and Machin both occur for China. Conder[60] interpreted the form *Magan* (signifying the region of Sinai) as a compound meaning the "place of strength," "walled land," or some such descriptive term.

The ordinary word in Assyrian and Babylonian for "land" or "country" is *matu*, often abbreviated to *mat*. And "the country of 'Gutu,'" according to Sayce,[61] appears in Assyrian inscriptions as *Mat Gugi*. He considers, therefore, that Gog is the Gugu of the Assyrian inscriptions and the Gyges of the Greeks (which I think is very doubtful, being far too late), the compound form "Magog" meaning the "land of Gog," i.e., *Mat Gugi*.

There is some indication that Marco Polo[62] understood the word "Mungul" to be a broken-down form of the word "Magog," since he came across an association of names "Ung" and "Mungul," which were considered the counterparts of Gog and Magog. He appears to be referring to a time prior to the migration of the Tartars. It is just conceivable that the word "Mongol" was originally attached to a people descended from Gog and of Indo-European stock. Curiously, small pockets of people have been reported still retaining an Indo-European form of language in areas now completely dominated by Mongols.[63]

Bochart[64] derived the word "Caucasus" from a compound form "Gog" and "Chasan" meaning "the stronghold of Gog." According to Josephus, the descendants of Gog were later known as the Scythians, whom he says were otherwise known as Magogites. These people subsequently formed the greater part of Russian stock. Mention is made of Gog in Ezekiel (38:2 ff.) as "the chief prince of Meshech and Tubal." It may be observed that "rosh" (רֹאשׁ), which in this passage is translated "chief prince," signified the inhabitants of Scythia. From it the Russians

---

59 Lloyd, J., *An Analysis of the First Eleven Chapters of the Book of Genesis,* Samuel Bagster & Sons, London, 1869, p. 114.

60 Conder, C. R., commenting on a paper by T. G. Pinches, "Notes on Some Recent Discoveries in Assyriology, etc.," *Trans. Vict. Inst.,* 26 (1897): 180.

61 Sayce, A. H., op. cit., p. 45.

62 Marco Polo, *Travels of Marco Polo,* Library Publications, N.Y., n.d., p. 87.

63 I regret that I have mislaid the source of this observation. It was given in a paper in the *Trans. Vict. Inst.*

64 Bochart, "Gog and Magog," *Chamber's Encyclopedia,* Vol. 4, Chambers, London, 1868, p. 813.

derive their name. Russia was known as Muskovi until the time of Ivan the Terrible, a name undoubtedly connected with Meshech. The Russian Empire was created by the Muskovite princes who were the first Grand Dukes of Moscow, but it was Ivan (1533-1584) who really consolidated and extended that great Empire until it reached the White Sea on the north and the Caspian Sea in the south and was thenceforth called Russia.

As stated at the outset, there is very little certainty about any of this but such fragments as we do have point in the same general direction, i.e., the area commonly referred to today as Russia has a population that is probably to be traced back largely to Gog.

Madai and Javan: The part that these play in early history is very well defined and can be stated without the complications that are attached to most of the previous names.

It is reasonably clear that the Madai appear subsequently as the Medes and Javan gave rise to the Ionians. In his book, *Races of the Old Testament,* Sayce says that the Medes claimed a relationship with the Aryans of north India, and on the Persian monuments (for example, the Behistun inscriptions) they are referred to as the "Mada" — from which the Greek form, Medes, comes.[65] There is no doubt that Persia was their general area of initial settlement. In Assyrian inscriptions they are mentioned as the Ma-da-ai.[66]

Now it has already been observed that before there arose a complete separation of the various nationalities — Medes, Persians, Greeks, Celts, etc. — the Japhethites were first divided into two major bodies. One of these comprised the ancestors of the Indians and Persians, whereas the second was the aggregate of those tribes which afterwards composed the nations of Europe. Thus the word "Indo-European" well sums up our ethnological origins.

That the separation of these two groups had probably preceded the smaller division into nationalities is suggested by the early rise of names distinguishing these two great divisions. The ancestors of the Indo-Persians claimed for themselves alone

[65] Behistun Inscriptions: *Records of the Past,* Vol. 1, Bagster, London, 1873, p. 111, para. 1, section 6. In the original, Mada appears in the English translation as Media.

[66] Spurrell, G. J., *Notes on the Text of the Book of Genesis,* Clarendon Press, Oxford, 1886, p. 97.

the old title, "Aryas," and they gave to the other body the name, "Yavanas,"[67] a word which may possibly be related to our word "Young," although to my mind it is clearly a recollection of the name Javan. Thus Javan and Madai, in a manner of speaking, may stand collectively for the two branches of the Indo-European family.

Orientals seem to have used the term Yavan for the Greek race as a whole. The Assyrians called the Greeks of Cyprus the "Yavnan." The Persians refer to the Greeks of Asia Minor and the Aegean Islands as the "Yuna." The terms "Greek" and "Hellene," "Achaean," and "Dorian" seem to have been unknown in Asia, according to Rawlinson.[68]

In the days when Egyptian monarchs of the IVth dynasty were erecting their pyramids, the Mediterranean was already known as the "Great Circle of the Uinivu,"[69] which is equated by same with the Javan.

Larned suggests that the Italian peninsula was occupied by peoples of a stock who had traveled into Greece, later crossing the Apennines and spreading southward along the western coast.[70] It is evident that in the name "Javan" we have a very early reference to the basic stock out of which Greece, and perhaps part of Italy, was first settled, for the Greeks in later periods used other patronymics to refer to themselves. And it would seem, on the other hand, that in the Medes we have an equally early reference to those who settled India, since in Genesis 10 there is no mention, for example, of the Persians who in later records were nearly always associated with the Medes. Indeed, as with the Greeks, whose more ancient name, Ionians, has long since disappeared, so in modern times the word "Persia" has remained but the name "Madai" has disappeared. What we have is a general term for those who became Indians, Medes, and Persians.

Elishah: The number of possible identifications of the descendants of this son of Javan is considerable. Most of them are probably correct. For example, it is quite generally agreed that the

---

67 Keary, C. F., *Outlines of Primitive Belief Among the Indo-European Races,* Scribner, N.Y., 1882, pp. 163ff.

68 Rawlinson, G., op. cit., p. 173.

69 Sayce, A. H., *The Higher Criticism and the Verdict of the Monuments,* S.P.C.K., London, 1895, p. 20.

70 Larned, J. N., *A New Larned History,* Vol. 6, Nichols, Springfield, Mass., 1923, p. 4636.

more familiar "Hellas" is a corrupted form of an original "Elishah" and, according to Rawlinson,[71] from about the time of the Persian War, Hellas came to be a name commonly applied to the Greeks as a whole.

Another form of this ancient name is believed, by many authorities, to be "Aioleis" (Ἀἰολεῖς), i.e., the Aeolians. This view was held also by Josephus.[72] The Jerusalem Talmud, the Midrash, and the Targums read for Elishah the form "Elis" or "Eolis," although scholars such as Skinner[73] and Driver[74] consider this quite groundless. The Tell el Amarna tablets include several people from *Alasia*. The *Eilesion* of the Iliad (II, I, 617) is doubtless a further reference. It is almost certain that the name reappears in the Ugarit tablets[75] in which there is a Canaanite reference to the Cyprians under the title "Alasiyans." In Ezek. 27:7, it is said that purple stuffs were brought to Tyre from the "Isles" (or coasts) of Elishah. The mussel from which the purple dye was obtained in antiquity abounded on the coasts of the Peloponnese, confirming the general area settled by this grandson of Japheth.

It is confusing to find a people broadly referred to as the "Greeks" being traced back and, without distinction, referred to both as the people of Hellas and as Ionians. This is analogous, however, to referring to Englishmen as descendants of Normans, Picts, Scots, or Celts, etc. The fact is that in both cases a few families have given rise to large clans or tribes, which in the ebb and flow of migration and conquest became united in various mixtures, so that a historian with one preference may emphasize one originating stock while another historian emphasizes a different one. And both are correct.

Tarshish: Not too much can be stated with certainty about the identity of Tarshish, another son of Javan. There are statements elsewhere in Scripture which confuse the issue somewhat. For example, it was the opinion of Sayce[76] (as it has been of a num-

---

[71] Rawlinson, G., op. cit., p. 184.

[72] Josephus, F., *Antiquities of the Jews,* Book 1, Chap. 6, section 1.

[73] Skinner, J., op. cit., p. 198.

[74] Driver, S. R., op. cit., p. 116.

[75] Harris, Zellig S., "Ras Sharma: Canaanite Civilization and Language," Ann. Report Smithsonian Instit., 1937, p. 485: R. J. Forbes, *Metallurgy in Antiquity,* Brill, Leiden, 1950, p. 346.

[76] Sayce, A. H., *Races of the Old Testament,* Rel. Tract Soc., London, 1893, p. 47.

ber of other scholars) that Tartessos in Spain was probably one of the initial settlements of Tarshish. However, the Old Testament speaks of ivory, apes, and peacocks being brought by the ships of Tarshish (II Chron. 9:21). Such creatures would not be expected from Spain. But Sayce argues that the implication is merely that merchants from Tartessos, or Tarshish, traded in these items, which they perhaps picked up somewhere in Africa and sold elsewhere in the Middle East. The Septuagint renders Tarshish in Isaiah 23:1 as Karkedonos (Καρχηδόνος), which was the Greek form of the name "Carthage" in North Africa.

While the Phoenicians seem to have had many trade dealings with Tartessos, the original port itself could not, according to Genesis 10, have been founded by them, for the Phoenicians were not descendants of Japheth. In Genesis 10:15 one of their major settlements was founded by a son of Canaan, and in the Old Testament the Phoenicians and Canaanites are described as descending from Ham. The Carthaginians, as Phoenician colonists, maintained even in the days of Augustine that they were Canaanites.[77] On the other hand, many colonies were also established by the Phoenicians in Spain. Here is one of the difficulties, for certain biblical references to Tarshish (II Chron. 9:21 and 20:36) have led some scholars[78] to suppose that there must have been another Tarshish in the Indian Ocean which could be reached via the Red Sea. Although this idea is now generally rejected, it underscores the fact that Tartessos in Spain is not an altogether satisfactory identification. That is to say, the Spanish settlement does not on the face of it seem to have been a Japhetic one, nor do the products which are said to have come from it seem proper to it.

However, Kalisch[79] believed that there was sufficient evidence to justify identifying Tarshish as the original settler of the whole Spanish peninsula "so far as it was known to the Hebrews, just as Javan is used to designate all the Greeks," the Phoenicians arriving later. Cook[80] believed that a small tribe of Javanites settled at the mouth of the Guadalquiver river in Spain,

---

[77] Carthaginian Canaanites: See article, "Phoenicia and the Phoenicians," *Popular and Critical Bible Encyclopedia*, Vol. 2, Howard-Severance, Chicago, 1912, p. 1342, end of section 5.

[78] So Jerome in his work, *On Jeremiah*, X, 9; and since then by Bochart and many others.

[79] Kalisch, M. M., op. cit., p. 243.

[80] Cook, F. C., *The Holy Bible with Explanations and Critical Commentary*, Vol. 1, Murray, London, 1871, p. 85.

thus initiating the colony of Tarshish. Bochart[81] says that both Cadiz and Carteia, which was in the Bay of Gibraltar, were in ancient times called Tartessos; and he thinks that the former was built by Tarshish, grandson of Japheth, immediately after the dispersion, and the latter, long afterwards, by the Phoenicians. He refers to the fact that, according to Herodotus,[82] when the Phoenicians first arrived, Tartessos was already in existence, and the king of that country was named Arganthonius.

In summary, then, it is possible that Tarshish, grandson of Japheth, settled in Spain and established a capital city and a kingdom which later on became a trading point much used by the Phoenicians, who stopped there on their way to the eastern Mediterranean ports bringing their wares picked up elsewhere. These wares may have come partly from Spain and partly from Africa. It is not at all impossible that they may even have come in part from India round the Horn of Africa, for there is plenty of evidence that the Phoenicians were superb navigators.

Kittim: This is another son of Javan and his descendants. There can be little doubt that by Kittim, or Chittim as it sometimes is spelled, the Hebrews understood the people dwelling in Cyprus. Josephus[83] observes that the island was called by the Greeks Kition and its inhabitants were known as Kitieis, or Kittiaeans. In the course of time the name came to have a larger meaning, being extended from Cyprus to the other islands of the Aegean, and from them to the mainland of Greece and even to Italy. For example, in I Maccabees 1:1, Alexander the Great is described as coming from the land of Kittim, and in I Maccabees 8:5, Perseus is referred to as the King of the Kittim. In Daniel 11:30 both the Vulgate and the Septuagint translate Chittim as Romanos. Although I have not seen elsewhere any reference to the possibility, it appears to me that the land of Chittim might be found in the form "Ma-Chettim" "Ma," as we have already observed, is a prefix for "place." If so we may have the original form of the more familiar "Macedon," the land of Alexander the Great's birth.

There is not much of substance in these remarks, but in a general sense they confirm the impression given throughout this

[81] Bochart: quoted by J. Lloyd, *Analysis of the First Eleven Chapters of Genesis,* Bagster, London, 1869, p. 117, n.

[82] Herodotus, Book 1, chap. 163.

[83] Josephus, F., *Antiquities of the Jews,* Book 1, chap. 6, section 1.

portion of Genesis 10, that the Japhethites were very much at home along the shores of the Mediterrranean and throughout its islands, as well as up into and across Europe.

Dodanim: Not very much can be written about this, except that it seems to appear elsewhere in Scripture with the initial D replaced by an R (cf. I Chron. 1:7). If Rodanim is the preferred form, it would appear that the Island of Rhodes formed one link in a series of settlements by the descendants of Javan.

The River Rhodanus, i.e., the Rhone, may have received its name from a branch of this family which settled at its mouth.[84] In Epirus there is to be found the city of Dodona and the county of Doris. Bochart suggested that the first settlement of the Dodanim was in southwest Asia Minor in that part of the country called by the Greeks Doris. It is possible also that a more corrupted form of the name is the Dardan, found in the inscriptions of Ramses II, signifying a people of Asia Minor not far from the Lycians, and just possibly providing us with the origin of the term "Dardanelles." In the present state of our knowledge of antiquity, little more can be said about the descendants of Dodanim.

Meshech and Tubal: These two names occur rather frequently as a couplet (See, for example, Ezek. 32:26, 38:2, 3). Meshech is found on the Assyrian monuments in the form of "Muskaa," probably pronounced Muskai. Classical writers were in the habit of calling them the Moskhi, and in the time of Ezekiel the position of these people is probably that described by Herodotus (III, 94), i.e., in Armenia where a mountain chain connecting the Caucasus and Anti-Tauraus was named after them, the Moschici Montes. Here, according to Strabo (XI, 497-499), was a district named Moschice.

In the Assyrian inscriptions the word Tubal occurs as Tubla, whereas it seems to have been known to classical geographers as Tibareni. According to Rawlinson,[85] these two — the Mushki and the Tibareni — dwelt in close proximity to each other on the northern coast of Asia Minor and were at one time among the most powerful people of that area. The Moschian capital was known to Josephus and was called by the Romans

---

84 Greenwood, George, *The Book of Genesis: An Authentic Record*, Vol. 2, Church Printing Co., London, 1904, p. 29.

85 Rawlinson, G., op. cit., p. 173.

"Caesarea Mazaca." Josephus[86] also says that the Iberians of Italy were descendants of Tubal. As he put it, "Thobel founded the Thobelites, now called Iberis." It also is possible that in the River Tiber we have a recollection of this same ancestor. According to Forbes,[87] the Moschi and Tibareni are included in the 19th satrapy of Darius. They were redoubtable enemies of the Assyrians in the early half of the first millennium B.C.; Tiglath Shalmaneser II mentions tribute paid to him by "24 kings of the land of Tabal."[88]

By classical times, these people had moved northwards,[89] although Xenophon[90] and his Greek troops still found remnants of them south of the Black Sea. Much later in history we meet the word Meshech in the form Muskovy. It is possible that the two famous cities of Moscow and Tobolsk still preserve the elements of the names Meshech and Tubal.

Tiras: According to Josephus and the Targum, the descendants of Tiras became the Thracians. Smith[91] says that one offshoot of the Thracians were the Getae or Goths. King Darius conquered them in 515 B.C. By the time of Alexander the Great (c. 330 B.C.) they dwelt at the mouth of the Danube.[92] But they maintained sufficient independence to unite with the Dacians in the early part of the first century B.C., thereafter harassing the Roman legions until they were conquered by Trajan in A.D. 106 and incorporated into the Roman Empire.

One of the problems here is that we have no further occurrence in Scripture of Tiras. There is this one brief mention of his name and then, unlike Gomer, Meshech, or Tubal, he disappears entirely. If the Thracians were really descendants and if they were, as Rawlinson[93] says, widely scattered with many offshoots such as the Bithynians and Phrygians, one might have expected that Scripture would make some reference to Tiras

[86] Josephus, F., *Antiquities of the Jews,* Book 1, chap. 6, section 1.

[87] Forbes, R. J., *Metallurgy in Antiquity,* Brill, Leiden, 1950, p. 280.

[88] Schrader, E., *The Cuneiform Inscriptions and the Old Testament,* Williams and Norgate, London, 1885, p. 64.

[89] Sayce, A. H., *Races of the Old Testament,* Rel. Tract Soc., London, 1893, p. 48.

[90] Xenophon, *The Anabasis,* trans. by J. S. Watson, Harper, N.Y., 1861, Book V, chap. 5, section 1, p. 159.

[91] Smith, R. Payne, *Commentary on Genesis,* ed. by Ellicott, Zondervan, Grand Rapids, Mich., n.d., p. 149.

[92] "Getae," *Everyman's Encyclopedia,* Vol. 6, Dent, London, 1913.

[93] Rawlinson, G., op. cit., p. 174.

Fig. 2. The basic centers of civilization which underlie all others. Each of these cultural centers of the early world was Hamitic in origin.

North America

Amerindian

South America

Asia

Indus

Sumer

European culture

Egypt

Africa

subsequently. On the other hand, it may be said that a general belief exists among ethnologists, which is nevertheless not susceptible of proof, that the Thracians ultimately gave origin to the Teutons. Thus Rawlinson observes:[94]

> The Thracian tribe of the Getae seems to have grown into the great nation of the Goths, while the Dacia (or Dacini) seem to have been the ancestors of the Danes. The few Thracian words that have come down to us are decidedly teutonic.... There is also a resemblance between the Thracian customs, as described by Herodotus (V, 4-8) and those which Tacitus assigns to the Germans.

Once again we have to admit that these are slender lines of evidence, yet in many respects they have a general concordance with all else that we know of the descendants of Japheth as a whole; and there is, therefore, every likelihood that the descendants of Tiras made as large a contribution to the population and civilization of Europe as the rest of his immediate family.

Out of this intricate network of possibilities and probabilities, there emerges a reasonably clear picture in which a single family beginning with Japheth multiplied in the course of time and peopled the northern shore of the Mediterranean, the whole of Europe, the British Isles and Scandinavia, and the larger part of Russia. The same family settled India displacing a prior settlement of Hamites who had established themselves in the Indus Valley. Isolated groups of this same people seem to have wandered further afield towards the East, contributing to small pockets of Japhethites which in the course of time were almost, if not wholly, swallowed up by Hamites. It is possible that some of them contributed characteristics found in the people of Polynesia, and it is conceivable that in the Ainu of northern Japan there is a remnant of Japhethites.

Noah had said that God would enlarge Japheth (Gen. 9:27). It seems that this enlargement began very early in Japheth's history, but it has been a continuing process and occurring in every part of the world with the exception of the Far East. The children of Japheth have tended to spread and multiply at the expense of other racial stocks. As we shall see in the last chapter, this enlargement did not mean that Japhethites were the first to migrate far and wide, for wherever they have spread, whether in prehistoric or historic times, they have been preceded by even earlier settlers whose racial origin was not Indo-European. This pattern of settlement of the habitable areas of the world

---

[94] Rawlinson, G., op. cit., p. 178.

has had a profound significance in the development of civilization, a significance which is considered in some detail in another Doorway Paper.[95] In the meantime, it has been established by many lines of evidence that the actual names provided in Genesis 10:1-5 were indeed real people whose families carried with them recognizably, though often in corrupted form, clear recollections of their respective forebears, so that they have survived to the present day still bearing the kind of relationships that are implied in this ancient Table of Nations. And they often preserve unmistakably even the patriarchal name.

---

[95] Part V, "A Christian World View: The Framework of History."

Chapter 3

THE DESCENDANTS OF HAM

THE DESCENDANTS of Japheth and the descendants of Shem are traced reasonably clearly in subsequent history, but the descendants of Ham present problems which are not shared by these other two. It is true that a certain number of listed descendants of Ham are also easily traceable, for example, Mizraim, Canaan, and Heth. And a number of the cities related to Ham in Genesis 10 present no problems, having become household words to Bible students. But there are many names here, about which we have very little information, yet which may have been ancestors of very substantial portions of the present world's population. It is certain of these names we propose to examine, for they bear upon the origin of the so-called "colored races."

We have already proposed that Japheth was indeed "enlarged" to an exceptional degree in his descendants, not merely in the number of nations ultimately derived from his family, but in their very wide spread over the face of the earth. Also, this enlargement was gradual enough to occur without seriously disrupting the natural development of dialectic differences, which in due course became distinct languages within the family. In another Doorway Paper[96] it is suggested that the confusion which occurred at Babel served chiefly as an affliction for the children of Ham, whose languages have proliferated bewilderingly from very early times to the present day, a proliferation contributing in no small measure to the fragmentation of the original family. The changes which took place in the Semitic family of languages were remarkably small. And though the changes which took place in the Japhetic family of languages were somewhat

---

[96] "The Confusion of Languages" (Part I of Doorway Papers Vol. VI, *Biblical Studies: I*) .

greater, they were nevertheless so orderly as to allow linguists to reconstitute both families with considerable assurance. In neither of these two families of language is there any real evidence of "confusion" in their development. On the other hand, in the languages of the Hamitic line there is a great deal of confusion, if by "confusion" we allow the term to mean that dialects rapidly developed between neighboring and related tribes as they multiplied, rendering their speech unintelligible to one another in a remarkable short space of time. This subject is explored in the Doorway Paper mentioned above and will not be pursued here, but it is necessary to introduce this because it bears on the lack of persistence through passing centuries of Hamitic ancestral names compared to those in the lines of Japheth and Shem. This makes it much more difficult to establish lines of connection by the means of names. In fact, the most important members of Ham's family bore names which disappeared completely except as preserved in ancient documents. The names of Ham's sons are not preserved even in corrupted form in modern times. The sons of Ham were Cush, Mizraim, Phut, and Canaan, but not one of these is held today by any living representatives in any recognizable form whatever. Cush subsequently became identified with Ethiopia, Mizraim with Egypt, Phut with Libya, and Canaan with Palestine, but the old names passed completely out of use.

On the other hand, many of the names were bywords for a long time not because there were numerous descendants, as in the case of Japheth, but rather because of some single notable achievement. Nimrod was remembered for his hunting prowess. Many of the cities which are listed as having been founded by Ham's descendants had notable histories. But they, too, for the most part ceased to have importance long before modern times. A notable exception is the city Jerusalem, which of course is not actually mentioned at all even under its older name Jebus.

How, then, can one provide substantiating evidence for the claim that from Ham were descended the colored races? The answer is, Only by inference. For example, while there was a Cush in or near Mesopotamia at the very beginning, the most prominent settlement established by descendants of this patriarch was in Ethiopia. The Ethiopians have been habitually considered true blacks, which is recognized indirectly in Scripture when the prophet asks, "Can the Ethiopian change his skin?" (Jer. 13:23). The first son of Cush was Seba, and according to Jervis, this patriarch was reputedly the founder of the Kingdom of Jemameh in Arabia. He says:[97]

> His tribe, extending eastward, occupied the coast of Oman, from Cape Musandam to the neighborhood of Ras-el-Had, on the extreme east border of the peninsula: they are mentioned by Ptolemy under the name of Asabi. The commercial greatness of this nation is attributed to their possession of Littus Hammaeum or Gold Coast, and of the port of Maskat, which, from the infancy of navigation, must have attracted and commanded the commerce of India.
>
> It appears that, from thence, they spread into Africa, across the straits of Bab-el-Mandeb. Josephus attests that Saba was an ancient metropolis of the kingdom of Meroe, in the very fertile region between the Nile and Astaboras (or Bahr-el-aswad) ; and that it ultimately received the name of Meroe after a sister of Cambyses King of Persia, although Meroe seems rather to be a word of Ethiopic derivation. The ruins of the ancient Meroe lie four miles to the north-east of Shendy, in Nubia.

There are other native African tribes which trace themselves back traditionally to Ham. The Yoruba[98] who are black skinned, for example, claim to be descendants of Nimrod, whereas the Libyians, who are "white" skinned, are usually traced back to Lehabim, a son of Mizraim. And the Egyptians were direct descendants of Mizraim. It is therefore possible that all of Africa, despite the different shades of color of its native populations, was initially settled by various members of this one Hamitic family.

There still remains, however, the vast aggregate of peoples who are generally classified as Mongoloid, who settled the Far East and the New World. Do they really appear in this genealogical tree, or must we admit that the Table of Nations is not comprehensive here?

There are two names which I think may conceivably provide us with clues. That they should be so briefly referred to in the genealogy may seem surprising if — as we are proposing — they gave rise to such enormous populations. We are referring specifically to Heth, a son of Canaan, and the Sinites, a tribe presumably descended from Sin, a brother of Heth.

Heth was, without question, the father of the Hittites. Except for the work of archaeologists, however, we should never have known how important the descendants of this man really were at one point in history, for the Hittite empire disappeared

---

[97] Jervis, J. J-W., *Genesis Elucidated*, Bagster, London, 1872, p. 167.

[98] Yoruba: see K. C. Murray, "Nigerian Bronzes: Work from Ife," *Antiquity*, England, Mar., 1941, p. 76.

completely from view—or nearly completely. This qualification is necessary if we allow any weight to an observation made by C. R. Conder.[99] It was his contention that when the Hittite empire crumbled, all the Hittites of importance were either killed or fled eastwards. Conder's view was that the word "Hittite," which appears in Cuneiform as "Khittae," was borne by the fleeing remnant of this once powerful nation to the Far East and was preserved through the centuries in the more familiar form "Cathay."[100] He assumes that they became a not unimportant part of early Chinese stock. Certainly there are curious links between them, for example, their modes of dress, their shoes with turned-up toes, their manner of doing their hair in a pigtail, and so forth. Representations show them to have possessed high cheek-bones, and craniologists have observed that they had not a few characteristics of the Mongoloids. More recently, another possible corroborating link appears in the discovery that the Hittites mastered the art of casting iron and the taming of horses, two achievements of great importance, and recurring very early in Chinese history[101]—long before reaching the West.

It should be observed that linguistic evidence exists for a Japhetic component in the Hittite empire.[102] In view of the fact that their initial expansion took place in Asia Minor, it is not too surprising that there may have been a mixture of races within the Empire. It could well be that there was an Indo-European aristocracy, just as at one point in Egyptian history there was a Shepherd King (Shemite) aristocracy. George Barton observed:[103]

> Some features of their speech clearly resemble features of the Indo-European family of languages, but other features seem to denote Tartar (i.e., Mongol) affinities. In a number of instances the influence of the Assyrian language can clearly be traced. The same confusion presents itself when we study the pictures of Hittites as they appear in Egyptian reliefs. Two

---

[99] Conder, C. R., "The Canaanites," *Trans. Vict. Instit.*, London, 24 (1890): 51.

[100] Chinese used rocket weapons for the first time, called them "Alsichem Al-Khatai" or "Chinese Arrows." See Willey Ley, "Rockets," in *Sci. American,* May, 1949, p. 31.

[101] Needham, J., *Science and Civilization in China,* Cambridge, 1954, Vol. 1, for horses, pp. 81, 83, etc., and for cast iron, pp. 1, 235, etc.

[102] Hittite Indo-Europeans: See for example, O. G. Gurney, *The Hittites,* Pelican Books, London, 1952, chap. 6, p. 117. And see the conclusion of George Barton, *Archaeology and the Bible,* Amer. Sunday School Union, Phila., 6th ed., 1933, p. 92, fn.

[103] Barton, George, op cit., pp. 90, 91.

distinct types of face are there portrayed. One type has high cheekbones, oblique eyes, and wears a pigtail, like the people of Mongolia and China. The other has a cleancut head and face which resemble somewhat the early Greeks.

This brings us to Heth's brother whose name was, presumably, Sin. Of this name there are many occurrences in variant forms through the Middle East and towards the Far East. One of the characteristics of Hamitic peoples — using the term "Hamite" in its strictly biblical sense and not as anthropologists currently employ it — is a tendency to deify their ancestors. It has been suggested that the Ammon of the Egyptians is a case in point, in which Ham himself has been deified: the combination in that same land of No-Ammon may be an extension of this practice back to Noah himself, who is then associated with his son in the dual title. The point of direct concern here is that the word "Sin" became the name of a very important deity, appearing from quite early times until quite late in Assyrian history. The last King of Sumerian Ur was named "Abi-Sin." The word appears, of course, in the name Sennacherib (Sin-ahe-erba, i.e., "May the god Sin multiply [my] brothers"), and as Naran-Sin, etc.

Sin was important enough not only to have been deified but to have been given the title "Lord of Laws."[104] In a hymn from Ur, it is said of him that it was "he who created law and justice so that mankind has established laws," and again, "the ordainer of laws of heaven and earth." Another remarkable circumstance may stem from this, for if some of his descendants traveled south into Arabia and settled in a district subsequently known as Sin-ai, then possibly his reputation as a great codifier of law led to a tradition which associated Sinai as a place where law was originated. It is possible that there is some connection between this circumstance and God's choice of Mount Sinai as the place where He gave the Ten Commandments. Moreover, according to Boscawen, the title "Lord of Laws," attributed to the deified Sin is, in the original hymn of Ur, Bel-Terite, and the first syllable is a form of the more familiar "Baal." And the word "Terite" is the plural of the form "tertu" meaning "law," which itself is the equivalent of the Hebrew "Torah" ("law").

In spite of the fact, therefore, that the patriarch Sin receives scant mention in Genesis 10, he was a very important individual.

---

[104] Boscawen, W. St. Chad, *The Bible and the Monuments*, Eyre and Spottiswoode, London, 1896, p. 64.

He may further have had his name preserved in the modern term "China." Although Perry espoused a view of culture growth which has come into general disrepute because of its over-simplification, he nevertheless may be essentially correct in the statements which he makes showing the Chinese civilization as having come from the West. Not a few Cuneiform scholars have noted how similar, in some respects, was Sumerian to Chinese. Now, Perry says:[105]

> There is one significant feature concerning the possible mode of origin of Chinese civilization that well merits attention. The place most closely associated by the Chinese themselves with the origin of their civilization is the capital of Shensi, namely, Siang-fu (Father Sin). Siangfu, on the Wei, a tributary of the Yellow River, is near important gold and jade mines.

It is surely significant that Sinai was equally important as a place of mines. The name "Sin," according to Dillmann,[106] is met with in Assyrian in the form "Sianu." It would not be diffi-cult for "Father Sin" to become "Father Sian" or, with a slight nasalization, "Siang," in Chinese "Sianfu." The Chinese have a tradition that their first king, Fu-hi, made his appearance on the Mountains of Chin immediately after the world had been cov-ered with water.[107] Sin himself was the third generation from Noah, a circumstance which, if the identification is justified, would provide about the right time interval.

Moreover, the people who early traded with the Scythians and who came from the Far East were called "Sinae," and their most important town was "Thinae," a great trading emporium in western China.[108] This city is now known as "Thsin" or simply "Tin," and it lies in the province of Shensi.

The Sinae became independent in western China, their princes reigning there for some 650 years before they finally gained dominion over the whole land. In the third century B.C. the dynasty of Tsin became supreme in the Empire. The word itself came to have the meaning of "purebred." This word was assumed as a title by the Manchu Emperors and is believed to have been changed by the Malays into the form "Tchina" and

105 Perry, W. J., *The Growth of Civilization*, Pelican Books, London, 1937, p. 125.

106 Dillmann, A., op. cit., Vol. 1, p. 367.

107 Inglis, J., *Notes on the Book of Genesis*, Gall and Inglis, London, 1877, p. 89, fn. to verse 28.

108 Fausset, A. R., "Sinim," *Bible Cyclopedia: Critical and Expository*, Funk and Wagnalls, London, n.d., p. 655.

from them through the Portuguese brought into Europe as "China." Some years ago the newspapers regularly carried head-lines with reference to the conflict between the Japanese and Chinese in which the ancient name reappeared in its original form, for they commonly spoke of the Sino-Japanese war.

Arrian in A.D. 140[109] speaks of the Sinae or Thinae as a people in the remotest parts of Asia. One is reminded of the reference to the Sinim in Isaiah 49:12 as coming "from afar," but specifically not from the north and not from the west.

Reverting once more to Conder's observation with respect to the "far Cathay" of Medieval reference, it would make sense to suppose that the remnants of the Hittites after the destruction of their Empire traveled towards the East and settled among the Sinites who were relatives, contributing to their civilization cer-tain arts, chiefly metallurgy (especially the casting of iron) and being so absorbed subsequently as to disappear entirely from history as a distinct people.

The finding of prehistoric man in the Choukoutien Caves with skeletal remains variant enough to bridge from the western limits of types in China to types in the New World has seemed to many to be clear evidence that those who settled the New World passed through China. That the New World was peopled by a Mongoloid stock is generally agreed, although there is some evidence of a small Negroid component.[110] The evidence, it is true, is slim, but what evidence there is appears to me to point consistently in the same direction, supporting our initial conten-tion that not only Africa with its black races, but the Far East and the Americas with their colored races were all descendants of Ham.

There is one further illustration of how the descendants of Ham may have contributed uniquely to Japhetic civilization, in this case, the Roman. The contribution made to Japhetic culture by the Sumerians, the Egyptians, the Cretans, and later the Chi-nese, and the American Indians, is explored in detail in Part IV of this volume, "The Technology of Hamitic People." The contribution made by the Etruscans is similarly pointed out in that Paper. The origin of the Etruscans, even though they have

[109] Arrian: as quoted by C. A. Gordon, "Notes on the Ethnology and Ancient Chronology of China," *Trans. Vict. Inst.*, London, 23 (1889): 170.

[110] Taylor, Griffith, *Environment, Race and Migration*, Univ. of Toronto, 1945, p. 256. See also E. A. Hooten, *Apes, Men and Morons*, Putnam's Sons, London, 1937, p. 185.

been studied and puzzled over intensively for over a hundred years, is still a mystery. I should like to suggest that there is one name in the list of Ham's descendants which might conceivably be a reference to their forebear, namely Resen (v. 12).

Resen is said to have been a city. It is characteristic of the earliest towns and cities mentioned in Genesis that they were named after their founders or their founders' children. Cain built a city and called it after the name of his son, Enoch, according to Genesis 4:17. There is little doubt that the Unuk, and later Uruk, of Cuneiform inscriptions reflects this. As we have shown elsewhere, this early settlement became known as Erech in due time, and much later as Warka. It gave rise to a word meaning "city"[111] which has come into English as "burg." We have noted also that Sidon is first mentioned as the firstborn son of Canaan, but a few verses later as the name of a city (vv. 15 and 19). Similarly, the Jebusites, presumably descendants of a man named Jebus, lived in a stronghold named originally after their ancestor. So I think it quite probable that when Nimrod went up from southern Babylonia into Assyria and built Nineveh and Resen, among other towns, he was naming the city of Resen either from a forebear or after an immediate relative. It is not strictly required to demonstrate that the Etruscans were a kind of colonizing fragment originating from this particular settlement founded by Nimrod. All I am proposing is that an ancestor whose name was Resen not only achieved sufficient importance to have an ancient city named after him in Assyria, but also to have given rise to a people who grew powerful enough and large enough to migrate up into Europe and into the north of Italy, from which they multiplied, and became wealthy and cultured enough to inspire the Japhetic Romans to adopt a very large part of their art, law, custom, and technology as their own, making scarcely any improvement on it.

The question is, Can we reasonably establish the propriety of deriving the more familiar word "Etruscan" from an ancient Resen; of tracing these same people back to the Middle East and close proximity to Assyria; and of establishing their racial affinity as neither Indo-European nor Shemitic. The answer to all three of these questions can be stated in the affirmative with some assurance on the following grounds.

To begin with, it can be stated simply that the people of

---

111 City: Eisler, R., "Loan Words in Semitic Languages Meaning 'Town'," *Antiquity*, Dec., 1939, pp. 449ff.

Etruria or Tuscany were called by the early Greeks Tyrsenoi. By the early Romans they were called Etrusci. But in classic Latin times, they called themselves Rasena.[112]

According to Herodotus,[113] these people came from Lydia. They claimed to have invented, during a very protracted famine in the land, a series of games, including dice. These were subsequently introduced into northern Italy and into Greece as a result of the following circumstance. The situation finally became so serious that it was decided to divide the nation in half, one half emigrating from Lydia in the hope of saving the other. The king's son was named Tyrrhenus, and he became the leader by appointment of that half of the nation which left Lydia. After sailing past many "countries," they came to a place which Herodotus calls "Umbria" (apparently almost the whole of northern Italy is intended) where they built cities for themselves. They laid aside their former name of Lydians and called themselves after the name of the king's son, Tyrrheneans.

That these people, the Etruscans, did come from Asia Minor is confirmed on linguistic and other grounds. Professor Joshua Whatmough[114] says, "There is scarcely room any longer to doubt the Anatolian affinities of the Etruscans." Raymond Bloch[115] on the basis of linguistic evidence believes that the Etruscans belonged to a loosely interrelated family of people who inhabited the shores of the Mediterranean, including those of Asia Minor, before the Indo-European invasion upset the patterns of the region, an invasion which came in the second millennium B.C. He considers the Etruscans to be a "pocket" of such displaced people, and that this explains the similarity between their religious and social customs and those of certain peoples of Asia Minor.

Many years ago, Prof. E. St. John Parry[116] presented evidence to show that the Pelasgians who, like the Etruscans, built Megalithic monuments, may have been disturbed at the same time by the same circumstance and moved out from Asia Minor along with them, subsequently being confused with them by early historiographers.

---

[112] Rouse, M. L., op. cit., p. 93.

[113] Herodotus, *History*, Vol. 1, Everymans, London, 1936, pp. 50, 51.

[114] Whatmough, Joshua, in a review of "The Foundations of Roman Italy," *Antiquity*, Vol. 11, 1937, p. 363.

[115] Bloch, Raymond, "The Etruscans," *Sci. American*, Feb., 1962, p. 87.

[116] Parry, E. St. John, "On Some Points Connected With the Early History of Rome," *Canad. Jour.*, Apr., 1854, p. 219.

One thing seems well established, and that is their language was neither Indo-European nor Semitic.[117] It seems fairly safe to assume (though language is by no means a safe guide in the matter) that they were themselves racially distinct from the Indo-Europeans.[118] A relationship has also been proposed with certain other "pockets" — the Basques, for example.[119]

We have mentioned the tradition which ascribes to the Etruscans or Racena the invention of dice. Years ago a pair of dice were found with the numbers apparently written out upon them instead of merely being indicated by dots. Shortly after their discovery, the Rev. Isaac Taylor presented a paper[120] before the Victoria Institute in London in which he showed that the most probable interpretation of the numerals was to be found by reference to allied terms in Finnic, Altaic, and Basque. A few years later, while the subject was still a very live issue — as indeed it still is — a paper was presented by a Mr. R. Brown[121] before the same Institute in which, in an appendix, some further Etruscan words are compared to certain Sumerian words. We are, then, coming perhaps even nearer to the ancient Resen of Genesis 10.

In his *Origin of Nations*, Rawlinson[122] draws attention to the fact that certain Etruscan bronzes are decorated or adorned with figures in rows, exhibiting sphinxes and human beings which, he suggests, are not unlike similar processions of figures found near Nineveh. These Assyrian parallels were discovered by Layard and reported in his famous work, *Discoveries in the Ruins of Babylon and Nineveh*. Of these, Layard wrote as follows:[123]

> A second bowl, 7½ inches in diameter and 3¾ inches deep, has in the centre a medallion and on the sides in a very high relief two lions and two sphinxes . . . wearing a collar, feathers, and a headdress formed by a disc with two uraei. Both bowls are remarkable for the boldness of the relief and the archaic

[117] Fiesel, Eva, "The Inscriptions on the Etruscan Bulla," *Am. Jour. of Arch.*, June, 1935, p. 196.

[118] MacIvor, D. R., "The Etruscans," *Antiquity*, June, 1927, p. 162.

[119] Basques: *Everyman's Encyclopedia*, Vol. 5, Dent, London, 1913, p. 544.

[120] Taylor, Isaac, "On the Etruscan Languages," *Trans. Vict. Instit.*, London, 10 (1876): 179-206.

[121] Brown, R., special note on "The Etruscans," *Trans. Vict. Inst.*, London, 14 (1881): 352-354.

[122] Rawlinson, G., op. cit., p. 123.

[123] Layard, A. H., *Discoveries in the Ruins of Babylon and Nineveh*, Murray, London, 1853, p. 189.

treatment of the figures, in this respect resembling the ivories previously discovered at Nimroud.

They forcibly call to mind the early remains of Greece, the especially the metal work and painted pottery found in very ancient tombs in Etruria, which they so closely resemble not only in design but in subject, the same mythic animals and the same ornaments being introduced, that we cannot but attribute to both the same origin.

Layard emphasizes this impression by illustrating his point with woodcuts in the text, which show that the figures found on a bronze pedestal at Powledrara in Etruria "are precisely similar to those upon a fragment of a dish brought from Nineveh." A thread of evidence carries us back, therefore, to the very environs of Nineveh where the city of Resen was situated.

There is a further piece of evidence leading us back to the same earlier source. It is of a slightly different nature though equally suggestive. The Romans annually celebrated a festival called the "Festival of Saturnus," or "Saturnalia," during which law courts were closed, schoolchildren had a holiday, and all business was suspended. One remarkable custom was the "liberation" or "freeing" of all slaves, who were allowed to say whatever they wished about their masters, took part in a banquet attired in their masters' clothes, and were waited upon by them at table. This period of freedom lasted about one week.

The origin of this festival, according to *Smith's Dictionary of Greek and Roman Antiquities,* is not certain.[124] In one legend it was attributed to the Pelasgians. In view of the fact that so many of the features of earlier Roman culture, including their ceremonies, are directly attributable to the Etruscans, and that the Etruscans and Pelasgians were sometimes confused with one another, it seems possible that this strange practice of giving slaves a week of complete liberty, indeed of licence, was originally introduced by the Etruscans.

It is therefore highly significant, I think, that when Prof. Pinches read a paper before the Victoria Institute entitled, "Notes upon Some of the Recent Discoveries in the Realm of Assyriology," he referred to one inscription of the famous Gudea who stated that after he had built Eninnu (a house or temple), he "released bonds and confirmed benefits. For seven days obedience was not exacted, the maid was made like her mistress,

---

[124] "Saturnalia," *Smith's Dictionary of Greek and Roman Antiquities,* Vol. 2, Murray, London, 3rd ed., 1901, p. 600.

and the manservant like his lord." In commenting on this, Prof. Pinches[125] remarks:

> Of course, the Sumerians were slave-holders, but they seem to have been of a kindly disposition, and to have treated their slaves well. In this case seven days' holiday are said to have been given them, and this is the only Cuneiform record known of such a thing.

It is indeed remarkable that there should be such a hiatus of so many centuries of absence of reference to this custom from Gudea to Roman times, yet evidently the custom was transmitted somehow, and it would seem most logical to assume that the transmitters were the Racina, the descendants of a certain Resen who were familiar with Assyrian culture.

In summary, then, we have a people calling themselves Rasena, after an ancestor whose name could easily be a form of the more ancient Resen, starting in Assyria, settling in Lydia from which they later emigrated to northern Italy, speaking a language neither Semitic nor Indo-European, preeminently city-builders (as though continuing the tradition of their ancestor), and still producing works of art for which quite exact parallels have been found in the very locality in which Genesis 10 states the city of Resen was built.

It may be that just as Sidon was remembered by a city named for him, so the city of Resen commemorated a patriarch whose descendants, long after the city had disappeared from view, multiplied and carried on their inherited tradition of city life as well as the name of their forebear and settled in Etruria, where they made a tremendous contribution to the basic Roman civilization which has become in time our own.

---

[125] Pinches, T. G., "Notes Upon Some of the Recent Discoveries in the Realm of Assyriology with Special Reference to the Private Life of the Babylonians," *Trans. Vict. Inst.*, London, 26 (1892): 139.

Chapter 4

THE DESCENDANTS OF SHEM

IN SPITE of the fact that in the line of Shem were to follow the Lawgivers, Prophets, Priests, and Kings with whose history the rest of the Old Testament is concerned, there is less to say about this part of the genealogy. One or two points are worth noticing, however, partly because the authenticity of the Table is supported here also, and partly because there is particular interest in one individual, Peleg, who is singled out for special mention, as Nimrod was in the previous section.

First, we have Elam listed as apparently the firstborn of Shem. The country named after him to the east of southern Mesopotamia was for many years believed to have been settled by people who were clearly not Shemites, and the biblical statement here was challenged. Subsequent excavations, however, have shown that the very earliest people to settle here were indeed Shemites. It is so often true that things appear to stand against the Word of God at first, but in the end further light completely vindicates it. The person who accepts it is like a man who appears to be losing every battle but still enjoys the absolute assurance of winning the final victory. This is a much happier position to be in, in the long run, than to be enjoying apparent victory only to find out in the end that one must lose. No less an authority than S. R. Driver,[126] although he underscores the fact that in later times the Elamites were entirely distinct racially from the Shemites (their language, for instance, being agglutinated), was forced to admit that "inscriptions recently discovered" seem to have shown that in very early times Elam was peopled by Shemites. He could not help but add that the biblical statement probably originated because Elam was dependent in

---

[126] Driver, S. R., op. cit., p. 128.

113

much later times upon Semitic Babylonia; he assures his readers that "it is very unlikely" that the original author of Genesis 10 could possibly have known what we now know. But since Driver's time, further excavation has provided very strong evidence of direct cultural links between some of the earliest cities in Babylonia and the lowest strata at Susa, the capital of Elam.[127]

The evidence now seems to indicate clearly the presence in Mesopotamia in very early times of three distinct groups of people, the Sumerians (Hamites), the earliest Babylonians (Shemites), and a group of people whom both Childe and Mallowen properly refer to as Japhethites (i.e., Indo-Europeans). As Childe put it:[128]

> From later written records, philologists deduce the presence of three linguistic groups — "Japhethites" (known only inferentially from a few place-names); Semites (speaking a language akin to Hebrew and Arabic); and the dominant Sumerians.

The picture as presented elsewhere by Childe[129] reveals that the first people to enter Mesopotamia came from the East and were not Sumerians, but were in fact Shemitic Elamites, who founded such early cities as Al-Ubaid and Jemdet Nasr. These people established themselves first in the south and gradually spread toward the north, but without losing the cultural links which take us back to Elam. Childe then proposes that a second wave of immigrants into Mesopotamia followed, who this time were not Shemites but Sumerians, i.e., Hamites. These people brought new civilizing influences with them which led to considerable cultural advance, until by the time of the Uruk period, though still a minority, they had become the rulers. Meanwhile, further to the north, i.e., in Assyria, the Shemites continued their slow development until there arose in the south a man whom Scripture names Nimrod, in the line of Ham. He established himself as lord of the South and then traveled up into Assyria, or as Scripture has it, "went forth out of that land into Asshur and added it to his kingdom." At the same time he founded a number of cities mentioned in Genesis 10 in connection with Nineveh.

Mallowen emphasizes the distinctions between these two

---

[127] First observed by E. A. Speiser excavating at Tepe Gawra in 1927 and reported in *Annual of the American Schools of Oriental Research,* 9 (1929): 22ff.

[128] Childe, V. G., *What Happened in History,* Pelican Books, 1948, p. 81.

[129] Childe, V. G., *New Light on the Most Ancient East,* Kegan Paul, London, 1935, pp. 133, 136, and 145-146.

dominant types, the Sumerians and the Akkadians, i.e., the Hamites and Shemites, in this early period of the country's development.[130] At the same time he also underscores the fact that there was another group, whose existence is well attested on linguistic grounds. Speiser[131] proposed that name Japhethite for these people, known very early in the hill country east of the Tigris. They were noted especially for their fairness of skin. That they did penetrate southern Mesopotamia at least in some numbers in very early times has been noted by Campbell Thompson[132] as well as by Speiser.

The general picture, then, although the details are not as clear as we would wish, nevertheless supports the implications of Genesis 10, even allowing us to detect reverberations of the exploits of Nimrod who is otherwise still unidentified. Someone established a southern ascendency in the north: perhaps Nimrod.

The second thing to notice in this section of the genealogy is the note about Peleg: "in whose days the earth was divided." The interpretations of this brief note has been both broad and interesting. Recently it has begun to appear that the Pelasgians of antiquity, who were great sea-going merchants and sometimes pirates, in earliest times may have received their name from Peleg. Surviving in a multitude of forms is a determinative appended to many words that has the effect of converting the word into a patronymic. This appears, for example, as "-icus" in the word "Germanicus," also "-ic" in the word "Britannic," "ski" in many familiar Russian names, possibly "-scans" in the word "Etruscans," and "scion" in English. Another one, which is the important point in this context, is "skoi," placed after the more ancient name "Peleg," giving the compound form "Pelegskoi." These are the "Pelasgians." The Pelasgians are very much of a mystery, for although they appear to have been quite powerful, it is not clear where they came from or what happened to them. When the Thracians descended to the Aegean from the north in the 14th century B.C., they displaced the Pelasgians from the territory which they held between the Hebrus and the Strymon. It is curious to find the Pelasgians occupying a territory adjacent to a river, the Hebrus, bearing a name so much reminiscent of Eber who, according to Genesis 10:25, was their father. After

[130] Mallowen, M. E. L., "A Mesopotamian Trilogy," *Antiquity*, June, 1939, p. 161.

[131] Speiser, E. A., *Mesopotamian Origins*, Phila., 1930.

[132] Thompson, Campbell, *Man*, Roy. Anthrop. Inst., xxiii, 1923, p. 81.

they were displaced, these people seem to have been swallowed up by the Greek population with whom they were subsequently confused. Munro says:[133]

> The Pelasgic nation ceased to exist as such and the Ionian name was adopted, probably among the mixed communities on the Asiatic side.

Perhaps because the Pelasgians were not Greek speaking people, they were the more readily equated by the Greeks, who tended to lump all foreigners together, with the Etruscans who were also non-Greeks. Yet they appear not to have been, in fact, the same people. We have, therefore, possibly a group of "Eberites" achieving some notoriety for a time in the early world, only to disappear by being displaced from their primary settlement and swallowed up in the melee of people who populated the Aegean area.

Their ancestor, Peleg, received his name because of an event which has been variously interpreted. In the Book of Jasher (2:11), which is ascribed to Alcuin and is very likely spurious, there is an interesting observation with respect to this man:

> It was Peleg who first invented the hedge and the ditch, the wall and bulwark: and who by lot divided the lands among his brethren.

Jamieson[134] in his Commentary believes that the event in view was a formal division of the earth made by Noah, acting under divine impulse, between his three sons. It is proposed that further reference to this event is to be found in Deuteronomy 32:8 and Acts 17:24-26. Peter Lange[135] refers to a work by Fabri entitled, "Origin of Heathenism," dated 1859, in which the author interprets the expression as having reference to a catastrophe which violently split up the earth into its present continental masses.[136] This was, of course, long before Wegener, Taylor, and Du Toit published their ideas on the subject of Continental Drift, a subject currently very much alive.

One more word about Peleg: In the *International Standard Biblical Encyclopedia* reference is made to a Babylonian geographic fragment (80-6-17, 504) which has a series of ideographs

---

[133] Munro, J. A. R., "Pelasgians and Ionians" in a communication in *Am. Jour. Arch.*, Apr.-June, 1935, p. 265.

[134] Jamieson, R., *Comm. Crit. Experimental and Practical on the Old and New Testament*, Vol. 1, Genesis-Duet., Collins, Glasgow, 1871, p. 118.

[135] Lange, Peter, *Commentary on Genesis*, Zondervan, n.d., p. 350.

[136] Doorway Paper No. 56, "When the Earth was Divided." Not included in this series of volumes.

tentatively read out as Pulukku, perhaps a modified form of Peleg. This is followed by the words "Sha ebirti," which could either signify "Pulukku who was of Eber," or it could be a composite phrase "Pulukku-of-the-Crossing." Conceivably a settlement of Pelegites was established on the river at a fordable point, this river afterwards receiving the name Hebrus. Whatever the truth of the matter, the word "Peleg" seems somehow to have come down to us also through Greek in the form *"pelagos,"* meaning "sea." If there is a real connection this might suggest a further idea, namely, that the "division" took place when men began to migrate for the first time by water. The phrase "the earth was divided" would be interpreted to mean "the peoples of the earth were divided," i.e., by water.

This is speculative indeed, yet on the whole one has the impression that "Peleg" was important enough to have his name retained in various forms which reflect the brief note which appears in Genesis 10.

A word should now be said about the sons of Joktan, thirteen in all, every one of whom appears to have settled in Arabia, chiefly in the south. Almodad is perhaps traceable to Al Mudad; Sheleph, in Yemen represented by Es Sulaf, and perhaps being the Salapeni of Ptolemy; Hazarmaveth, today Hadramaut; Jerah, adjoining the latter, being possibly found in the name of a fortress, Jerakh; Hadoram, represented by the Adramitae in Southern Arabia, mentioned by Pliny and Ptolemy; Uzal, which is probably the old name of the capital of Yemen; Diklah, a place of some importance in Yemen, known as Dakalah; Obal, preserved perhaps in several localities in south Arabia, under the name Abil; Abimael is completely unidentified; Sheba might suggest the Sabeans; Ophir, perhaps represented by Aphar, the Sabaean capital of which Ptolemy speaks under the name Sapphara (Geog. 6.7) and which is possibly modern Zaphar; Havilah, the district in Arabia Felix, known as Khawlan; and Jobab, usually identified with the Jobarites mentioned by Ptolemy among the Arabian tribes of the south, and which it is suggested was misread by him as *Iōbabitai,* instead of an original *Iōbaritai.*

The first boundary referred to in Genesis 10:30 perhaps refers to Massa (cf. Gen. 25:14), a northern Arabian tribe, about midway between the Gulf of Akaba and the Persian Gulf. On the other hand, there is a seaport called *Mousa,* or *Moudza,* mentioned by Ptolemy, Pliny, Arrian and other ancient geographers, perhaps representing the place mentioned here. This was a town of some importance in classical times, but has since fallen into decay, if the modern "Mousa" is the same place. Gesenius, from the latitude given by Ptolemy, places Mesha at Maushid, on the west coast of Yemen. If the latter is correct, then the second geographical locality is perhaps to be found in Sephar, a mount of the east, which is to be understood as being the Sipar, listed along with Elam and Susa, mentioned in a text found at Susa. This note in Genesis 10 would then mean that the thirteen sons of Joktan settled between these two points, and the location of Ophir would seem to be settled within the peninsula, not at the mouth of the Indus as some have thought.

There have been many occasions in the above remarks to observe what is only to be expected of this very early date, namely, the proximity to one another of representatives of the three branches of Noah's family. It is not to be thought for one moment that Shemites, Hamites, and Japhethites each went their own way without intermarriage and subsequent intermingling. It should not, therefore, surprise one to find in this Table that the same name may reappear in two different sections of Noah's family. Thus we read of two people named Sheba, one in verse 7 as a son of Cush and one in verse 28 as a son of Joktan. Rawlinson[137] explains how linguistic evidence demonstrates the early existence of at least two races in Arabia: "one, in the northern and central regions, Semitic, speaking the tongue usually known as Arabic; and another in the more southern regions, which is non-Semitic, and which from the resemblance of its language to the dialects of the aboriginals of Abysinnia, the descendants of ancient Ethiopians, deserves to be called Ethiopian or Cushite." This is not a case of erroneous duplication, therefore, but an indirect confirmation of the truthfulness of the record, since it would have been even more surprising if, at that time, there had been no such name-sharing among the different families.

Thus far, then, what evidence we do have bearing directly upon this ancient Table of Nations consistently tends towards its vindication as a document which is both etymologically sound and historically of great importance.

---

[137] Rawlinson, G., op. cit., p. 209.

Chapter 5

THE WIDENING CIRCLE

I T SEEMS unlikely, even making all conceivable allowances for gaps in the text, which some are persuaded must exist, that one could push back the date of the Flood and with it the date of the events outlined in this Table of Nations, beyond a few thousand years B.C. At the very most these events can hardly have occurred much more than 6000 years ago — and personally, I think 4500 years is closer to the mark. In this case, we are forced to conclude that, except for those who lived between Adam and Noah and were overwhelmed by the Flood and whose remains I believe are never likely to be found, all fossil men, all prehistoric peoples, all primitive communities extinct or living, and all civilizations since, must be encompassed within this span of a few thousand years. And on the face of it, the proposal seems utterly preposterous.

However, in this chapter I hope to show that there are lines of evidence of considerable substance in support of the above proposition. In setting this forth, all kinds of "buts" will arise in the reader's mind if he has any broad knowledge of current physical anthropology. An attempt is made to deal with some of these "buts" in four other Doorway Papers: "Fossil Man and the Genesis Record" (Vol. II of this series), "Primitive Cultures: Their Historical Origins" (Vol. II), "Longevity in Antiquity and Its Bearing on Chronology" (Vol. V), and "The Supposed Evolution of the Human Skull" (Vol. II). Yet some problems remain unsolved. However, one does not have to solve every problem before presenting an alternative view.

It is our contention that Noah and his wife and family were real people, sole survivors of a major catastrophe, the chief effect of which was to obliterate the previous civilization that had developed from Adam to that time. When the Ark grounded, there were 8 people alive in the world, and no more. Landing somewhere in Armenia, they began to spread as they multiplied, though retaining for some time a homogeneous cultural tradition. The initial family pattern, set by the existence in the party of three sons and their wives, gave rise in the course of time to three distinct racial stocks who, according to their patriarchal lineage, are most properly termed Japhethites, Hamites, and Shemites, but in modern terminology would be represented by the Semitic people (Hebrews, Arabs, and ancient nations such as Babylonians, Assyrians, etc.), the Mongoloid and Negroid Hamites, and the Caucasoid Japhethites.

At first they kept together. But within a century or so they broke up into small groups, and subsequently some of the family of Shem, most of the family of Ham, and a few of the family of Japheth arrived from the east in the Mesopotamian Plain (Gen. 11:2). Here it would appear from evidence discussed elsewhere that the family of Ham, who had become politically dominant, initiated a movement to prevent further dispersal by proposing the building of a monument as a visible rallying point on the flat plain, thus bringing upon themselves a judgment which led to an enforced and rapid scattering throughout the earth.

This circumstance accounts for the fact that in every part of the world where Japheth has subsequently migrated he has always been preceded by Ham — a fact which applies in every continent. In prehistoric times this is always found to be true, the earliest fossil remains being Negroid or Mongoloid in character, but those who followed were not. Indeed, in protohistoric times whatever cultural advances the pioneering Hamites had achieved tended to be swallowed up by the succeeding Japhethites. The record of Japheth's more leisurely spread over the earth has been marred by the destruction of both the culture and their Hamite creators wherever the Japhethites arrived in sufficient force to achieve dominion. This happened in the Indus Valley, it happened in Central America, it happened to the Indian tribes of North America, it happened in Australia, and only numerical superiority has hitherto preserved Africa from the same fate. The indebtedness of Japheth to Ham for his pioneering contribution in mastering the environment is amply explored and documented in Part IV of this volume, "The Technology of Hamitic People," and its complement, Part I, "The Part Played by Shem, Ham, and Japheth in Subsequent World History." The evidence will not be repeated here.

Now, in spite of South African discoveries of recent years, it still remains true that whether we are speaking of fossil man, ancient civilizations, contemporary or extinct native peoples, or the present world population, all lines of migration that are in any way still traceable are found to radiate from the Middle East.

The pattern is as follows: Along each migratory route settlements are found, each of which differs slightly from the one that preceded it and the one that follows it. As a general rule, the direction of movement tends to be shown by a gradual loss of cultural artifacts, which continue in use back along the line but either disappear entirely forward along the line or are crudely copied or merely represented in pictures or in folklore. When several lines radiate from a single center, the picture presented is more or less a series of ever increasing circles of settlement, each sharing fewer and fewer of the original cultural artifacts which continue at the center. At the same time completely new items appear, which are designed to satisfy new needs not found at the center. The further from the center one moves along such routes of migration, the more new and uniquely specific items one is likely to find which are not shared by other lines, but there remain some recollections of a few particularly important or useful links with the original homeland. Entering such a settlement without previous knowledge of the direction from which the settlers came, one cannot be certain which way relationships are to be traced. There is, however, usually some dependable piece of evidence which allows one to separate the artifacts which have been brought in from those that have been developed on the site. This is particularly the case whenever complex items turn up requiring materials which would not be available locally. Sometimes the evidence is secondhand, existing in the presence of an article which is clearly a copy and has something about its construction which proves it to be so. For example, certain Minoan pottery vessels are clearly copies of metal prototypes, both in the shape they take and in their ornamentation.[138] Where the pottery handles of these vessels join the vessel itself, little knobs of clay are found which serve no functional purpose, but which are clearly an attempt to copy the rivets which once secured the metal handle to the metal body of the prototype. These prototypes are found in Asia Minor, and it is therefore clear

---

[138] See on this J. D. S. Pendlebury, *The Archaeology of Crete*, Methuen, London, 1939, p. 68 and V. G. Childe, *Dawn of European Civilization*, Kegan Paul, 5th ed., 1950, p. 19.

which way the line of migration is to be traced, for it is inconceivable that the pottery vessel with its little knobs of clay provided the metal worker with the clues as to where he should place his rivets.

In the earliest migrations which, if we are guided by the chronology of Scripture, must have been quite rapid, it was inevitable that the tendency would be more markedly towards a loss of cultural items common to the center as one moves out, rather than a gain of new items.[139] Thus the general level of culture would decline, although oral traditions, rituals, and religious beliefs would change more slowly. In due time, when a large enough body of people remained in any one place, a new "center" would arise with many of the old traditions preserved but some new ones established with sufficient vigor to send out waves of influence both forwards and backwards along the line.

Accompanying such cultural losses in the initial spread of the Hamitic peoples would be a certain coarsening of physique. Not only do people tend to be in many cases unsuited for the rigors of pioneering life and be culturally degraded as a consequence, but the nourishment itself often is grossly insufficient or unsuitable, and their bodies do not develop normally either. As Dawson has observed,[140] the more highly cultured an immigrant is when he arrives, the more severely he is handicapped and likely to suffer when robbed of the familiar accouterments of his previous life. This has been noted by those who have studied the effects of diet on the human skull for example, and this subject is dealt with in some detail in "The Supposed Evolution of the Human Skull" (contained in Vol. II of this series) ; and with respect to culture, in "Primitive Cultures: Their Historical Origins" (in Vol. II) .

The occasional establishment of what might be called "provincial" cultural centers along the various routes of migration has greatly complicated the pattern of relationships in protohistoric times, yet the evidence which does exist, for all its paucity at times, strongly supports a Cradle of Mankind in the Middle East from which there went out successive waves of pioneers who were neither Indo-Europeans nor Shemites. These were Hamitic pioneers, either Mongoloid or Negroid in type with some admixture, who blazed trails and opened up territories in every

---

[139] Perry, W. J., op. cit., p. 123.
[140] Dawson, Sir William, *The Story of the Earth and Man,* Hodder and Stoughton, London, 1903, p. 390.

habitable part of the earth and ultimately established a way of life in each locality which at a basic level made maximum use of the raw materials and resources of that locality. The Japhethites followed them, building upon this foundation and taking advantage of this basic technology in order to raise in time a higher civilization, sometimes displacing the Hamites entirely, sometimes educating their teachers in new ways and then retiring, and sometimes absorbing them so that the two racial stocks were fused into one.

So much for the broad picture. We shall now turn to a more detailed examination of the evidence that (a) the dispersion of man took place from a center somewhere in the Middle East, and (b) that those who formed the vanguard were of Hamitic stock.

Before man's evolutionary origin was proposed it was generally agreed that the Cradle of Mankind was in Asia Minor, or at least in the Middle East. Any evidence of primitive types elsewhere in the world, whether living or fossil, were considered proof that man became degraded as he departed from the site of Paradise. When Evolution seized the imagination of anthropologists, primitive fossil remains were at once hailed as proof that the first men were constitutionally not much removed from apes. One problem presented itself however, the supposed ancestors of modern man always seemed to turn up in the wrong places. The basic assumption was still being made that the Middle East was the home of man and therefore these primitive fossil types, which were turning up anywhere but in this area, seemed entirely misplaced. Osborn, in his *Men of the Old Stone Age*, accounted for this anomaly by arguing that they were migrants.[141] He asserted his conviction that both the human and animal inhabitants of Europe, for example, had migrated there in great waves from Asia and from Africa. He wrote, however, that it was probable that the source of the migratory waves was Asia, north Africa being merely the route of passage. This was his position in 1915, and when a third edition of his famous book appeared in 1936, he had modified his original views only slightly. He had a map of the Old World with this subscription, "Throughout this long epoch Western Europe is to be viewed as a peninsula, surrounded on all sides by the sea and stretching westwards from the great land mass of eastern Europe and Asia — which was the chief theater of evolution, both of animal and human life."

---

[141] Osborn, H. F., *Men of the Old Stone Age*, N.Y., 1936, pp. 19ff.

However, in 1930, and contrary to expectations, Prof. H. J. Fleure had to admit:[142]

> No clear traces of the men and cultures of the later part of the Old Stone Age (known in Europe as the Aurignacian, Solutrean, and Magdalenian phases) have been discovered in the central highland of Asia.

The situation remained essentially the same when W. Koppers in 1952 observed:[143]

> It is a remarkable fact that so far all the fossil men have been found in Europe, the Far East, and Africa, that is, in marginal regions of Asia that are most unlikely to have formed the cradle of the human race. No remains are known to us from central Asia where most scholars who have occupied themselves with the origin of men would place the earliest races.

It is true that some fossil men have now been found in the Middle East, but far from speaking against this area as being central to subsequent migration, they seem to me to speak indirectly — and therefore with more force — in favor of it. We shall return to this subsequently.

Prof. Griffith Taylor of the University of Toronto, speaking of migratory movements in general, whether in prehistoric or historic times, wrote:[144]

> A series of zones is shown to exist in the East Indies and in Australasia which is so arranged that the most primitive are found farthest from Asia, and the most advanced nearest to Asia. This distribution about Asia is shown to be true in the other "peninsulas" (i.e., Africa and Europe, ACC), and is of fundamental importance in discussing the evolution and ethnological status of the peoples concerned. . . .
>
> Which ever region we consider, Africa, Europe, Australia, or America, we find that the major migrations have always been from Asia.

After dealing with some of the indices which he employs for establishing possible relationships between groups in different geographical areas, he remarks:[145]

> How can one explain the close resemblance between such far-distant types as are here set forth? Only the spreading of racial zones from a *common cradle-land* (his emphasis) can possibly explain these biological affinities.

---

[142] Fleure, H. J., *The Races of Mankind*, Benn, London, 1930, p. 45.

[143] Koppers, W., *Primitive Man and His World Picture*, Sheed and Ward, N.Y., 1952, p. 239.

[144] Taylor, Griffith, op. cit., p. 8.

[145] Ibid., p. 67.

Then, subsequently, in dealing with African ethnology, he observes:[146]

> The first point of interest in studying the distribution of the African peoples is that the same rule holds good which we have observed in the Australasian peoples. The most primitive groups are found in the regions most distant from Asia, or what comes to the same thing, in the most inaccessible regions. . . .
>
> Given these conditions its seems logical to assume that the racial zones can only have resulted from similar peoples spreading out like waves from a common origin. This cradleland should be approximately between the two "peninsulas," and all indications (including the racial distribution of India) point to a region of maximum evolution not far from Turkestan. It is not unlikely that the time factor was similar in the spread of all these peoples.

In a similar vein Dorothy Garrod wrote:[147]

> It is becoming more and more clear that it is not in Europe that we must seek the origins of the various paleolithic peoples who successfully overran the west. . . . The classification of de Mortillet therefore only *records the order of arrival* (my emphasis) in the West of a series of cultures, each of which has originated and probably passed through the greater part of its existence elsewhere.

So also wrote V. G. Childe:[148]

> Our knowledge of the Archaeology of Europe and of the Ancient East has enormously strengthened the Orientalist's position. Indeed we can now survey continuously interconnected provinces throughout which cultures are seen to be zoned in regularly descending grades round the centres of urban civilization in the Ancient East. Such zoning is the best possible proof of the Orientalist's postulate of diffusion.

Henry Field in writing about the possible cradle of Homo sapiens, gives a very cursory review of the chief finds of fossil man (to that date, 1932), including finds from Pekin, Kenya Colony, Java, Heidleberg, (Piltdown), and Rhodesia, and then gives a map locating them; and he remarks:[149]

---

[146] Ibid., pp. 120, 121.

[147] Garrod, Dorothy, "Nova et Vetera: A Plea for a New Method in Paleolithic Archaeology," *Proc. Prehist. Soc. of East Anglia*, Vol. 5, p. 261.

[148] Childe, V. G., *Dawn of European Civilization*, Kegan Paul, London, 3rd ed., 1939. In the 1957 edition, Childe in his introduction invites his readers to observe that he has modified his "dogmatic" orientation, a little but he still concludes at the end of the volume (p. 342), "the primacy of the Orient remains unchallenged."

[149] Field, Henry, "The Cradle of Homo Sapiens," *Am. Jour. Arch.*, Oct.-Dec., 1932, p. 427.

It does not seem probable to me that any of these localities could have been the original point from which the earliest men migrated. The distances, combined with many geographical barriers, would tend to make a theory of this nature untenable. I suggest that an area more or less equidistant from the outer edges of Europe, Asia, and Africa, may indeed be the centre in which development took place.

It is true that these statements were written before the recent discoveries in South Africa, or in the Far East at Choukoutien, or in the New World. Of the South African finds little can be said with certainty and there is no unanimity as to their exact significance. The finds at Choukoutien, as we shall attempt to show, actually support the present thesis in an interesting way. As for the New World, nobody has ever proposed that it was the Cradle of Mankind. Thus the Middle East still retains priority as the probable original Home of Man. Nevertheless, as to dating, it must be admitted that no authority with a reputation at stake would ever propose it was a homeland *so recently* as our reckoning of only 4500 years ago. The time problem remains with us and at the moment we have no answer to it, but we can proceed to explore the lines of evidence which in all other respects assuredly support the thesis set forth earlier in this chapter.

Part of this evidence, curiously, is the fact of diversity of physical type found within what appear to have been single families. This has been a source of some surprise and yet is readily accounted for on the basis of a central dispersion. Some years ago, W. D. Matthew made the following observation:[150]

> Whatever agencies may be assigned as the cause of evolution in a race, it should be at first most progressive at its point of original dispersal, and it will continue this process at that point in response to whatever stimulus originally caused it, and will spread out in successive waves of migration, each wave a stage higher than the preceding one. At any one time, therefore, the most advanced stages should be nearest the centre of dispersal, the most conservative stages the furthest from it.

Some comment is in order on this observation because there are important implications in it. Lebzelter[151] pointed out that "where man lives in large conglomerations, race (i.e., physical form) tends to be stable while culture becomes specialized: where he lives in small isolated groups, culture is stable but spe-

---

[150] Matthew, W. D., "Climate and Evolution," *Annals of the New York Acad. of Sci.*, 24 (1914): 180.

[151] Lebzelter, quoted by W. Koppers in his *Primitive Man*, p. 220. His view was sustained by LeGros Clark, *JRAI*, 88, Pt. 2 (July-Dec., 1958): 133.

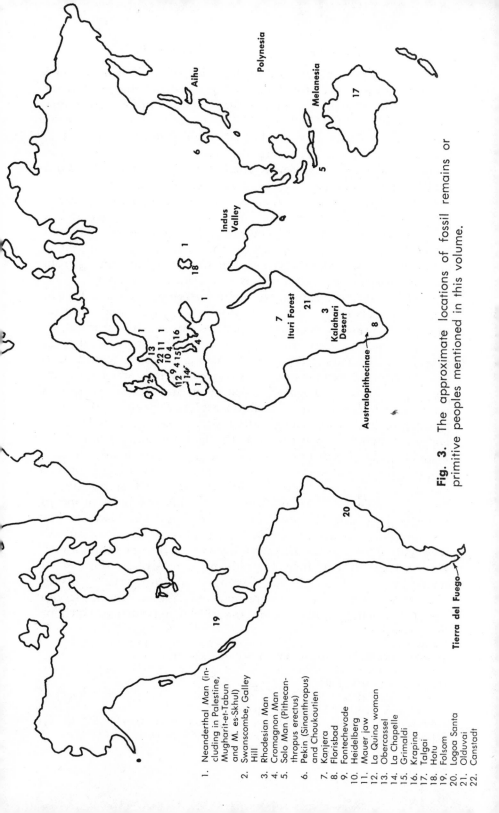

Fig. 3. The approximate locations of fossil remains or primitive peoples mentioned in this volume.

Polynesia

Aihu

Melanesia

17

Indus Valley

18

Ituri Forest

21

7

Kalahari Desert

3

Australopithecinae 8

13
22 11
10 4
9 15 16
12 4
2 14
1

1

1

1

1

19

20

Tierra del Fuego

1. Neanderthal Man (including in Palestine, Mugharit-et-Tabun and M. es-Skhul)
2. Swanscombe, Galley Hill
3. Rhodesian Man
4. Cromagnon Man
5. Solo Man (Pithecanthropus erectus)
6. Pekin (Sinanthropus) and Choukoutien
7. Kanjera
8. Florisbad
9. Fontechevade
10. Heidelberg
11. Mauer jaw
12. La Quina woman
13. Obercassel
14. La Chapelle
15. Grimaldi
16. Krapina
17. Talgai
18. Hotu
19. Folsom
20. Lagoa Santa
21. Olduvai
22. Canstadt

cialized races evolve." According to Lebzelter, this is why racial differentiation was relatively marked in the earlier stages of man's history. The explanation of this fact is clear enough. In a very small closely inbreeding population, genes for odd characters have a much better chance of being homozygously expressed so that such characters appear in the population with greater frequency, and tend to be perpetuated. On the other hand, such a small population may have so precarious an existence that the margin of survival is too small to encourage or permit cultural diversities to find expression. Thus physical type is variant but is accompanied by cultural conformity, whereas in a large and well-established community, a physical norm begins to appear as characteristic of that population, but the security resulting from numbers allows for a greater play of cultural divergence.

At the very beginning, we might therefore expect to find in the central area a measure of physical diversity and cultural uniformity: and at each secondary or provincial center in its initial stages, the same situation would reappear. The physical diversity to be expected on the foregoing grounds, would, it is now known, be exaggerated even further by the fact (only comparatively recently recognized) that when any established species enters a new environment it at once gives expression to a new and greater power of diversification. Many years ago, Sir William Dawson remarked upon this in both plant and animal biology.[152] From a study of post-Pliocene molluscs and other fossils, he concluded that "new species tend rapidly to vary to the utmost extent of their possible limits and then to remain stationary for an indefinite time." An explanation of this has been proposed recently by Colin H. Selby in the *Christian Graduate*.[153] The circumstance has been remarked upon also by Charles Brues,[154] who adds that "the variability of forms is slight once the population is large, but at first is rapid and extensive in the case of many insects for which we have the requisite data." Further observations on this point were made by Adolph Schultz in discussing primate populations in the 1950 Cold Springs Harbour Symposium.[155]

---

[152] Dawson, Sir William, op. cit., p. 360.

[153] Selby, Colin H., in a "Research Note," in the *Christian Graduate*, IVF, London, 1956, p. 99.

[154] Brues, Charles, "Contribution of Entomology to Theoretical Biology," *Sci. Monthly*, Feb., 1947, pp. 123ff., quoted at p. 130.

[155] Schultz, Adolph, "The Origin and Evolution of Man," *Cold Springs Harbour Symposium on Quantitative Biology*, 1950, p. 50.

Thus we have in reality three factors, all of which are found to be still in operation in living populations, which must have contributed to the marked variability of early fossil remains, particularly where several specimens are found in a single site as at Choukoutien for example, or at Obercassel, or Mount Carmel.

These factors may be summarized as follows: (a) A new species is more variable when it first appears; (b) A small population is more variable than a large one; (c) When a species or a few members of it shift into a new environment, wide varieties again appear which only become stable with time. To these should be added a fourth, namely, that small populations are likely to be highly conservative in their culture, thus maintaining many links though widely extended geographically.

Fossil remains constantly bear witness to the reality of these factors, but this has meaning only if we assume that a small population began at the center and, as it became firmly established there, sent out successive waves of migrants usually numbering very few persons in any one group, who thereafter established a further succession of centers, the process being repeated again and again until early man had spread into every habitable part of the world. Each new center at the first showed great diversity of physical type but as they multiplied a greater uniformity was achieved in the course of time. Where such a subsidiary center was wiped out before this uniformity had been achieved but where their remains were preserved, the diversity was, at it were, captured for our examination. At the same time, in marginal areas where individuals or families were pushed by those who followed them, circumstances often combined to degrade them physically so that fossil man tended toward a bestial form — but for secondary reasons. On the other hand, in the earliest stages of these migrations cultural uniformity would not only be the rule in each group but necessarily also between the groups. And this, too, has been found to be so to a quite extraordinary degree. Indeed, following the rule enunciated above, the most primitive groups — those which had been pushed furthest to the rim — might logically be expected to have the greatest cultural uniformity, so that links would not be surprising if found between such peripheral areas as the New World, Europe, Australia, South Africa, and so forth, which is exactly what has been observed.

Such lines of evidence which we shall explore a little further, force upon us the conclusion that we should not look to these marginal areas, to primitive contemporaries or to fossil remains, for a picture of the initial stages of man's cultural position. It is exactly in these marginal areas that we shall *not* find them. The logic of this was both evident to and flatly rejected by E. A. Hooten who remarked:[156]

> The adoption of such a principle would necessitate the conclusion that the places where one finds existing primitive forms of any order of animal are exactly in the places where these animals could not have originated....
>
> But this is the principle of *lucus a non lucendo*, i.e., finding light just where one ought not to do so, which pushed to its logical extreme would lead us to seek for the birthplace of man in that area where there are no traces of ancient man and *none of any of his primate precursors* (my emphasis).

William Howells has written at some length on the fact that, as he puts it, "all the visible footsteps lead away from Asia."[157] He then examines the picture with respect to the lines of migration taken by the "Whites" and surmises that at the beginning they were entrenched in southwest Asia "apparently with the Neanderthals to the north and west of them." He proposes that while most of them made their way into both Europe and North Africa, some of them may have traveled east through central Asia into China, which would possibly explain the Ainus and the Polynesians. He thinks that the situation with respect to the Mongoloids is pretty straightforward, their origin having been somewhere in the same area as the Whites, whence they peopled the East. The dark skinned peoples are, as he put it "a far more formidable puzzle." He thinks that the Australian aborigines can be traced back as far as India, with some evidence of them perhaps in southern Arabia. Presumably, the African Negroes are to be derived also from the Middle East, possibly reaching Africa by the Horn and therefore also via Arabia. However, there are a number of black-skinned peoples who seem scattered here and there in a way which he terms "the crowning enigma," a major feature of which is the peculiar relationships between the Negroes and the Negritos. Of these latter, he has this to say:[158]

> They are spotted among the Negroes in the Congo Forest, and they turn up on the eastern fringe of Asia (the Andaman Islands, the Malay Peninsula, probably India, and possibly

---

156 Hooten, E. A., "Where Did Man Originate?" *Antiquity*, June, 1927, p. 149.

157 Howells, Wm., *Mankind So Far*, Doubleday Doran, 1945, pp. 295ff.

158 Ibid., pp. 298, 299.

formerly in southern China), in the Philippines, and in New Guinea, and perhaps Australia, with probable traces in Borneo, Celebes, and various Melanesian Islands.

All of these are "refuge" areas, and undesirable backwoods which the Pygmies have obviously occupied as later more powerful people arrived in the same regions....

Several things stand out from these facts. The Negritos must have had a migration from a common point....And it is hopeless to assume that their point of origin was at either end of their range....It is much more likely that they came from some point midway, which is Asia.

There is, then, a very wide measure of agreement that the lines of migration radiate not from a point somewhere in Africa, Europe, or the Far East, but from a geographical area which is to be closely associated with that part of the world in which not only does Scripture seem to say that man began peopling the world after the Flood physically, but also where he began culturally. Looking at the spread of civilization as we have looked at the spread of people, it is clear that the lines follow the same course. The essential difference, if we are taking note of current chronological sequences, is that whereas the spread of people is held to have occurred hundreds and hundreds of thousands of years ago, the spread of civilization is an event which has taken place almost within historic times.

One might postulate that those whose migration took place hundreds of thousands of years ago and whose remains supply us with fossil man and prehistoric cultures (Aurignacian, etc.) were one species; and that those who initiated the basic culture in the Middle East area — the watershed of all subsequent historic cultures in the world — were another species. Some have tentatively proposed a concept such as this by looking upon Neanderthal Man as an earlier species. or subspecies who was eliminated with the appearance of so-called "modern man."[159] The association of Neanderthals with moderns in the Mount Carmel finds seems to stand against this conception.[160] And indeed, there is a very widespread agreement today that, with the exception of the most recent South African finds, all fossil, prehistoric, primitive, and modern men are one species, Homo sapiens.

Ralph Linton viewed the varieties of men revealed by fossil

[159] Weidenreich, Franz von, *Palaeontologia Sinica*, whole Series No. 127, 1943, p. 276; and see F. Gaynor Evans in *Science*, July, 1945, pp. 16, 17.

[160] Romer, Alfred, *Man and the Vertebrates*, Univ. of Chicago Press, 1948, pp. 219, 221.

finds to be due to factors which we have already outlined. As he put it:[161]

> If we are correct in our belief that all existing men belong to a single species, early man must have been a generalized form with potentialities for evolving into all the varieties which we know at present. It further seems probable that this generalized form spread widely and rapidly and that within a few thousand years of its appearance small bands of individuals were scattered over most of the Old World.
>
> These bands would find themselves in many different environments, and the physical peculiarities which were advantageous in one of these might be of no importance or actually deleterious in another. Moreover, due to the relative isolation of these bands and their habit of inbreeding, any mutation which was favorable or at least not injurious under the particular circumstances would have the best possible chance of spreading to all members of the group.
>
> It seems quite possible to account for all the known variations in our species on this basis, without invoking the theory of a small number of distinct varieties.

Viewed in this light, degraded fossil specimens found in marginal regions should neither be treated as "unsuccessful" evolutionary experiments towards the making of true Homo sapiens types, nor as "successful," but only partially complete phases or links between apes and men. Indeed, as Griffith Taylor was willing to admit,[162] "the location of such 'missing' links as Pithecanthropus in Java, etc., seemed to have little bearing on the question of the human cradleland." He might in fact also have said the same on the question of human origins. He concludes, "They are almost certainly examples of a...type which has been pushed out to the margins."

Thus the way in which one studies or views these fossil remains is very largely colored by one's thinking whether it is in terms of biological or historical processes. Prof. A. Portmann of Vienna remarked:[163]

> One and the same piece of evidence will assume totally different aspects according to the angle — palaeontological or historical — from which we look at it. We shall see it either as a link in one of the many evolutionary series that the paleontologist seeks to establish, or as something connected with remote

---

161 Linton, Ralph, *The Study of Man,* Student's ed., Appleton, N.Y., 1936, p. 26.

162 Taylor, Griffith, op. cit., p. 282.

163 Portmann, A., "Das Ursprungsproblem," *Eranos-Yahrbuck,* 1947, p. 11.

historical actions and developments that we can hardly hope to reconstruct. Let me state clearly that for my part I have not the slightest doubt that the remains of early man known to us should all be judged historically.

This same approach toward the meaning of fossil man has been explored in some detail by Wilhelm Koppers who thinks that "primitiveness in the sense of man being closer to the beast" can upon occasion be the "result of a secondary development."[164] He believes that it would be far more logical to "evolve" Neanderthal Man out of Modern Man than Modern Man out of Neanderthal Man. He holds that Neanderthal was a specialized and more primitive type, but *later* than modern man, at least in so far as they occur in Europe.

Such a great authority as Franz von Weidenreich[165] was also prepared to admit unequivocably, "no fossil type of man has been discovered so far whose characteristic features may not easily be traced *back* to *modern man*" (my emphasis). This agrees with the opinion of Griffith Taylor,[166] who observed, "Evidence is indeed accumulating that the paleolithic folk of Europe were much more closely akin to races now living on the periphery of the Euro-African regions than was formerly admitted." Many years ago, Sir William Dawson pursued this same theme and explored it at some length in his beautifully written, but almost completely ignored work, *Fossil Man and Their Modern Representatives*. Though at one time the unity of man was questioned, we see that it was not questioned by all.

On almost every side we are now being assured that the human race is, as Scripture says, "of one blood," a unity which comprehends ancient and modern, primitive and civilized, fossil and contemporary man. It is asserted by Ernst Mayr,[167] by Melville Herskovits,[168] by W. M. Krogman,[169] by Leslie White,[170]

---

[164] Koppers, W., op. cit., pp. 220, 224.

[165] Weidenreich, Franz von, *Apes, Giants and Man,* Univ. of Chicago Press, 1948, p. 2.

[166] Taylor, Griffith, op. cit., pp. 46, 47.

[167] Mayr, Ernst, "The Taxonomic Categories in Fossil Hominids," *Cold Springs Harbour Symposium,* 15 (1950): 117.

[168] Herskovits, Melville, *Man and His Works,* Knopf, N.Y., 1950, p. 103.

[169] Krogman, W. M., "What We Do Not Know About Race," *Sci. Monthly,* Aug., 1943, p. 97, and subsequently, Apr., 1948, p. 317.

[170] White, Leslie, "Man's Control over Civilization: An Anthropocentric Illusion," *Sci. Monthly,* Mar., 1948, p. 238.

by A. V. Carlson,[171] by Robert Redfield,[172] and indeed by
UNESCO.[173] At the Cold Springs Harbour Symposium on "Quantitative Biology" held in 1950, T. D. Stewart,[174] in a paper entitled, "Earliest Representatives of Homo Sapiens," stated his
conclusions in the following words, "Like Dobzhansky, therefore,
I can see no reason at present to suppose that more than a single
hominid species has existed on any time level in the Pleistocene."
Alfred Romer[175] observed in commenting on the collection of
fossil finds from Palestine (Mugharet-et-Tabun, and Mugharet-
es-Skuhl), "While certain of the skulls are clearly Neanderthal,
others show to a variable degree numerous neanthropic (i.e.,
"modern man") features." Subsequently he identifies such neanthropic skulls as being of the general Cro-Magnon type in
Europe—a type of man who appears to have been a splendid
physical specimen. He proposes later that the Mount Carmel
people "may be considered as due to interbreeding of the dominant race (Cro-Magnon Man) with its lowly predecessors (Neanderthal Man)." Thus the picture which we once had of ape-
like half-men walking with a stooped posture, long antedating
the appearance of "true" Man, has all been changed with the
accumulation of evidence. These stooped creatures now are
known to have walked fully erect,[176] their cranial capacity usually
exceeding that of modern man in Europe (if this means anything) ; and they lived side by side with the finest race (physically
speaking) which the world has probably ever seen.

As an extraordinary example of the tremendous variability
which an early, small isolated population can show, one cannot
do better than refer to the finds at Choukoutien in China,[177]
from the same locality in which the famous Pekin Man was

---

171 Carlson, A. V., in his retiring address as President of the Amer. Assoc.
Adv. Sci., *Science,* 103 (1946): 380.

172 Redfield, Robert, "What We Do Know About Race," *Sci. Monthly,*
Sept., 1943, p. 193.

173 UNESCO: Provisional draft: given as of May 21st, 1952, in *Man, Roy.
Anthrop. Inst.,* June, 1952, p. 90.

174 Stewart, T. D., Vol. 15, 1950, p. 105.

175 Romer, Alfred, op. cit., pp. 219, 221.

176 Neanderthal erect: first reported by Sergio Sergi in *Sci.,* supplement 90
(1939): 13; contrast with M. C. Cole, *The Story of Man,* Chicago, 1940,
frontispiece facing p. 13: and note that Cole's reconstruction of a stooped
Neanderthal, for popular consumption, appeared one year *later* than the report in *Science.*

177 For a useful and early summary report, see "Homo sapiens at Choukoutien," News and Notes, *Antiquity,* June, 1939, p. 242.

found. These fossil remains came from what is known as the Upper Cave, consisting of seven individuals, who appear to be members of one family: an old man judged to be over 60, a younger man, two relatively young women, an adolescent, a child of five, and a newborn baby. With them were found implements, ornaments, and thousands of fragments of animals.

Study of these remains has produced some remarkably interesting facts. The most important in the present context is that, judged by cranial form, we have in this one family a representative Neanderthal Man, a "Melanesian" woman who reminds us of the Ainu, a Mongolian type, and another who is rather similar to the modern Eskimo woman. In commenting on these finds Weidenreich expressed his amazement at the range of variation:[178]

> The surprising fact is not the occurrence of paleolithic types of modern man which resemble racial types of today, but their assemblage in one place and even in a single family, considering that these types are found today settled in far remote regions.
>
> Forms similar to that of the "Old Man," as he has been named, have been found in Upper Paleolithic, western Europe and northern Africa; those closely resembling the Melanesian type, in the neolithic of Indo-China, among the ancient skulls from the Cave of Lagoa Santa in Brazil, and in the Melanesian population of today; those closely resembling the Eskimo type occur among the pre-Columbian Amerindians of Mexico and other places in North America, and among the Eskimos of western Greenland of today.

Weidenreich then proceeds to point out subsequently that the upper Paleolithic melting-pot of Choukoutien "does not stand alone."[179] In Obercassel in the Rhine Valley were found two skeletons, an old male and a younger female, in a tomb of about the same period as the burial in Choukoutien. He says, "The skulls are so different in appearance that one would not hesitate to assign them to two races if they came from separate localities." So confused is the picture now presented that he observes:[180]

> Physical anthropologists have gotten into a blind alley so far as the definition and the range of individual human races and their history is concerned. . . .
>
> But one cannot push aside a whole problem because the methods applied and accepted as historically sacred have gone awry.

---

[178] Weidenreich, F., op. cit., p. 87.
[179] Ibid., p. 88.
[180] Ibid.

This extraordinary variability nevertheless still permits the establishment of lines of relationship which appear to crisscross in every direction as a dense network of evidence that these fossil remains for the most part belong to a single family.

Griffith Taylor links together Melanesians, Negroes, and American Indians.[181] The same authority proposes a relationship between Java Man and Rhodesian Man.[182] He relates certain Swiss tribes which seem to be a pocket of an older racial stock with the people of northern China, the Sudanese, the Bushmen of South Africa, and the Aeta of the Philippines.[183] He would also link the Predmost Skull to Aurignacian folk and to the Australoids.[184] Macgowan[185] and Montagu[186] are convinced that the aboriginal populations of central and southern America contain an element of Negroid as well as Australoid people. Grimaldi Man is almost universally admitted to have been Negroid even though his remains lie in Europe,[187] and indeed so widespread is the Negroid type that even Pithecanthropus erectus was identified as Negroid by Buyssens.[188]

Huxley maintained that the Neanderthal race must be closely linked with the Australian aborigines, particularly from the Province of Victoria;[189] and other authorities hold that the same Australian people are to be related to the famous Canstadt Race.[190] Alfred Romer relates Solo Man from Java with Rhodesian Man from Africa.[191] Hrdlicka likewise relates the Oldaway Skull with LaQuina Woman; LaChapelle and others to the basic African stock,[192] and holds that they must also be related to

---

181 Taylor, Griffith, op. cit., p. 11.

182 Ibid., p. 60. His argument here is based on head form, which he considers conclusive.

183 Ibid., p. 67. He feels only a "common cradle-land" can possibly explain the situation.

184 Ibid., p. 134.

185 Macgowan, K., Early Man in the New World, Macmillan, N.Y., 1950, p. 26.

186 Montagu, Ashley, Introduction to Physical Anthropology, Thomas, Springfield, Ill., 1947, p. 113.

187 Weidenreich, Franz, op. cit., p. 88.

188 Buyssens, Paul, Les Trois Races de l' Europe et du Monde, Brussels, 1936. See G. Grant MacCurdy, Am. Jour. of Arch., Jan.-Mar., 1937, p. 154.

189 Huxley, Thomas, quoted by D. Garth Whitney, "Primeval Man in Belgium," Trans. Vict. Inst., 40 (1908): 38.

190 According to Whitney, op. cit., p. 38.

191 Romer, Alfred, op. cit., p. 223.

192 Hrdlicka, Ales, "Skeletal Remains of Early Man," Smithsonian Inst., Misc. Collections, 83 (1930): 342ff.

Indian, Eskimo and Australian races. Even the Mauer Jaw is held to be Eskimo in type.[193]

We cannot do better than sum up this general picture in the words of Sir William Dawson who, far in advance of his time, wrote in 1874:[194]

> What precise relationship do these primitive Europeans bear to one another? We can only say that all seem to indicate one basic stock, and this is allied to the Hamitic stock of northern Asia which has its outlying branches to this day both in America and in Europe.

While it is perfectly true that the thesis we are presenting has, in the matter of chronology, the whole weight of scientific opinion against it, it is nevertheless equally true that the interpretation of the data in this fashion makes wonderful sense and, indeed, would have allowed one to predict both the existence of widespread physical relationships as well as an exceptional variableness within the members of any one family. In addition to these physiological linkages there are, of course, a very great many cultural linkages. As a single example the painting of the bones of the deceased with red ochre, a custom which not so very long ago was still being practiced by the American Indians, has been observed in prehistoric burials in almost every part of the world. Surely such a custom could hardly arise everywhere indigenously on some such supposition as that "men's minds work everywhere pretty much the same...." It seems much more reasonable to assume it was spread by people who carried it with them as they radiated rapidly from some central point.

This brings us once more to the question of the geographical position of this Cradle. Evidence accumulates daily that as a cultured being the place of man's origin was somewhere in the Middle East. No other region in the world is as likely to have been the Home of Man, if by man we mean something more than merely an intelligent ape. Vavilov[195] and others[196] have repeatedly pointed out that the great majority of the cultivated

---

[193] Ibid., p. 98. And see William S. Laughlin, "Eskimos and Aleuts: Their Origins and Evolution," *Science,* 142 (1963): 639, 642.

[194] Dawson, Sir William, "Primitive Man," *Trans. Vict. Inst.,* London, 8 (1874): 60-61.

[195] Vavilov, N. I., "Asia, the Source of Species," *Asia,* Feb., 1937, p. 113.

[196] Cf. Harlan, J. R., "New World Crop Plants in Asia Minor," *Sci. Monthly,* Feb., 1951, p. 87.

plants of the world, especially the cereals, trace their origin there. Henry Field remarks:[197]

> Iran may prove to have been one of the nurseries of Homo sapiens. During the middle or upper Paleolithic periods the climate, flora, and fauna of the Iranian Plateau provided an environment suitable for human occupation. Indeed, Ellsworth Huntington has postulated that during late Pleistocene times southern Iran was the *only* (his emphasis) region in which temperature and humidity were ideal, not only for human conception and fertility but also for chances of survival.

Many speculations exist as to the routes taken by Caucasoids, Negroids, and Mongoloids, as the world was peopled by the successive ebb and flow of migrations. Howells,[198] Braidwood,[199] Taylor,[200] Goldenweiser,[201] Engberg,[202] Weidenreich,[203] Cole,[204] and others,[205] have tackled the problem or have expressed opinions based on the study of fossil remains; and of course, Coon's *Races of Europe* is largely concerned with the same problem.[206] Not one of these can really establish how man originated, but almost all of them make the basic assumption that western Asia is his original home as a creature of culture.

From this center one can trace the movements of an early migration of Negroid people followed by Caucasoid people in Europe. From this same area undoubtedly there passed out into the East and the New World successive waves of Mongoloid people. In Africa Wendell Phillips,[207] after studying the relationships of various African tribes, concluded that evidence already existed making it possible to derive certain of the tribes from a

---

197 Field, Henry, "The Iranian Plateau Race," *Asia,* Apr., 1940, p. 217.

198 Howells, Wm., op. cit., pp. 192, 203, 209, 228, 234, 238, 247, 289, and 290.

199 Braidwood, Robert, *Prehistoric Man,* Nat. Hist. Museum, Chicago, 1948, pp. 96, 106.

200 Taylor, Griffith, op. cit., pp. 88, 115, 123, 164, and 268.

201 Goldenweiser, Alexander, *Anthropology,* Crofts, N.Y., 1945, pp. 427, 492.

202 Engberg, Martin, *Dawn of Civilization,* University of Knowledge Series, Chicago, 1938, p. 154.

203 Weidenreich, Franz von, op. cit., p. 65.

204 Cole, M. C., *The Story of Man,* University of Knowledge Series, Chicago, 1940.

205 See, for example, Boule, M. and H. V. Vallois, *Fossil Man,* Dryden Press, N.Y., 1957, pp. 516-522, an evaluation of various views.

206 Coon, C. S., op. cit., see Chapter 5.

207 Phillips, Wendell, "Further African Studies," *Sci. Monthly,* Mar., 1950, p. 175.

single racial stock (particularly the Pygmies of the Ituri Forest and the Bushmen of the Kalahari Desert), which at a certain time must have populated a larger part of the African continent only to retreat to less hospitable regions as later Negroid tribes arrived in the country. Prof. H. J. Fleure held that evidence of similar nature towards the north and northeast of Asia and on into the New World was to be discerned by a study in the change of head forms in fossil remains.[208] Wherever tradition is clear on the matter, it invariably points in the same direction and tells the same story.

Thus we conclude that from the family of Noah have sprung all the peoples of the world — prehistoric, protohistoric, and historic. And the events described in connection with Genesis 10 and the prophetic statements of Noah with respect to the future of his three sons together combine to provide us with the most reasonable account of the early history of mankind, a history which, rightly understood, does not at all require us to believe that man began with the stature of an ape and only reached a civilized state after a long, long evolutionary history.

In summary, then, what we have endeavored to show in this chapter is as follows:

(1) The geographical distribution of fossil remains is such that they are most logically explained by treating them as marginal representatives of a widespread and in part forced dispersion of people from a single multiplying population established at a point more or less central to them all, and sending forth successive waves of migrants, each wave driving the previous one further toward the periphery;

(2) The most degraded specimens are those representatives of this general movement who were driven into the least hospitable areas, where they suffered physical degeneration as a consequence of the circumstances in which they were forced to live;

(3) The extraordinary physical variability of fossil remains results from the fact that the movements took place in small, isolated, strongly inbred bands; but the cultural similarities which link together even the most widely dispersed of them indicate a common origin for them all;

(4) What I have said to be true of fossil man is equally true of living primitive societies as well as those which are now extinct;

---

[208] Fleure, H. J., op. cit., pp. 43, 44.

(5) All the initially dispersed populations are of one basic stock—the Hamitic family of Genesis 10;

(6) The initial Hamitic settlers were subsequently displaced or overwhelmed by Indo-Europeans (i.e., Japhethites), who nevertheless inherited, or adopted, and extensively built upon Hamitic technology and so gained an advantage in each geographical area where they spread;

(7) Throughout the great movements of people, both in prehistoric and historic times, there were never any human beings who did not belong within the family of Noah and his descendants;

(8) Finally, this thesis is strengthened by the evidence of history which shows that migration has always tended to follow this pattern, has frequently been accompanied by instances of degeneration both of individuals or whole tribes, usually resulting in the establishment of a general pattern of cultural relationships which parallel those archaeology has revealed.

The tenth chapter of Genesis stands between two passages of Scripture to which it is related in such a way as to shed light on both of them. In the first, Genesis 9:20-27, we are given an insight into the relationship of the descendants of the three sons of Noah throughout subsequent history, Ham doing great service, Japheth being enlarged, and Shem's originally appointed place of responsibility being ultimately assigned to Japheth. We are not told here the nature of Ham's service, nor how Japheth would be enlarged, nor what special position Shem was ultimately to surrender to his brother. In the second passage, Genesis 11:1-9, we are told that there was but a single language spoken by all men until a plan was proposed that led to the dramatic scattering of the planners over the whole earth.

In the center stands Genesis 10, supplying us with vital clues to the understanding of these things by telling us exactly who the descendants were of each of these three sons. With this clue, and with the knowledge of history which we now have, we can see the significance of both passages. We now understand in what way Ham became a servant of his brethren, in what way Japheth's spread over the earth could be called an enlargement rather than a scattering, and in what circumstances Shem has surrendered his position of special privilege and responsibility to Japheth. We could not fully perceive how these prophetic statements had been fulfilled without our knowledge of who among the nations were Hamites and who were Japhethites. And this knowledge we derive entirely from Genesis 10.

Furthermore, the real significance of the events which surrounded and stemmed from the abortive plan to build the Tower of Babel would similarly be lost to us except for the knowledge that it was Ham's descendants who paid the penalty. This penalty led to their being scattered very early and forced them to pioneer the way in opening up the world for human habitation, a service which they rendered with remarkable success but no small initial cost to themselves.

Moreover, if we consider the matter carefully, we shall perceive also the great wisdom of God who, in order to preserve and perfect His revelation of Himself, never permitted the Shemites to stray far from the original cultural center in order that He might specially prepare one branch of the family to carry this Light to the world as soon as the world was able to receive it. For it is a principle recognized in the New Testament by our Lord when He fed the multitudes before He preached to them and borne out time and again in history, that spiritual truth is not well comprehended by men whose struggle merely to survive occupies all their energies.

Thus where Ham pioneered and opened up the world to human occupation, Japheth followed at a more leisurely pace to consolidate and make more secure the initial "dominion" thus achieved. And then — and only then — was the world able and prepared to receive the Light that was to enlighten the Gentiles and to cover the earth with the knowledge of God as the waters cover the sea.

Footnote on the time taken for early migrations.

Kenneth Macgowan shows that with respect to a Middle East "Cradle of Man," the most distant settlement is that in the very southern tip of South America, 15,000 miles approximately. How long would such a trip take? He says that it has been estimated that men might have covered the 4000 miles from Harbin, Manchuria, to Vancouver Island, in as little as 20 years (*Early Man in the New World*, Macmillan, 1950, p. 3 and map on p. 4).

What about the rest of the distance southward? Alfred Kidder says, "A hunting pattern based primarily on big game could have carried man to southern South America without the necessity at that time of great localized adaptation. It could have been effected with relative rapidity, so long as camel, horse, sloth, and elephant were available. All the indications point to the fact that they were." (*Appraisal of Anthropology Today*, Univ. of Chicago Press, 1953, p. 46.)

INTRODUCTION

THIS IS a very short paper. Yet there are some points of importance to consider in the light of it.

It shows how necessary it sometimes is to be able to escape one's own culture and enter into the spirit of another culture that is structured differently, in order to see the real motives which lie behind even our own judgments at times.

It also shows that the great figures of old, heroic though they may seem to have been, were very ordinary mortals really! This assumes, of course, that our interpretation is correct.

Another lesson is that each correction of some fundamental untruth is itself in time distorted until it too becomes untrue.

And finally, it demonstrates how wonderfully Scripture holds together with an inner concordance that still renders it its own best interpreter.

PART III

Why Noah Cursed Canaan Instead of Ham: A New Approach to an Old Problem

Chapter 1

WHY NOAH CURSED CANAAN

And Noah began *to be* an husbandman, and he planted a vineyard:

And he drank of the wine, and was drunken; and he was uncovered within his tent.

And Ham, the father of Canaan, saw the nakedness of his father, and told his two brethren without.

And Shem and Japheth took a garment, and laid *it* upon both their shoulders, and went backward, and covered the nakedness of their father; and their faces *were* backward, and they saw not their father's nakedness.

And Noah awoke from his wine, and knew what his younger son had done unto him.

And he said, Cursed *be* Canaan; a servant of servants shall he be unto his brethren.

And he said, Blessed *be* the LORD God of Shem; and Canaan shall be his servant.

God shall enlarge Japheth, and he shall dwell in the tents of Shem; and Canaan shall be his servant.

THE STORY appears in Genesis 9:20-27. Noah, apparently, cultivated a vineyard and whether intentionally or accidentally, ended up with an intoxicating drink. Like many others in this condition, he had removed his clothes because of the sensation of overheating which results from the dilation of the veins at the surface of the skin. Drunkenness and nakedness have been closely associated throughout history. In a drunken stupor the old man lay indecently exposed and his son Ham "saw his nakedness" (v. 22).

Some people believe that this phrase means more than appears on the surface and that on the basis of Leviticus chapters 18 and 19, the implication is that homosexuality was involved. On the other hand, Ham's immediate behavior seems to tell against this, for he would hardly proceed to tell his two

144

brothers outside (v. 22) if he had committed such a terrible offense against his father. Moreover, the behavior of Shem and Japheth in taking a garment and carefully covering the nakedness of their father with their faces averted so that "they saw not their father's nakedness" (v. 23) suggests that in both instances the words mean simply what they say.

Later on, Noah awoke and somehow found out what his younger son had done. Like many others who have lost their own self-esteem and are angry at themselves, Noah became enraged against his son. But he did not curse him; he cursed his grandson, according to verse 25. And herein seems to lie the injustice, and the widespread conviction that the text is in error. Shem and Japheth are blessed, Ham is ignored and a grandson, Canaan, who can surely have had no responsible part in Ham's misbehavior, suffers the full brunt of his grandfather's anger.[1]

Several explanations have been offered as to why, when Noah had thus been wronged by Ham, he pronounced a curse upon Canaan instead. I should like to suggest a reason which seems to have been overlooked.

In Exodus 20:5, God declared that He would "visit the iniquities of the fathers upon the children unto the third and fourth generations...." There is nothing arbitrary, barbaric, or even surprising about this. The sins of the fathers are reflected in the behavior of their children, and these children in their turn pay the penalty. What is surprising, however, is that men will distort the truth and make it a falsehood of the most malicious kind. It soon comes to mean that a child is not to be blamed for his sins — his environment and his heredity being held chiefly responsible. We say easily enough, "It is our fathers who are to be blamed, the generation which educated us. We are simply the children of our own age." Thus, even today a more sympathetic view is being taken of Adolph Hitler and some would even try to picture him as a child who was wronged and might otherwise have been a great hero. And in any case he is not to be blamed for what he did.

Curiously enough, this inverted process of reasoning is exactly what the Israelites applied to Exodus 20:5. By the time of Jeremiah they were saying, "The fathers have eaten sour

---

[1] Paul Hershon, in his *Rabbinical Commentary on Genesis*, (Hodder and Stoughton, 185, p. 54) quotes a passage in which the child Canaan is said to have first seen Noah uncovered, and then to have told his father Ham about it.

grapes and the children's teeth are set on edge" (Jer. 31:29).
In other words, it was not the children's misdoings which had
brought all these misfortunes upon them. It was all their fathers'
fault! But the Lord said in effect to Jeremiah, "You must correct
this; it is quite wrong. Tell them that 'every one shall die for
his own sin; every man that eateth sour grapes, his *own* teeth
shall be set on edge'" (Jer. 31:30).

It might be thought that this would have settled the matter
and straightened things out once for all. But in the course of
time, the truth was again distorted in another way and people
came to interpret this to mean that any misfortune which over-
took a man was due to his own sinfulness. Not unnaturally, this
had the effect of destroying all sympathy, for a man who was in
trouble or sickness was simply receiving his just deserts. It served
him right.

This is what created the peculiar problem for the disciples
when they were brought face to face with a man born blind in
John 9:1ff. It seems doubtful if it was sympathy that made them
question the Lord about his case, but rather a kind of theological
curiosity. Here was a man who had suffered a great misfortune.
He had been born blind. But since he was *born blind,* it seemed
impossible to attribute the fault to the man himself. On the
other hand, Jeremiah had made it clear that Exodus 20:5 did
not mean that it was his parents' fault. So they asked, "Who did
sin, this man or his parents?" Their question reflected their
attitude towards suffering. The Lord, however, while not denying the truth of the implications in their question, nevertheless
pointed out that in this instance the blind man was a privileged
person who providentially was permitted to show forth the glory
of God. There are at least three reasons why people suffer: because of the wickedness of their parents, because of their own
sinfulness, or simply for the glory of God.

Now, in other cultures than our own, and for reasons which
are not always clear, it is customary to attach the blame for a
man's failings upon his parents. But by the same token, it is also
customary to give *them* the credit for his successes. This principle
is recognized by most of us, in fact, but mostly without explicit
formulation. In these other cultures, both ancient and modern,
the principle has been publicly recognized.

It is an attitude which is quite remarkably reflected in
Scripture. Perhaps the clearest illustration is to be found in the
story of Saul and David, I Samuel 17:50-58. In this instance,

David had performed a deed of great national importance by destroying Goliath. David himself was no stranger to Saul for he had on many occasions played his harp to quiet the king's distracted spirit. Yet we find that when Saul saw David go forth against Goliath (v. 55) he said to Abner the captain of his hosts, "Abner, whose son is this youth?" And although Abner must certainly have known David by name, he replied, "As thy soul liveth, O King, I cannot tell."

This has always seemed a strange remark both for the king and his commanding officer to have made. But the explanation lies in a proper understanding of the social significance of verse 58. "And Saul said unto him, Whose son art thou, young man? And David answered, I am the son of thy servant Jesse, the Bethlehemite." This is simply an occasion upon which, following the social custom of his own day, Saul sought to give credit where credit was due, namely, to the father. Because David was Jesse's son, Jesse was to receive recognition.

Another illustration will be found in I Kings 11:9-12:

> And the Lord was angry with Solomon, because his heart was turned from the Lord God of Israel which had appeared unto him twice, and had commanded him concerning this thing, that he should not go after other gods: but he kept not that which the Lord commanded.
>
> Wherefore the Lord said unto Solomon, Forasmuch as this is done of thee and thou hast not kept my covenant and my statutes, which I have commanded thee, I will surely rend the kingdom from thee and will give it to thy servant.
>
> Notwithstanding in thy days I will not do it for David thy father's sake: but I will rend it out of the hand of thy son.

This is a beautiful example, because it is so specific in statement. Solomon was to be punished: but he could not be punished personally without bringing discredit on David his father, and this the Lord was not willing to do. The only way in which Solomon could be punished appropriately without injuring David's name was therefore to punish Solomon's son.

In the New Testament we find another instance. It is quite obvious that while a man can publicly seek to give credit to the father of a worthy son, a woman could not discreetly make reference to the father in complimentary terms for fear of being misunderstood. She therefore refers instead to the son's mother who rightly shares in the worthiness of her children. This fact is reflected clearly in Luke 11:27, where we read of a woman who suddenly perceiving the true greatness of the Lord Jesus

Christ, cried out in spontaneous admiration, "Blessed is the womb that bare Thee and the breasts which Thou hast sucked."

When we apply this principle to the story given in Genesis 9:20-27, the significance of the cursing of Canaan rather than Ham at once becomes clear. But because the principle has not been applied by commentators, the apparent injustice of Noah has puzzled people at least since the beginning of the Christian era when the commentators began to take notice of it. It appears that Jewish rabbis had access to a copy of the Septuagint (the Greek translation of the Old Testament, made in the third century B.C. by the Jews in Alexandria and which appears to form the basis of a number of quotations in the New Testament from the Old Testament) in which the name "Canaan" was replaced by the name "Ham." It is proposed by some authorities that this was the original reading and that the text was tampered with by Hebrew scribes who wished to add to the degradation of the Canaanites by showing that they were the subjects of a divine curse.

However, it is quite possible to explain the text exactly as it is, as a reflection of the social custom which we have been considering above. To begin with, there may have been a reason for Ham's behavior, other than mere disrespectfulness.

Without becoming involved in the technicalities of genetics, it is possible that Ham may himself have been a mulatto. In fact, his name means "dark" and perhaps refers to the color of his skin. This condition may have been derived through his mother, Noah's wife, and if we suppose that Ham had himself married a mulatto woman, it is possible to account for the preservation of the negroid stock over the disaster of the Flood.[2] It seems most likely that Ham had seen the darkness of his mother's body, for example, when being nursed. But he may never have seen the whiteness of his *father's* body.

When Charles Darwin visited the Tierra del Fuegians during the Voyage of the Beagle, he remarks how interested the natives were in the color of his skin. Naturally his face and his hands were bronzed by exposure to the weather after the long voyage, but when he rolled up a sleeve and bared his arm, to use his own words, "they expressed the liveliest surprise and admiration at its whiteness."[3]

---

[2] See Chapter Two.

[3] *The Darwin Reader,* Scribner, New York, 1956, extract dated as of Dec. 17, 1832, paragraph 10.

The same may have been true in the case of Ham and his father. His own body and that of Noah's wife being quite dark, he may have gone away reflecting upon the difference and forgetting his filial duty. In fact, this could conceivably be the reason he went to tell his brothers, for he may have supposed that they would be as surprised at this discovery as he was himself.

If this was the case, it may be argued that this was a small offense to receive such a pronounced judgment. But it is not at all certain that the form of the curse was as severe as it appears to be. That his posterity were to be servants, yes — but the Hebrew can just as readily be translated "servants par excellence." This actually is more likely, for we have in Hebrew plenty of instances of the superlatively excellent expressed in this manner, involving the reduplication of the key word as "Holy of Holies," "Lord of Lords," etc.[4] But where we find in Hebrew a comparable phrase in which the author is referring to that which is superlatively base (as in Dan. 4:17), the Hebrew uses an entirely different form of construction. In other words, wherever Hebrew employs a reduplication of a word, the concept intended is one of "excellence," much as in English we may say "very, very good." But while we may also say "very, very bad," the Hebrew evidently does not adopt this, but depends upon another form of construction. In short, what we are saying is that the phrase "servant of servants" may have meant that his descendants would perform a great service to their brethren. The judgment, in so far as it was a judgment, lies in the fact that they rendered this service to others and benefited little themselves.

However, the point is not essential to this essay, and in any case, it is the subject of two extended studies appearing as other Doorway Papers.[5] What is important to note is that Noah could not pronounce judgment of any kind upon his own son, Ham, the actual offender, without passing judgment upon himself, for society held him, the father, responsible for his son's behavior.

---

[4] Compare: God of Gods, Dan. 2:47; Holy of Holies, Heb. 9:3; King of Kings, Rev. 19:16; Heaven of Heavens, Neh. 9:6; Hebrew of Hebrews, Phil. 3:5; Lord of Lords, Rev. 19:16; Song of Songs, Song of Sol., 1:1; Age of Ages, Eph. 3:2.
Note: the references in the New Testament are either quotes from the Old Testament, or are Hebrew thoughts expressed in Greek. In any case, it is clear that the highest, not the lowest is intended by the writer.

[5] Part IV, "The Technology of Hamitic People," and Part I, "The Part Played by Shem, Ham and Japheth in Subsequent World History" in this volume.

To punish Ham, then, he must of necessity pronounce a curse upon Canaan, Ham's son.

On the other hand, when it came to blessing, the situation was very different. In pronouncing a benediction upon Shem and Japheth, he was, in fact, doing himself an honor! Such is human nature — and such is probably the explanation of this otherwise puzzling incident.

Chapter 2

WAS CANAAN A TRUE BLACK?

L IKE SOME other parts of this paper, this appendix is also speculative. As long as this is clearly understood, no harm will be done, provided the speculation is not divorced entirely from the evidence. The general title of these Doorway Papers was intended to suggest that they could provide room for new approaches to old problems.

No one has ever suggested, to my knowledge, that the Sumerians were negroid — nor do any of the reconstructed "Sumerian Life and Times" series such as have appeared in the *National Geographical Magazine,* or *Life,* ever so portray them. Yet there is some evidence to suggest that they may have been black skinned.

According to Samuel Kramer *(From the Tablets of Sumer,* Falcon's Wing Press, 1956, p. 60), they refer to themselves as "the blackheaded people." Actually the Sumerian original reads "head-of-black people," the symbol for head (SAG) being a cone shaped hat hiding all but the neck of the wearer, thus:

◁╞═ which turned through 90° becomes △

Hammurabi in his famous Code of Laws, also refers to the natives of Mesopotamia (Deimel's transcription, 1930, R. 24, line 11) as:

A-NA SALMAT GAGGADIM
i.e., "blackheaded ones."

Such descriptive phrases are, I think usually taken to mean

151

merely "dark-haired." But it seems likely that 95% or more of all the people who made up the early Middle East cultures were black-haired, whether Semitic or Sumerian, and the feature was hardly a distinguishing one. Indo-Europeans (from Japheth, whose name possibly means "fair") played little part in it till much later. But the Semitic population according to A. H. Sayce (*Fresh Light from the Ancient Monuments,* London, 1893, p. 26) distinguished themselves with racial pride from other peoples by their own light colored skin, and claimed that Adam too was a white man. They were his racial descendants. Yet they had black hair like the Sumerians and would not be different in this feature, and might therefore just as well have been termed "blackheaded people." But they apparently never were.

Evidently, then, it would be no mark of distinction to refer to the hair color, but it would definitely be such to refer to skin color. And the Sumerians were apparently proud of their black skin. In his *Sumerian Reader,* Gadd says they came to equate the term "blackheaded people" with the idea of "men" as real people by contrast with other human beings who are not really men at all.

It is further to be noted that the founders of the wonderful Indus Valley cultures were black skinned, and not merely black haired. The Rig Veda makes frequent reference to the fact that the conquering Aryans triumphed over these black and noseless (!) enemies (S. Pigott, *Prehistoric India,* Pelican, 1950, p. 261, and Lord Arundell of Wardour, *Tradition: Mythology, and the Law of Nations,* 1872, p. 84). But there was some real connection if not racial identity, between the Sumerians and these Indus Valley people. It may well be therefore that the phrase does really refer to skin color.

Now in the famous six sided prism of Sennacherib, the king refers to the conquered Canaanites as "blackness of head people."

GIM-RI SAL-MAT KAKKAD-DU-U

In this case it seems that Canaan could have been a black child, the homozygous offspring of his mulatto parents, Ham and his wife. The black people have a quite remarkable series of high cultures to their credit, and are almost born metallurgists. So were these ancient Canaanites.

PART IV

The Technology of Hamitic People

INTRODUCTION

IF YOU enjoy reading catalogs, now and then, you will probably enjoy this paper, although it is dull indeed if read merely as literature. But if treated as intended, namely, as a list of technical achievements, it may come as a surprise to find how many, how varied, and how fundamental have been the inventions of Hamitic people, and how great a service they have rendered to mankind in the field of technology.

Hitherto our ethnocentrism in the writing of history has obscured this fact, but we now have a sufficient and ever-growing body of documented materials to justify this presentation.

Some of these achievements may be considered slight by those who have never actually contributed anything new to the sum total of human invention. But one should not be deceived by simplicity: it may be the hallmark of genius. It could also be argued that if we can only point to one invention of note in some particular tribe, that people can hardly be termed inventive. However, if we have only mentioned one invention that does not mean it was their sole achievement. It was mentioned only because it illustrated a particular aspect of native ingenuity.

Scarcely an anthropologist can be found who would not at once agree that even the most primitive of people are peculiarly ingenious in finding practical solutions to practical problems. That they do not invent more is merely because they do not see the need for more inventions. When needs arise their solutions tend to be uncannily effective and simple.

What may be said with a fair degree of certainty is that up until the time when Indo-Europeans, i.e., Japhethites, began to make extensive contacts with other cultures, Western man's technology was poor in the extreme. We have been great borrowers, and somewhat tardy in acknowledging the debt. Some of the reasons why this borrowed technology has been advanced in such an extraordinary way are considered in Part V.

THE INVENTIVENESS OF THE
HAMITIC PEOPLES

I BELIEVE THAT it was Luther who complained that his opponents demanded in the very first paragraph a full explanation of everything he was about to discuss, before they would allow him to proceed any further! I find myself in somewhat the same position.

This Doorway Paper is actually one in a series of four, the first entitled "The Part Played by Shem, Ham, and Japheth in Subsequent World History" (Part I). The other three play a supporting role and are very necessary for the validation of the thesis presented in the first one. Without reading them, it is likely that many informed readers will be continually aggravated because certain basic assumptions, essential to the argument, are set forth as if unquestionable, whereas in fact they require very careful substantiation. But, like Luther, one soon finds the opening paragraph cannot be written at all if it must answer all the objections raised against it before proceeding any further: no more can any *one* of these particular Doorway Papers.

In the first of this series, a "framework" of history was predicated on the assumption that the present population of the world is to be wholly derived from the three sons of Noah— Shem, Ham, and Japheth. It was further hypothesized that the Indo-Europeans are Japhethites, which few will challenge; that the Semites are of Shem, which scarcely anyone will question; and that the colored races (black, brown, "red," and yellow) are from Ham, which *many* will deny. But granted this premise, the pattern of the subsequent history of these three divisions of mankind is remarkably reflected in Scripture in a number of surprising ways, as suggested in Part I.

In this paper my purpose is only to seek to substantiate a rather bold claim made for the descendants of Ham, namely, that

155

as the inventors of almost everything basic to World Civilization (in its mechanical as distinct from its spiritual aspects), they have indeed been "servants of servants," servants par excellence.

The people whose inventiveness is to be explored and illustrated quite extensively are all assumed to be neither Shemites nor Japhethites, and therefore descendants of Ham. This, in a word, includes all who are Negroid or Mongoloid, which comprehends, as a matter of fact, the founders of virtually all ancient civilizations in the Middle East, Africa, the Far East, and the New World, as well as presently existing or recently extinct primitive people. Hamites, it can be shown, have been in unexpected ways the world's great innovators, though very few people, except perhaps archaeologists, ethnologists, and cultural anthropologists, have been aware of it. The acknowledgment of our own debt to them is long overdue.

The arts and architecture of such people have been recognized and admitted as remarkable enough, but their technology is commonly believed to have been of little account except for an occasional odd device like the compass. In due time, when it was discovered that Eskimos, a people who are generally held to be as nearly representative of paleolithic man as one could expect to find, could be trained to operate and even repair such delicate and complicated devices as sewing machines or clocks more readily and more rapidly than it was possible to train the "white man," considerable surprise was expressed. Eventually, the ingenuity of these so-called primitive people became increasingly apparent and writers began to vie with one another in their search for superlatives to enlarge upon their native ingenuity. But it soon became evident that the Eskimos were not the only "backward" people who were intensely practical. Their wilderness of ice and snow and their inhospitable environment is shared in a different way by other primitive people, whom it now turns out have proved themselves to be quite as ingenious in making the most of the immediately available resources of their surroundings. For example, there are the Indians of the Sonoran Desert in Southern Arizona. Considering their situation, it is quite amazing to find what they have succeeded in extracting out of it. Throughout this discussion of primitive culture, and in much of the treatment of more highly complex civilizations of non-Western tradition, it is necessary to bear in mind that the greatest displays of ingenuity frequently appear in the ex-

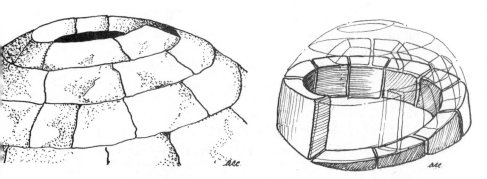

Fig. 4. Igloo construction. The original structure on which the drawing is based was seventeen feet in diameter. The spiral form of the construction is evident.

Fig. 5. Eskimo snow goggles. Various types are made from wood and bone.

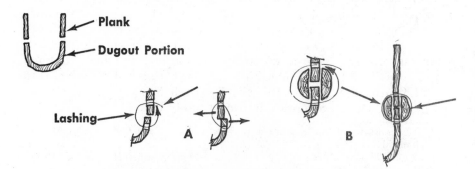

Fig. 6. Polynesian canoe building. Planks lashed insecurely (A) can slide to either side, thus loosening the caulking. By adding a piece split to form two half-rounds (B), the planks are tied in such a way that movement is virtually impossible. The whole is then caulked.

ploitation of the *immediate* resources of the environment rather than the secondary or less immediate resources.

This recognition of their resourcefulness, given somewhat belatedly, is now being accorded at high levels. Claude Levi-Strauss, speaking officially for UNESCO, made the following admission in attempting to establish who has made the greatest contribution to the world's wealth:[1]

> If the criterion chosen had been the degree of ability to overcome even the most inhospitable geographical conditions, there can be scarcely any doubt that the Eskimo on the one hand and the Bedouin on the other, would carry off the palm.

He might equally well have used the Indians of the Sonoran Desert in place of the Bedouin. And one could have included another rather rugged environment, the high altitudes of the Peruvian Andes, where the Aymara have shown themselves well able to hold their own with the Eskimo, the Bedouin, and the Indians of Arizona.

Let us examine very briefly some of the achievements of such people. One of the best modern authorities of this aspect of Eskimo life is Dr. Erwin H. Ackerknecht who writes:[2]

> The Eskimo is one of the great triumphs of our species. He has succeeded in adapting himself to an environment which offers to man but the poorest chances of survival. . . .
> His technical solution of problems of the Arctic are so excellent that white settlers would have perished had they not adopted many elements of Eskimo technology.

Frederick R. Wulsin,[3] an authority on clothing problems for cold climates, says candidly that "there seems to be no doubt that Eskimo clothing is the most efficient yet devised for extremely cold weather." Of this we have had personal experience, and can affirm its truth without hesitation. Moreover, to the Eskimo must probably go the credit for developing the first "tailored clothing" and, not unnaturally perhaps, the first thimbles.[4] In addressing a Scientific Defence Research Symposium in Ottawa in 1955, Dr. O. Solandt admitted frankly that:

---

[1] Levi-Strauss, Claude, *Race and History,* The Race Question in Modern Science, UNESCO, Paris, 1952, p. 27.

[2] Ackerknecht, Erwin H., "The Eskimo's Fight Against Hunger and Cold," *Ciba Symposia,* 10 (July-Aug. 1948): 894.

[3] Wulsin, Frederick R., "Adaptations to Climate Among Non-European Peoples," in *The Pysiology of Heat Regulation and the Science of Clothing,* ed. L. H. Newburgh, Saunders, Phil., 1949, p. 26.

[4] Jeffreys, C. W., *A Picture Gallery of Canadian History,* Vol. 1, Ryerson, Toronto, 1942, p. 113.

The White Man has not introduced a single item of environmental protection in the Arctic which was not already being used by the natives, and his substitute products are not yet as effective as the native ones. Only in his means of production has he the edge.

Ackerknecht continued subsequently:[5]

A very short review of the Eskimo's hunting techniques has already revealed an extraordinary number of well conceived implements. Eskimos are described as very "gadget-minded" and are able to use and repair machinery such as motors and sewing machines with almost no instruction. It is impossible to give here a complete list of aboriginal Eskimo instruments the number of which and quality of which have been emphasized by all observers. . . .

The best known type of Eskimo house is undoubtedly the dome-shaped snow-house with its ice window. With extraordinary ingenuity, the very products of the cold are used here as a protection against it.

It might be thought that once the idea was conceived, the construction of such a house would be comparatively simple. Actually it is remarkably difficult to construct a dome, without any means of supporting the arch while in the process of completing it. As the wall rises, it converges upon itself. Each new block overhangs more and more until near the top they rest almost in a horizontal plane. The problem is to hold each block in place until the next one ties it in, and then to hold that one until it, too, is tied in place.

Given enough hands the process is not so difficult, but the Eskimos have overcome the problem so effectively that one individual can, if he has to, erect his own igloo single-handed, without too much difficulty. The solution is to carry the rising layers of blocks in a spiral instead of in a series of horizontal levels. This is shown in Fig. 4. Thus as each block is added it not only rests on the lower level, but against the last block. One block would simply tend to fall in and, by experience, so do two or even three, when a new layer is started if the tiers are horizontally laid. But the Eskimo method entirely overcomes the problem.

The solution is, of course, amazingly simple — once it is known. . . . Most solutions are, when someone has discovered them for us. The problem is to visualize the solution before it exists. We tend to assume we would discover the way quite quickly, but experience shows that this is not true. A. H. Sayce has put it so

---

[5] Ackerknecht, E. H., op. cit., p. 897.

well, "One of the most significant lessons of Archaeology is that man is not essentially creative but destructive," and among ourselves at least "constructiveness belongs to the few."[6] H. M. Davies reminds us of this fact when he pointed out:[7]

> We drive an automobile because it is nearly foolproof, with little appreciation to the hidden, beautiful mechanism that powers it, and with no conception of the creative thought that went into its development: meanwhile we demand the family airplane. We listen to a radio receiver whose operation is utter magic to us and demand the even more complex television. We are a race of lever-twiddlers, button-pushers, and knob-twisters, enjoying the prodigious technical labors of a comparatively few men.

And Sayce joins with Davies in the article which was quoted above:[8]

> As compared with the mass of mankind, the number of those upon whom the continuance of civilization depends is but small; let them be destroyed or rendered powerless, and the culture they represent will disappear.

Returning to the Eskimo again, we have to realize that his environment offers him little in the way of raw materials, and his solutions must always seem simple by nature. It is all the more to his credit that he has achieved so much. Dr. Edward Weyer in an article rightly entitled, "The Ingenious Eskimo," put the matter this way:[9]

> Take the Eskimo's most annoying enemy, the wolf, which preys on the caribou and wild reindeer that he needs for food. Because of its sharp eyesight and keen intelligence, it is extremely difficult to approach in hunting. Yet the Eskimo kills it with nothing more formidable than a piece of flexible whalebone.
>
> He sharpens the strip of whalebone at both ends and doubles it back, tying it with sinew. Then he covers it with a lump of fat, allows it to freeze, and throws it out where the wolf will get it. Swallowed at a gulp the frozen dainty melts in the wolf's stomach and the sharp whalebone springs open, piercing the wolf internally and killing it.
>
> When the Eskimo gets a walrus weighing more than a ton

---

[6] Sayce, A. H., "Archaeology and Its Lessons," in *Wonders of the Past*, Vol. 1, ed. Sir John Hammerton, Putnam's Sons, London, 1924, p. 10.

[7] Davies, H. M., "Liberal Education and the Physical Sciences," *The Sci. Monthly*, May, 1948, p. 422.

[8] Sayce, A. H., op. cit., p. 11.

[9] Weyer, Edward, "The Ingenious Eskimo," *Nat. History* (Nat. Hist. Museum, N.Y.) May, 1939, pp. 278, 279.

on the end of a harpoon line, he is faced with a major engineering problem: how to get it from the water on to the ice. Mechanical contrivances belong to a world in whose development the Eskimo has had no part. No implement ever devised by him had a wheel in it. Yet this does not prevent him from improvising a block and tackle that works without a pulley. He cuts slits in the hide of the walrus, and a U-shaped hole in the ice some distance away. Through these he threads a slippery rawhide line, once over and once again. He does not know the mechanical theory of the double pulley, but he does know that if he hauls at one end of the line, he will drag the walrus out of the water onto the ice.

The deceiving thing about all his ingenuity is its very simplicity. He makes all kinds of hunting devices that are effective, inexpensive in time, easily repaired and uses only raw materials immediately available. His harpoon lines have floats of blown-up skins attached, so that the speared animal is forced to come to the surface if he dives. To prevent such aquatic animals from tearing off at high speed dragging the hunter and his kayak, he attaches baffles to the line which are like small parachutes that drag in the water. A bone hoop and a skin diaphragm stretched over it, some thongs, and this is all that he needs.

To locate the seal's movements under the ice he has devised a stethoscope, which owes nothing to its modern Western counterpart, working on the same principle.[10] And recently a native "telephone" was discovered in use, made entirely from locally available materials, linking two igloos with a system of intercommunication, the effectiveness of which was demonstrated on the spot to the Hudson's Bay Agent, D. B. Marsh who discovered it. Marsh added at the end of his report this statement:[11]

> The most amazing thing of all was that no one in that camp had ever seen a telephone, though doubtless they had heard of them from their friends who from time to time visit Churchill.

Nevertheless, it is exceedingly unlikely that any friends who had seen a telephone would have seen the kind of arrangement this Eskimo had developed which, of course, used no batteries. We used to make a similar kind of thing as children with string and ordinary cans, but they were never of very much use, and in any case we got the idea from someone else. In this case, the Eskimo

---

[10] An illustration of such an instrument is given by Alexander Goldenweiser, *Anthropology*, Crofts, N.Y., 1937, p. 85, fig. 23.

[11] Marsh, D. B., "Inventions Unlimited," in *The Beaver* (The Hudson's Bay Co.) Dec., 1943, p. 40.

had used fur around the diaphragm to cushion it, and the sound
came through remarkably well.

Finally, a word about Eskimo snow goggles. An illustration
of one of these will be found in Fig. 5 on page 157. They
are well known to explorers and no one will travel in the
Arctic without them— or something to replace them — if he wishes
to escape the very unpleasant ailment of snow blindness. Like
everything else the Eskimo makes, they are very effective, and
often so designed that he does not need to turn his head to see to
either side of him. This is important, since the game he usually
hunts would catch the movement.

Turning now to the Indians of the Sonoran Desert, Macy
H. Lapham has written illuminatingly of their genius for making much of little. He said:[12]

> To the stranger, these desert wilderness areas seem to have
> little to contribute to the subsistence of the native Indian....
> Notwithstanding this forbidding aspect, to the initiated there is
> a veritable storehouse of the desert, from the widely scattered
> resources of which essentials in food, clothing, shelter, tools,
> cooking utensils, fuel, medicine, and articles of adornment or
> those sacred in ceremonial rites, have contributed for genera-
> tions, and still are contributing to the needs of the Indian....

Lapham gives many excellent photographs in which various
plants are identified and the products which the Indians have
extracted from them are also listed. These lists are very impressive. He remarked:

> The desert ironwood, a small tree, is known for its ex-
> tremely hard wood, is prized for the campfire, and has been used
> for arrow heads and implements.... The beans of the Mesquite
> are made into meal and baked as cakes. The split and shredded
> inner bark, along with similar materials from the willow and
> cotton wood, furnish the fibres and strands for building and for
> woven baskets. Some of these baskets are so finely woven that
> coated with gum and resins obtained from desert plants they
> may be used for liquids....
> Condiments and seasonings for food, before the present era
> of the tin can, were obtained from native mints, peppergrass,
> sage and other herbs. Ashes of the salt bush which grows in
> saline soils, were used as a substitute for baking powder. Other
> plant products containing sugar and mucilaginous substances
> yielded substitutes for candy and chewing gum...
> Wild cotton was cultivated and harvested by the Indians
> before the White Man and his wool-bearing animals found

---

[12] Lapham, Macy H., "The Desert Storehouse," *The Sci. Monthly,* June,
1948, pp. 451ff.

their way into the desert. In his arts and crafts the Indian used gums and resins from the Mesquite and the creosote bush, as adhesives; awls made from the cactus spines and sharpened bone; and dyes from species of the indigo bush, mesquite, the fetid marigold, seeds of the sunflower, and from minerals.

In the absence of the family drugstore, the Indian resorted to a range of desert plants for cures of various ailments. Some of these were of doubtful value, but others are to be found on the shelf of the modern druggist. These remedies included materials for poultices and infusions, and decoctions of the manzanita, creosote bush, catnip, canaigre or wild rhubarb, verba santa or mountain balm, berba mansa, the inner bark of the cotton wood, winter fat, golden aster, goldenrod, yarrow, horsebrush, and species of the sunflower. They were used for sore throats, coughs, respiratory diseases, boils, toothaches, fevers, sore eyes, headaches, and as tonics and emetics. Mullein leaves were smoked and used for medicinal purposes; while roots of the yucca, winter fat, and four o'clock, and leaves of the seepweed, were used as laxatives and for burns and stomach ache. There was even an insecticide — a sweetened infusion of the leaves of the Haplophyton or cockroach plant which was used as a poison for mosquitos, cockroaches, flies and other pests.

Even such random excerpts from Lapham's article might be sufficient indication of the "inventiveness" of these so-called primitive people. But there is much more to wonder at. A photograph of a Mesquite thicket in a river bed is accompanied by this observation: "Mesquite thickets supply fuel, poles, timbers for buildings and fences, and fibres and strands for baskets and binding materials. From the Mesquite's bark, seed pods, and bean-like seeds come food, browse for livestock, medicine, gums, dyes, and an alcoholic beverage."

The roots of the Yucca trees supply drugs and a "soap substitute." Like the pioneer farmers, it seems that they used everything but the noise! He concluded:

> Thus, as the Indian made his rounds of this self-help commissary in an apparently empty wasteland, he found an impressive stock to be harvested and added to his market basket. We can only marvel at the wisdom and vast store of knowledge accumulated by these primitive people as they made the desert feed, clothe and shelter them.

This is a long quotation. But it serves to indicate what ingenuity can do with an otherwise unpromising environment. It is difficult indeed to conceive of a more complete exploitation of the primary resources of the desert in which they have been content to live.

One wonders if Lapham's use of the word "found" is really

just. They seem virtually to have exhausted their environment, extracting from it wisely, ingeniously, and effectively all it could possibly afford. Would *we* have "found" much of this? The point I should like to emphasize particularly here is that such people, for so long supposedly unimaginative and dull, have demonstrated a remarkable genius for this kind of thing. Their ingenuity has been overlooked so often because those who surveyed their works were themselves unaware of the effort required to invent *anything*. It all seems so obvious. Their solutions to mechanical problems in particular are always characterized by a peculiar simplicity that is completely deceiving.

To digress for a moment, we may use as an illustration of this aspect of primitive technology, a method used by the Polynesians to bind the plank walls of their canoes. Anyone who has ever tried to bind two planks together edgewise so that they will be tight and rigid — and will remain so — will have quickly discovered how difficult it is. It is, in fact, almost impossible. Yet the Polynesian canoe builders do it easily. Fig. 6 shows how it was done. In a sense, it really takes an engineer to see the genius of this. By using gums and resins in the joint, a perfectly rigid, strong, and watertight union is effected. The solution seems obvious enough. Such ingenuity was exercised wherever their comparatively simple needs were not completely satisfied because of some mechanical obstacle.

Perhaps one more such "simple" solution may be in order here. The Indians of North America used leather for clothing — the familiar buckskin. However, one problem of all such materials is that after a while the edges begin to curl up or to roll in such a way as to be both unsightly and ill-fitting, and of course colder in winter. This was overcome by making a series of cuts into the edge and at right angles to it, each cut being about two inches long, and spaced about one-sixteenth of an inch to one-eighth of an inch apart. This imparted to the edges the familiar "frill" effect, which is both decorative and fundamentally useful. It required virtually nothing to do it — except ingenuity in the first phase. It prevents edge-curling entirely.

Desert areas always seem to hold so little promise of survival to the sophisticated European. The very appearance of barrenness seems to hinder the processes of thought which would otherwise find how to render it more habitable. But it seems to have been no great problem to non-Indo-European people, whether ancient or modern.

In his UNESCO paper, Levi-Strauss mentions the Bedouin along with the Eskimo, and archaeological exploration in the desert area of Transjordania has revealed a remarkable triumph of desert conquest by Bedouin peoples of early times.

Michael Evenari and Dov Koller reported recently on the results of their work in Negev. They wrote:[13]

> The idea that anyone could have farmed a desert as arid as this is today, seemed so incredible that many authorities concluded the climate of the region must have been more lush in the time of the Nabataeans. Nelson Glueck went to Palestine in the 1930's and to Transjordania, to re-explore the Nabataean Culture, and what he found led him to acclaim the Nabataeans as "one of the most remarkable people that ever crossed the stage of history." Their cities did indeed bloom in the midst of a seemingly hopeless desert. Nowhere in all their houses was there a stick of wood to show that any trees had ever grown in the region. . . .

The authors then explain how these ancient people achieved a greater mastery of the desert than any other people since, and they underline the fact that the Nabataeans "avoided the mistake" of trying methods which are are universally accepted Indo-European ones, namely, the use of dams. Their method was cheaper, more effective, more readily controlled, and brought a greater area of desert land under successful cultivation. They so prospered, in fact, as to be able to build and support the very famous city of Petra. The authors then describe the method of irrigation these people employed. In summing up, they remarked —to quote their own words:

> The more one examines the Nabataeans' elaborate system, the more impressed one must be with the precision and scope of their work. Engineers today find it difficult enough to measure and control the flow of water in a constantly flowing river, but the Nabataean engineers had to make accurate flow estimates and devise control measures for torrents which rushed over the land only briefly for a few hours each year. They anticipated and solved every problem in a manner which we can hardly improve upon today. Some of their structures still baffle investigators.

Records tell that the yield was often seven or eight times the sowing. The authors concluded:

> The Nabataeans' conquest of the desert remains a major challenge to our civilization. With all the technological and

---

[13] Evenari, Michael, and Dov Koller, "Ancient Masters of the Desert," *The Sci. American,* Apr., 1956, pp. 39ff.

scientific advances at our disposal, we must still turn to them for some lessons. . . . The best we can do today is no more than a modification of the astute and truly scientific methods worked out more than 2000 years ago by the Nabataean masters of the desert.

Snowy waste or sandy desert, bitter cold or stifling heat — we have little to contribute to such people in the conquest of such environments.

Returning to the New World again, J. Grahame Clark, speaking of the contributions made by the Indians of North and South America to the Old World, had this to say:[14]

> Baron Nordenskiold, unlike some European theorizers who found it difficult to credit the aborigines with the ability to raise their own civilization independently of the Old World inspiration, had spent many long and arduous years in the field of South American archaeology, and his conclusions carried with them outstanding authority. In addition to many technical inventions he attributed to the American Indian the achievement of domesticating the animal and plant life of his habitat so effectively that during the four centuries since the Discovery, the White Man had failed to make a single contribution of importance. The native fauna gave poor scope, but from it he domesticated the llama, alpaca, guinea pig, and turkey. Of plants he domesticated hundreds. . . .

Matthew Stirling, Chief of the American Bureau of Ethnology, spoke of this contribution from plant life.[15]

> Among the plants developed by these ancient botanists are maize, beans (kidney and lima), potatoes, and sweet potatoes, now four of the leading foods of the world. Manioc, extensively cultivated by the natives of tropical America is now the staff of life for millions of people living in the equatorial belt. Other important items, such as peanuts, squash, chocolate, peppers, tomatoes, pineapples and avocados might be added.
>
> In addition, the Indian was the discoverer of quinine, cocaine, tobacco and rubber, useful commodities of modern times. Maize or Indian corn was one of the most useful contributions of the American Indian to mankind. Over a considerable portion of the Americas, it is the staff of life.

Kenneth Mackoman added to this list, the custard apple, strawberry, vanilla bean, chickle, and cascara, besides a number of others less familiar. [16] His whole list of important plants made up

14 Clark, J. Grahame, "New World Origins," *Antiquity*, June, 1940, p. 118.
15 Stirling, Matthew, "America's First Settlers, the Indians," *Nat. Geog. Magazine*, Nov., 1937, p. 592.
16 Macgowan, Kenneth, *Early Man in the New World*, Macmillan, N.Y., 1950, p. 199.

by the Indian's agriculture is impressive, for it contains 50 items, not one of which is an Old World species. Every one of them can be cultivated with a hoe, requiring no draft animals whatever. He also mentions one other accomplishment which is very difficult to account for. The Indian devised a method of extracting a deadly poison (cyanide) from an otherwise useful plant, manioc, without losing the valuable starch it contained. Macgowan says that Henry J. Bruman called this "one of the outstanding accomplishments of the American Indian." The remarkable thing about it is that they should ever have thought of making use of a plant which, as they found it, contained a deadly poison.

M. D. C. Crawford gave a list of vegetables which were cultivated by the American Indians prior to 1492, which adds the following to the above:[17]

Aloe	Cacao	Pineapple
Alligator Pear	Chili pepper	Indian fig (Prickly pear)
Arrowroot	Jerusalem Artichoke	Pumpkin
Star Apple	Cotton (gossypium barbadense Linn.)	

J. L. Collins wrote more recently:[18]

> The pineapple shares the distinction accorded to all major food plants of the civilized world, of having been selected, developed, and domesticated by people of prehistoric times, and passed on to us through one or more earlier civilizations. The pineapple, like a number of other contemporary agricultural crops ... originated in America and was unknown to the people of the Old World before its discovery.

Just where the Indians found the original plants which they improved upon to produce modern pineapples, we do not know. None of the existing varieties compares with the domesticated plant, and Collins observes, "None of these can be singled out now as the form or forms which gave rise to the domestic pineapples of today, or even of those varieties in the possession of the Indians at the time of the Discovery of America." This was no accident then, but a deliberate and intelligent breeding process which progressed so far before we knew anything about

---

[17] Crawford, M. D. C., *The Conquest of Culture*, Fairchild, N.Y., 1948, pp. 145, 146.

[18] Collins, J. L., "Pineapples in Ancient America," *The Sci. Monthly*, Nov., 1948, p. 372.

it, that we cannot now retrace the steps by which it was first accomplished.

Melville Herskovits points out that the North American Indians increased the fertility of their land artificially, by putting a fish in each maize hill, and practiced multi-planting highly successfully.[19] In each hill planted with maize, they placed squash and bean seeds together, so that the bean plants could climb the corn stalks and the squash vines run along the ground. The same practice is apparently found in West Africa, where gourds take the place of squashes. Their reasoning here, as Herskovits points out, is different from ours: they held that a plant which grows erect, one that climbs, and one that hugs the earth, must each have a different nature and therefore extract a different food from the earth. They will not compete with each other for the goodness of the soil.

Considering the Orient, Dr. F. H. King, who has made a very careful examination of the farming methods practiced by the Chinese, the Koreans, and the Japanese, draws special attention to their painstaking care in maintaining or enhancing the fertility of their soils, using all kinds of fertilizers and other special means.[20]

Necessity is the mother of invention (although laziness helps!) and food is a necessity. Primitive people have shown extraordinary ingenuity in obtaining food. We have already mentioned one or two devices used by the Eskimo, the spring bone for killing wolves, for example. In other parts of the world there is the same remarkable ingenuity, and not the least remarkable element is the variety.

For example, according to George P. Murdock, the Ainu of Northern Japan use dogs to do their fishing for them.[21] There are shoals of fish in the shallow waters along some of their coasts, and to catch these they have trained their dogs to swim straight out to sea in a line until a given signal. The dogs then wheel around and come back in an arc towards the shore, barking and making a big splash, thus driving the fish into even shallower

---

[19] Herskovits, Melville, *Man and His Works,* Knopf, N.Y., 1950, p. 250.

[20] King, F. H., *Farmers for 40 Centuries,* Rodale Press, Emmaus, (Pa.), reviewed by W. M. Myers, "Those Clever People," *The Sci. Monthly,* Dec., 1949, p. 448.

[21] Murdock, George P., *Our Primitive Contemporaries,* Macmillan, N.Y., 1934, p. 167.

water where each dog seizes one in his mouth, runs ashore, and drops it at his master's feet — receiving a fish's head as a reward.

Ralph Linton speaks of one device for catching wild fowl, which he feels should certainly be awarded top prize for simple ingenuity.[22] A flat stone of about 18 inches in diameter is given a small raised rim of mud or clay. Then certain nuts are placed in the enclosure. These nuts are a particular delight of the local guinea fowl. But the natives of several parts of Africa where these birds are found take care to ensure that the nuts are just too large for the fowl to pick up in their beaks. Attracted to the food, the birds try again and again to get a nut in their mouth, each time striking the flat rock with their beak instead. But they are persistent creatures, so they keep it up until their heads are swollen and they have literally knocked themselves silly. Each day the owner of the stone calls by and picks up the stupefied birds from the immediate neighborhood. Poultry farmers have found that the same thing can happen to chickens fed on a concrete floor. But there is no evidence that Indo-Europeans ever put this observation to any practical use.

We may mention a further example of native ingenuity, found in certain parts of Oceania, where there are cuttlefish which have long sucker-tipped arms that are stretched out to catch fish. The natives attach these cuttlefish to lines and use them to catch food for themselves instead.[23]

Lord Raglan tells how in some areas of Oceania, the natives of Java, of the Banda Islands, and the Dobuans, catch a particular species of fish that is difficult to approach, by using fishing-kites.[24] The kite is flown on a line of some length, and the fish hook dangles from the tail of the kite, thus allowing the fisherman to keep a considerable distance from the fish which would otherwise evade him.

It is well known that the Japanese have for years used Cormorants to do their fishing for them.[25] The birds seem to be well trained and to enjoy themselves immensely. The Samoans use a native plant drug which, when poured on the water, makes

[22] Linton, Ralph, *The Tree of Culture*, Knopf, N.Y., 1956, p. 83.

[23] Cotton, Clare M., "Animals: Old Hands at Angling," *Sci. News Letter*, Mar. 6, 1954, p. 155.

[24] Raglan, Lord, *How Came Civilization?* Methuen, London, 1939, p. 130.

[25] Gudger, E. W., "Fishing with the Cormorant in Japan," *The Sci. Monthly*, July, 1929, pp. 5ff.

the fish dopey and easy to catch.[26] According to Carleton Coon, the Australian aborigines poison the water holes with a mild drug that similarly makes the animals who drink from them stupified.[27] By such means, they easily catch the swift-footed emu, for example. A paper published by the Smithsonian Institute lists hundreds of such poisons used by primitive people in all parts of the world to catch game.[28]

The Tierra del Fuegians have so many different traps and other devices for catching ducks and geese, etc., that it would be wearying to detail them. Coon refers to them as being many and ingenious, and varying according to the nature of the locality.[29] They are, moreover, characterized by a remarkable degree of originality, so that it becomes difficult to imagine any further alternatives. Yet these same Tierra del Fuegians were considered by Darwin, when he visited them during his voyage with the Beagle, to be the very lowest of all humans, hardly people at all.[30] Sir John Lubbock shared this opinion.[31] Yet their inventiveness, where it had to be exercised, knew almost no limitations. I should like to draw attention to this point here. Inventiveness was exercised where needs arose, seldom otherwise. And this inventiveness did not (as ours so often does) display itself by merely modifying the products of others. The results were as diverse as they were original, and they are almost always characterized by a grand simplicity that is completely misleading to the Westerner whose products are so terribly complicated. Yet simplicity is the hallmark of genius.

Take as an illustration of this, the bola. Here is a weapon that is effectiveness itself in bringing down small rapidly moving game. The device is composed of a number of stones (usually about 2 inches to 3 inches in diam.), around each of which a cord is fastened in a groove with a free end about 12 inches to 18 inches long. From 4 to 8 such stones form the weapon which

---

26 Murdock, G. P., op. cit., p. 51.

27 Coon, Carleton S., A Reader in General Anthropology, Henry Holt, N.Y., 1948, p. 220.

28 Heizer, Robert F., "Aboriginal Fish Poisons," Paper No. 38 in the series Anthropological Papers, Bulletin 151, (Smithsonian Inst., Washington, 1953), pp. 225-283. Several hundred specific poisons are listed.

29 Coon, C. S., op. cit., p. 220.

30 Darwin, Charles, Journal of Researches, Ward, Lock, and Co., N.Y. (preface dated 1845), pp. 206ff.

31 Lubbock, Sir John, Prehistoric Times, New Science Library, Hill, N.Y., 1904, p. 201.

is made by tying together the free ends of the long cords. Holding these cords at their junction, the native swings the stones around like a windmill and lets the whole affair fly at the flock of birds, or rabbits, or any such small game. The stones tend to part company in flight, but only of course to the extent of the cords which tie them to one another. The weapon is thus widely spread by the time it reaches the game, and the chance of a hit is greatly increased. The same effect is, of course, obtained with shot. However, if any one of the stones or cords make contact, the whole weapon at once wraps itself around the victim. Down it comes. What could be more effective? These bolas are found in many parts of the world and even in prehistoric sites, a testimony to the inventiveness even of prehistoric man,[32] for its seems hard to believe that they were invented only once and that all modern instances are derivatives.

Of all primitive people, perhaps the Australian aborigines have aroused the most interest, not merely because they are so well known and among the last to retain a great part of their ancient skills and traditions, but also because of the extraordinary simplicity of their material culture. Virtually the whole of a man's worldly wealth can normally be carried with him, often in one hand! Of added interest, of course, is the fact that they seem to be negroid, and yet they have much body hair and bushy beards, which Negroes never have. Thus their origin is an intriguing mystery still.

But their ingenuity is also undoubted in so far as they have cared to exercise it. Probably the supreme example of this is the boomerang. It is also found in other parts of the world, and even in prehistoric sites.[33] As a weapon, it is remarkable: quite justly been called the first "guided missile." Of course, all thrown objects are guided in a sense; but the boomerang can be so controlled in the hands of an expert that it will do extraordinary things in the air, and return to the sender if it misses the target, a great saving of effort and a real advantage in war.

George Farwell recently authored an official Australian Government paper in which the design of this weapon was carefully

---

[32] Bolas: see Robert Braidwood, *Prehistoric Men*, Nat. Hist. Museum, Chicago, 1948, p. 56.

[33] Boomerangs: these have also been reported from Egypt at Badari by V. G. Childe, *New Light on the Most Ancient East*, Kegan Paul, London, 1935, p. 65; and in Europe, by Herbert Wendt, *I Looked for Adam*, Weidenfeld and Nicolson, London, 1955, p. 356.

considered.[34] It is much more complex than would appear to the casual observer. Its response to controlled flight is outlined by the author who then explains how this is possible. Even if its special construction features were purely accidentally discovered at first, it is still true that the inventor dis-covered his discovery; this is not merely a play upon words. Of the boomerang Farwell wrote:

> There are sound reasons for its design features. The under-sides of the arms are flat, the upper have a slight camber, a factor which provides lift. There is also a twist from the horizontal at the outer end of each arm, one upward, the other down, perhaps not more than two degrees in all.
>
> It may seem unreal to discuss a prehistoric weapon in terms of aerodynamics, but therein lies the remarkable achievement of the aborigine. His practical mind and acute observation anticipated certain ideas of the 20th century aircraft designers.
>
> Sir Thomas Mitchell, the explorer, made the characteristic twist of the boomerang the basis for a new type of ship's propeller, which he patented 100 years ago. Early in this century G. T. Walker of Cambridge University spent no less than ten years of research into the boomerang's properties, evolving certain theories on gyroscopic flight.

Farwell then elaborates somewhat on the dynamics of its flight and gives some examples of feats which the natives can achieve with little effort. He presumes that it was perhaps by observing the flight of falling leaves with their curled edges that they came to the idea. This sounds rather weak to me. At any rate, they created a very ingenious weapon, and we have found no way to improve it yet.

George Sarton used this weapon as an illustration of "the uncanny ingenuity of 'primitive' people."[35] To this he added the elastic plaited cylinder of jacitara palm bark, called a tipiti, which is used to extract the poison cyanide from the manioc, to which reference has already been made. As a third illustration he referred to prehistoric Chinese pottery vessels which took the form of a tripod, the legs of which were hollow and formed the containers. It thus anticipated by thousands of years the modern trisection aluminum wares. The shape, of course, permitted the cooking of three separate dishes at the same time.

In the Peruvian Andes, living at an elevation of 14,000 feet

34 Farwell, George, "The First Known Guided Missile," reprinted in *The Globe and Mail*, Toronto, Sat. Aug. 29, 1953, p. 17, as a feature article from the Australian Government publ. *South West Pacific*.

35 Sarton, George, *A History of Science*, Harvard, 1952, p. 5.

approximately, are the Aymara — believed to be the remnants of the creators of the Inca Empire. They are a rather impatient and ill-tempered people according to some observers, possibly by reason of the rarified atmosphere in which they live and possibly on the same account they do not care to exert themselves much to improve their condition — although obviously this was not true in the past. But they have developed their medical skill quite extensively and have so organized the profession that there are specialists in various fields of medicine, who refer patients to one another as seems necessary.[36] Like most primitive people, they mix magic with their medicine: but they evidently realize that the magic has mainly a psychological value. This is also true of other such native people. A. P. Elkin has written on this point at some length and is convinced that the witch doctor is often a man, as he put it, of "High Degree," by which he means relatively of Ph.D. calibre in the context of his own culture.[37] It is, in fact, becoming increasingly apparent that the non-Indo-European far anticipated us in their medical practices, as well as in the field of psychology. I think this is particularly true in certain areas, such as in dealing with fear. Of African medical skill, Grantly Dick Read has pointed out:[38] "They had cures for diseases which modern science still finds difficult to heal — and sometimes the knowledge of a good witch doctor could be of very good use to modern psychology." Frequently, of course, they did not reflect much upon the psychology they used, but it was always very practical in its application, representing a kind of deep wisdom which modern physicians sometimes lack.

There are often amusing and revealing illustrations of this. In two areas in particular they explored widely: in person-to-person relationships, especially with near relatives; and in dealing with the supernatural. For example, they insist as a rule that a man go to live with his wife's people. There are a number of very good reasons for this, not the least of which is the fact that they recognized that most emotional tensions revolve around the lady of the house. When a man goes to his wife's home, the lady

---

[36] Tschopik, H., Jr., "The Aymara," in the *Handbook of South American Indians,* Vol. 2, Bulletin 143, Bureau of American Ethnology, 1946, pp. 501-573.

[37] Elkin, A. P., "Aboriginal Men of High Degree," 1944 Queensland Univ. John Murtagh Macrossan Memorial Lectures, Australasian Publications, 1946.

[38] Read, Grantly Dick, "No Time for Fear," as reviewed by W. A. Deacon in the Sat. Review of Books, *Globe and Mail,* Toronto, Aug. 11, 1956.

of the house "gains" a son. If, however, the wife goes to the husband's house to live, the lady of the house "loses" a son! This can be a serious thing—the root of much jealousy, causing emotional tensions which they sought to avoid if possible.

As an illustration of a second area in which psychology is applied, one may cite a case that occurred in a Pueblo village after the last war. Many young Hopi volunteered for service overseas. This often badly confused their traditional cultural behavior patterns. One anthropologist noting this, suggested to a Hopi veteran that he'd still be afraid to sleep in one of their ancient cemeteries. He laughingly denied this. So he, and an old villager, agreed to a test. The old man selected a spot to sleep, performed several little rites, sprinkling seed around his bed and urinating on the seed. With a brief prayer, he then lay down and slept like a child. The young man no longer believed in such things—neither the spirits (so he said) nor the magic. He tossed and turned, quite unable to sleep—pretending to be unafraid and having no longer any accepted means to offset the fears he denied. He finally got up and returned to the village. A. P. Elkin has given many instances of this kind of thing in Australia, and says that he often spoke to the old men about their faith in the magic they used and was surprised to find how clearly they understood its psychological value. Some of the witch doctors were "Ph.D.'s" in psychology, rather than medical doctors with an "M.D.," according to Elkin.

But even in the use of drugs that do actually work chemically the non-Indo-European has often been far ahead of us. Aldous Huxley has written of the use of such drugs as tranquilizers and other remedies for anxiety.[39]

> Certain chemical compounds produce certain changes of consciousness and so permit a measure of self-transcendence and a temporary relief of tension. Thus, the so-called "tranquilizing" drugs are merely the latest addition to a long list of chemicals which have been used from time immemorial for changing the quality of consciousness and so making possible some degree of transcendence. Let us always remember that, while modern pharmacology has given us a host of new synthetics, it has made no basic discoveries in the field of the natural drugs; it has merely improved the methods of extraction, purification, and combination. All the naturally occurring sedatives, narcotics, euphorics, hallucinogens, and excitants were discovered thou-

---

[39] Huxley, Aldous, "History of Tension," *Sci. Monthly*, July, 1957, pp. 4, 5.

sands of years ago before the dawn of civilization. This is surely one of the strangest facts in that long catalog of improbabilities known as human history. Primitive man, it is evident, experimented with every root, twig, and leaf, and flower, with every seed, nut and berry, and fungus, in his environment. Pharmacology is older than agriculture. There is good reason to believe that even in paleolithic times, while he was still a hunter and a food-gatherer, man killed his animals and human enemies with poisoned arrows. By the late Stone Age he was systematically poisoning himself. The preserved heads of poppy in the kitchen middens of the Swiss Lake Dwellers shows how early in his history man discovered the techniques of self-transcendence through drugs. There were dope addicts long before there were farmers.

As an example of the extent to which some people went, it may be mentioned that the Jagga even developed a truth serum.[40]

Claude Levi-Strauss has underscored another aspect of this psycho-medical contribution:[41]

> The West, for all its mastery of machines, exhibits evidence of only the most elementary understanding of the use and potential resources of that supermachine, the human body. In this sphere, on the contrary, the East and Far East are several thousand years ahead; they have produced the great theoretical and practical summae represented by Yoga in India, and Chinese breath-techniques, or the visceral control of the ancient Maoris. . . .
>
> In all matters touching on the organization of the family, and the achievement of harmonious relations between the family group and the social group, the Australian aborigines, though backward in the economic sphere, are so far ahead of the rest of mankind that, to understand the careful and deliberate system of rules they have elaborated, we have to use all the refinements of modern mathematics. . . .
>
> The Australians, with an admirable grasp of the facts, have converted this machinery into terms of theory, and listed the main methods by which it may be produced, with the advantages and the drawbacks attaching to each. They have gone further than empirical observation to discover the laws governing the system, so that it is no exaggeration to say that they are not merely the founders of modern sociology as a whole, but are the real innovators of measurement in the social sciences.

Not all sociologists would agree with Levi-Strauss, of course, but there is no doubt that the social aspects of human relationships have here been subjected to unusual scrutiny. It seems

---

[40] Truth Serum: referred to by Robert Lowie, *Social Organization*, Rinehart, N.Y., 1948, pp. 168, 169.

[41] Levi-Strauss, C., op. cit., p. 27.

almost a rule, in fact, that the simpler the culture in its materials, the more elaborate its formalized social structure is apt to be, including its rituals. And conversely, the more physically complex the civilization, the less formal its social patterns are likely to be. Ralph Linton has written of one occasion in an Australian tribe, where it happened that the regulations had become so involved that a time came when it was found nobody could properly get married any more.[42]

The American Indians also had an extensive medical knowledge. Their surgical skill was remarkable, and like non-Indo-Europeans in many other parts of the world, ancient and modern, they practiced such delicate operations as trepanation with remarkable success.[43]

Such extremely delicate surgery implies the use of some kind of anaesthetic. Robert Lowie has reminded us that we owe this very fundamental discovery to the South American Indian. He has said, "What is absolutely certain is that our local anaesthetics go back to the Peruvian Indian's coca leaves, whence our Cocaine."[44]

Another important invention from the same source is the enema. Robert Heizer, in an issue of a well-known publication, which was devoted to the history of this instrument, stated that:[45]

> The medical practices of the Indians of North and South America prior to the shattering of their cultures by Caucasian wars and exploitation, were truly amazing in their magnitude and excellence. Our fractional knowledge of these attainments derives from early historical records, ethnobotanical works by botanists and pharmacologists, and from intensive study of skeletal materials by trained observers. Included in the roster of medical techniques was the administration of enemas and lavements by means of a number of instruments — bulb and piston type syringes and clyster tubes.

E. Nordenskiold, writing of the American Indian as an inventor, has referred to such enema syringes, one of which he described

---

42 Linton, Ralph, *The Study of Man*, Student's Ed., Appleton Century, N.Y., 1936, p. 90.

43 Popham, Robert, "Trepanation as a Rational Procedure in Primitive Surgery," *Univ. of Toronto Medical Journal*, Feb., 1954, pp. 204-211.

44 Lowie, Robert, *An Introduction to Cultural Anthropology*, Farrar and Rinehart, 2nd ed., 1940, p. 336.

45 Heizer, Robert, "The Use of the Enema by the Aboriginal American Indians," *Ciba Symposia*, 5 (Feb., 1944): 1686.

Fig. 7. A modern reed house from the Middle East.

Fig. 8. The first toothbrush? This is reproduced from a Chinese manuscript which dates its invention to 25 June 1498.

Fig. 9. A rubber-bulbed enema syringe from the Omagua Indians of Guiana and the Upper Amazon Basin.

Fig. 10. One of the Parthian batteries as reconstructed from remnants found near Baghdad, Iraq.

in detail.[46] The accompanying illustration, Fig. 9, is taken from his work, and shows how little we have been able to improve upon it. Even the decorative scheme is in excellent taste, and its mode of manufacture was copied exactly when Indo-Europeans first began to exploit the native development of rubber latex.

The same author also mentions the invention of tweezers for medical purposes, for which he gives the credit to the Araucanians, another Peruvian tribe. The Jivaro Indians use the pincers of living ants for the purpose of suturing wounds, a most extraordinary procedure that has been observed in other parts of the world also.[47] The skin is drawn together, the small ant is so applied that it seizes the suture and holds it tightly closed in its strong mandible, and then the animal's body is quickly snipped off. So a series of fine pincers along the wound hold the skin lesions together till healing takes place. Erwin Ackerknecht, in writing of this technique, concludes that it is a witness to "the great inventive power that the 'savage' develops in all those fields that he deems worthy of interest."[48]

We have mentioned rubber enema bulbs. According to Nordenskiold, these appear to have been a secondary development arising out of the making of hollow rubber balls for games.[49] Such balls were made by forming a core of clay or some such material and then dipping this repeatedly in a solution of latex allowing each coating to dry before applying the next one. When the skin was thick enough, a small round hole was cut through the rubber to the clay core, and the latter was removed through the hole, a small amount at a time. The hole was then plugged with another wad of latex, in a semi-hard condition, and the ball redipped once more in latex thus sealing the air inside the ball. Solid balls were also made, which weighed as much as 25 pounds. These were used in the well-known games played by the Maya in such open courts as have been found at Chichen Itza, Mexico, and elsewhere.

---

[46] Nordenskiold, E., "The American Indian as an Inventor," *Jour. of Roy. Anthropol. Instit.,* 59 (1929): 273ff.

[47] Ants used for saturing: see a review of Lewis Cotlow's *Amazon Head Hunters* by E. A. Underwood, in *Nature,* Feb. 19, 1955, p. 318.

[48] Ackerknecht, Erwin, *Ciba Symposia,* 10 (July-Aug., 1948): 924, in a note under the title, "An Ingenious Device for Stitching Wounds." The same author has a paper entitled, "Primitive Surgery," *Am. Anthropologist,* New Series 49, Jan.-Mar., 1947, in which he gives a bibliography on the subject containing 204 references.

[49] Rubber enemas: this is the opinion of E. Nordenskiold, in his paper, "The American Indian as an Inventor," p. 298, referred to above.

An article in a rubber journal recently pointed out that these balls are only one example of the use made by the American Indian of this material.[50] He also made watertight shoes, flasks, ponchos, and dolls. The same article states that "the development and use of natural rubber by the American Indian is impressive, for in 300 years his 'civilized' conquerors made little improvement in the ancient method of rubber manufacture." The natives used a certain sap of a vine (Iponoea bona-nox) or from a liana (Catonyction speciosum) to coagulate the latex. Certain trees have the latex in the form of rubber in suspension in water. The water can be evaporated and the rubber remains, without any need for a catalyst.

The story of Charles Goodyear's effort to take over the development of rubber from the natives of Brazil and exploit it in America and elsewhere, is well known. The problem was to treat it so that it would retain its structure even in hot weather. Their own rubber served the Indians well enough, especially since they had the secret of curing it by using local products as catalysts. Goodyear, again and again, brought himself, his family, and his backers to the point of ruin and bankruptcy because he could not cure the stuff out of which he was trying to make raincoats, mail bags, and overshoes.

As soon as warm weather came, his products turned into a sticky, useless mess. Of course, he finally discovered how to cure by vulcanizing, using sulfur as a catalyst.[51] But it seems probable that many of his heartbreaks never would have occurred if he had gone back to the originators of rubber articles and asked them to teach him what they knew first. Moreover, it is very doubtful if Goodyear or anyone else of his cultural background would have seen in the Brazilian forest what the natives had seen, i.e., a natural product requiring only mixing it with another natural product to supply a remarkably versatile and useful material.

In Textiles, Indo-Europeans have been borrowers in almost every detail. G. P. Murdock has said that the Central American Indian excelled here also.[52]

> In skill and technique in the textile arts the ancient Peruvians have had no equals in human history. They wove plain webs, double faced cloths, gauze and voile, knitted and crocheted

---

[50] Article in *Rubber Age*, Nov. 1956, p. 365.

[51] Charles Goodyear: see on this, H. Stafford Hatfield, *The Inventor and His World*, Penguin Books, Harmondsworth, Eng., 1948, pp. 41-44.

[52] Murdock, G. P., op. cit., pp. 428, 429.

fabrics, feather work, tapestries, fine cloths interwoven with gold and silver threads, employing in short, every technique save twilling known to the Old World, in addition to some peculiar to themselves. . . .

They employed methods identical with those used in the famous Gobelin and Beauvais tapestries; they nevertheless in harmony of colours, fastness of dyes, and perfection of technique, far surpassed the finest products of Europe.

C. Langdon White has said that the best of their fabrics were made from the wool of the vicuna, softest of all animal fibers, with 270 threads to the inch as compared with 140 threads, otherwise considered to be outstanding.[53] M. D. C. Crawford,[54] writing in 1948 before certain recent developments, underscores this achievement of the Indians. He made a particular study of this aspect of their art and skill, and concludes:

As a matter of fact, Europe had never produced a single original natural textile fibre or any dye except perhaps woad. She has not contributed a single fundamental or original idea to the basic mechanics of textiles, nor a single original and fundamental process of finishing, dyeing, or printing. . . .

In the broader world history of textiles and cloth, the ingenious English inventions of the 18th century (led by Kay's fly-shuttle) are but incidental, mechanical modifications and developments of older ideas which grew out of the social conditions in England, and were directly due to the importation of cotton and silk fabrics from the Far East during the 16th and 17th centuries. No new basic principles either in spinning, weaving, or fabric construction, nor new methods of decoration, dyes, colors, or designs, are involved in the English machines. The ancient principles of twisting and elongating masses of fiber into yarn, the principle of interlacing one set of filaments held in place between parallel bars of a second set of filaments, remains undisturbed. No new raw materials are involved: flax, hemp, wool, cotton, and silk, remain the principle fibres. And for colour the dyes of antiquity were still employed. As a matter of fact, all the dye raw materials of antiquity, both from Asia and America, were still mentioned in English dyer's manuals in the late part of the 19th century, and years after Perkin's experiment with coal tar derivatives in 1856.

Silk, of course, came to us from China, felt from Mongolia,[55] materials made from pulps were developed in Polynesia (tapa

---

[53] White, C. Langdon, "Storm Clouds Over the Andes," *The Sci. Monthly,* May, 1950, p. 308.

[54] Crawford, M. D. C., op. cit., pp. 184, 185.

[55] Felt: see M. C. and Fay Cole, *The Story of Man,* Cuneo Press, Chicago, 1940, p. 374.

cloth, etc.). These last are coming into their own in our day, the capacity for greater production being about our only claim for credit. And even here, the claim may be somewhat premature, because considerable difficulty has been experienced thus far in the manufacture of such materials on a large scale. The native products are hand-made, of course. Moreover, their methods of decoration, by tie-dyeing, batique, and silk-screen, are simply not applicable to mass production methods at present. We do not have time for tie-dyeing.

Furthermore, as we shall see when we come to consider the textile "industries" of ancient Sumeria, virtually the whole concept of mechanization, of large mills and hundreds of specialized workers each doing a single kind of operation, was well developed at least five thousand years ago in the Middle East. Meanwhile, the Egyptians succeeded in weaving such fine fabrics that they are still equal to our own best products woven by the very latest mechanical means. Some of the garments associated with King Tutankhamen's tomb have 220 threads to the inch, compared with our common handkerchiefs of today which show only about 60 to 70 threads per inch, or far less than the Egyptian prototype.

Native pottery has always been a source of amazement, whether in the New World or the Old. Chinese pottery has long been prized for its beauty of form, color, and texture. Central American pottery is remarkable for its complete freedom of form, and for its ingenuity. In an environment where evaporation rates are high, it is desirable to cut down the size of the opening at the top. But this makes pouring more difficult. The air rushing in suddenly causes the water to flow out unevenly and to spill. But in many places water is too precious to be wasted in this way. The Peruvians and the Maya overcame this by putting two spouts on the pot so that one became both a handle and a separate air inlet. The variations of this theme were both ingenious and aesthetically pleasing. Not content with this, they even went further and so designed the passages that when water was poured out, the air rushing in caused a whistle to blow. In some cases it is difficult to see why this was done (unless it was to warn the adults when children were robbing them of a rather precious commodity). Other types seem clearly to have been whistling kettles, a further effort to conserve waste by warning the lady of the house that the precious water was boiling away.[56] Many vessels are shaped as heads, faces, animals,

---

[56] Whistling Kettles: on this see, T. Athol Joyce, "Marvels of the Pot-

and even whole people, so lifelike in many cases that they must surely have been actual portraits. Their artistry and skill seem to have known no limits.

The same is true of Middle East pottery. In Minoan Crete the wares are of such delicacy that it seems they must be copies of originals made in hammered metal. Even "rivets" are sometimes indicated. They reveal that the metal prototypes were sometimes formed by a process akin to deep drawings as we technically understand it now. Some of the pottery from the earliest levels at Tell Halaf and Susa is astonishing in its complete freedom of form and delicacy. We shall refer to this subsequently.

The fame of the Central American Indians in road building has been reported. Cement pavements and other types of surfaced roads, suspension bridges spanning up to 450 feet, anchored at each end by massive stone pillars and capable of carrying cattle and pack animals, were built in some of the most rugged country in the world. These bridges were often 6 to 8 feet wide. The ropes by which these slender structures were supported are known to have been up to 12 inches in diameter.[57] One of the most famous builders was the Inca Mayta Capac who is generally dated from A.D. 1195 to 1230.

Although these Indians used wheels on toys, for some reason they did not employ wheeled vehicles. At least there are no remains of them, pictures, or references in their traditions or literature. Yet they did use road-rollers, weighing up to 5 tons.[58] Moreover, they had extensive and regular postal systems along these highways, and an excellent quality of paper in use for writing letters and keeping records.

Archaeologists have discovered that the Maya were making true paper approximately 3000 years ago.[59] Before these artisans disappeared, the Aztecs had learned the secret. This same process was handed down from generation to generation and today is used by the Otomi Indians in Mexico. The inner bark of the fig tree is soaked in running water until the sap jells and can be

ter's Art in South America," in *Wonders of the Past,* Vol. 2 ed. by Sir John Hammerton, London, Putnam's Sons, 1924, pp. 464, 465.

[57] Ropes: see Alexander Goldenweiser, *Anthropology,* Crofts, N.Y., 1937, p. 402. Also V. W. Von Hagen, *Realm of the Incas,* New American Library, N.Y., 1957, pp. 186, 187 for illustrations.

[58] Road Rollers: see Marshall H. Saville, "The Ancient Maya Causeways of Yucatan, *Antiquity,* Mar., 1935, p. 73.

[59] Paper in S. America: see Victor W. Von Hagen, "The First American Papermakers," *The Paper Industry and Paper World,* Dec., 1944, p. 1133.

scraped off. The fibrous residue is then boiled in lime, washed once more, and laid on a flat wooden surface like a breadboard, where it is pounded to a pulp. The pulp is left on the board and sun-dried. The ancient Aztecs went one step beyond the 20th century Otomis. Their process was identical up to this point, but after the paper was dry they sized it, and calendered it with hot stones to produce surfaces readily adaptable for printing. They then printed on it with a crude kind of movable type!

Although many of these original developments have long since been lost sight of, there still remains sufficient on record to suggest that in Central America a place of remarkable technical excellence, where natural resources were being widely exploited, mathematics had been developed (including the use of zero and a place system for numbers), and an extensive literature (among the Maya, at least) was published to satisfy the demands of a cultured leisure class.

Gilbert Lewis has written:[60]

> Probably the most remarkable achievements of the American Indians were in the fields of arithmetic, astronomy, and the Calendar. Two of the greatest inventions of arithmetic, the zero and the sign of numerical position, were regularly employed in America long before they were known to have occurred elsewhere....
>
> It may be noted that a few apparently unrelated items which I have discovered in literature may, when put together, suggest the possible use of astronomical instruments in early America. Both in Mexico and Peru concave mirrors were found, articles that had not been seen in Europe at the time of the Conquest. In Peru, these concave mirrors were employed in a solar rite. Periodically all old fire was extinguished and a new fire was started by the priests who, with these mirrors focussed the rays of the setting sun on a wisp of cotton. Among the Aztecs new fire was produced at night by the fire drill. However, that they had recollections of a practice akin to the Peruvian is suggested by the name of one of their chief gods, "Smoking Mirror."

Writing of Peruvian surgery, J. Alden Mason, quoting the well-known paleopathologist R. L. Moodie, has said:[61]

> I believe it to be correct to state that no primitive or ancient race of people anywhere in the world had developed such a field of surgical knowledge as had the pre-Columbian Peruvians.

---

[60] Lewis, Gilbert, "The Beginnings of Civilization in America," *Am. Anthropologist,* New Series 49, Jan.-Mar., 1947, p. 8 and footnote.

[61] Mason, J. Alden, *The Ancient Civilizations of Peru,* Penguin, Harmondsworth, 1957, pp. 222, 223.

Their surgical attempts are truly amazing and include amputations, excisions, trephining, bandaging, bone transplants (?), cauterizing, and other less evident procedures.

He then speaks of the use of anaesthetics and possibly hypnotics. He remarks that some skulls show the result of operations on the frontal sinus. Their "operating rooms" were first cleared and purified by the sprinkling and burning of maize cornflour, first black, and finally white.

Mason has thought that it is literally impossible to exaggerate the technical achievements of these Peruvian highlanders in the field of textiles. He holds that this is not the view merely of enthusiastic archaeologists, but of textile manufacturers themselves. Their skill he terms "incredible." They even had invisible mending in place of patching. The Aymara still do. In metallurgy they were not far behind.

Among their textiles, according to Mason, have been found "twining, plain cloth, repp, twill, gingham, warp-faced and weft-faced or bobbin pattern weave, brocade, tapestry, embroidery, tubular weave, pile knot, double cloth, gauze, lace, needle-knitting, painted and resist-dye decoration, and several other special processes peculiar to Peru and probably impossible to produce by mechanical means." It is even possible that they may have watered some crops with colored liquids to produce naturally dyed fibers that were indeed sun-worthy.

Nor is this inventiveness limited to Central America, although for climatic reasons this may have been the best environment to encourage high civilizations. The Iroquois had invented "rifled" arrow-heads long before they found themselves face to face with or in possession of rifled fire arms.[62] It does not seem likely that the spiraling is sufficient to rotate the arrow rapidly enough that the need for feathers was eliminated. This, at least, has not proved to be the case with my own sample. Evidently such was not the objective. What is clearly achieved is a far more serious wound. Like the outlawed dumdum bullets of World War I, the form of the head is such that the arrow does not pass

[62] Rifled Arrowheads: I have one of these in my possession. There are several references to them in the literature and some examples in Museums in Canada and the United States. There may have been a family, a kind of Iroquois Krupps, which supplied friend and foe alike, at a price! E. B. Tylor refers to them, *Anthropology*, Hill, N.Y., 1904, p. 155. Also, Sir William Dawson, *Fossil Men and Their Modern Representatives,* Hodder and Stoughton, London, 1883, p. 124. There seems to be no doubt about their intentional design.

right through (where it could easily be withdrawn) but buries itself in the flesh and stops there. The energy of the arrow is absorbed as the head corkscrews into the body.

The Aymara of Peru today build sailing boats and use them on lakes two and a half miles above sea level. Yet there is scarcely a tree to be found at this elevation. These vessels are made entirely of local bulrushes, and even the sails are mats woven from the same materials. The masts are built up of small pieces of wood spliced together. Provided these vessels are permitted to dry out every little while, they will carry a considerable load.[63]

The pre-Inca Indians were master architects, building great monuments and immense fortifications of stones set into each other by being laid and lapped together right on the spot. How they were erected is still a mystery, for many of the stones are huge. But this certainly is the only genuinely earthquake-proof architecture in Middle America.

One of the most surprising things about the great Ball Court of Chichen Itza is its acoustical properties. Recently the editor of an American magazine visited this court and reported on its unexpected characteristics. He wrote:[64]

> We climbed to the vantage point of one of the stands for the thrones of the priests at the southern end, while our guide went to the other. We were five hundred feet apart. We talked in low tones, no louder than a couple would use sitting in the living room of an average home. We could hear each other perfectly. We reduced our voices to a mere murmur: we could still hear each other perfectly....
>
> The General Electric Company, we were told, brought a large group of engineers to Chichen Itza to carry on acoustical experiments in the big ball court. They attempted to duplicate the court elsewhere but did not get the same acoustical effect because they had not built of limestone.

The tools of the pre-Columbian builders were no less remarkable than their buildings. It is believed now that they may have used glass cutting edges for saws, etc., in place of steel, the glass being a natural volcanic residue. Recent experiments demonstrate that such tools can be most effective. The idea is suggested by the form of certain fighting weapons.[65]

---

[63]Aymara boats: see Stewart E. McMillin, "The Heart of Aymara Land," *Nat. Geog. Magazine,* Feb. 1927, pp. 213-256.

[64] Barnhouse, Donald G., "The Editor Visits Mexico's Mayan Ruins," *Eternity Magazine,* May, 1956, p. 35.

[65]Glass saws: under the title, "Glass-toothed Saw Cuts Wood: and In-

They had even developed a specialized form of dental repair, using a kind of Portland Cement filling which has remained firm and intact in tooth cavities for 1500 years. Of this discovery Sigvad Linné remarks:[66]

> The findings of archaeologists have revealed to us some of the inventiveness and technical skill possessed by the Indians. The practical aids of these unknown technicians may have been primitive yet it could scarcely have been "primitive peoples of nature" that with such simple means achieved results before which their later-born Swedish colleagues sometimes stand in dumb amazement.

One might mention that a recent report from Washington states that there is now evidence of the habitual use of some kind of cleaning agents on the teeth of prehistoric skulls.[67] Since the Chinese had by at least A.D. 1500 developed a toothbrush that looks remarkably like its modern counterpart, there is surely nothing new under the sun.[68] For a picture of this toothbrush see Fig. 8.

Nordenskiold adds to the credit of the American Indians the invention of the hammock (New Guinea),[69] children's go-carts (Northwestern Brazil),[70] cigar holders,[71] the chain,[72] and an ingenious self-acting water-pump (Colombia), which the Spaniards adopted and converted into a bilge pump.[72] We might create a tiresome catalogue if we were to go on listing isolated instances of native ingenuity such as the use of the skin of the ray-fish by the Polynesians as a "sand-paper";[74] the use of giant

---

genious Hand-made Tool May Provide a Solution for an Ancient Scientific Puzzle," *Science News Letter*, July 13, 1957.

[66] Tooth filling: see Sigvad Linne, "Technical Secrets of American Indians," *Jour. of Roy. Anthrop. Instit.*, 87 (July-Dec., 1957): 152, 153, and 163.

[67] Toothpaste: *Sci. News Letter*, Dec. 23, 1956, in a series of brief notes written anonymously under the heading, "Anthropology-Archaeology."

[68] Toothbrush: see Curt Proskauer, "Oral Hygiene in the Medieval Occident," *Ciba Symposia*, 8 (Nov., 1946): 468. The illustration is from a woodcut in the Lei Shu Ts'ai Hiu, a Chinese Encyclopedia.

[69] Nordenskiold, E., "The American Indian as an Inventor," p. 281.

[70] Ibid., p. 302, from Northwestern Brazil.

[71] Ibid.

[72] Ibid., used by a small tribe, the Hurari, in Matto Grasso, and found nowhere else in South America.

[73] Ibid., p. 300.

[74] Sand paper: see Leonard Adam, *Primitive Art*, Penguin, Harmondsworth, 1949, p. 162.

fireflies,[75] called Cucuyo, tied to the feet by the natives in the West Indies to light their way along the jungle paths at night, and so forth.

So much importance is attached to inventors and their inventions that they were held in great veneration and quite often ultimately deified. The only encyclopedias that the Chinese had originally dealt with the heroic figures who were famous because they invented something.[76] Indeed in some cultures this kind of talent is so generally expected of the males that the would-be son-in-law must win his bride by performing some almost impossible task set by the family calling for nothing short of inventive genius.[77]

It may well be asked then, Why did these people never progress beyond a certain level of civilization which we tend to think of as essentially "primitive"? Why did they stop where they did? Were the causes circumstantial ones, or did they arise because of wars, forced migrations, and so forth? In other words, do we have any grounds for suspecting the limitations to have been inherent in something which may perhaps be termed a "Hamitic trait," or was it simply that they had no leisure, no security, little accumulated wealth, and very limited natural resources?

Such limitations can scarcely be applied to the higher cultures of China, India, Sumeria, Egypt, Crete, or Anatolia, yet these also halted apparently on the very threshold of a scientific revolution, achieving an extraordinarily high degree of technical skill and "know-how" which nevertheless seemed also to lead into a blind alley. Stagnation was followed by decay; and decay led to eclipse. Climate was right, records were extensive, natural

[75] Fireflies: see Donald C. Peattie, "The Miracle of the Firefly," *The Reader's Digest*, Oct., 1949, p. 102.

[76] Needham, J., *Science and Civilization in China*, Vol. 1, Cambridge, 1954, p. 54.

[77] Prof. T. F. McIlwraith, Head of the Dept. of Anthrop. in the Univ. of Toronto, gave a lecture on the various means adopted by different people to test aspiring husbands. The Arawak of Central Africa adopt this method, as do other widely scattered tribes. An early chapter of Genesis (Gen. 4:17-21) gives prominence to the first city-builder, the first agriculturalist, the first tent-dweller, the first musician, and the first metal worker. The latter is referred to as Tubal-Cain, which some authorities feel may be the original form of the word Vulcan, who was (like many Chinese inventors) subsequently deified.

resources abundant enough, had they cared to exploit them. For some reason, they stopped short.

It is, of course, very possible that our own age of far greater technical knowledge will in time pass away and be forgotten, as theirs. But I do not believe that such will happen this time for reasons which are considered in Part V. But let us here examine some of the achievements of these "higher" cultures.

There is little doubt that the basic cultures in Sumeria (and later on, in Babylonia and Assyria), in Egypt, and in the Indus Valley, were all non-Indo-European. The root elements of Mesopotamian civilization in later times when the Babylonians and Assyrians (both Semitic in origin) had achieved ascendancy, were still essentially Sumerian. It is pretty well agreed that these Sumerians were not Semites, being clean shaven and comparatively hairless like the Egyptians. And from their language it is quite clear that they were not Indo-European. Their civilization developed very rapidly and achieved a remarkable level of technical competence. In the earliest stages of their history, they seem to have shared many features with the Indus Valley people who were later overwhelmed by the Aryans,[78] and also with the first settlers in Northern Syria, and even with the earliest Egyptians. As further development took place in each of these areas, cultural similarities became obscured. All these cultures seem to spring into being already remarkably well organized, with skills in weaving and pottery making, in the erection of defensive structures and temple buildings, and with some use of metals from the very first. It is assumed that the Sumerians were organized into city-states before the Egyptians were, although it was once held that the oldest center of civilization was along the Valley of the Nile. Although there is, as yet, no evidence of the Sumerians without basic elements of civilization, it is believed that they came from the North and East, and it is expected that the origins of these people (and of the Egyptians and Indus Valley people also) will in due time be discovered in the general direction of Jarmo, Sialk, etc. What is now fairly clearly established is that civilization, the arts and trades, and organized city life, with the division of labor, social stratification, a leisure class, written records, and so forth, began, in so far as the Middle East is concerned, with these Sumerians.

The Sumerians knew what percentages of metals to use to

---

[78] Childe, Vere Gordon, "India and the West Before Darius," *Antiquity*, Mar., 1939, p. 15.

achieve the best alloys, casting a bronze with 9 to 10% of tin exactly as we find best today; their pottery was often paper-thin, tastefully shaped and decorated, and with a ring like true china evidently having been fired in controlled-atmosphere ovens at quite high temperatures. Their methods of production led very early to a measure of automation including powered agricultural equipment that was in the strictest sense "mechanical"; the control of quality production was early established by systems of inspection; their factories were highly organized, and price and wage controls were established by law. They developed loan and banking companies with outlandish interest rates, yet still legally controlled; their record keeping and postal systems were evidently efficient, mail even being carried in envelopes.

In addition, the upper classes lived quite sumptuously, well supplied in many cases with home comforts and "modern conveniences" — including running water in some instances, tiled baths, proper disposal of sewage, extensive medical care, etc. Even libraries existed and well-organized schools. By comparison, their descendants did not sustain their inheritance, but came to live in that filthy squalor, precarious poverty, and constant threat of disease, which misled earlier generations of Europeans to suppose mistakenly that they themselves were the creators of this superior civilization.

The greatness of Egypt was more monumental: Sumerians did not build with stone, for they did not have it in sufficient quantity, but they left another kind of monument — imperishable written records. Once these began to be deciphered, something of their achievements became apparent. It is by such means that we know, for example, of their mathematics. Dr. T. J. Meek has told us:[79]

> Like the Egyptians the early Sumerians used the additive method to multiply and divide, but before 2000 B.C., they had evolved multiplication tables and tables of reciprocals and of squares and cubes, and other powers, and of square and cube roots and the like. They had attained a complete mastery of fractional quantities and had developed a very exact terminology in mathematics. The correct value of Pi, and the correct geometrical formula for calculating the area of rectangles were known before 3000 B.C., and in the years that followed came the knowledge of how to find the area of triangles and circles, and irregular quadrangles, polygons, and truncated pyramids;

---

[79] Meek, T. J., "Magic Spades in Mesopotamia," *Univ. of Toronto Quarterly,* Vol. 7, 1938, pp. 243, 244.

also cones and the like. By 2000 B.C., the theorem attributed to Pythagoras was familiar and they could solve problems involving equations with two, three, and four unknowns.

According to one of the best authorities in this area, they even had developed an equivalent to our logarithm tables.[80] George Sarton,[81] writing some 20 years later than Meek, could add to this accomplishment, their knowledge that the angle in a semi-circle is a right-angle, that they could measure the volume of a rectangular paralleliped, of a circular cylinder, of the frustrum of a cone, and of a square pyramid. He has summed up this achievement thus:

> The Sumerians and their Babylonian successors left three legacies, the importance of which cannot be exaggerated:
> (1) The position concept in numeration. This was imperfect because of the absence of zero; (2) the extension of the numerical scale to submultiples of the unit as well as to the multiples. This was lost and was not revived until A.D. 1585, with reference to decimal numbers; and, (3) the use of the same base for numbers and metrology. This too was lost, and not revived till the foundations of the metric system in 1795.

Later, he wrote of what we borrowed indirectly from this source:

> Many other traces can be detected in other cultures, even that of our own today — sexagesimal fractions, sexagesimal divisions of the hours, degrees, and minutes, division of the whole day into equal hours, metrical system, position concept in writing of numbers, astronomic tables. We owe to them the beginnings of algebra, of cartography, and of chemistry.

Perhaps the greatest surprise of all is to find that the Greeks did not do so very well in transmitting this heritage usefully. Thus Sarton concluded:

> The Greeks inherited the sexagesimal system from the Sumerians but mixed it up with the decimal system, using the former only for submultiples of the unit, and the latter for multiples, and thus they spoiled both systems and started a disgraceful confusion of which we are still the victims. They abandoned the principle of position, which had to be reintroduced from India a thousand years later. In short, their understanding of Babylonian arithmetic must have been very poor, since they managed to keep the worst features of it, and to overlook the best. . . .

---

[80] Neugebauer, O., and A. Sachs, *Mathematical Cuneiform Texts,* American Oriental Society, Yale Univ. Press, 1946, p. 35.

[81] Sarton, George, *A History of Science,* Harvard, 1952, pp. 73, 74, 99, 118.

The Greeks used their intelligence in a different way and did not see simple [i.e., practical] things that were as clear as day to their distant Sumerian and Babylonian predecessors.

It might be thought that if the Sumerians were really practical people they would have adopted a decimal system from the first, and quickly abandoned the sexagesimal system. But there is much to be said for the use of 12 instead of 10 as a base number. Ten has only two factors, 2 and 5. But 12 has 2, 3, 4 and 6, or twice as many: and in the higher multiples such as 60, the number of factors is, of course, greater than the corresponding 20 of the decimal system. Learning to think in terms of such a system would be difficult for us now that we are so accustomed to the decimal system, but there are some highly competent mathematicians who hold that the change could be made and would be advantageous. This is a matter of opinion, of course, but since we have 10 fingers the choice of 10 as a base seems more natural. And one must suppose therefore that these practical people saw a real advantage in using 12 instead. Yet it was purely a practical matter, and not a theoretical one.

The Greeks were more interested in theory than practice. The contrast between the Sumerian and the Greek attitude is seen in their treatment of problems of Astronomy. In this connection, O. Neugebauer has said:[82]

> A careful analysis of the assumptions, which must be made in order to compute our texts, shows nowhere the need for specific mechanical concepts such as are familiar to us from the Greek theory of eccentrics or epicycles, or from the corresponding planetary models of Tycho Brahe or Kepler.... At no point can we detect the introduction of an hypothesis of a general character.

Samuel Kramer makes frequent reference to the fact that the Sumerians were an entirely practical people, with no urge to search for truth for its own sake, among whom there was not the slightest tendency either to theorize or generalize, who sought for no underlying principles, and undertook no experiments for verification.[83]

Sarton gives some illustrations to show how their mathematics arose out of a practical need, i.e., business records and

---

[82] Neugebauer, O., "Ancient Mathematics and Astronomy" in *A History of Technology,* Vol. 1, ed. by C. Singer et al., Oxford, 1954, p. 799.

[83] Kramer, Samuel N., *From the Tablets of Sumer,* Falcon's Wing Press, Indian Hills, 1956, pp. xviii, 6, 32, 58 and 59.

transactions. In the same way geometry reached the Greeks, after being developed to satisfy entirely practical needs by the Egyptians. This is why Thales termed it Geometry, for it was required originally to measure the land in order to reestablish property boundaries obscured each year by the flooding Nile.[84]

Among the Sumerians and Babylonians, banking houses sprang up and became the forerunners of world economics as represented by our international banking institutions. Two such banks were known from cuneiform records by the names of Engibi and Sons, established about 1000 B.C., and lasting some 500 years, and Murasha Sons, founded about 1464 B.C., and dissolved finally in 405 B.C. The latter established a system of mortgaging.[85]

Glass was known to the Sumerians by 2700 B.C., and both they and the Egyptians were experts in the working of it.[86] For drilling such substances they used diamond drills, or some soft material coated with emery or corundum.[87]

A tablet found a few years ago is inscribed by a certain Dr. Lugal-Edina, dated about 2300 B.C., and in it we are told how surgeons of the day had already learned to set broken bones, make minor and major incisions, and even attempt operations on the eyes. Sicknesses are given names, and symptoms carefully noted. Waldo H. Dubberstein of the Oriental Institute of the University of Chicago, in reporting on this, has written:[88]

> One hundred years of exploration and research in the field of ancient Near Eastern history have yielded such astounding results that today it is unwise to speculate on the further capacities and resources of these early people along any line of human endeavor.

Medicine was a carefully regulated profession with legally established fees for various operations and very stiff penalties for failure or carelessness, evidently intended to protect the customer

---

[84] Jourdain, Philip E. B., "The Nature of Mathematics," in *The World of Mathematics,* Vol. 1, ed. by James R. Newman, Simon and Schuster, N.Y., 1965, pp. 10-13.

[85] Reavely, S. D., "The Story of Accounting," *Office Management,* Apr., 1938, pp. 8f.

[86] Wiseman, P. J., *New Discoveries in Babylonia about Genesis,* Marshall Morgan and Scott, London, 2nd ed., rev., n.d., p. 30.

[87] Boscawen, St. Chad, in discussing a paper by Sir William Dawson, "On Useful and Ornamental Stones of Ancient Egypt," in the *Trans. Vict. Instit.,* 26 (London, 1892): 284.

[88] Dubberstein, Waldo H., "Babylonians Merit Honour as Original Fathers of Science," *Sci. News Letter,* Sept. 4, 1937, pp. 148, 149.

and prevent charlatanism. This certainly suggests that the profession was not simply a "School of Magicians."

Although their buildings have largely disappeared, they were noteworthy examples of the use of local materials, mud-dried brick and reeds. The former are easily visualized as promising materials; the latter are not. But as a matter of fact, "reed huts" (mentioned in some of the very earliest tablets) are capable of a surprising beauty and spaciousness. There is every reason to believe that the design has not greatly changed through the centuries that intervened. Floor plans as revealed by excavation seem to indicate similar structures. See Fig. 7.

By the time the Sumerians arrived in Mesopotamia, they had domesticated as many animals as were ever domesticated in that area, with the exception of the horse which was tamed by the Hittites — although they did have a draft animal, a mountain ass. And the same may be said of grains. N. I. Vavilov always considered that the Highland Zone to the north and east whence they had come, was for this reason the most likely home, with few exceptions, of all such domesticated plants and animal species as are commonly in use today. He called it the "Source of Species."[89]

Written records appear at the very earliest levels, and even at Sialk there seems to have been no period when they were without the use of metals.[90] The same story is found to be true of Egypt. Here again there is no true "beginning." The Egyptians, like the Sumerians and the founders of Tell Halaf in Northern Syria, appear to have been culturally creative from the very beginning, and to have developed their technology exceedingly rapidly. Pastoral societies are slower to develop, and the Semites, who were largely pastoral, contributed little and borrowed much. Indo-Europeans, meanwhile, did not even have a word of their own for "city"; the organization of urban community life with all that this entails in terms of civilization did not originate with them. It has been shown that all of their words for city, town, etc., are loan-words.[91]

Samuel N. Kramer has recently published a volume resulting from a lifetime of cuneiform studies which he titles, *From the*

---

[89] Vavilov, N. I., "Asia the Source of Species," *Asia*, Feb. 1937, p. 113.

[90] Childe, V. G., *What Happened in History*, Penguin, Harmondsworth, 1942, p. 64.

[91] Eisler, Robert, "Loan Words in Semitic Languages Meaning 'Town'," *Antiquity*, Dec., 1939, pp. 449ff.

Tablets of Sumer, and his subtitle takes the following form: "Twenty-five Firsts of Man's Recorded History."[92] It is an impressive collection of "firsts." One will feel at times that he has introduced a few cases which are only rightly termed so, by a kind of special pleading. However, on the whole his collection shows that their inventiveness was by no means limited to mechanical things, but applies equally well to forms of literature. and indeed to the very idea of collecting libraries, writing histories, and cataloguing books for reference.

The speed with which Egyptian civilization developed was equally astonishing. P. J. Wiseman, who has spent a lifetime in the area studying its past history closely in touch with the work of archaeologists, has said in this regard:[93]

> No more surprising fact has been discovered by recent excavation than the suddenness with which civilization appeared.... Instead of the infinitely slow development anticipated, it has become obvious that art, and we may say "science" suddenly burst upon the world.
>
> For instance, H. G. Wells acknowledges that the oldest stone building known is the Sakkara Pyramid. Yet as Dr. Breasted points out, "From the Pyramid at Sakkara to the construction of the Great Pyramid less than a century and a half elapsed."
>
> Writing of the latter, Sir Flinders Petrie stated that, "The accuracy of construction is evidence of high purpose and great capability and training. In the earliest pyramid, the precision of the whole mass is such that the error would be exceeded by that of a metal measure on a mild or a cold day; the error of levelling is less than can be seen with the naked eye."

The same famous Egyptologist stated that the stone work of the Great Pyramid is equal to optician's work of the present day.[94] The joints of the masonry are so fine as to be scarcely visible where they are not weathered, and it is difficult to insert even a knife edge between them.

Vere Gordon Childe, speaking of their earliest earthenware, has remarked:[95]

> The pottery vessels, especially those designed for funerary use exhibit a perfection of technique never excelled in the Nile

[92] Kramer, Samuel N., *From the Tablets of Sumer,* Falcon's Wing Press, Indians Hills, 1956.

[93] Wiseman, J. P., op. cit., pp. 28, 31 and 33.

[94] Petrie, Sir Flinders, *The Wisdom of the Egyptians,* British School of Archaeology, Publ. No. 63, 1940, p. 89.

[95] Childe, V. G., *New Light,* p. 67.

Fig. 11. Plumbing at the palace in Knossos, Crete, dated Middle Minoan I, about 2000 B.C. (A) The sections made of baked clay had handles for convenience of installation. (B) Packing was used for smooth joints, ensuring free flow and little turbulence. (C) Serrated couplings retained filler material securely.

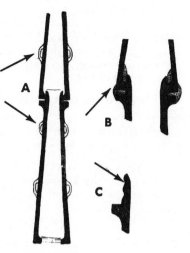

Fig. 12. A native loom whose design is common to many parts of the world. It is used only for those materials available in the locality.

Finished Cloth

Foot Pedals

Fig. 13. Chinese rocket launchers, with a capacity of forty to one hundred rocket arrows, may have been used as early as A.D. 1232. These rockets are said to have had a range of four hundred feet.

Valley. The finer ware is extremely thin, and is decorated all over by burnishing before firing, perhaps with a blunt toothed comb, to produce an exquisite rippled effect that must be seen to be appreciated.

J. Eliot Howard has stated that the hieroglyphics of the earliest periods indicate that pottery, metallurgy, rope making, and other arts and techniques were already well developed,[96] and W. J. Perry — quoting de Morgan — has written:[97]

> What appears at a very early date in Egypt is perfection of technique. The Egyptian appears from the time of the earliest Pharaohs as a patient, careful workman, his mind like his hand possessing an incomparable precision...a mastery that has never been surpassed in any country.

A carved (or ground?) diorite head from Egypt was sold in London some years ago for the sum of $50,000, and it was considered by the experts at the time "never to have been surpassed in the entire history of sculpture."[98]

It is hard to decide which of these two civilizations produced the most remarkable metal wares. The jewelled weapons of their noble dead are simply beautiful. There are no essential metallurgical techniques which they had not mastered very early in their history. These include filigree, mold and hollow casting, intaglio, wire-drawing, beading, granulation (in water?), welding, inlaying of one metal with another, sheeting hammered so thin as to be almost translucent, repoussee, gilding on wood and other materials, possibly spinning of metal — and later, even electroplating using a form of galvanic cell catalyzed with fruit juices and housed in a small earthenware jar.[99] One of these is illustrated in Fig. 10 on page 177.

Sir Arthur Evan's researches in Crete have revealed the same pattern of history.[100] The magnificent Palace of Minos with its system of hot and cold running water, its rooms often decorated

---

[96] Howard, J. Eliot, "Egypt and the Bible," *Trans. Vict. Instit.*, 10 (London, 1876): 345.

[97] Perry, W. J., *The Growth of Civilization*, Penguin, Harmondsworth, 1937, p. 54.

[98] Macoffin, Ralph N., "Archaeology Today," *The Mentor*, Apr., 1924, p. 6

[99] Reported in "Batteries B.C." *The Laboratory*, 25, No. 4, 1956 Fisher Scientific Co., Pittsburgh, quoting Willard F. M. Gray of the General Electric Co. Gray reconstructed these batteries on the basis of archaeological materials.

[100] Evans, Sir Arthur, *The Palace of Minos*, Macmillan, London, in 4 vols., plus Index Vol., beginning publ. in 1921.

with a kind of wall-paper effect done (as it is done today) with a sponge,[101] its extraordinary architecture, its beautiful pottery — in many cases patterned upon metal prototypes — its highly organized court life, and its evidence of extensive trade and commerce overseas — all these achievements demonstrate clearly that the craftsmen of the ancient Minoan Empire were in no whit behind the Egyptian and Sumerian in technical competence. Two sections of their water piping are illustrated in Fig. 11. Like the drainage and sewage systems of the Indus Valley cities of Mohenjo Daru and Changu Daru, they are equal in effectiveness to anything we can install today. The underground sewage disposal system with its perforated street drain above from Syria is likewise evidence of a highly organized city life that indicates the same kind of technical achievement and recognition of community responsibility. Indeed, according to T. J. Meek, the people of Tell Halaf in Syria were never without metals, and their finely fired pottery "no thicker than two playing cards" and beautifully designed, is equal to the best that the Sumerians produced.[102] It is closely paralleled by some of the earliest pottery found at Susa by de Morgan,[103] a city which was closely tied in with the Sumero-Egyptian-Indus Valley "Archaic Civilization," as W. J. Perry aptly called it.

Here, in these areas, lie the roots of all Western Civilization in its earlier stages of development. From these centers, sometimes directly, sometimes indirectly (as via the Etruscans), Europe derived the inspiration of its culture.

The indebtedness of the Greeks to the Minoans is now fully appreciated.[104] The Minoans had in turn derived much of their

[101] See *Bulletin of the Royal Ontario Museum of Archaeology*, No. 11, March, 1932, p. 7.

[102] Meek, T. J., "The Present State of Mesopotamian Studies," in the Haverford Symposium of Archaeology and the Bible, American Schools of Oriental Research, New Haven, 1938, p. 161.

[103] Spearing, H. G., "Susa, the Eternal City of the East," in *Wonders of the Past*, Vol. 3, ed. by Sir J. Hammerton, Putnam's, 1924, p. 582.

[104] Bibliography on Aegean pre-history:
Blegen, Carl W., *Zygouries: a Prehistoric Settlement in the Valley of Cleonae*, Harvard, 1928.
Bosanquet, R. C., *Excavations at Phylakopi in Melos*, Macmillan, 1904.
Dinsmoor, W. B., *The Architecture of Ancient Greece*, Batsford, 1950.
Evans, Sir Arthur, *The Palace of Minos*, Macmillan, 4 vols., 1921-1935.
Heurtley, W. A., *Prehistoric Macedonia*, Cambridge, 1939.
Holmberg, Erik J., *The Swedish Excavations at Asea in Arcadia*, Leipzig, 1944.

culture from the Egyptians. Some influences reached Greece directly from Asia Minor. Between these three sources can be divided almost everything in Greek culture that has a technical connotation: mathematics, architecture, metallurgy, medicine, games, and even the inspiration of much of their art — all was borrowed from such non-Indo-European sources. Even their script was borrowed. In fact, one might say their very literacy, for influential figures like Socrates, far from contributing anything to the art of writing, actually strongly opposed it as a threat to the powers of memory.

The same is true of Rome. The part played by the Etruscans in the foundation of Roman Civilization is immense. Sir Gavin de Beer, in a recent broadcast in England said:[105]

> It may seem remote to us (to ask who the Etruscans were), and yet it affects us closely for the following reason. We regard the Romans as our civilizers, and we look up to them as the inventors of all sorts of things they taught us. But it is now clear that, in their turn, the Romans learned many of these things from the Etruscans.

De Beer holds that whatever else might be said about these interesting people, their language at least was non-Indo-European, and they were not related either to the Romans or the Greeks. With this agrees M. Pallottino, an authority on the Etruscans.[106] George Rawlinson, the great Orientalist and classical scholar, says in this respect:[107]

> The Romans themselves notwithstanding their intense national vanity acknowledged this debt to some extent and admitted that they derived from the Etruscans their augury, their religious ritual, their robes and other insignia of office, their

Mylonas, George, *Prehistoric Macedonia,* Studies in honour of F. W. Shipley, Wash. Univ. Series, Lang. and Lit., No. 14, 1942, pp. 55f.

Pendlebury, J. D. S., *The Archaeology of Crete,* Methuen, London, 1939.

Seager, Richard B., *Explorations in the Island of Mochlos,* Amer. School of Class. Studies, at Athens, publ. in Boston, 1912.

Valmin, M. Natan, *The Swedish Messenia Expedition,* Oxford, 1938.

Wace, A. J. B., *Prehistoric Thessaly,* Cambridge, 1912.

Weinberg, Saul, "Neolithic Figurines and Aegean Interrelations," the *Am. Jour. of Archaeol.,* Apr., 1951, pp. 121ff.

Xanthoudides, Stephanos, *The Vaulted Tombs of Mesara,* Liverpool Univ. Press, and Hodder and Stoughton, London, 1924.

[105] De Beer, Sir Gavin, "Who Were the Etruscans," *The Listener,* BBC, London, Dec. 8, 1955, p. 989.

[106] Pallottino, M., *The Etruscans,* Penguin, Harmondsworth, 1955.

[107] Rawlinson, George, *The Origin of Nations,* Scribner, N.Y., 1878, p. 111.

games and shows, their earliest architecture, their calendar, their weights and measures, their land surveying systems, and various other elements of their civilization. But there is reason to believe that their acknowledgment fell short of their actual obligations and that Etruria was really the source of their whole early civilization.

To this list, D. Randall MacIver adds their martial organization — and even in all probability the very name of the city itself.[108]

Out of Africa has come to us far more than just the Egyptian contribution, even were this not a sufficient one. One does not think of Africa as particularly inventive. As a matter of fact, however, so many new things came from that great continent during Roman times that they had a proverb, *"Ex Africa semper aliquid,"* which freely translated means, "There is always something new coming out of Africa."[109] Among other things out of Africa came "Animal Tales" — the Fables — from Ethiopia. Edwin W. Smith and Andrew M. Dale have pointed out:[110]

> It might indeed be claimed that Africa was the home of animal tales. Was not the greatest "literary inventor" of all, an African, the famous Lokman, whom the Greeks not knowing his real name called Aethiops (i.e., Aesop)?

Even in medicine Africans have some remarkable achievements to their credit. To mention but two: the pygmies of the Ituri Forest had invented an enema quite independently of its South American Indian counterpart,[111] and it is known that Caesarean operations were successfully undertaken in childbirth emergencies before the White Man had succeeded in doing it.[112] Out of Ethiopia came also coffee.[113] And quite recently African art has been the "inspiration" (for good or ill) of new forms of art. Very recently a kind of rocking stool inspired by an ingenious African prototype came into popularity.

Their engineering skill is often revealed in very simple things. A sedan chair is so designed that the rider receives a

---

[108] MacIvor, D. Randall, "The Etruscans," *Antiquity,* 1 (June, 1927): 171.

[109] Editorial in *Endeavour,* April, 1945, p. 41.

[110] Smith, Edwin W., and Andrew M. Dale, *The Ila Speaking Peoples of Northern Rhodesia,* Vol. 2, Macmillan, London, 1920, p. 342.

[111] Coon, C. S., *A Reader in General Anthropology,* Holt, N.Y., 1948, p. 340.

[112] Ackerknecht, Erwin, "Primitive Surgery," *The Am. Anthropologist,* New Series 49 (Jan.-Mar., 1947): 32.

[113] Anonymous, "The Story of Coffee," *The Plibrico Firebox,* Plibrico Firebrick, Toronto, 22 (July-Aug., 1948): 4, 5.

Fig. 14. Sumerian drinking straws.

Fig. 15. The earliest known cast-iron stove, as shown in an advertisement by the Borg-Warner Corporation in the "Saturday Evening Post," 8 September 1951. Adapted from Ripley's "Believe It Or Not!" Reprint permission granted by © Ripley International, Inc.

Fig. 16. Cast probably in A.D. 953, this may well be the largest single cast-iron figure in the world. It stands in the yard of the Kai-Yuam Monastery in Ts'ang-chow, China, and is approximately twenty feet high.

minimum of jolts and rockings due to the unevenness of the ground. It is a kind of super-whiffle-tree sling that equalizes the load and guarantees smooth passage.

As a further witness to the same kind of genius for simplified construction an African loom is shown on page 195. It makes the most effective use of locally available raw materials, and in fact uses their actual form to the best advantage.

Almost every African community of any size has its own smelting furnace and smithy. No part of this iron working art has been borrowed from Europe. The whole process (and the refinements found in some cases) is a native invention. The bellows used to increase the oxygen supply and thereby the heat at the hearth, are of native design and manufacture, and are very varied in form. The pipes which convey the air into the furnace are also homemade. Suitable clay is plastered around pieces of wood of the proper size and shape (curved, straight, or even forked) and then the whole is burned in a fairly hot fire. This reduces the wooden insert to ashes and leaves the desired pipe form, shaped and baked, ready for use. When the ore has been reduced and the metal is removed from the dismantled furnaces, it is worked by hand. The metal may be hammered into sheets, drawn into wire, or forged into other forms, such as vessels and blades, as desired. It is not surprising that we, having largely learned from Africa the basic techniques of ironworking, should refer to our iron metalworkers as Blacksmiths. R. J. Forbes says that although today African smiths often obtain their raw materials from European sources, the Negro smiths "are very ingenious craftsmen in inventing and using new tools and types of bellows."[114]

Among the literary achievements of the Egyptians must be listed what was surely the first "moving-picture" sequence,[115] and the first Walt Disney Cartoon.[116] Gloves and camp-stools are found first in Crete,[117] soap in Egypt,[118] virtually all carpenter's

[114] Forbes, R. J., *Metallurgy in Antiquity,* Leiden, 1950, p. 64.

[115] "A Cinematograph Touch in Ancient Egyptian Art: Wall-paintings that Suggest Moving Pictures," reproduced from P. E. Newberry, *Beni Hasan,* in *The Illustrated London News,* Jan. 12, 1929, pp. 50, 51.

[116] Hambly, Wilfrid D., "A Walt Disney In Ancient Egypt," in a letter to the editor, *Sci. Monthly,* Oct., 1954, pp. 267, 268; Has illustrations of "animated animal figures" behaving like people!

[117] Gloves and campstools: see Axel Persson, *The Religion of Greece in Prehistoric Times,* Univ. of California, 1942, p. 77.

[118] Soap: see a paper on this by Rendel Harris, *Soap,* Sunset Papers, published privately in England, in 1931.

tools (saws, squares, bucksaws, brace and bit, etc.) from the Etruscans[119]— with a novel brace and bit[120] — and the "level" from Egypt.[121] The Etruscans invented lathes.[122] The Egyptians built a pipe-organ using water apparently to obtain a uniform air pressure.[123] Folding umbrellas and sunshades were first designed in China[124] and were not introduced into England till centuries later, where the introducer apparently almost lost his life. The Sumerians used straws for drinking[125] (Fig. 14) and bequeathed to their successors chariot wheels which were made of plywood using the same technique for the manufacture as we use today.[126] Africans were using vaccines long before the White Man adopted them.[127] And there is a record of the invention of a malleable glass, the secret of which was destroyed by the ruling monarch, along with the originator, for fear of upsetting the economy.[128] Every form of building technique now commonly used (including concrete) is found among non-Indo-Europeans, and in many cases long antedating the Romans, especially the arch, barrel vault, dome, and cantilever principle of construction. The barrel vault was achieved in Babylonia without the need of a supporting scaffold under it, by starting against an upright wall which was later removed. The cantilever principle was used by the Egyptians, among others, in strengthening their larger sea-going vessels, to prevent them from "breaking their backs," as marine engineers term it.

---

[119] Tools: see George M. A. Hanfmann, "Daidalos in Etruria," *Am. Jour. of Ach.*, Apr.-June, 1935, pp. 192ff.

[120] Brace and bit: an illustration of this is given in *The Illustrated London News*, April 12, 1930, p. 623, in a series of articles by G. H. Davis and S. R. K. Glanville entitled, "Life in Ancient Egypt: Astonishing Skill in Arts and Crafts."

[121] Levels: see George Sarton, *A History of Science*, Harvard, 1952, p. 124, n. 94.

[122] Lathes: see Charles Singer, et al., *A History of Technology*, Vol. 1, Oxford, 1954, pp. 192, 518.

[123] Apel, Willi, "Early History of the Organ," *Speculum*, 23 (1948): 191-216.

[124] A number of bronze castings used in the construction of these large umbrellas are to be seen in the Royal Ontario Museum, Toronto.

[125] Well known from the monuments and from seals. The line drawing in the illustration is probably from a seal (Fig. 14).

[126] Linton, Ralph, *The Tree of Culture*, Knopf, N.Y., 1956, p. 114.

[127] Vaccines: see Melville Herskovits, *Man and His Works*, Knopf, N.Y., 1950, p. 246.

[128] Malleable glass: the details of this are given by Stanko Miholic, "Art Chemistry," *Sci Monthly*, Dec., 1946, p. 460.

James Hornell, an authority on watercraft as developed by primitive and ancient people, opened a paper on the subject with these words:[129]

> There can be no doubt that to Asiatic ingenuity we owe the beginnings of the world's principle types of Water Transport. Early man in Asia invented means of extraordinary diversity to enable him to cross rivers, etc.

The vessels illustrated or referred to include every type of small craft from mere floats to coracles and large outrigger sailing vessels, etc. If we bear in mind that China gave us the stern-post rudder, the watertight compartment construction, as well as canal locks for inland waterways,[130] and that the Koreans built the first true battleship, with iron cladding — notwithstanding the claims made for "Old Ironsides" in Boston Harbor — it will be seen that we have not contributed a great deal basically to marine engineering. Isabella L. Bishops has said of this Korean warship, that it was named Tortoise Boat, and was "invented by Yi Soon Sin in the 16th century, enabling the Koreans to conquer the great Japanese General Hideyoshi in Chinhai Bay."[131]

Naphtha gas was first used by the Sumerians,[132] eyesalves in multiple tubes probably by the same people,[133] but spray-painting by paleolithic man![134] Cigarettes were known to the North American Indians long before Europeans had ever heard of tobacco;[135]

---

[129] Hornell, James, "Primitive Types of Water Transport in Asia: Distribution and Origins," in *Jour. of Royal Asiatic Soc.*, London, 1946, Pts. 3 and 4, pp. 124-141.

[130] Needham, J., op. cit., Vol. 1, pp. 240-243.

[131] Article "Koreans" in the Ency. Brit., 14th Ed., 1937, Vol. 13, p. 489, with illustration.

[132] Naphtha: as we have already mentioned, the Chinese piped this gas as early as 450 B.C. But it was also used by the Babylonians for divination purposes according to R. J. Forbes, p. 251, *A History of Technology*, Vol. 1, ed. by Charles Singer, et al. By the same author, it is said to have been used by the Sumerians, probably, in furnaces for heating metals, *Metallurgy in Antiquity*, p. 111.

[133] Forbes, R. J., *A History of Technology*, Vol. 1, p. 293.

[134] Leakey, L. S. B., in *A History of Technology*, Vol. 1, p. 149. This is possibly begging the point a little! It is assumed from the nature of certain paintings that they were done by blowing (or splattering) the paint from the mouth (!) using baffles to limit it as required. Certainly it does seem to have been sprayed, somehow.

[135] Cigarettes: see an editorial note, in "The Sacred Cigarette," *Discovery*, June, 1958, p. 262. Found by the thousands. . . . We have already mentioned cigar-holders: and, of course, the Indians were originators of the pipe for tobacco smoking.

spectacles are probably a Chinese invention;[136] and safety pins came from the Etruscans.[137] The Chinese did many things with glass, for, according to Bruno Schweig,[138] there is evidence of glass mirrors as early as 2000 B.C., and although the source of my information here is not the best, there is a reference to the first "windows" of glass in a collection of Chinese Stories. It is said that in the reign of Emperor Ming, a man named Wing Dow invented a "device" which he called Looking-through-the-Walls, whence it is claimed we now derive our word Window, a corruption of the inventor's name.[139]

Although the abacus seems a very slow and primitive way of making calculations, recent experiments undertaken by experts in both the ancient instrument and the modern electrically operated comptometer, have shown that in the hands of a skilled operator it can hold its own against all mechanical devices (excluding computers) except in one particular type of calculation.[140]

Le Comte de Nouy, after a backward look at the "rostrum of ingenuity" which meets the eye from antiquity, expresses the conviction:[141]

> Intelligence does not seem to have increased radically in depth during the last 10,000 years. As much intelligence was needed to invent the bow and arrow, when starting from nothing, as to invent the machine gun, with the help of all anterior inventions.

One demonstration of the wisdom of this observation is that the experts find it quite impossible to determine now how the first bow ever came to be invented. Their reconstructions are as varied as can be: which tends to show that such a weapon would certainly not occur easily to its originator, since we cannot even imagine how it originated with one right in front of us.

---

[136] Spectacles: see Ethel J. Alpenfels, anthropologist with the Bureau for Intercultural Education, in an article entitled, "Our Racial Superiority," abstracted in *The Reader's Digest*, Sept., 1946, p. 81, from *Catholic World*, July, 1946, p. 328ff.

[137] Safety pins: illustrated in an article by D. Randall MacIvor, "The Etruscans," *Antiquity*, 1 (June, 1927): 170.

[138] Schweig, Bruno, "Mirrors," *Antiquity*, Sept., 1941, p. 259.

[139] Windows: see Phyllis R. Feuner, *Giants, Witches, and a Dragon or Two*, Knopf, N.Y., 1943, p. 185.

[140] Abacus: these experiments were reported as a note under "Misplaced Conceit," in *His* (Inter-Varsity Christian Fellowship, Chicago) Oct., 1957.

[141] Du Nouy, Le Comte, *Human Destiny*, Longmans Green, N.Y., 1947, p. 139.

Finally, we come to the great contribution made by China.[142] If we should ask today what three things above all have contributed to or are contributing to our present conquest of the earth, we might possibly agree that printed matter, a convenient medium of exchange of some kind (i.e., currency), and powered propulsion are fundamental. All of these — and of course hundreds besides — we have derived from China, though often indirectly, via the Arab world.

For our wheeled vehicles we initially used draft animals domesticated in the Middle East, but because of the inefficiency of harnessing methods, these draft animals could not pull nearly as much as they do now, due to the lack of an effective harness which was meanwhile being developed in China. But we have, of course, long since passed out of the draft horse age into the jet-propulsion era. The motive power for such high-speed engines was likely inspired by the Chinese. In the air, China and the Far East anticipated us in virtually every form of airborne vehicle or device, including rockets, but also kites, gliders, balloons, parachutes, weather forecasting, and even the helicopter in the form of a toy.

The fact that we have obtained from China silk, porcelain, explosives, paper, printing with movable type, paper money, the magnetic compass, and mechanical water clocks, is so well known that it needs little or no elaboration. That the Chinese anticipated us in the use of gas for cooking and heating, cast iron, flame weapons in warfare, and, as has been stated above, the initial conquest of the air, is possibly less well known. But in addition to this, they initiated the use of fingerprinting for identification purposes, chain pumps, the cross-bow and a repeating bow with 12 shots per load, gimbal suspension systems, the draw loom, the rotary fan and a winnowing machine, piston bellows, wheel-barrows, stirrups, a greatly improved harness for draft animals that enabled them to pull almost twice as heavy a load, deep drilling methods, and much more.

Marco Polo gives us quite an extensive account of the use of paper money.[143] He says it was issued in various denominations, stamped authoritatively by the Governor of the Mint, and circulated as the only form of valid currency over a very wide

---

[142] Under "Science and Civilization in China," in the section "The Progress of Science," *Discovery*, Nov., 1957, p. 458.

[143] Polo, Marco, *The Travels of Marco Polo*, Library Publications, N.Y., n.d. Chap. 24, pp. 137-140.

geographical area. The bills, he says, were quite remarkably strong and did not tear easily; any which had been torn, however, or had suffered defacement, were recalled to the Mint and replaced. Strikingly reflecting our own bills of a few years ago, they contained a promise that they would be redeemed for certain fixed quantities of either precious stones or metals upon request. Foreign merchants could not sell their jewels or precious metals on the open market, but were required to turn them in at the Mint, where they received recompense in paper money.

Consider how great such an innovation really was. Marco Polo says, a man who wished to move could turn in hundreds of pounds (by weight) of valuable goods in personal property, walk away with a pocketful of money so light as to be hardly noticeable, with which in some other part of the Empire he could recover his hundreds of pounds of goods. Everywhere else in the world men were loaded down with the weight of their possessions, which often took such a form as to be almost worthless once the owner left his own locality. What such a scheme did for trade and commerce is incalculable. What paper money does for us today is virtually to keep our civilization running. Maybe we would have come to it anyway in time, but certainly we did not originate the idea. It originated in the 13th century with the Great Khan.

Needham has pointed out, it was often many centuries before such inventions reached the West from China. And he also notes that China received from the West very little in return: actually, only four items — the screw principle, a force pump for liquids, the crankshaft, and clockwork powered by a spring[144] Of these, only the screw principle and an alternative form of it (the windmill) seem actually to be to the credit of Indo-Europeans, possibly the Greeks for the screw and the Persians for the windmill. There is evidence that even the screw was obtained from Egypt.

Needham has pointed out that the art of drilling deep wells or boreholes as used today in exploiting oil reserves is specifically of Chinese origin.[145] He mentions that the use of graticules on maps to simplify the specifying and location of places, is probably of Chinese origin, although Ptolemy also employed this

---

[144] Needham, J., op. cit., Vol. 1, p. 241. But there is some question about the Screw Principle. Archimedes may have "borrowed" it from Egypt.
[145] Ibid., p. 244.

method.[146] For almost all Needham's illustrations, one thing can be said, to use his own words:[147]

> Firm evidence for their use in China antedates, and sometimes long antedates, the best evidence for their appearance in any other part of the world....

Then he has quoted Toynbee as having said —

> How ever far it may or may not be possible to trace back our Western mechanical trend toward the origins of our Western history, there is no doubt that a mechanical penchant is as characteristic of the Western civilization as an esthetic penchant was of the Hellenic.

Of this observation, Needham has said, "It is to be feared that all such valuations...are built on insecure foundations." The fact is, we simply do not have any such penchant if we judge our "racial" character by looking at our achievements prior to the time we began to borrow from non-Indo-Europeans. Since that time, racial mixture has taken place on such a scale, and with it, of course, "cultural" mixture also, that it is difficult to say for certain who is and who is not Indo-European in many cases. About all we can do is attempt to gain a certain measure of objectivity in this regard by looking more carefully at the actual achievement involved in many borrowed elements of our civilization which we now think simple and obvious.

Take as an example the preparation of silk. Sarton wrote:[148]

> Consider what the invention implied — the domestication of an insect, the "education" of silkworms, the cultivation of the white mulberry, the whole of sericulture!

It involved the recognition of the possibilities of the material in the first place. Spider web is one of the strongest known natural filaments, but it does not seem that anyone ever thought of cultivating spider web for this purpose. The idea of such a possibility is not enough. It requires considerable energy to turn it into a working industry, and although it seems highly improbable that it was done in a single step, somebody must have been alive to the practical advantages of making the effort and have demonstrated it could be done. But, having developed the "industry" until it was producing results, there it was left, with virtually no effort to extend it or improve the technique or seek for substitute insects or even attempt to make a synthetic material using the same kind of substance produced by other means.

---

[146] Ibid., p. 245.
[147] Ibid., p. 241.
[148] Sarton, George, *A History of Science,* Harvard, 1952, p. 5, n. 4.

This is the kind of thing that Indo-Europeans are good at; but the initial stimulation always seems to have come from somewhere else.

Needham has drawn attention to the fact that the Chinese have excelled in the arts of war, inventing many new weapons and new methods of attack or defense. The repeating, or "magazine" cross-bow, of which an example is to be found in the Royal Ontario Museum, is surely the world's first machine gun.[149] Credit (?) must also be given to them for the invention of flame weapons and smoke bombs. Although the former appeared in the Mediterranean area first in North Africa, being used against the Romans, there is no doubt that the Arabs derived them from the Chinese, for they called them "Darts of China." In a paper on chemical warfare published some years ago in the United States, Harold Lamb had this to say:[150]

A search through Oriental annals reveals other ancestors of present European weapons. But it is a little surprising to find the modern hand-grenade, flame-thrower, and cannon in use in Asia centuries ago.

In Roman days vases filled with a fire compound were employed by the Persians at the Siege of Petra. This compound was sulfur, asphalt, and naphtha; and the vases were cast by mangonels (a kind of giant catapult). The flames which sprang up when the vessel broke could not be extinguished. This was the origin of the much talked about Greek fire, which they, having borrowed it from the Arabs ... were surprised to find would continue to burn on water, a fact which mystified the early Crusaders.

Haram al-Raschid used sulfur-naphtha compound at the siege of Heraclea. ... At the siege of Acre, a Damascus engineer destroyed the wooden towers of the Crusaders by casting against them light clay vessels of the fluid until everything was well saturated. Then a flaming ball was thrown out and, as we read in one old Chronicle, "all was destroyed by flame, man, weapons, and all."

During the 13th century, flame weapons were highly developed by the Arabs. They had hand-grenades — small glass or clay jars that ignited when they broke; and a curious fire-mace, that was to be broken over the head of a foe, its owner keeping well to windward!

Flame throwers appeared in the form of portable tubes that could burn a man to ash at 30 feet. [We still cannot do much better — or worse — with modern weapons!] Some of the

[149] Repeating bow: this is described in "Crossbow," *Bulletin of the Royal Ontario Museum of Archaeology*, No. 10, May, 1931, p. 11.

[150] Lamb, Harold, "Flame Weapons," *Chem. Warfare Magazine*, Dec., 1927, p. 237.

names of these flame weapons, such as the Chinese Flower, and
so on, indicate that they had their origin in that country. In fact
we find the Chinese of the 13th century very familiar with destructive fire. They had the pao that belched flaming power, and
and fie-ho-tsing, the "spear of fire that flies."

It seems, then, that the Arabs borrowed much from the Far
East — paint brushes (but with the original pig bristles replaced
by camel hair — for religious reasons), paper manufacture, block
printing, silk, alchemy, and such weapons of war as the above in
addition to explosives. They were great carriers but apparently
somewhat uninventive except possibly during one short period
of their history.

Another document prepared by the Office of the Chief of
the Chemical Warfare Service (Washington, 1939) opens with
these words:[151]

> Ghengis Khan, famous ruler of the Mongols and of China,
> used chemicals in the form of huge balls of pitch and sulfur
> shot over the walls of besieged towns to produce combinations
> of screening smoke, choking sulfur fumes, and incendiary effects
> as a standard routine of attack.

Even "irritating" gases were used by the Arabs against the
Roman Legions in North Africa as early as A.D. 220. According
to Capt. A. Maude, the secret of this weapon was finally learned
by the Romans by Julius Caesar, through the capture of a Prince
of Mauritania named Juba II, subsequently married to Selene,
the daughter of Cleopatra.[152]

The Chinese, curiously enough, did not make much use of
their explosives in warfare by developing cannon until the idea
was suggested to them by Europeans. But they did make rocket
arrows, and their launching devices were certainly the predecessors of modern multiple rocket launchers. An illustration of
these, from a Chinese manuscript, is given in Fig. 13. Psychological weapons were developed — large arrows with whistling or
screaming heads on them, guaranteed to stampede horses. Some
of their bows were so beautifully designed that, as Klopsteg has
shown, they could shoot up to half a mile with them.[153]

Their gunpowder burned rather slowly and unevenly. Hence
it was not too effective in cannon. But this did not deter them.

[151] "The Story of Chemical Warfare," *Chem. Warfare Mag.,* Jan., 1939, p. 1.

[152] Maude, A., "Ancient Chemical Warfare," *Jour. of Royal Army Med.
Corps,* 62 (1934): 141.

[153] Klopsteg, Paul E., *Turkish Archery and the Composite Bow,* privately
published in Toronto, 1947.

They made use of this. They arranged the cannon's barrel so that it was free to move and then fastened the charge in it so that it stayed with the weapon. Thus they had a jet propelled rocket. They made the tube out of tightly wound paper to save weight and put a point on it for better flight. But they soon found that because of the uneven burning of the propellant, the rocket's flight was somewhat erratic. They overcame this by putting a trailing stick on it to steady it. At first this stick had feathers, but they found that the feathers were simply burned off. But these feathers proved unnecessary. However, regardless of the size of the rocket, they found that it had the best balanced flight when the stock was seven times as long as the rocket head. This is still found to be so.[154]

Willey Ley has written that the Arabs learned of these weapons from Chinese, and thus called them "Alsichem alkhatai," or Chinese Arrows.[155] The French Sinologist, Stanislas Julien, has found references to these rockets in China as early as A.D. 1232.

In metallurgy (and in alchemy) the Chinese were far ahead of the West. R. J. Forbes, a foremost authority on metallurgy in antiquity, has told us that they were making cast iron stoves by at least 150 B.C.[156] A picture of one such stove is given for interest's sake, though the original source of the illustration is not known (see Fig. 15). It was used by the Borg-Warner Corporation in an advertisement.

Another metallurgical journal gives a picture of a huge, single-piece, cast iron statue, which is believed to have been set up in A.D. 953. This is held to be one of the largest single iron castings ever made. It is shown in Fig. 16.

As a matter of interest, it is sometimes pointed out that the Hittites (possibly a non-Indo-European people with an Indo-European aristocracy), who vanished from history so completely that their very existence was once doubted, are referred to in cuneiform documents as the Khittai, and sometimes as the Khattai. C. R. Conder suggested that they disappeared because when their Kingdom came to an end, the people packed up and travelled East where they left their name associated with China and the Far East, in the form "Cathay."[157] The Arab call the

---

[154] Coggins, Jack, and Fletcher Pratt, *Rockets, Jets, Guided Missiles and Space Ships,* Random House, N.Y., 1951, p. 4, with foreword by Willey Ley.

[155] Ley, Willey, "Rockets," *Sci. American,* Mar., 1949, p. 31.

[156] Forbes, R. J., *Metallurgy in Antiquity,* Leiden, 1950, p. 442.

[157] Conder, C. R., "The Canaanites," *Trans. Vict. Instit.,* London, 24 (1890): 51.

Chinese Arrows as "Alkhatai," as we have seen. Forbes has held that the Hittites discovered cast iron even before the Chinese did. If this is true, it is possible the Chinese obtained their knowledge of it from the Hittites.

China also led in the conquest of the air. Francis R. Miller wrote that:[158]

> China enters first claim to the invention of the balloon — centuries before Europe knew it. The Chinese further claim to have had a system of signals by which different toned trumpets sounded from the tops of high hills and gave notice of impending changes of wind and weather, for use by navigators of dirigible balloons.

Miller has given an illustration from an official Chinese document of a large dirigible said to have been used at the coronation of the Emperor Fo-Kien, in 1306. It is large enough to carry 9 individual gondolas lowered to the ground with pulley systems.

In another place, Miller has reported:[159]

> A contemporary of Confucius (c. 550 B.C.) named Lu Pan, who was known as the "mechanician of Lu," is said to have made a glider in the form of a magpie from wood and bamboo which he caused to fly.

Miller also stated that kites, as precursors of airplanes first appeared in Chinese annals at a very early date. The Chinese who kept the records frequently refer to them. The earliest kites were used for military signaling, first recorded in warfare in the time of Han Sin who died in 196 B.C. He was one of the Three Heroes who assisted in founding the Han Dynasty. General Han Sin, plotting to tunnel into Wei-yang palace, flew a kite to measure the distance to it.[160] Needham wrote:[161]

> De la Loubere saw the parachute used by acrobats in Siam around 1688, and his description was read a century later by Lenormand, who then made some successful experiments and introduced the device to Montgolfier. This is not to deny that the idea of the parachute had been proposed in Europe at the time of the Renaissance, but there are Asian references to it much earlier still.

The first suspension bridges with iron chains were con-

---

[158] Miller, Francis T., *The World in the Air,* Vol. 1, Putnam's Sons, N.Y., 1930, p. 99.
[159] Ibid., p. 56.
[160] Ibid., p. 73.
[161] Needham, J., op. cit., Vol. 1, p. 231.

structed in China at least ten centuries or more before they were known and built in Europe.[162]

The story of printing and of paper manufacture is so well known as to need little consideration here. It came to Europe first with the old camel silk trains as a finished product, its secret of manufacture jealously guarded. Not until an Arab victory over the Chinese armies near Samarkand in A.D. 751, did paper settle in the West as an industry, set up by captured Chinese paper makers. Its use soon spread all over Europe.

The development of printing depended upon the manufacture of suitable ink. We have already mentioned the use of carbon black to strengthen rubber. This material was first made by the Chinese, who prepared it by burning oil and allowing the flame to impinge on a small porcelain cone, from which the deposited carbon was removed at frequent intervals with a feather. The famous stick ink resulted from the compounding of this with a strong glue solution.[163]

R. H. Clapperton has shown that the recent researches of Sir Aurel Stein and Sven Hedin prove beyond doubt that the Chinese were not only the inventors of rag paper, raw fiber (mulberry bark and bamboo paper), and paper made of a combination of raw fiber and rags, but also the inventors of loading and coating paper.[164] We formerly used a china-coated paper to obtain the best reproduction of photographs with a fine screen, though this has now been replaced with less expensive and possibly more durable plastic coatings. But the idea originated with the Chinese.

A recent Chinese author, Li Ch'iao-p'ing, points out that Chinese inventions opened up new fields of chemical manufacture in early times, but then remained stationary for centuries. One of their earlier contributions to medicine was the extraction of ephedrine from the herb Ephedra, a process credited to a very famous Emperor Shen Nung, who is supposed to have lived somewhere between 3000 and 2200 B.C.[165] A two thousand year old rig for drilling salt wells was recently cited as still a good

---

[162] Ibid.

[163] Stern, H. J., *Rubber: Natural and Synthetic,* Maclaren, London, 1954, p. 118.

[164] Clapperton, R. H., and William Henderson, *Modern Paper-Making,* 2nd ed., rev., Blackwell, Oxford, 1942.

[165] Bender, George A., *Pharmacy in Ancient China,* A History of Pharmacy in Pictures, Parke Davis, and Co., n.d.

model for the modern cable rig of today's oil fields.[166] Even in
the design of clothing, they seemed to have a genius for hitting
upon the best end-results, quite apart from the actual materials
they developed. Thus it has been recently shown that the so-called
"Chinese sleeve" which permits each forearm to be inserted into
the opposite sleeve, is more effective for keeping the hands warm
in cold weather than either Arctic mittens or a muff. Europeans
adopted muffs and mittens. But having investigated the Chinese
pattern thoroughly, it now appears they are not as effective.[167]

Although the "clock" motor principle was taken to the Chinese from the West, their water clocks long antedated the European systems of keeping accurate time, and were certainly more
dependable, especially when mercury was used in place of water.
The complexity of these water clocks has only recently been recognized. Some ancient documents describe them in sufficient detail to enable Needham and others to draw plans and diagrams
of their operation. This was reported recently in the British
Journal, Nature.[168] These devices were highly ingenious, involving gear trains of several kinds, the speed being very exactly
regulated by a very clever use of water or mercury. Knowledge
of these seems to have come into Europe during the Crusades.
The clocks were connected with astronomical observations, in an
endeavor to predict seasons more exactly. The interest was purely
of a practical nature.

As we have previously mentioned, the Chinese had already
discovered the uniqueness of finger prints, and quickly perceived
how useful this could be for identification purposes. They were
using them in the T'ang dynasty as early at A.D. 618.[169]

According to a special report on the use of natural gas, it is
said that the Chinese were the first to use it.[170] The story goes
that some villagers near Peiping were trying to put out a local
brush fire, when they found one flame that could not be extinguished with water. "The practical villagers then built a bamboo

[166] See a review of "The Chemical Arts of Old China," by Eduard Farber,
in the Sci. Monthly, June, 1949, p. 430.

[167] Annual Project Report (U.S. Quartermaster Stores) Jan.-Dec., 1956,
p. 430.

[168] Needham, J., and Wang Ling, and Derek J. Price, "Chinese Astronomical Clockwork," in Nature, Mar. 31, 1956, pp. 600, 601.

[169] Haddon, A. C., The History of Anthropology, Watts, London, 1934,
p. 33.

[170] Reported in The Telegram, Toronto, April 4, 1955, in a special section
devoted to the use of Natural Gas, under the title, "Gas and Pipeline too:
way back in 450 B.C."

pipeline from the outlet to the village, and used the gas for heating brine to make salt." This is said to have taken place somewhere about 450 B.C. Whether they can be said to have invented the use of natural gas or not is a questionable point, but certainly they were very quick to see its practical possibilities. This is in exact contrast to the Romans who produced cast iron in considerable quantities but threw it all away because they did not recognize it as a potentially useful product.[171] As we have already remarked, the basic technology of all metallurgy is entirely non-Indo-European. Even heat-treatment and case-hardening was known before we "discovered" it. Some processes of steel production have seemed clearly to be of our own devising, the Bessemer process, for example, which is a means of producing particularly pure forms of iron in preparation for the manufacture of certain types of steel. It has recently been shown, however, that immediately before William Kelly introduced the process into the United States, four Chinese workers were brought in, presumably as experts.[172]

In some instances we not only never have improved upon the products of our instructors, but actually have not even been able to improve upon their methods of manufacture, where we usually shine. Cire Perdu casting is still employed for small bronze statues of racing horses and such items, and even the use of cow manure for the mold has been retained from the most ancient times, to give the best results. This system is extraordinarily effective for casting hollow articles of intricate form, where the use of ordinary cores is quite impossible, and yet it is found in every primitive society that has any knowledge of metals, in every archaeological site bearing the remains of cultures who had developed metal casting skills, and virtually every high civilization with the exception of Indo-Europeans seems to have had a knowledge of the art — almost exactly as it is now done in Europe. We therefore use the same basic methods as non-Indo-Europeans for casting hollow objects in metal, just as we have adopted exactly the same method of molding objects in rubber (cored or slush-molded) as the natives of Central and South America.

Although it will be possible to quote authorities who do not hesitate to say in so many words that we have invented virtually

[171] Forbes, R. J., *Metallurgy in Antiquity*, p. 407.

[172] Needham, J., *The Development of Iron and Steel Technology in China*, reviewed by F. C. Thompson, in *Nature* (England), Dec. 12, 1959, p. 1830.

nothing, such sweeping generalizations need qualification. In the first place, racial mixture has proceeded so extensively in Europe and America that it is difficult to say who is truly Japhethic and who is a mixture of Shem and Ham as well. It is no longer always clear who is truly Indo-European and who is not. But it is true to say that whatever inventiveness we have shown in the past three or four centuries has almost always resulted from stimulation from non-Indo-Europeans. Our chief glory has been the ability to improve upon and perfect the inventions of others, often to such an extent that they appear to be original developments in their own right. We can also make some claim to have greatly advanced mass production methods. But it would surely be a great mistake to credit the improver with greater inventive ability than the originator. Moreover, the individual who tells the truth 99% of the time, but now and then tells lies, would hardly be termed a liar. By the same token, it does not seem proper to call a people "inventive" who once in a while do invent something, but who 99% of the time merely adapt the inventions of others to new ends.

Paul Herrmann has written an interpretive survey of man's conquest of the earth's surface from paleolithic times to the present day. It is the work of one man, no small undertaking, and has therefore not the comprehensiveness one might desire, but it has the advantage of being a unified treatment. In his foreword he has this to say:[173]

> A further aim in writing this book was to weaken the very widespread conviction that our progress in the technological aspects of civilization represents, in any *real* sense, a greater achievement than that of our forebears. The liberation of atomic energy probably means no more and no less than did the invention of the firedrill or the wheel in their day. Both discoveries were of immense importance to early man.

Needham says that the only Persian invention of first rank was the windmill, and apart from the rotary quern whose history is not quite certain, the only European contribution of value, mechanically speaking, is the pot-chain pump.[174] This gives us two claims to originality. Compared with the originality of other cultures prior, let us say, to the 15th century A.D., we certainly did not shine in this direction. Yet we have advanced technology so far ahead of all previous civilizations that there must be some

[173] Herrmann, Paul, *Conquest by Man*, Harper, N.Y., 1954, pp. xxi, xxii.
[174] Needham, J., *Science and Civilization in China*, Vol. 1, p. 240.

fundamental reason—a reason to be suggested in Part V of this volume.

Meanwhile, in the conquest of land, sea, and air, in agriculture and animal husbandry, in economics, trade, and commerce, in the creation of all that lies behind literature, the keeping of records, and the ordering of knowledge, in arts and crafts, in architecture, and the textile world, in metallurgy and medicine, in the planning of cities and the development of means of communication over long distances, in the invention of tools and the exploitation of power sources—in all these areas the foundations were laid by Hamitic people.

What we have since been able to do in elaborating this basic heritage is another story. It is necessary here only to establish something of the measure of our indebtedness. This catalog by no means exhausts the list. In fact, even in the use of electricity and internal combustion engines of the Diesel type, the initial inspiration seems likewise to have come from Hamites.

This paper has dealt with the contribution of descendants of Ham. The contribution of Shem was of another very special kind, essentially in the realm of the spirit. On the other hand, the contribution of Japheth has been in the realm of the intellect. Japheth took the technology of Ham and created science. But science unredeemed by a true spiritual perception is far from beneficial for man in the long run. Shem, Ham, and Japheth thus were each called to play a unique and vital part. When any one of them has failed to contribute, or when one has dominated the other two, civilization (though seeming to gain at first) has always suffered a decline. But when each has contributed in the proper measure, enormous strides forward are made and the development of civilization has been almost explosive. What, then, will world civilization become when the Lord Jesus Christ returns to establish a Kingdom of Righteousness in which not only the three sons contribute in perfect proportion, but their contribution will be entirely for peace and not for war? Surely this will be an age of wonders indeed!

PART V

A Christian World View:
The Framework of History

*The world was created for man's body, man's body for
his spirit, and man's spirit for God: the spirit that it
might be brought into subjection unto God, the body
unto the spirit, and the world unto the body.*

HUGO ST. VICTOR

PROLOGUE

THE KEY to the existence of a universe such as we live in lies, I believe, in the fact that God wished to show forth that aspect of His Being which the angels have never comprehended, namely, His love, yet without at the same time surrendering that part of His Being which they *do* comprehend, namely, His holiness. God's plan was therefore to create Man with such a nature and in such a situation that he would need to be redeemed, and so to order events that this redemption could only be achieved by the Incarnation and Self-sacrifice of the Creator Himself on man's behalf. Only at such a cost was it possible for God to make manifest His love for His creatures without diminishing His holiness. Both the Incarnation and the Crucifixion were dependent upon the existence of a physical order, a time-space world in which the creatures to be redeemed were embedded and in which the Creator Himself could also voluntarily confine Himself for a season. Granted this plan and granted a natural order in which reasoning mind could exist and physical death could be a meaningful reality, then man in God opens to us the meaning of the physical universe, because this was the basic framework within which the plan of Redemption was to be worked out. Athanasius has these words about the Incarnation:[1]

> The achievements of the Savior through His Incarnation are so astounding and so numerous that any one wishing to describe them in detail would be like one who gazes at the expanse of the sea, and attempts to count its waves.

So then, the Incarnation and Crucifixion, on man's behalf, are the key to the physical order in which man lives, and dies.

This is the basic thought that I put before the reader. The rest is an unfolding of it in terms of the Scriptures. It is my hope that the reader will find much to stimulate him and give him a fresh realization of the unfathomable riches to be found in the Word of God. The Lord grant that it may be so.

---

[1] Athanasius, *De Incarnatione*, Chapter 54.

INTRODUCTION

A RABBI WAS explaining to his pupils how strongly God condemns the worship of idols. One of them asked, "If God so abhors idolatry, why does He not destroy the idols that men worship?" The Rabbi replied, "Because some of them, the sun and the moon for example, are an essential part of the fabric of God's economy." After a moment's pause, the student said, "Then why does He not at least destroy those that are not essential?" To which the Rabbi answered, "Because it would then appear He was condoning the worship of the idols He did *not* destroy."

The literature of antiquity is full of little exchanges like this, neat, satisfying in a way, wise too, and not without genuine force. Such answers were common when men believed that the universe was created by God with man particularly in mind. It was assumed that God had created the heavens and that therefore He could "tamper" with it if necessary — for man's benefit: for, after all, man was of greater importance than the sun and the moon. It seemed self-evident to man, after the Incarnation, that the Earth was paramount among the heavenly bodies and that man was paramount on the earth. The heavens and the earth were created for man's sake.

But during the past hundred years the universe has been studied without reference to God as its Creator and without any thought that man might be its *raison d'etre*. It seems that as its immensity has become increasingly apparent so has man's insignificance in terms of size, until he has dwindled in importance virtually to the vanishing point: as Leslie Paul put it:[2]

> The entire term of humanity is but a minute episode in a scarcely longer history of life on a cooling planet which for the most of its existence knew no life at all. And that planet in the

[2] Paul, Leslie, *Annihilation of Man,* Harcourt Brace, N.Y., 1945, p. 154.

infinite immensity of the universe is a tiny scrap of matter rushing with all other scraps — and from all other scraps — at colossal speed to heaven knows what destination in the curvature of space.

In no one knows what time, though it will be soon enough by astronomical clocks, the lonely planet will cool, all life will die, all mind will cease, and it will all be as if it had never happened. That, to be honest, is the goal to which evolution is traveling, that is the "benevolent" end of the furious living and furious dying. . . . All life is no more than a match struck in the dark and blown out again. The final result . . . is to deprive it completely of meaning.

Significance has thus come to be defined either in terms of size — and man is very small relative to the vastness of the universe — or in terms of duration — and what is man's life relative to the four billion years or more estimated for its age? By every standard of assessment of which science is capable — and its standards can only ever be *quantitative* — man judges his own worth to be virtually nil.

But this very judgment is self-contradictory, for if man is of no consequence, then neither is his judgment of what is of consequence. His very opinion about the Cosmos can carry little weight in a Cosmos which scarcely recognizes his existence and would be no different if he ceased to exist altogether. These presumptuous statements about the insignificance of man, by writers like G. Gaylord Simpson, can logically be ignored for, by their own admission, if man *is* of no consequence so, then, are his opinions of no significance even if his knowledge of the "facts" is tremendous.

To an increasing number of people this philosophy of science, which is of necessity a philosophy of materialism, is proving to be quite inadequate for man because it is quite unable to deal effectively with purposes, and man must have purpose to live by. This is particularly true of young people whose power of dedication is strong and who feel the futility of modern life so keenly.

Some years ago Edmund Sinnott wrote eloquently on this matter. He points out how well dictators have learned this truth and how easily they can rally people who, having no other commitments and feeling the deadness of life, are eager to dedicate themselves to some cause. The inconsistencies, the cruelties, and the blind intolerances that are demanded of their followers can safely be ignored: enthusiasm will carry the day: as Sinnott wrote:[3]

---

[3] Sinnott, Edmund, "Ten Million Scientists," *Science* 111 (1950): 124.

Something precious outweighs all else, and to underestimate their tremendous appeal to the troubled and uncertain is folly. Today, when easygoing tolerance so often is the ideal attitude and security is commonly reckoned as the highest blessing, we may well forget man's tremendous capacity for dedication, his eagerness to nourish convictions.... The significance brought into his life by a cause and a creed often seems compensation enough for loss of freedom.

If we cannot understand how readily people may surrender their liberty, it is because we have forgotten how stimulating dedication can be. Sinnott believes that the "adventure" of a scientific career can be compensation and stimulus enough, and in his article he is therefore appealing to younger men and women to fling themselves into such a vocation. Yet the evidence in England and the United States (where surveys have been made) seems to show that young people are opting out of science courses and turning to the arts and the humanities with renewed interest, believing that the pursuit of science stultifies man's life rather than enriching it.[4] And much of the blame for this impoverishment is the philosophy of science that inevitably creates a sense of purposelessness by reducing man's importance in the universe almost to zero. To many thinking people, it is becoming apparent once again that there is much truth in Dryden's view of man as "the measure of all things," and that the universe has meaning only when man is made the key.[5] The size of man's body and the length of his earthly life cannot be used as guides

---

[4] The swing from Science to Arts courses has been reported from both the United States and England, where it is causing some concern because it increases the shortage of scientific and technical personnel (See "Dainton Report: British Youth Swings Away from Science," *Science,* 159 [1968]: 1214). The situation in England has been remarked upon several times in *The New Scientist* during recent years. See for the U.S., a report in *Science* 160 (1968): 396f.

[5] A simple illustration! Gabriel W. Lasker in his paper "The 'New' Physical Anthropology Seen in Retrospect and Prospect" in *Human Evolution,* edited by Korn and Thompson, Holt, Rinehart and Winston, N.Y., 1967, p. 15, remarks: "Several species of primates, above all in importance the gorilla, are near extinction, and it is of the utmost practical importance that these species be preserved. Even the common varieties of monkey are needed in such numbers for testing polio vaccines and the like that there is a real threat of depopulation. Some nonhuman primates may become as useful to man as domestic cattle have been, since they can synthesize substances similar to man's, just as the cow synthesizes a milk which can substitute for human milk, and the maintenance of herds of these animals is an urgent necessity." The assumption is that these nonhuman primates have no importance *in their own right.*

to his importance. Man as a creation of God is still the measure of the true significance of all else in the universe.

A. S. Aldis wrote recently, with proper insight:[6]

> All the philosophers say you cannot get an "ought" from an "is." Science establishes facts, but that doesn't give you the knowledge of what you ought to do. To make the transition, you need a third factor, teleology; if you are convinced that the developing universe disclosed by science has an ascertainable purpose, then you begin to get a standard by which to judge good and bad.

But such a "purpose" must be with specific reference to man, or it has no power to affect his behavior where selfish interests conflict, or to satisfy his mind in moments of solitary reflection when he comes face to face with ultimate things. Mascall has written eloquently on this:[7]

> The difficulty which civilized Western man in the world today experiences (is) in convincing himself that he has any special assigned status in the universe, and upon the sense of instability which this uncertainty produces. Many of the psychological disorders which are so common and distressing a feature of our time are, I believe, to be traced to this cause.

Since it is now held almost without exception by modern philosopher-scientists that man has quite by accident been thrown up in some blind and purposeless cosmic process, the unhappy consequences of such a view are at last being recognized and an effort is being made to engender some kind of *ersatz* purpose. Thus Julian Huxley speaks of the "glorious paradox"[8] of a process that through eons of time and quite without direction finally produced a creature, man, who by reason of his possession of self-consciousness and his ability to make delayed decisions is freed from the previous all-pervasive determinism of the natural order and can therefore undertake that which no creature before him had been able to undertake, namely, the directing of his own future. No goal has been set: only the promise that if he can think up a goal appropriate to his potential he can now do something toward the attainment of it and thus fulfill himself in a new way.

---

[6] Aldis, A. S., "Science — Its Own Arbiter?" a paper published by The Christian Medical Fellowship, London, 1967, pp. 9-10.

[7] Mascall, E. L., *The Importance of Being Human,* Columbia Univ., N.Y., 1958, p. 19.

[8] Huxley, Sir Julian, refers to this "glorious paradox" in the *Rationalist Annual,* 1946, p. 87.

Although the statement that no goal has yet been agreed upon is essentially correct when applied to individual effort, Huxley sees a goal "worthy" of the human race as a whole, and this goal is the ultimate production of a Super-race![9] Huxley nevertheless woefully admits that his "new religion" is still in need of a prophet to whip it into compelling shape and shake the world with it.[10] Bertrand Russell appears to be quite unenthused. He wrote mournfully:[11]

> That man is the product of causes which had no pre-vision of the end they were achieving; that his origin, his growth, his hopes and fears, his loves and beliefs, are but the outcome of accidental collocations of atoms; that no fire, no heroism, no intensity of thought and feeling, can preserve an individual life beyond the grave; that all the labours of the ages, all the devotion, all the inspirations, all the noonday brightness of human genius, are destined to extinction in the vast death of the solar system; and that the whole temple of man's achievement must inevitably be buried beneath the debris of a universe in ruins — all these things, if not quite beyond dispute, are yet so nearly certain, that no philosophy which rejects them can hope to stand.

The kind of goal such men do foresee is entirely unlike the goal which moved Augustine to write his *City of God* or Aquinas his *Summa Theologica* or Dante his *Divine Comedy*. Theirs was essentially a goal for man in God, as Bunyan's was a goal for man in Christ, and as such both had the power to inspire — which without a shadow of a doubt the goal of Simpson, Huxley, and a great host of other scientists of modern times does not have.

Many will object that we cannot now return to a Christian view because it was once and for all undermined by the expansion of knowledge. But it was not in itself the Christian philosophy of earlier days that was so much at fault as it was the proofs from the study of the order of Nature by which men sought to rationalize it. Far better would it have been to hold to the

---

[9] Huxley, Sir Julian, "New Bottles for New Wine: Ideology and Scientific Knowledge," *Jour. Roy. Anthrop. Instit.*, London, 80, Pts. 1 and 2 (1950): 20. Huxley's words are: "Man is enabled, and indeed, forced to view his destiny as the trustee, spearhead, or effective agent of any further evolutionary progress on this planet. He has been thrown up by the cosmic process as an instrument for the further carrying on of that process."

[10] Ibid., p. 20. It is clear that Huxley saw in Teilhard de Chardin this new prophet. Hence the enthusiasm which he exhibits in his Introduction to the latter's *The Phenomenon of Man*.

[11] Russell, Bertrand; as quoted by J. N. D. Sullivan, *Limitations of Science*, Pelican Books, England, 1938, p. 175.

spiritual view of man as an act of faith and allow thereafter that humanly derived knowledge might illuminate or elaborate the details of that faith, but never supply its foundations. Why should we fear to admit that our understanding stems in part from what we believe? Contrary to what many Christians suppose, science itself progresses by the formulation of hypotheses which are nothing less than acts of faith. The essential difference is that science demands that a hypothesis must be subject to experimental validation by the *uncommitted* experimenter. The kind of faith with which a Christian undergirds his philosophy is similarly experimentally verifiable, but not in the laboratory sense, for the rules are not the same. But this does not mean it is any less real or valid. The basic assumption which he makes is that God exists as a personal but purely spiritual Being, omniscient, omnipresent, and omnipotent. The existence of God can be demonstrated by any individual who is willing to accept the conditions which God Himself has imposed upon such an experiment: but *he can only make this demonstration with absolute certainty for himself.* In other words, there is a kind of knowledge here which each man must gain personally and cannot acquire vicariously. Hence demonstration is not of the same kind that exists in a laboratory situation. But it is real knowledge, and such knowledge is the key which gives meaning to history, both the history of the individual and of the universe.

Let us then once more boldly declare our faith that man is indeed the measure of all things, not man by himself but man in God. Hugo St. Victor so aptly stated it:[12]

> The world was created for man's body, man's body for his spirit, and man's spirit for God: the spirit that it might be brought into subjection unto God, the body unto the spirit, and the world unto the body.

And let us see what evidence there might be for such a tremendous claim that in the final analysis the very universe itself was made for man.

---

[12] Hugo St. Victor: quoted by H. O. Taylor, "Medieval Mind," in Bk. 2 *Early Middle Ages,* Macmillan, London, 1938, p. 91.

Chapter 1

MAN: THE KEY TO THE UNIVERSE

THE WORLD was made for the body, the body for the spirit, and the spirit for God. Everything ultimately, therefore, finds its purpose in God.

In any field of research it is most important to begin by asking the right questions. It is not infrequently stated, in fact, that asking the right question may be even more important than finding the right answer. But contrary to popular opinion very few people do ask questions at all. Most of us take things pretty much for granted, once we have passed childhood.

One question that is not often asked but is an important one for the present discussion is, Why did God need to create anything at all? Viewing the situation anthropomorphically, one might say that when *we* create something, we have a genuine sense of achievement which gives us pleasure, and therefore perhaps creative activity gives God pleasure. But a moment's reflection tells us that only when the thing we have created serves some purpose does it give us pleasure, though "purpose" can be defined in very broad terms. In fact, it is doubtful if we can create anything, pleasurably, which does not have a purpose directly related to man himself. Superficially, it would seem that one could find exceptions to this, but it can be shown that the exceptions are only apparent, and by contrast it is more readily demonstrated that creative activity is more purposeful and more pleasurable as it more directly serves some human interest. In other words, creation is for pleasure and that pleasure stems from the fact that it is purposeful in relation to man. It is doubtful if purpose has any meaning, ultimately, unless it *does* in some way relate to human destiny.

If God created the universe, we must assume, I think, that

225

He had a purpose in mind. It is inconceivable that He would create it merely for its own sake, for if He did, one might ask immediately, What would He do with it? If, on the other hand, we make the bold assumption that God's ultimate objective in creating the physical order was to place man within it, so that such a puny creature becomes the justification for such a tremendous act, then we have to find some way of explaining just how man could be so important to God. David asked this question when he looked at the heavens in all their magnitude and then said, "What is man that Thou art mindful of him?" (Ps. 8:4).

Is it possible that the creation of man really is the key to the meaning of the universe? To answer this question, we have to think about two matters of great importance: the first is, In what way is man unique in the universe, and the second is, In what way is he uniquely related to God. The answers to both questions are interdependent, yet they are also capable of separate treatment.

There are three orders of creatures which have conscious life: the angels, the animals, and man. About the angels, we know nothing except by revelation, but from revelation we learn that they are exceedingly numerous, that they can act upon the physical order if they choose — though they are not dependent upon it for their existence — and that some of them at least have sinned against God. If the argument from silence carries any weight in such matters, it would appear that they are not redeemable, for Scripture gives no intimation of such a thing. As we shall see, the reason for this appears to lie in the fact that redemption depends upon an act of God which, for very clearly defined reasons, involved the Incarnation. A great many connected lines of cause and effect are involved in the Incarnation and these must first be broadly set forth before it will be clear why the plan of Redemption revealed in Scripture does not allow for the redemption of purely spiritual beings without bodies. Turning to the animals, a similar argument from silence suggests that the plan of Redemption does not involve them either because, though they do have bodies, they are not held to be morally accountable before God. Thus the angels are not redeemed because they have no necessary corporeal existence, and the animals are not redeemed because they have no moral accountability.[13]

Between these two orders of created beings stands man who

---

[13] Animal Accountability: The possibility that animals are accountable is

has a corporeal existence — unlike the *angels* — which renders the Incarnation necessary to make his redemption *possible*. At the same time, the *necessity* for his redemption stems from the fact that he is morally accountable — unlike the *animals*. His possession of a body makes his redemption possible; the possession of a fallen spirit makes his Redemption necessary.

Man is therefore neither animal nor angel but a unique creature of God sharing something of both, the moral accountability of the angels and the dependence upon the physical order of the animals. He bears a relationship to God as a consequence of his uniqueness, which makes him higher than the angels. But this status which he may achieve, and for which I believe he was created, is possible only because he has a special kind of physical life, a special kind of mental capacity, and a special kind of spiritual potential. And the Bible is deeply concerned with the history of all three.

His spiritual potential can readily be shown to be dependent ultimately upon his special kind of mental capacity, and this in turn results from his possession of a special kind of central nervous system which is only partly shared by the animals. It is, however, dependent upon the world in which he lives, the physical order of things in which he moves and has his being, the air he breathes with its special composition, the fluid which forms so large a part of his body, the temperature of his environment, the gravitational forces which play upon him, in short, his very existence in the right kind of a world. And from here we move one step further and perceive that this is the right kind of world for him because it is appropriately set in the right kind of solar system and accompanied by the right kind of satellite — the moon. So we move from God to the human spirit, to the mind, to the human body, to the world which he inhabits, and on out into a larger realm.... And perhaps if we knew enough, into the galaxy of which our solar system is a part, and the universe within which our galaxy belongs. We do not know enough to be sure that our solar system bears some unique relationship to its galaxy or our galaxy to the universe, but I think it is likely that such unique relationships do exist and that we shall discover them in due time, just as we have come to learn how important the size of our earth is and how critical its distance from the sun is.

---

suggested by several passages of Scripture which have been examined in "The Extent of the Flood" (Part VI) in Vol. IX of the Doorway Papers (*Miscellaneous Studies*).

But all these are ultimately related to man. This is what makes them significant. Perhaps they might be matters of interest in themselves, but I suspect that if we made inquiry we should soon find, as indeed many students do find, that the mere study of astronomy, geology, or any other science for its own sake tends to lose its power to inspire action, unless it is related to human destiny in some way. When one is young the concept of "human destiny" may be adequately defined in terms of personal ambition, but as ambition in terms of success in this life tends for all but a very few people to become tarnished and inadequate, there comes a time when human destiny has to be defined in terms that are much broader, indeed that are transcendental. It is then that men begin to feel the need for a sense of purpose that reaches beyond personal ambition. It is at such times that the possession of an adequate World View proves to be so important. Without it life is impoverished, for man does not live by bread alone. Even Julian Huxley admits the inadequacy of the present scientific philosophy:[14]

> Some system of beliefs is necessary. Every human individual and every human society is faced with three overshadowing questions: What am I, or what is man? What is the world in which I find myself, or what is the environment which man inhabits? And, What is my relation to the world, or what is man's destiny?
> Men cannot direct the course of their lives until they have taken up an attitude to life: they can only do that by giving some sort of answer to these three great questions; and their belief system embodies that answer.

It seems virtually impossible to create such an adequate World View unless man is made the key or the end for which the world was made, and the world the end for which the universe was made. How beautifully simple it is to believe that God made man for Himself, the world for man, and the universe for the world. Such a simple framework makes such a tidy neat little bundle out of experience. Perhaps it is naive to hold such a belief in this day and age. Yet it is surprising how much of what we know can be woven smoothly, reasonably, satisfyingly, indeed even excitingly, into such a World View.

I know that there are many intelligent people who feel no

---

[14] Huxley, Sir Julian, op. cit. (ref. 9), p. 16. The whole question of the need for a personal philosophy of life or world view is dealt with at length by contrasting medieval times with the present, in Vol. VIII of the Doorway Papers, Part III, "Medieval Synthesis and Modern Fragmentation of Thought."

real need for this kind of philosophy of life. But there are many who do feel a genuine dis-ease whenever they read, as one does with increasing frequency these days, that the universe and man are pure accident, and that God is nonexistent. To my mind, the evidence of purpose is everywhere to be seen provided that one makes the single bold assumption that purpose does exist, that it exists in relation to man, and that it exists in relation to man as a special creation of God. At any rate, we are making this assumption only because I believe it is an entirely scriptural one; and we propose to explore it without further apology. This exploration will involve the study of the universe as a setting for man viewed as a creature uniquely equipped for a certain kind of understanding which makes possible a special relationship with God that sets him apart from both animals and angels.

And so we begin with God Himself. The character of any plan which God may have with respect to man will naturally depend upon what kind of a "Person" God is. The Bible tells us that God is both love and light. We cannot understand God's love for us except in terms of human relationships, but our experience of human relationships is unfortunately distorted by the fact that man is a fallen creature and all our relationships are on this account troubled. We can only see His love through the filter of our own nature as it now is. Had we lived when Jesus Christ walked the earth and had we been able to observe how He behaved towards men, we imagine our vision would have been quite clear; seeing Him, we would have seen God and our understanding of what God is like would have been perfect. But this is not true. The disciples lived with Jesus daily, week after week, month after month, and still did not see what He was really like or that God was really like Him. Philip said, "Show us the Father and it sufficeth us." And the Lord answered, "Who hath seen me hath seen the Father." But they had not seen Him at all, as His words to Philip clearly show (John 14:9).

We have in the New Testament, especially in the Gospels, a portrait of what God is like. Nevertheless we still see through a glass darkly. But this much is certain: God loves man and seeks his company even at unimaginable cost to Himself; and for all our indifference, His delight is still with the sons of men. From Scripture as a whole it is clear that God created man because He sought an order of beings capable of entering into a unique relationship with Himself, a relationship that was to result from an experience which man was to undergo, an experience involving (1) a Fall from a state of innocence to a state of conscious guilt, and then (2) a redemption to an entirely new level of virtue and fellowship with God as a direct consequence of that Fall. The special relationship was therefore "special" because it involved redemption.

It is apparent that angels worship God and rejoice with Him and in some sense form His "Court": yet I think it is implied in Scripture that while they may be *company* they can never achieve the status of *companions,* for they neither comprehend nor respond to His love, knowing only His holiness.[15] Yet love is the very essence of God's being. Angels cannot experience the redemptive power of God as men are able to, and accordingly they lack any personal realization of the love of God. It seems that in some way, incomprehensive though it is, God also felt this lack and therefore determined to create a being towards whom He could make manifest His love and not merely His holiness, by one single act that depended upon the existence of a physical world and which, on this account necessitated its creation.

As far as we know, there was only one way in which the love of God could be displayed comprehendingly, and that was by sacrifice, a sacrifice in which God Himself would become like His creatures in order to enter into their world, experience their kind of life, and finally assume their guilt and translate His great love into comprehensible terms by becoming responsible for the very sin which had been a necessary element of the experience.

The fact is that we can have, and do have, no other clear proof of the reality of God's love for man except that which was displayed at Calvary,[16] and if man had not sinned, there could have been no occasion for the Cross. It is foolish to speak of the love of God while at the same time ignoring the meaning of the death of Jesus Christ His Son. The world is full of contradictions of the idea that God *loves* man. Apart from Calvary, the evidence of God's care for man is easily overwhelmed by the facts of his-

---

[15] Worship, of angels: the only indications in Scripture of the attitude of angels toward God reveal recognition of His holiness and His wisdom. At the completion of the initial creation the angels "shouted for joy" (Job 38:7), and in Isaiah's vision they are worshipping God and saying, "Holy, holy, holy" (Isa. 6:3).

[16] I John 3:16: "Hereby perceive we the love of God, because he laid down his life for us." This passage is especially remarkable because the wording of it is such that the reader cannot but go away with the realization that it was *God* who laid down His life in order to demonstrate His love, thereby leaving no doubt as to who it was who sacrificed Himself on our behalf.

tory which suggest rather His total indifference. Indeed, among the Jewish people there are those today who believe that God could not have remained silent in the face of Belsen and Dachau unless He really is *dead*. They have their "God is dead" people, too. The lot of man through the centuries does not confirm faith in the love of God. Only at Calvary does proof appear unequivocally. And this fact alone is sufficient to show that *here*, therefore, is the pivotal point in God's dealings with man.

We only deceive ourselves when we suppose that the love of God is self-evident, that the Christian understanding of the death of Jesus Christ is not essential to the proclamation of God's love, that we can forget Calvary and persuade men of God's love without reference to it. The man of the world knows better. He contemplates the world about him and seeing its tragedy and its pain, its poverty and hate and destruction, he is not moved by assurances of God's benevolence.

But Scripture properly sees the key to all history in this ultimate revelation of God's thoughts towards Man, the death of Jesus Christ. And it is a comprehensible revelation, a revelation which is bound up in historical events occupying time and space in man's time-and-space world. It was the climax of divine planning and preparation. It was no accident. A whole series of circumstances were required to make it possible, and these prerequisite conditions are analyzable; and their analysis involves not merely the most rewarding of all intellectual exercises, namely, theology, but also the study of natural science and history.

To fulfill God's desire for the true companionship of creatures capable of responding to His love, no other being seems to have been possible than such a one as Man is. And such a being cannot be conceived without taking into account his unique capacities as well as the physical environment in which he lives out his life. These circumstances invite us to examine the relationship between man and the universe in this light. And his varied capacities require us to examine how God undertook to preserve him against destroying himself completely after he had sinned, while His purposes were being carried through to completion. The animals do not belong in the spiritual world as far as we know, and angels do not belong in the physical world; but man belongs in both, and in this is neither animal nor angel. He is unique because he is redeemable, and the mode of his redemption is the key to the existence of the time-space universe of which he is a part.

But first one might ask, Is there any other way that man might have been redeemed? Centuries ago, Anselm wrote in answer to this question:[17]

> If God were unwilling that the human race should be saved, except through the death of Christ, when He could have saved them by His simple will, see how, in so judging, you question His wisdom; for even if man were for no sufficient reason to do with great labour that which he could have done with ease, he would certainly not be judged wise by any one.

In other words, why did God adopt so painful a way to redeem man when He might have accomplished it merely by an act of will? But, Anselm argues, since we cannot doubt God's wisdom as we might doubt a man's, we must think of the plan of Redemption taking the form that it did as an objective "desirable to God's love, which infinite power, guided by infinite wisdom, could not accomplish by a simple act of the divine will, an objective by which God could show that He was prepared to pay the great cost and self-sacrifice it involved."

The easy way of merely exercising His infinite power and saying "Let Man be redeemed," much as He had said "Let there be light," would never have served to show *at what personal cost God* was prepared to effect man's redemption as a showing-forth of His love. The hard way was necessary: for otherwise there was no justification for the creation of a race of men who were capable of falling into sin. No good could have come out of the tragedy of human experience, only the undoing of it.

And so we must examine carefully the mode of our Redemption,[18] requiring as it did that God become Incarnate in the world He had created and there subject Himself to many of its laws for man's sake.

The Crucifixion stands as the pivotal point upon which all else depends. All events, and all achievements, acquire their significance only in its light. It was a unique event requiring that

---

[17] Anselm puts these words into the lips of Boso in his *Cur Deus Homo?* Book I, Chapter 6.

[18] The Incarnation: Heb. 10:4-7 speaks first of the body prepared to make the Incarnation *possible,* and then it proceeds to show that because the sacrifice of such creatures as were appointed in the Levitical code were totally inadequate to take away sins, the Incarnation was *necessary.* I can never read this passage without being reminded of Isa. 9:6, "For unto us a child is born, unto us a Son is given...." where the "child born" looks forward to John 1:14, whereas perhaps the "Son *given*" looks forward to John 3:16.

certain circumstances should come about which can be considered from two points of view: First, there are those circumstances which relate to the historical setting, the theater as it were, upon the stage of which the Lord at one particular and appropriate time in history entered into the stream of human affairs and sacrificed Himself. Secondly, there are those which relate to the manner in which His physical death actually came about, circumstances which bear critically upon the nature of Adam's body when he was first created,[19] and therefore upon the kind of physical world which had to be planned for him from the very beginning.

The more I reflect upon the matter, the more convinced I am that if there is meaning to the universe, the key to that meaning is to be found in the birth and death of Jesus Christ, the Second Adam, because the physical world itself was required in order that these two unique events could take place. And these unique events were required that God might by a process of Redemption show forth His love toward an order of beings whose very existence was made dependent upon the creation of just such a physical world. Thus the birth and death of Jesus Christ were not accommodated to a physical order already independently in existence, but quite the reverse. The physical order was deliberately structured to make these two events possible. These events were the *cause* not the *consequence* of creation. They preceded it: as Revelation 13:8 says, Jesus Christ was slain from the foundation of the world.

Moreover, in the course of time, acting according to the predeterminate counsel and foreknowledge of God,[20] it was these same creatures who brought to pass the very event by which they themselves were to be redeemed, having after 4000 years or so of historical development under the guiding hand of God, perfected the cultural setting in which that event was to occur.

---

[19] Directly bearing on this issue is "If Adam Had Not Died," in Vol. V of the Doorway Papers.

[20] Acts 2:23: "Him, being delivered by the determinate counsel and foreknowledge of God, ye have taken, and by wicked hands have crucified and slain." Note that it was not merely by God's foreknowledge but part of His predeterminate counsel. The omnipotence of God in the affairs of men is explored in depth, depending almost entirely upon a very large number of biblical references (over 200 passages are quoted) in "The Omnipotence of God in the Affairs of Men," in Vol. VI of the Doorway Papers. In this study the fact emerges from Scripture that human history, both the good and the bad in it, has been overruled by God for His own purposes to an extent which few of us are probably aware.

The Incarnation and the Crucifixion together are, therefore, the cause of all that is related to the planning of the natural order, and of the creation of man as its most important member. For God's love is not shown forth here in a way which is self-evident so that angels or even animals could understand it merely by witnessing it, but in such a way that only a creature such as man could comprehend it. For this comprehension depends upon a certain kind of spiritual and mental constitution, with the power to see its meaning in the light of personal need, a need which neither the animals nor the angels are aware of. This need does not relate solely to the spirit, for then perhaps the angels would have understood; nor does it relate solely to the body, for then the animals might have been brought within its compass. It relates to a *need* which is both spiritual and physical. It relates to a *death* which is both spiritual and physical, a death of a representative Man, which was not "natural" in the sense that other events in the universe are "natural," but which was necessary in order to abolish the death[21] which all other men now suffer "unnaturally," and in so doing to demonstrate the love of God whose Son became that representative Man.

The death of Jesus Christ was unique — even from the physiological point of view. The uniqueness of it was possible only because of the Virgin Birth. The Virgin Birth was possible only because of the manner of the creation of Adam as a potentially immortal creature out of whom Eve was taken while he was yet in an immortal state. It is important to understand that immortality here means not that Adam could not die, for he did so; but rather that he need not have died if he had maintained the conditions of life originally appointed to him. In another Doorway Paper[22] the significance of taking Eve out of Adam while he was yet unfallen has been carefully explored from the physiological point of view. What emerges from this study is that while Eve partook of the same forbidden fruit as Adam and thus like him became a mortal creature, the poison in one important re-

---

[21] Heb. 2:9: "But we see Jesus, who was made a little lower than the angels for the suffering of death, crowned with glory and honour; for he by the grace of God should taste death for every man," and II Tim. 1:10: "But is now made manifest by the appearing of our Saviour Jesus Christ, who hath abolished death, and hath brought life and immortality to light through the gospel."

[22] The derivation of Eve out of Adam has been made the subject of a special study from the point of view of genetics in "The Nature of the Forbidden Fruit," in Vol. V of the Doorway Papers.

spect affected their bodies in a different way. It poisoned Adam's body, including the seed he carried. Eve's body, however, was so structured by divine appointment that the same corruption did not reach the seed which she carried. The consequence was that in all succeeding generations every woman's seed when naturally fertilized by the male seed has been corrupted by it and this "infection" has resulted in the birth of a *mortal* child. But because of what has been appropriately termed "the continuity of the germ plasm" (here, the still uncorrupted seed of woman), the possibility has always remained that this uncorrupted seed of woman, if brought to life apart from the introduction of the male seed, would lead to the birth of an immortal Child, who would thus have escaped the poison stream of death which has rendered all other men mortal. This is the significance of the term "the seed of the woman," as opposed to "the seed of the man." Yet because Eve was taken out of Adam's body in its unfallen state, her seed was originally part of the uncorrupted seed of Adam whence she herself came, and thus in the final analysis this same seed *was* initially Adam's seed and the Savior a lineal descendant of Adam though escaping Adam's corruption. Such is the wisdom and power of God. The Incarnation was therefore itself possible only because of the way that the genetics and chemistry of human life and procreation have been ordered, this "ordering" being clearly dependent upon the natural order and clearly necessary to make the Incarnation possible. So it came about that the *whole* plan of Redemption was intimately bound up with the created world which herein finds its *raison d'etre*.

In the light of revealed truth, man therefore stands apart from the rest of creation because though he is now a mortal creature and seemingly little different from the rest of the animal world, yet he was not created as such in the beginning. Death is quite natural for other creatures but not for man. And indeed he has always been persuaded that he need not or should not die at all — or that if he must die he will still live on in some other way. The death of a human being has an element of tragedy about it which the death of an animal in old age has not. As for the angels who, in their normal estate, are purely spiritual beings, we do not know what the meaning of "death" to them could be. We do know from Scripture that some angels have sinned. But we have no idea whether it would be possible for God to find some means of redeeming them. To redeem man,

God became Man and not angel,[23] because the process of Redemption required the sacrifice of a life which was like that of the subjects to be redeemed. It is not within our power to conceive of a vicarious sacrifice made on a purely spiritual level by a purely spiritual being which would not at the same time bring about the very cessation of the existence of the one who made it. It had to be possible for God's love to be displayed by a Sacrifice of Himself which would not lead to His own annihilation. The Resurrection of Jesus Christ is an absolutely essential part of His Crucifixion, and it depended entirely upon the fact that it took place within the framework of a physical order of things. The universe as a substantial reality was therefore needed not merely for the initiation of the redemptive act in terms of Crucifixion but also for its completion in the terms of a bodily Resurrection. It is in this sense that I believe the universe has meaning. It has meaning because it was essential to the plan whereby God displayed His love, and because man was the special object of that display. Man becomes the key to the universe, not man in himself but man as the special creature of God's love for whom the physical world is essential to his being.

As explored elsewhere,[24] the death of Jesus Christ also involved certain conditions which demanded crucifixion rather than some other form of legal death. No other kind of death would have satisfied these conditions, for no other form of death would have permitted the Lord to decide when He would dismiss His spirit as a purely voluntary act while at the same time satisfying the legal requirements of the death penalty being imposed. In any other kind of death (poisoning, strangling, drowning, thrusting through), only by a miracle could He have remained alive once the process had been initiated. As it was, it was only by a miracle that He died on the Cross when He did, for He died *on* the Cross but not *because* of it. His death was entirely an act of His own will, and not merely a willing surrender to circumstance. On the Cross He did not simply choose the *time* of dying, which would have been merely to commit suicide — something any man may do. But rather, having power not to die at all, He chose nevertheless to do so, by dismissing

---

[23] Heb. 2:16: "For verily he took not on him the nature of angels; but he took on him the seed of Abraham."

[24] The reasons why no other form of capital punishment would have satisfied the requirements of the Lord's sacrificial death have been examined in "The Unique Relationship Between the First and the Last Adam" in Vol. V of the Doorway Papers. See also "How Did Jesus Die?" in Vol. V.

His life as a man dismisses a servant. He never was, like us, subject to death. He deliberately chose to become so — which no other man can ever do.

This event involved the voluntary surrender — more precisely, the active termination — of a physiologically constituted life process which, unlike the life processes of all other animal forms including that of man as he now is, was not subject to natural death at all. As man now is, the spirit leaves the body when the body can no longer support it. Jesus Christ dismissed His spirit by an act of will that rendered His body thereby inviable. We are subject to death by our fallen nature, He *became* subject to death by an act of will. Had He willed, He might have lived on indefinitely. As it was He submitted to a form of capital punishment but dismissed His life *before* that penalty could take its naturally expected effect.

But because this choice, the choice of living on or of dying, had to be available to Him in order to make His Sacrifice vicarious, it was also required that that for which He substituted must at first have been similarly constituted. Thus the creature upon whom God wished to bestow His grace and to whom He wished to prove His love, had to be so constituted at first as unfallen that the Son of God could truly represent him. Otherwise, He would not have been a properly constituted substitute. The Second Adam, an immortal Creature who need never have died, truly represented the First Adam, an equally immortal creature who need never have died. He thus stood as an exact counterpart of the First Adam, accomplishing for man by an act of will what the First Adam by an act of will failed to do. Unless the Second Adam was physiologically so constituted as to be an immortal creature, He could not have *surrendered* His immortality on man's behalf; but unless the First Adam had once been an immortal creature, the surrender of immortality by the Second Adam would not have been substitutional *for man*. We thus find that the Crucifixion was only possible because it took place within the framework of physical and not merely spiritual life, and we must conclude therefore that the creation of man as a physical and not merely a spiritual being was essential in order to make possible God's plan of Redemption. A purely spiritual human being, some kind of human creature living independently of the physical world, would not have provided God with the "means," the *modus operandi,* of a plan of Redemption which was to serve as a display of His love through an act of Incarnation and Self-sacrifice.

So the First Adam's creation was in such a form that in due time the Second Adam could both represent him perfectly as a substitute and die for him vicariously as a Savior. The demands of the Cross, seen in the light of its total theological context, involved not merely the creation of a certain type of "first man" but also a certain type of physical order in which he could be imbedded, though transcending it. For him was needed a special kind of body, a special kind of mind, and a special kind of spirit. And, in turn there was needed a special kind of total environment for these to operate in. Nor can we isolate this environment from the solar system, nor the solar system from the universe. It is all of a piece, it is a uni-verse we live in, where every thing relates to every other thing and no thing is unnecessary. In a newsletter, recently, one writer said: "Biologists tell us that not a leaf falls in the forest or a raindrop into the sea but that the consequences of each happening must go on for all time and spread through all space." With pure poetic insight Francis Thompson has that wonderful couplet which reads, "Thou canst not stir a flower, without troubling a star." And more prosaically, but nonetheless significantly, we find Sir C. N. Hinshelwood saying:[25]

> It may not be wholly unreasonable to fancy that to almost every element there falls some unique and perhaps indispensible role in the economy of nature.

It is customary to look upon man's body as a burden to him, as though only his spirit had eternal significance. And yet Scripture is very clear in stating that the Crucifixion, by which his eternal destiny was determined, was dependent upon One who sacrificed His *body*. He was made flesh (John 1:14 and I Tim. 3:16) that He might bear our sins in His own *body* on the tree (I Pet. 2:24). We are reconciled now in the *body* of His flesh through death (Col. 1:21, 22), and perfected for ever by the offering of His body (Heb. 10:10). Man is not a spiritual creature who happens to have a body. His body is as much a part of his total being as the Lord's glorious body of His total glory; and man's bodily resurrection is as essential to his completion as the Lord's bodily Resurrection was to His Sacrifice.

---

[25] Hinshelwood, C. N., "Some Aspects of the Chemistry of Hydrocarbons," Presidential address to the Chemical Society, 1948, reported in *Jour. Chem. Soc.*, Pt. I, 1948, p. 531.

For though we have already been re-created in spirit, we still wait to be completed by the adoption of, i.e., the redemption of, the *body* (Rom. 8:25) which is to be refashioned like His glorious body (Phil. 3:21). It is this fact which forces us to look for a vital connection between man and the physical order, and to find in man its ultimate significance.

But the processes of history also have special significance because the Crucifixion could not be merely an isolated event, occurring in some dark age of lawlessness and barbarism, or in some corner of the earth where knowledge of it might filter back into the world only by accident. It was an event which had to be appropriately witnessed and recorded, which had to be performed in an orderly legal way according to an accepted standard of behavior and judgment to which mankind as a whole would give rational assent. It had to occur at a time when the event itself would be sufficiently public (one might say, publicized) that there could never be any doubt about it having happened. It had to come to pass when there was a sufficiently sophisticated and dependable means of communicating the news to a large population that was not merely numerous but fluid, so that word of it would be carried far and wide. It required the existence of a legal code of wide application to a large number of people, so that the "justice" of the event would be comprehensible in the same terms to them all. Roads for travel had to exist and be maintained in safety. A "police force" (the military) had to exist, with sufficient strength to prevent a lawlessness that would quickly have turned the trial into a lynching. A lingua franca was needed which could interpret the record of these events in the light of the Old Testament so that the message would, culturally speaking, be a universal and not merely a Jewish one. These circumstances may have occurred repeatedly since that time and perhaps upon occasion in an even more "effective" way. But it seems almost certain that this was the *first* time the circumstance had occurred. The Roman Empire guaranteed, at least for a short while, a world ideally ordered as a proper setting, both culturally and legally.

Consequently, as we shall try to show, the course of history has been overruled in a way which has not hitherto been observed by any philosopher of history (even those with Christian persuasion) which once again demonstrates what a wealth of insight is sometimes unexpectedly to be found by the serious study of Scripture.

Chapter 2

MAN'S LIFE: SPIRITUAL, INTELLECTUAL, AND PHYSICAL

ALTHOUGH DETERMINED efforts are being made to reduce man to the terms of physics and chemistry, to eliminate all vital forces which could conceivably exist in their own right outside the physical order, to derive consciousness from the inanimate forces of Nature and self-consciousness in turn from consciousness, it appears to me that God by the very act of creation must have introduced something which was not derived from the mere substance which it inhabits, otherwise why speak of creation at all in reference to man? And yet it seems that this created "soul" is so constructed that the physical housing which it inhabits is in some way essential to it. Thus while by the very statement "Let us create man" one must suppose that some essential part of man is created in entire independence of his physical body (though this, too, was created), God saw fit to design a creature who bridged the gap between the purely spiritual and purely physical orders of being. It is this which makes man neither animal nor angel but something of both and having the capacities in part of each.

The uniqueness of man considered as a total spirit-body entity has become increasingly more apparent as the determination to reduce him to the status of a mere animal has gathered momentum. When evolution first became widely popular in its appeal, there was a tendency to fit man into its scheme by emphasizing his purely animal characteristics and largely overlooking his possession of certain other capacities, particularly his capacity for language and for self-consciousness. The whole burden of research tended to be absorbed in the study of bone structure, and the search for fossil remains assumed tremendous importance since it was believed — and popularly still is believed — that such bones could prove man's descent from some purely animal ancestor. Culture was considered to be merely an extension of his strictly animal behavior. It was something only quantitatively different from animal habit, not qualitatively different.

But in the course of time, certain aspects of human culture began to appear in a new light as being uniquely human and not easily, if at all, derivable from some counterpart on a lower scale in the animal world. Two related cultural phenomena were soon freely admitted in this class: the first was the power of creative activity — the ability to make things, to make fire, to make tools, and to make purely artistic objects; and the second was the possession of self-consciousness and with it the power of speech.

Every effort has been made to find the counterparts of these things in the animal world, to find evidence of *self*-consciousness as opposed to mere consciousness, evidence of true language in the propositional sense and not merely in the use of signs, evidence of the creation of weapons and tools and not merely the incidental use of things that lie at hand, and evidence of a conscious striving for beauty in design and not merely instinctive orderliness of construction such as is to be observed in the honeycomb, for instance.

Not only has the search for animal origins for these things so far proved fruitless but in some cases has turned out to be so pointless that, in the case of language for example, the search has been almost abandoned.[26] Yet it is these very things which have constituted those elements of human nature that make man uniquely able to respond to the overtures of God, to enter into fellowship with Him, to worship Him fittingly, and in some measure to think His thoughts after Him.

The study of human physiology has served increasingly to emphasize the fact that man's body constitutes a temple of a very special design such that the unique characteristics and capacities of man, as opposed to the animals, can express themselves. He is equipped with a combination of faculties and functions which operate harmoniously and subserve one another, and which in the event of the failure of any one of them tend to reduce him

---

[26] Langer, Susanne, *Philosophy in a New Key*, Mentor Books, N.Y., 1952, p. 88. Her words are: "The problem is so baffling that it is no longer considered respectable."

not to an animal level but to something far worse. His possession of a central nervous system with capacities and complexities far greater by many orders of magnitude than that to be observed in the most intelligent animals constitutes only one of these. He is equipped with binocular vision combined with manual dexterity and truly opposable thumbs, and with tactile sensitivity that allows his hands to serve as an extension of his mind in a way quite unobserved in any other creature. He has two hands and two feet — appropriate to an erect posture which makes his body capable of maneuvers that are unique. All other creatures have either four hands or four feet; and although this might not appear of very great importance it is actually profoundly so. Man's central nervous system is of such a nature that the destruction of some parts of it does not merely reduce him somewhat so that his behavior approaches more nearly that of other creatures, but rather tends to destroy him entirely — to disorganize his whole being. Animals will recoved from brain operations in which whole sections are rendered inoperative and can in time recover a large number of their former animal capacities, evidently by some process of substitute control in some other part of the brain. Man's brain is so complex that the possibilities of this kind of substitution are virtually absent.

Many purely anatomical features of the human body differ in critical ways from the corresponding structures in other animals. These structures are presumed related in such a way that, superficially, the difference is slight and inconsequential, but in fact the differences are often critical (e.g., in structure of the feet) and essential for the proper functioning of the whole man viewed as a culture bearing creature.[27]

In the development of human organs there are also important differences. The rate of maturing of the animal brain is so fast, relatively, that the animal's period of plasticity is enormously reduced when compared with the long span of maturing and adolescence in man. In most animals plasticity remains for only

[27] The differences between man and other animals, physiologically speaking, are far greater than is popularly supposed. Standard textbooks of comparative anatomy tend to obscure the fact by emphasizing the homologues, since current theories of animal ancestry render these of more immediate interest. But actually the differences are so numerous and so important that a separate Doorway Paper, "Is Man An Animal?" (Part V of *Evolution or Creation?* which is Vol. IV of this series) examines the matter, with quotations and graphs and charts and tables from a very large number of authoritative sources — as a corrective against current popular assumptions.

a few months or perhaps a year. In man it is normally 15 to 20 years, and by proper cultivation it may last up to 50 years. Thus it is always possible for a human being to relearn and therefore to change in nature. In animals this is never true. In human beings the period of fertility, especially in the female, is limited in such a way that children are not likely to be born before they can be cared for in the first few critical years nor after the mother has reached such an age that she can no longer care for them to maturity. Most animals are on their own within a few months and consequently the female may continue to be fertile until within a few months of the terminus of her normal life span. But this extremely long and slow process of coming to maturity in man is largely responsible for allowing him to develop with the unique capacities that he enjoys, and it ultimately relates to his ability to respond to the overtures of God. As men and women grow older and begin to approach the stage of mental set which the animals reach in so much shorter a time, they begin to find it more and more difficult to respond to God unless they already have entered into true fellowship with Him. This in itself is evidence that the slow maturing process in humankind is a gracious provision by God, making more possible the end for which man was created in the beginning.

The possession of self-consciousness which very early enables a growing child to see himself in relation to those of his own family and to the community at large provides him with the experimental base upon which to perceive his possible relationship to God as His child, and to other Christians in the fellowship of a brotherhood. Although animals clearly recognize their own kind and distinguish them from those creatures which are of another species, and although for a season there is a sense of "family" when the young are being raised, it is fairly clear that family relationships in this sense are not merely allowed to lapse when the young can shift for themselves, but are actually destroyed, the young being thereafter treated as competitors and intruders.[28] The bonds of blood relationship (that is to say, all family bonds except those of mating) are loosely held within a few months and then rejected entirely. If it should be argued that this cannot be applied to man because he is helpless for so long a period, the answer is surely that this helplessness is part

---

[28] This aspect of animal behavior has been studied and written about in a quite fascinating and most informative way by Konrad Lorenz in a most readable work entitled *On Aggression*, Bantam Books, N.Y., 1967, 306 pp.

of the economy of God whereby He has established family bonds for man in an entirely new way.

Thus one can see that the uniqueness of human nature, of human capacity, and of human relationships is in each case not a uniqueness of a purely spiritual kind that might have originated by some entirely cultural process, but is dependent upon the kind of anatomy and physiology that human beings have. Man is a unique body-spirit entity, and the uniqueness of his body is understandable in terms of the uniqueness of his spirit, and the uniqueness of his spirit in the terms of the uniqueness of his relationship among other created beings to God. And that this physiological uniqueness stems from spiritual integrity is surely borne out by the fact that when the spirit has been degraded, the body no longer serves as a beautifully organized instrument for survival — as is everywhere to be seen otherwise in nature — but as a faulty, inefficient, diseased agent of destructiveness. Clearly it was intended to serve the higher purpose.

It must always be borne in mind that if man was to be created with a potential for saintliness when surrendered to the Spirit of God, this same potential must exist for devilishness when surrendered to Satan. There is none of the uniformity of animal behavior about man. He has capacities for extremes which in healthy animals are quite unknown. This was an inevitable consequence for a creature capable of loving God, as we know man can do. He is capable of passionate devotion, but not always to the good. His powers of dedication are tremendous, and therefore all the more disastrous if wrongly directed. Thus the course of history is full of surprises, of deeds of extraordinary nobility and deeds of appalling savagery.[29] And those who have shown themselves capable of such things often did not seem distinguishable in prospect, but only afterwards.

Man's nature tends either up or down, depending upon the grace of God. And hence, as a precaution, God has so constituted him that he is able to create from within himself, even in his fallen estate, certain correctives which provide a measure of restraint to the ravaging tendencies of his fallen nature. These correctives may be examined under two headings: Civilization

---

[29] The potential of man for good and for evil has been set forth in "The Fall Was Down" (Part I of Vol. III of the Doorway Papers), where it is shown that in every man there is the capability of appalling wickedness that only accidents of birthplace and social environment prevent from being realized. The importance of culture as a restrainer of human wickedness is here examined.

and Culture. It is important to establish meanings for these terms that will allow some precision in the discussion of them. For the sake of clarity in the present context, we define "civilization" *as the mechanics of a culture* which allow a society to eat, live, multiply, and have dominion over the immediate environment; and we define "culture" *as the "spirit" of a civilization,* its value system and its "artistic" refinement and elaboration — using art in the widest sense as embellishment beyond mere utilitarianism. In a manner of speaking, civilization is the "body" and culture the "spirit," and both are required to make life meaningful and worthwhile. They do not necessarily coincide. A very wealthy and affluent society can become "uncultured" for all its high civilization, and a primitive people whose civilization is at a bare subsistence level can nevertheless be highly cultured in their social behavior patterns and "genteel" in their own way. Ideally, the two should go together, each interacting with the other for good. A man should have a sufficient margin of survival that he can appreciate the song of a bird or a tree blown in the wind, but some societies have been reduced to such a low level by the struggle to keep body and soul together that they have not survived at all. Yet the reverse can happen, too. There have been societies which enjoyed almost total immunity from the struggle to survive because of the lushness and temperateness of their environment. Yet they were in a state of chronic warfare so disruptive of settled and peaceful existence that the arts were in danger of almost total disappearance.

As Christians we have often tended to equate culture with "worldliness." This is a mistake. Culture is what curbs the less pleasant aspects of human nature — including bad manners, for instance. By culture, base impulses and motives, if not "virtuously" suppressed, are at least hypocritically concealed. In day-to-day social relations such suppression, and even such concealment, is desirable. If we have disrespect for someone, it is not necessarily a good thing to make our disrespect obvious merely on the grounds that this is being more honest. Completely frank people are not so much to be praised for their fearless honesty as they are to be pitied for their lack of self-control. Ideally, civilization provides man with the means to cultivate what remains of the finer and more creative side of his life by relieving him of the consuming problem of getting food and shelter. But culture is what directs the energies thus set free into useful, helpful, and constructive channels. It does not so much *produce good* as it does open the way for good to be done by suppressing or discouraging the evil propensities in human nature. In the absence of culture, man may be simply a barbarian, and a barbarian society does not permit the free development and expression of man's potential in body, mind, and spirit. It reduces him to an animal level where mere survival is paramount.

Man does indeed need to survive; he does have a body that demands preservation and care, but he also has a spirit that refuses to have its aspirations and its fears ignored. He has, besides a body and a spirit, a *mind*. He lives in three realms at once; in the physical world to which he must to some extent conform if he is to survive, in a realm that is spiritual where he also seeks to come to terms with "spirit forces" and "powers" rather than physical things, and in a world of thought. His spiritual life, his mental life, and his corporeal existence may each be treated separately. The religious man may feel keenly about spiritual things and live in hope or fear of the hereafter with or without a sense of worthiness, and yet do very little thinking in the sense that a philosopher thinks about things dispassionately. The life of the spirit and of the mind are not to be confused. Philosophers may be profound in their thinking, yet profoundly unreligious or unconcerned about spiritual matters, just as spiritual people may be quite unresponsive to philosophical ideas.[30] Faith and reason are often diametrically opposed. One may have either — or neither; for there are men whose whole life is animal in its orientation, caring neither for the musings of the philosopher nor the aspirations of the saint.

But there is no question that the whole man is at his best

---

[30] While it is important to distinguish between the mental life and the spiritual life of man, there is a further division which has not been made in the present paper in order to avoid complicating the subject matter more. Whenever we are dealing with the "spiritual" history of mankind, it is well to recognize that there is a difference between a man's *spiritual* life (as the Christian understands it) and his *religious* life. From the scriptural point of view every man has something of a religious life but a spiritual life does not appear until a man is born again. This distinction is quite fundamental and when properly recognized provides an insight into some remarkable passages of Scripture which have to do with the symbolism rigorously adhered to in both the Old and the New Testaments, in connection with Israel's history. A Doorway Paper "Three Trees: And Israel's History" (Part II of *Biblical Studies: I,* Doorway Papers Vol. VI), shows how remarkably consistent the Bible has been throughout in treating of Israel's national, religious and spiritual history under the symbolism of the vine, the fig tree, and the olive, respectively.

when each area of his life, his bodily needs, his mental capacity, and his spiritual awareness, are allowed to balance one another and grow together to maturity. And what I wish to show is that in a remarkable way God has taken care to see that these three facets of man's needs, as man, are each properly nourished and preserved so that the effects of the Fall may be always held in check and man never allowed to completely destroy himself while God has yet some purpose to work out with respect to him and while history thus pursues its course.

Man has a spiritual, a physical, and an intellectual life, each of which interacts with the other, yet each of which may usefully be considered as a separate entity. Scripture has provided us with an insight into the manner in which God has divided the responsibility for each of these three aspects of human potential, allocating to the three sons of Noah, Shem, Ham and Japheth, the responsibility for man's spiritual welfare, physical well-being, and intellectual development, respectively. And the manner in which each has fulfilled his task and has contributed to the whole provides the framework of history, which forms an essential part of this paper.

Chapter 3

MAN'S POTENTIAL:
IN SHEM, HAM, AND JAPHETH

HUGH DRYDEN, writing on "The Scientist in Contemporary Life,"[31] remarked: "Man's life at its fullest is a trinity of activity — physical, mental, and spiritual." Dryden was not speaking of the theological concept of man as a trichotomy of body, soul and spirit; and it is important in the present context to observe the distinction quite clearly. If in his article he were concerning himself with the concept of "soul," he would have included it under the heading of man's *spiritual* nature, not his intellectual capacity. What he is seeking to point out is that there are three areas of human involvement which must all be taken into account and nurtured if man is to develop his personality to the full. He must live in the sense of surviving as a viable entity, which means food and warmth and shelter and so forth. He must be allowed to stretch his mind and explore with his intellect whatever attracts his attention, which means mental stimulation and challenge. And he must not overlook the fact that there is a spiritual side to his nature which is not satisfied either by bread alone nor by intellectual exercise or rational argument, but something which transcends them both. This side of his total being seems to be somewhere within both body and mind, and yet can be entirely contrary to the interests of either. A healthy body and a healthy mind do not guarantee, but may contribute to, spiritual well-being. It is not solely a matter of emotions and yet it must involve the emotions to be satisfying. For most men it is best described under the general heading of

---

[31] Dryden, Hugh, "The Scientist in Contemporary Life," *Science*, 120 (1954): 1054.

248

Religion, a vague but comprehensive term that can mean almost anything or nothing, yet is normally concerned neither with man's body nor with his mind, but with what is most simply described as his soul.

In a similar vein, Viktor E. Frankl wrote,[32] "Man lives in three dimensions: the somatic (physical, i.e., bodily), the mental, and the spiritual." The thought behind both these quotations can be expressed in innumerable ways. While the life that an individual lives in these three realms can be mapped discreetly for purposes of analysis, they are seldom distinguished in everyday experience. But man *does* have a capacity for physical life, for mental life, and for spiritual life. And as a result of these capacities has elaborated culture in three directions: He has developed technology to satisfy his bodily needs, philosophy to organize and elaborate his mental life, and religion to provide for his spiritual life.

Research into the factors which influence personality development has shown that whenever these three "needs" are appropriately cultivated, character develops in a normal and healthy way. But when one of them is neglected or denied the individual becomes somehow unbalanced. It would be wrong to suppose that, as man is constituted at present, any one of these three "capacities" is more important than the other. The overly spiritual man is no more a balanced person than the overly sensual. It may seem that he would be a preferred type, but experience shows that the mystic can be quite as unbearable at close range as the "trousered ape" (to use Lewis' phrase). Neither does the purely intellectual prove to be any more desirable — at close quarters. It is difficult to know which is most unpleasant, spiritual or intellectual pride, but both can be insufferable. In a curious way the trousered ape, boorish and uncultured as he is, may be the least unbearable, if one has a choice. But virtually every distortion or abnormality of character can be equated with imbalance in one of these three directions.

Thus as an individual, man can live in any one of the three realms almost to the exclusion of the other two with virtually no awareness of his own loss. He can become almost entirely sensual, or almost entirely intellectual, or almost entirely a mystic. In the first case he is likely to be looked upon as crude, in short, an animal dedicated to his own physical comforts. In the second

---

[32] Frankl, Viktor E., quoted in *The Digest of Neurology and Psychology.* (Institute of Living, Hartford, Conn.) Feb., 1955, p. 74.

case he is likely to be thought of as impractical, a "brain." In the third case he is likely to be looked upon as other-worldly, a man whose feet are not on the ground. Of course, there are many combinations, though there are limits to these. There may be a man whose animal tastes are strongly defined and yet who has a keen mind. Such a man "succeeds" in the worldly sense of the term. He is a clever creature. On the other hand, the man who is both a "brain" and spiritually inclined is apt to be a theological type, a success in his chosen field. But a combination of the animal and the spiritual is hard to conceive; the bridge between the spiritual and the physical lies in the intellect, which can be joined to either of the other two or can unite them all.

As with the individual, so with a society, a culture, or a nation as a whole: when the "body," the "mind," and the "spirit" of a people receive equal encouragement and cultivation, the society enjoys a measure of health and well-being which is not only reflected in a higher level of creative activity but in a reduction of the evil effects of the Fall. By contrast when any one of these three components dominates (or is seriously neglected) the effects of sin in human nature become in some way aggravated. This is particularly clear when a society becomes dedicated to the satisfying of its animal instincts, the things of its "body." It ends up by degenerating; it becomes barbaric. It is not quite so obviously detrimental when a society turns "intellectual" to the exclusion of all else, and we probably have little to go on from a study of history. The Golden Age of the Greek philosophers may be a case in part, and at times "intellectuals" have possibly dominated life in India. There is little question that such societies do not or cannot survive for long. The needs of the body must be recognized, and these needs can only be ignored by the few if they are in a position to demand that the many take care of the matter for them. Intellectual elites survive only while a lower class is willing to serve their need, and history shows that human beings will not perform this kind of service indefinitely.

Nor does a purely spiritual society do very well, either. Not a few such experiments have been made, retreats from the world, cloisterings in out-of-the-way places. (The corruption which has soon set in has appalled even the acolytes themselves after a while.) The greatest danger has been spiritual pride, and spiritual pride is surely even more disastrous to man's total health than intellectual pride is, for it has no self-correctives.

What is true of the individual, history therefore has shown to be true of whole cultures. And nations also have personalities. Whether this is genetically determined or not is a matter of debate. There are those who argue strongly against this concept as food for racists. Nevertheless the existence of Modal Personality, the idea that there is a recognizable English, French, or Chinese stereotype, can be forcibly argued. I am convinced that God not only foresaw the consequences of such potentially one-sided emphasis as we may observe in individuals, but foresaw also that mankind as a whole would always be tending in the same direction. This was a foreseeable part of the consequences of the Fall, as the world was peopled and history ran its course.

And I believe that God took special steps to control this tendency while the human experiment was being conducted. God's object was to prevent society from becoming completely oriented toward one to the exclusion of the other two, or even two things to the exclusion of the third. And my belief is that He did this by allotting to each of the three sons of Noah a specific "responsibility" for human welfare, a responsibility which was to belong not merely to Shem, Ham, and Japheth as individuals, but to their descendants, the Semites, the Hamitic peoples, and the Japhethites.[33] To Ham was allotted responsibility for man's physical well-being, the provision of a sufficient margin of dominion over the physical world to set him free from the constant need to fend against hunger, cold, heat, storm, disease, and other challenges: this margin of safety to leave him with some free energies. To Japheth was allotted the responsibility for the full development and full exploration of man's mental capacities, a kind of intellectual dominion. And to Shem was allotted responsibility for man's spiritual development: out of the family of Shem were to arise in a unique way men who would be concerned with man's religious needs, and some of these men founded *false* religions.

Out of the family of Ham have arisen, as can be shown from a wealth of evidence, the producers of the world's technology, a technology catering to and guaranteeing man's mastery of the physical world. From the descendants of Japheth, equated with-

---

[33] This subject has been explored in two other Doorway Papers which contribute to the present volume, the three being complementary: namely, Part I, "The Part Played by Shem, Ham and Japheth in Subsequent World History," and Part IV, "The Technology of Hamitic People," the latter being a study of some 200 inventions and techniques and processes which are basic to the modern world and which were originated by Hamitic people.

out much controversy with the Indo-European peoples, have arisen the individuals and groups who have contributed uniquely to man's intellectual needs. And certainly spiritual leadership has come from the Semites. Thus the contribution of Ham has been a technological one, of Japheth an intellectual one, and of Shem a spiritual one. When Japheth applied his philosophical genius to the technology of Hamitic peoples, a technology to which he had, up till the 14th or 15th century, contributed virtually *nothing*, there arose that new phenomenon of human creativeness, science. For science is, after all, philosophy applied to technology. Similarly, when the "Gentiles" entered into "the tents of Shem" to assume for a time a dual responsibility in history, then in a new way they applied their philosophical bent to the religious truth which they inherited from Shem, and theology arose. For theology is, after all, philosophy applied to spiritual truth.

Thus each contributed to the whole of man's capacity and in so far as they *have* each done so in a balanced way and *whenever* they have done so, tremendous advances in culture and civilization have resulted. This was true in the very beginning when the evidence shows that Shem, Ham, and Japheth were still together, and it perhaps accounts for the tremendous speed with which civilization developed in the earliest period in the Middle East. It is possible that it accounts for several other notable periods of advance in Europe and in England, and even more dramatically in the New World. But whenever any one of the three contributions fails, then society is impoverished, the effects of sin become more and more manifest and terrifying, the great strides forward in civilization begin in some strange way to bog down just when least expected to — often "unaccountably." And upon a number of occasions in the past an almost total eclipse of the culture has ensued.

Revival is not always merely spiritual. It may be intellectual, too. In some circumstances the physical side of man's life has been so badly neglected that a frightful poverty has resulted and the consequent desperately small margin of survival (characteristic of some primitive cultures of recent times which have recollections of much happier days) contributes to the decay of the other capacities as well. Revival in intellectual life and revival in spiritual life are both apt to be observed anew when the burden of physical life has also been eased.

A society strong only in any two areas can, however, be unexpectedly weak when attacked by a society which is strong in the third area. For example, technical superiority overwhelmed the Central American civilizations, who could not save their religiously oriented culture when attacked by the more materially minded Spaniards. But sometimes it seems as though a people with mental vigor can bring to nought the attacks of otherwise overwhelming physical superiority.

The principle here is recognized in the New Testament, for it is not recommended that man be offered the Gospel so long as he can barely keep body and soul together. The Lord fed men first. But the temptation for man now to fulfill the easier part of this twofold responsibility is great indeed, and social service ministering to the body all too easily overshadows the spiritual ministry. And I think, if a search is made, evidence will appear in the Gospels that the Lord was most careful to meet man on the level of his mind as well. He was always willing to reason with man, and Peter encourages us to have "reasons" for our faith. Paul speaks of the importance of the renewing of the mind (Rom. 12:1) and assures us that soundness of mind is part of Christian experience (II Tim. 1:4). The Epistle to the Romans is surely an example of the application of the intellect to spiritual truth, and I think it is worthy of note that it was Paul who was called upon to write it. For although Paul was strictly of the family of Shem and might therefore be supposed to have preeminently spiritual rather than intellectual insight, he was separated from his own people and made an apostle to the Gentiles, adopting a Japhetic language in which to cast the Christian theology he was guided to formulate.

Nations have personalities, by which I mean that for reasons which are to some extent identifiable, groups of people viewed as societies, nations, and even as racial stocks, develop certain characteristic temperaments and ways of viewing things, because of a shared history, a shared cultural background, and most important of all, a shared language.

That nations do have personalities will be admitted readily enough when it is made clear that by this we do not mean to imply any superiority: only that specific groups of people have contributed uniquely to the total cultural wealth of the world, each in an identifiable way, and that this contribution has been a kind of natural result of what seems to be a peculiar bent of the people as a whole. Differences of contribution cannot be converted into superiorities of contribution. In so far as national character leans in one direction or the other, it may be superior or otherwise in some particular circumstance. For example, stubbornness is probably useful in a pioneering people who must battle against overwhelming odds, and a nation with a tendency towards stubbornness may be specially suited to a pioneering role. Again, a highly inventive and practical people may be best for one situation, whereas a philosophically minded people may be better for another. Sometimes patience is a weakness, sometimes a strength. Much depends upon the demands of the environment which thus tends to favor some and disfavor others, and so, acting as a kind of cultural selective pressure, it tends to bring about a social milieu in which children grow up to be adults with particular bents in one nation and different bents in another.

Thus arise not superiorities so much as differences in modal personality. It enables one to speak of the typical American, Canadian, Frenchman, Indian, or Chinese. Such "stereotypes" do exist, though identifying them with sufficient precision to be able to write a specification is often very difficult. It is equally difficult to write down a precise description of facial type, the face of a Chinese as opposed to that of a Scotsman, for example. All descriptive terms that have been thought up have proved quite inadequate, since one can find Welshmen who fit the description of the Chinese, and even Ainu who perfectly fit the Scotsman's description. Those who have studied this question of racial type, physiologically viewed, know the truth of this only too well. And yet for all this, one can tell a Chinese from a Scotsman at a glance. Personality types, i.e., modal personality types, are even harder to state precisely, yet there is no doubt that people who share a language and a culture and an environment and a history do develop to a large extent the same attitudes, mannerisms, and ways of speaking.

One *very* important factor in this process is language, and language has been held to be one of the most specific barriers to the breakdown of national character that exists.[34] The cultural dialogue in Canada between the English and the French segments of the population is an excellent illustration, for there is

---

[34] Kroeber, A. L., *Anthropology*, Harcourt Brace, N.Y., 1948, p. 221. In their book *Introducing Social Change*, C. M. Arensberg and A. H. Niehoff (Alpine, Chicago, 1966, p. 30) remark in this connection, "A language is inextricably linked to all aspects of a Culture. Nothing more clearly distinguishes one culture from another than its language."

a real difference between the sentiments and attitudes toward many aspects of daily life between the English and the French, who nevertheless share the same environment. So important is language that the French people in Canada who have felt their language threatened, have felt their very *selves* to be threatened. Language forms a vehicle of thought, and it is questionable whether thought is possible without language. And since thought is the mainspring of action except where emotion overrules it, language becomes a fundamental factor in action. As a people speak, so they think; as they think, so they act: in this order. We learn to speak *before* we learn to think about things in any depth; not, be it noted, before we feel about things but before we reflect upon them. Helen Keller, who certainly could claim to have a profound knowledge, held that a wordless thought was impossible.[35]

Thus if we assume that God allotted to each of the three families of Noah a growing diversity of speech, diversity which was at first scarcely observable but continually widened the gap between the three families, it would be a simple matter for Him providentially to bring into being three families of man, each of whom had a World View that increasingly directed their energies differently. This, I suggest, is exactly what happened. Although we suppose that all the languages of man were at one time rooted in a single stock, it was a stock that was capable of developing into three distinct "families" now clearly recognized as such in two of its branches, the Semitic and the Indo-European. That there is some justification for grouping all other languages than these into a one-time single family is explored in another Doorway Paper.[36] To my mind, the evidence is quite substantial and of such a nature as to suggest that within the Hamitic family there existed something which has not been found in the Semitic or Japhetic families, namely, a strong tendency towards fragmen-

---

[35] The editor of her biography, John A. Macy, wrote: "The ordinary man will never be rid of the fallacy that words obey thought, that one thinks first and phrases afterwards" (*The Story of My Life*, Grosset & Dunlap, N.Y., 1904, p. 419). The crucial importance of language to man is explored in "Who Taught Adam to Speak?" (Part VI of Doorway Papers Vol. II). The subject is a fascinating one and remarkably few people are aware of what has been said on the subject of the origin of this unique human faculty during recent times.

[36] The possibility that all languages known to man have been derived from a single basic language is examined in some detail in "The Confusion of Languages" (Part I in Doorway Papers Vol. VI).

tation. The Semitic family is still, after all these years, easily identifiable as such. The same is true of the Japhetic or Indo-European family of languages.

The only thing that can be said with certainty about the Hamitic family of languages is that they share in common a clear difference in structure and in "World-View" from each other from either the Semitic or Indo-European families. Whether one would accept them as a single family, Hamitic in origin, depends on whether one believes that the Table of Nations in Genesis 10 is describing the origin of the *whole* population of the world as I do, or that it sets forth merely some segments known to the writer in his own day to be actually related or at least near neighbors. Personally, I am quite convinced that the object of Genesis 10 is to contribute towards a philosophy of history which is implicit in the rest of Scripture by showing how the human race was finally divided up. And while the evidence for my belief in this respect has been set forth at considerable length in another Doorway Paper (documented from over 200 sources), it still will not convince those who take a much more limited view of the Table of Nations.[37]

So then, for the sake of discussion and not without reason, we can assume that there are three families of man and that they are still definable. And having made this assumption, the contribution that each family has made to the sum total of human civilization and culture is also identifiable. The *order* in which they spread out from the central Cradle of Civilized Man in the Middle East, and the *way* in which they went out, are both matters of some importance in the light of subsequent history.[38] The biblical record takes cognizance of, and may indeed account in a way for both.

The evidence that from the family of Japheth have arisen the great philosophical systems so characteristic of Western Cultures is overwhelming, whether we study the history of India,

---

[37] An extended analysis of the tenth chapter of Genesis has been undertaken in Part II, "A Study of the Names in Genesis 10," in which an attempt has been made to show that this really is a comprehensive Table of Nations covering the population of the whole world and not merely the nations surrounding Israel with whom they were personally acquainted.

[38] "Fossil Man and the Genesis Record" (see Doorway Papers Vol. II) is a study of the distribution of these remains and the light they throw upon the spread of Noah's family throughout the whole world after the Flood. In this study, evidence is presented to show that the world's first settlements were always established by members of the family of Ham, and not by either Shemites or Japhethites.

the Greek or Roman world, or the rest of Europe in later times. Here we find the roots of philosophy. We do not find these roots in Africa or China or the New World. This aspect of the subject has been explored in depth by many historians and a large part of the evidence has been accumulated in a Magnum Opus by the author which he hopes one day to publish.

The religious contribution of the family of Shem is not difficult to document. The false religions of the world, taking the word "religion" to mean man's attempt to relate himself to the supernatural and to make preparation for the hereafter, have all originated from a Middle East prototype that was entirely Babylonian (i.e., Semitic) in origin. Judaism and Islam likewise sprang out of Shem — as did Christianity. Everywhere else religion has been very largely of a highly practical nature with very practical intentions: the bringing of rain, the defeat of one's enemies, the obtaining of personal success, and so forth. Religion in the sense of aspiration after holiness or the presence of the gods is not the objective of native religions. Native religious practices are much more earthy in the nature of a contract between near-equals. This subject, too, is explored in greater depth in one of the Doorway Papers[39] and much more extensively in the Magnum Opus referred to previously. It is sometimes difficult to distinguish between "practical wisdom" that is characteristic of Confucianism and much of the so-called religious literature of the ancient South American cultures, which is more "canny" than spiritual. Certainly Judaism, Christianity, and Islam are Semitic in origin. And anyone who will study, even if with some measure of skepticism, the text of Hislop's *The Two Babylons*,[40] will realize that paganism is similarly Semitic in origin, being a corruption of the truth that was once the preserve of the family of Shem.

The contribution of the family of Ham, always bearing in mind that I am using the term in its biblical sense, is tremendous. It is essentially technological. It is safe to say, I think, that until about 450 years ago neither Semites nor Indo-Europeans had contributed a single basic invention or material or process or food or product of any kind to the world's civilization. Of a veritable host of writers who have in recent years been studying

[39] On the native concept of "contract" between God and man, see "Nature as Part of the Kingdom of God" (Part II in Doorway Papers Vol. III).

[40] Hislop, Alexander, *The Two Babylons*, Loizeaux Bros., N.Y., 1953, 330 pp., ill.

the origins of our technology in some detail, not one that I know of has been able to credit to us anything of importance with the sole possible exception of the invention of the windmill. The statement sounds so unbelievable to anyone who has not had the opportunity of reviewing the evidence for themselves that one is tempted to try and support it on the spot. The reader will find a very substantial collection, fully documented, of brief histories of some 200 or more basic inventions attributable to the Hamitic people, from whom we borrowed them without acknowledging the debt, in another Doorway Paper.[41]

It appears that God had a clear objective in view in thus dealing with the family of Noah. In order to open up the world for human habitation, God appears to have thrust out from the Center the members of one family, the Hamites, who were peculiarly fitted as pioneers by reason of their highly practical nature. Wherever they went, they seem to have had a remarkable skill in at once recognizing and seizing upon the immediate raw materials of their environment which would best serve for food, clothing, weapons, and shelter essential for survival.[42] There are some extraordinary examples of native ingenuity under circumstances in which it might be thought human survival would be

---

[41] Part IV of this volume, "The Technology of Hamitic People."

[42] In his latest work, *The Savage Mind,* Weidenfeld and Nicolson, London, 1966, p. 3, Claude Levi-Strauss, the French social anthropologist, has a series of quotations from various sources which give some indication of why these Hamitic people succeeded in doing so much more with their environment than the far less practically minded Japhetic people. Speaking of the Hawaiians, he writes, "These native Hawaiians' utilization of their available natural assets was well-nigh complete — infinitely more so than that of the present commercial era which ruthlessly exploits the few things that are financially profitable for the time being, neglecting and often obliterating the rest." Speaking of the natives of Cape York Peninsula in North Australia, he wrote: "The natives are acutely aware of the characteristic trees, underscrub, and grasses of each distinct 'association area,' using this term in its ecological sense. They are able to list in detail and without hesitation, the characteristic tree in each, and able to record the string, resin, grasses, and other products used in material culture, which they obtain from each association, as well as the mammals and birds characteristic of each habitat" (p. 45). He concludes (p. 45) by saying that this intense and detailed knowledge of the available resources of the habitat is common to native people the world over.

A truly extraordinary illustration of this thoroughness in exploiting the environment is to be found in an article on the Indians of the Sonoran Desert by Macy H. Lapham, entitled, "The Desert Storehouse," *Sci. Monthly,* June, 1948, pp. 451f. A summary of his paper will be found in Part IV of this volume, "The Technology of Hamitic People."

impossible, particularly in desert and Arctic conditions. The price paid for this pioneering effort at first was some measure of physical and cultural degeneration. Nevertheless wherever the Hamites went, they ultimately effected permanent settlements and more or less established their dominion over the earth. Centuries later Japhethites followed them at a more leisurely pace, taking with them cultural refinements which ultimately led to the emergence of far higher civilizations. These refinements were not of the ingenious kind but rather with those aspects of culture which could never have survived had the way to survival not already been opened up for them by the Hamites who preceded them. Man's physical and mental life were now secure.

It appears that the world in pre-Flood times shared a measure of spiritual truth which was presumably revealed at the very beginning but had increasingly become corrupted due to man's sinful disposition and his tendency to worship what he himself creates. At the time of the Flood, it may have been true that Noah was the only man left with any measure of purity of faith and spiritual understanding. One gathers from Genesis 9 that Shem shared more of his father's spiritual insight and love of God than either Japheth or Ham, and Shem's godly disposition seems to be the source from which arose the subsequent stream of spiritual insight that remained after the Flood. However, by the time of Abraham this stream had narrowed down almost to one man, and God called Abraham out and took him under His wing in a special way. He prospered him until his family was enlarged and the reservoir of his own spiritual understanding increased. In due course this family grew to be a nation, and this nation was welded into a self-conscious people by the bitterness of their experience in Egypt and the wonders of their redemption out of it. This people was then brought into a land capable of giving them physical security, once it was subdued. And there, by a succession of revelations brought to them through a line of prophets specially commissioned, the light which had almost died out was formalized, written down, and guaranteed for posterity in the Old Testament.[43]

---

[43] A remarkable little book entitled *The Philosophy of the Plan of Salvation* was published by James B. Walker in 1885 (Walden & Stowe, N.Y., 276 pp). The author shows the rationale of God's dealings with Israel from the call of Abraham to the coming of the Messiah. He underscores the fact that God's dealings with Israel were guaranteed to bring about the formation of a nation which was to stand in a pagan world as a testimony to the

If we briefly summarize the historical process, it is clear that God then took steps to complete the revelation of Himself to mankind through His people by sending His own Son to be their King, in order that He might set them at the head of the nations as the spiritual leaders of the world, had they been willing.

We cannot tell what might have happened if they had risen to the call and accepted their Messiah. Perhaps the millennium would have followed, a period of cultural achievement, the nadir of civilization that would have revealed the full potential of human nature in the cooperative effort of Shem, Ham, and Japheth together. But, as Noah predicted, descendants of Shem defaulted and Japheth took over part of the responsibility which was initially allocated to them.[44] The result has been a period referred properly to as "the times of the Gentiles," since, as it happens, in Genesis 10 the children of Japheth are actually identified as "the Gentiles." But this period, as I read Scripture, is a special period, a kind of parenthesis which will be concluded when the Messiah returns again to assume His rightful position over the family of Shem, and Shem recovers his originally appointed position within the family of nations.

I believe Scripture is full of this threefold division. As we have explored elsewhere,[45] Abraham had three wives, a Semite, a Hamite, and a Japhethite; there are three Gospels written specifically, one each for Shem, Ham, and Japheth respectively, that is, Matthew, Mark and Luke; three "groups" came seeking Jesus in a special way, first the shepherds (Shemites), the Wise Men (Hamites), and finally "certain Greeks" (Japhethites); in the Crucifixion Shem, Ham, and Japheth joined hands, Shem as the instigator, Ham in the transport of the Cross (Mark 15:21), and

Oneness of God amidst the polytheism of the Old World. The book is certainly worth acquiring, though difficult to obtain now.

[44] Gen. 9:26-27: And Noah said, "Blessed be the Lord God of Shem; and Canaan shall be his servant. God shall enlarge Japheth, and he shall dwell in the tents of Shem; and Canaan shall be his servant." It appears that the phrase "he shall dwell in the tents of Shem" quite possibly means he shall assume for a season the rightful position of Shem, this phrase being rather analogous to our "sitting in the seat of." It is noteworthy that in the Authorized Version the children of Japheth as listed in Genesis 10 are identified as "the Gentiles," which at once brings to mind the New Testament circumstance in which Jerusalem was to be "trodden down by the Gentiles" until their time was fulfilled (Luke 21:24).

[45] This threefold division of the family of man as recognized throughout Scripture is elaborated upon in Part I, "The Part Played By Shem, Ham and Japheth in Subsequent World History."

Japheth in the execution. Even in Acts the Gospel was preached first to Shem, then by a strange circumstance to one who belonged to the family of Ham (the Ethiopian eunuch), and finally to the family of Japheth. All this is surely more than coincidence, and there are other such triads.

As we have already seen, the Fall of man enters the overall picture as an essential part of God's plan to reveal His true character by a redemptive act. While this process of education, this demonstration to mankind of His love was being worked out through history, it was essential that the effects of the Fall be held in check. Without the restraint of civilization and culture, the wickedness of man would have known no limit and the world would become a scene of barbarism totally destructive of anything in human nature that might have provided a context for the grace of God. Imagine for one moment what would have been the consequence at the time of our Lord's appearing if the whole world was a morass of unrelieved wickedness and cruelty, without order, without law, without restraint upon human nature — every man a monster of iniquity. It is not an impossible situation to conceive. The Incarnation would manifestly have been ineffective; there would have been no context for the Cross, nor even words capable of explaining what God meant by it in terms of His love.

Thus for the conducting of the divine plan, it was essential that in some way man should be civilized; and the means whereby God ensured this would happen seems to me to have been set forth in Scripture implicitly by reference to the circumstances of the emergence of three families equipped for and appointed to three specific kinds of contribution. In the narrower sense of the term this, as I see it, is the framework of history, and while it is true that racial and cultural mixture have both taken place on a global scale it is still possible to sort out these threads and see the hand of God. It is not true to say that all the descendants of Shem have been wholly absorbed with a religious World View. And certainly the Japhethites have not all been philosophers. Yet it *is* true that from Shem sprang the great monotheistic faiths and from Japheth the great philosophical systems. As for those who form the third branch of the family of man, there is no longer any question that from them has arisen the world's basic technology. Thus the total potentiality of Man was not entrusted to one family.

Now what I mean by total potential is simply what man is

capable of. He is capable of building a Gothic cathedral, of
smashing an atom, of writing a Handel's *Messiah,* of putting a
space vehicle gently down on the far side of the moon, of painting a *Creation of Adam,* of carving a *Thinker,* of formulating an
equation like $E = Mc^2$, of building a Parthenon or a Pyramid, of
making a Flemish tapestry or a Ming vase or a bust of Nephertiti,
of writing an "Elegy in a Churchyard" or *Les Miserables...*
and alas, of planning a Belsen or a Dachau. What if all of this
potential creativeness were to find expression for good? Perhaps
if Israel had accepted their Messiah and preserved for the world
the spiritual balance which Shem was intended to contribute in
a full and perfect way, the world of the Roman Empire days
would have formed the basis of a World Empire, under the Lord
as King, in terms of prosperity undreamed of. And perhaps when
the Lord returns this will be part of the meaning of the term
"Millennium."

But Man is not the creature he should have been, and every
great gift he has can be, and usually is, corrupted and turned to
evil use. So it is well that these potentials should have been
divided. Imagine a race, all the members of which possessed the
brains of an Aristotle, the inventive genius of an Edison and a
da Vinci, and the great religious zeal of a Loyola to give the
"spiritual" drive to all the other forms of energy. And then
imagine this dedicated to serve the selfish and hence the strongest
instincts in Man. What would one have? What could man
achieve? what *would* man achieve under the wrong leadership?
and who would their leader prove to be? The Anti-Christ, perhaps?

Chapter 4

RELIGION, PHILOSOPHY, AND TECHNOLOGY

WHAT WE have been trying to show is that the historical process reflects the interaction between three families of people descended respectively from the three sons of Noah to whom God appears to have apportioned specific responsibilities and equally specific capabilities for the fulfillment of them: to Shem, responsibility for man's religious and spiritual well-being; to Japheth, his mental well-being; and to Ham, his physical well-being. By this apportionment it is not implied that every Semite has tended to be more religiously minded, and every Japhethite more interested in intellectual exercise, and every Hamite more mechanically inclined or more practical than members of the other two families. All that is intended is that the great religions of the world — true and false[46] — had their roots in the family of Shem, all true philosophical systems have originated within the family of Japheth,[47] and the world's basic technology is a Hamitic contribution. We have then noted that *when these three worked together in balanced harmony, civilization as a whole has advanced because maximum restraints have been placed upon the evil consequences of sin while the purposes of God are being carried forward.*

---

[46] The paganism of the Old World, rooted in Babylonian religious beliefs (see Hislop, ref. 40): Mohammedanism; and Judaism, with its outgrowth Christianity. Hinduism is not a religion in the sense that these are, but a religiously colored philosophy.

[47] I think it is noteworthy that the gods of the Hamitic peoples have tended to be gods of power; the god of the Aryans, a god of intellectual enlightenment; and the God of Israel, a God of the salvation of the soul.

It is important to observe that all *three* are necessary for this. If any one element is given overemphasis the ultimate effect is detrimental. No society prospers which is overly materialistic, or overly intellectual, or overly spiritual. Man is neither an animal nor an angel. He cannot dedicate himself to mere physical survival and the exploitation of his animal appetites. Nor can he dedicate himself to nurturing his soul to the neglect of his body. And by the same token, of course, he cannot retire to an ivory tower either, for then he must starve in body *and* soul.

One of the effects of the Fall is to rob man of a proper balance. He becomes a creature of extremes, of improper enthusiasms, of unbalanced dedications, and correspondingly of a tendency to fatal neglect. Many neglect their spiritual life in our materialistically oriented culture. Many neglect the needs of the body in the mystically oriented cultures of India. Many neglect the exercise of their minds, as primitive peoples have often been accused of doing.[48] Any such neglect violates human nature and severely hinders the normal development of the whole man. Both excess and neglect are equally unhappy in their consequences and serve rather to heighten than to restrain the disastrous effects of the Fall. Neither the spiritual contribution of Shem, nor the intellectual contribution of Japheth, nor the technological contribution of Ham really benefit man as they were intended to do without the balancing constraint of the other two.

We have also noted that only when the contribution of Japheth is effectively brought to bear upon the contribution of Shem does theology emerge; and theology does not emerge without it. Moreover, when this same intellectual contribution of Japheth is applied to the technology of Ham, then science emerges, and science does not emerge without it. This does not really mean that the contribution of Japheth is more important than the other two, for it might just as easily have been stated in reverse. The philosophizing of Japheth leads nowhere without the pabulum of technology supplied by Ham, and this pabulum *far antedates* any scientific philosophizing of Japheth, as we shall

---

[48] I do not mean by this that primitive people are potentially any less intelligent: only that they seem to rest content with a thorough knowledge of the total wisdom of their culture without challenging, exploring, or seeking to understand the rationale of it. They neglect mental activity for its own sake. The important difference between intelligence and accumulated knowledge is explored in an interesting way in "Establishing a Paleolithic IQ" (see Doorway Papers Vol. II), which deals with early man as well as modern primitives.

show. By the same token, human intellect does not do well in its reach after spiritual truth apart from revelation; indeed, it leads rather into darkness and general skepticism. Between Malachi and Matthew God remained silent, while at the same time the outworkings of Greek philosophy were permitted to run their course in the search for ultimate reality and spiritual understanding. And how did it end? It ended in almost total skepticism summed up in Pilate's cynical and yet perhaps honest question, "What is truth?" I suggest that this is why Paul, after visiting Athens and seeing there their altar to "an Unknown God" (Acts 17:23), suddenly realized with new force how hopeless it was even for the best intellects in the world and under ideal conditions to arrive at a true understanding of the nature of God and man's relationship to Him. This, I suggest, is why he wrote later to the Corinthians and said, *"After that,* in the wisdom of God, the world by wisdom knew not God," *then* God sent forth His Son (I Cor. 1:21). Thus did God permit Japheth to discover for himself the inadequacy of the contribution he could make apart from the revelation of God which came through Shem.

However, it is in harmony with this view of history that after the revelation of Himself had been established through the Old Testament — the nature of true religion, of *true* worship, of what God required of man and of what man might hope for in God — and after God had completed (really, "fulfilled") the Old Testament revelation in the Person of Jesus Christ His Son and seen to it that the details of His message and lifework were sufficiently preserved in a record, the Gospels — then God turned to the Gentiles, the Japhethites, to take this body of religious truth and set it forth as a Christian theology. God used Hebrew for the Old Testament and probably a form of Semitic speech, viz., Aramaic, as the basis of the Gospel record.[49] But then He turned to a Japhetic language in order to convert this revelation into a structured organic systematized faith, in short, into a theology.

It will be worth examining to what extent scholars have recognized the uniqueness of Semitic forms of speech, and particularly of Hebrew, as a vehicle for the presentation of truth which concerns man's soul, and then to explore Japhetic lan-

---

[49] On this question, see Edouard Naville, *Archaeology of the Old Testament: Was the Old Testament Written in Hebrew,* Scott, London, 1913, 212 pp., and see especially pp. 3-29; and also George M. Lamsda, *The Four Gospels According to the Eastern Version Translated from the Aramaic,* Holman, Phila., 1933, Introduction, pp. v-xxii.

guages as the most perfect vehicle for the organization of this revealed truth into a Christian theology.

The Influence of Language on Thinking

It is perhaps significant that of all peoples who can trace themselves back or who can *be* traced back to Japheth, the Greeks have been most forward in recognizing him as their great progenitor, under the name Japetos. It is as though God wished us to know in no uncertain terms that it was Shem through whom the initial revelation came to us, and Japheth through whom that revelation was finally set in order. Yet the two languages are fundamentally different. In a study of the contrast between Greek and Hebrew thought, Thorlief Boman has gone to great lengths to show how different are these two modes of speech and consequently how different are the ways of thinking which these two languages allow. One might even say *predetermined*.[50] In a critical study of Boman's views, Professor James Barr in spite of his hostility towards them, has nicely summarized the position taken by Boman and others, as follows:[51]

First, the contrast is made between "the static and the dynamic." The Greeks were ultimately interested in contemplation, in withdrawing *from* "doing," in order to be free to meditate and to reason. The Hebrews were not interested in philosophy *per se,* but only in action. Their religious zeal was dynamic. Secondly, the contrast is between the "abstract" and the "concrete." Barr states it:[52]

> It is a characteristic procedure of Greek thought to work with abstractions. Abstract terms of the kind we call qualities and properties are essential in this kind of discussion.... Hebrew thought, on the other hand, does not work with abstractions; its terms are always related to the actual object or situation and not to an abstraction from it.... The contemplative approach, by contrast, means dissociation of the mind from involvement in action. In Hebrew thought the thinking object is the acting person.

Thirdly, the contrast is in "the conception of man," as Barr puts it:[53] "In Greek thought man is seen as a duality, with an immortal soul imprisoned or confined in a mortal body; the two are

---

[50] Boman, Thorlief, *Hebrew Thought Compared with Greek,* SCM Press, London, 1960.
[51] Barr, James, *The Semantics of Biblical Language,* Oxford, 1962.
[52] Ibid., p. 11.
[53] Ibid., p. 12.

only temporarily or accidentally related. In Hebrew thought the soul *is* the living person in his flesh."

This dualism versus monism has been viewed as analogous to the difference between a rider (the soul) on a horse (the body), and a centaur, a soul-body entity. In the Old Testament, and not unnaturally to some extent in the Gospels, the soul is without hesitation taken as the whole man. Thus by inspiration and looking forward to the Lord's Resurrection David said, "Thou wilt not leave my soul in Hell": and in saying this he meant as much his spirit as he did his body. In the Epistles, by contrast, man is taken apart, the body, the soul, and the spirit, being concretely — or perhaps one should say, discretely — divisible (Heb. 4:12). Such a prayer as that our whole soul and body and spirit might be preserved blameless is a Greek concept of man rather than a Hebrew one, though God saw fit to set forth both concepts in Scripture. Thus it comes about that in the New Testament the construction of biblical psychology in this matter is quite possible and certainly worth attempting. But the Old Testament does not encourage the making of such an attempt, though it provides the basic framework in a different form. The two complement each other, and the complementarity resides ultimately in the difference between the two languages, not merely in vocabulary but in mode of expression, way of thinking, in its view of reality.

The extent to which this difference *is* dependent primarily upon language and secondarily upon the kind of mentality which emerges as an individual matures while speaking that language is noted by Barr. The point at issue here is very similar to the old question of the hen and the egg: which came first? Only in this case, I think the answer is clearer. It is the language which we learn as children that orders our thought processes as we mature, until we come to equate the two and to presume that we are thinking first and then finding words to express our thought, while all the time the vocabulary and grammar of our language is determining for us how we shall view reality. As B. L. Whorf rightly observed,[54] we see things not as *they* are but as *we* are, a fact of fundamental importance which every once in a while becomes startlingly clear when we come to discuss some subject of mutual interest with a person whose language differs from our own.

---

[54] Whorf, Benjamin Lee, "Science and Linguistics," *Technology Review* 42 (1940).

It is perfectly true that we do think first and then put our thoughts into words whenever we are trying to communicate in a language which is not our own. Indeed, it is universally agreed that we do not really master any language until we think in it, without any need for translation, a circumstance which proves the point I am making, i.e., that we think in words.

It will be worth pausing for a moment at this point before proceeding to examine the implications of this, to consider a few opinions on the matter from those best qualified to speak, namely, the linguists.

Although the intimate relationship between word and thought has been remarked upon and studied since the time of Humboldt, it is only in recent years that the matter has become a subject of study in its own right and not merely as a side issue in general linguistics. Two names stand out preeminently in relation to this, namely, Ernst Cassirer and Benjamin Lee Whorf. As an introduction to what Whorf called metalinguistics, the following quotations are taken from miscellaneous writings of his, and although they are extracts from a number of separate papers, they can be read consecutively as though they were a continuum. In a paper entitled, "Science and Linguistics," he wrote:[55]

> Talking, or the use of language, is supposed only "to express" what is essentially already formulated (in the mind). Formulation is an independent process, called thought or thinking, and is supposed to be largely indifferent to the nature of particular languages. Languages have grammars which are assumed to be merely norms of conventional and social correctness but the use of language is suppose to be guided not so much by them as by correct, rational, or intelligent *thinking*.
>
> Thought, in this view, does not depend on grammar but on laws of logic or reason which are supposed to be the same for all observers of the universe — to represent a rationale in the universe that can be "found" independently by all intelligent observers, whether they speak Chinese or Choctaw.

Subsequently, he continues:[56]

> When linguists became able to examine critically and scientifically a large number of languages of widely different patterns ... it was found that the grammar of each language is not merely a reproducing instrument for voicing ideas *but rather is itself the shaper of ideas* [my emphasis], the programme and guide for the individual's mental activity, for his analysis of impressions. ...

55 Ibid., p. 3 of reprint.
56 Ibid., p. 5 of reprint.

Formulation of ideas is not an independent process ... but part of a particular grammar, and differs as between different grammars. We dissect nature along lines laid down by our native languages. The categories and types that we isolate from the world of phenomena we do not find there simply because they stare every observer in the face: on the contrary, the world is presented in a kaleidoscopic flux of impression which has to be organized by our minds — and this means largely by the linguistic systems in our minds....

This fact is very significant for modern science for it means that no individual is free to describe nature with absolute impartiality, but is constrained to certain modes of interpretation even while he thinks himself most free. The person most nearly free in such respects would be a linguist familiar with very many widely different linguistic systems. As yet no linguist ever is in any such position. We are thus introduced to a new principle ... which holds that all observers are *not* [my emphasis] led by the same physical evidence to the same picture of the universe unless their linguistic backgrounds are similar or can in some way be calibrated.

This rather startling conclusion is not so apparent if we compare only our modern European languages.... Among these tongues there is an unanimity of major pattern which at first seems to bear out natural logic. But this unanimity exists only because these tongues are all Indo-European dialects cut out of the same basic plan, being historically transmitted from what was long ago one speech community....

When Semitic, Chinese, Tibetan, or African languages are contrasted with our own, the divergence in analysis of the world becomes more apparent; and when we bring in the native languages of the Americas where speech communities for many millennia have gone their ways independently of each other and of the Old World, the fact that languages dissect nature in many different ways becomes patent. The relativity of all conceptual systems, ours included, and *their dependence upon language* [my emphasis] stands revealed.

What surprises most is to find that various grand generalizations of the Western World, such as time, velocity, and matter, are not essential to the construction of a consistent picture of the Universe.

In another paper of his entitled "Language and Logic," Whorf wrote:[57]

We cut up and organize the speed and flow of events as we do largely because, through our mother tongue, we are parties to an agreement to do so, not because nature itself is segmented in exactly that way for all to see. Languages differ not only in how they build their sentences but in how they break down

[57] Whorf, Benjamin Lee, "Language and Logic," *Technology Review*, 43 (1941): 21.

nature to secure the elements to put in those sentences. . . . For as goes our segmentation of the face of nature, so goes our physics of the Cosmos.

Then in a further paper entitled "The Relation of Habitual Thought and Behaviour to Language," Whorf wrote:[58]

> How does such a network of language, culture, and behaviour come about historically? Which was first, the language patterns or the cultural norms? In the main they have grown up together, constantly influencing each other. But in this partnership the nature of the language is the factor that limits free plasticity and rigidifies channels of development in the more autocratic way.

Thus far, then, we see the direction in which modern thinking about the relationship between language and thought, language and World View, language and how people perceive the world about them has been going. In a volume of the Collected Works of Whorf we may extract one or two further insights. With respect to the question of whether thought is possible without some kind of verbalization, Whorf wrote, "The linguistic side of *silent* [his emphasis] thinking, thinking without speaking, is of a nature as yet little appreciated."[59] At this point there is a footnote as follows:

> Some have supposed thinking to be entirely linguistic. Watson, I believe, holds or held this view, and the great merit of Watson in this regard is that he was one of the first to point out and teach the very large and unrecognized linguistic element in silent thinking. His error lies in going the whole hog; also, perhaps, in not realizing or at least not emphasizing that the linguistic aspect of thinking is not a biologically organized process . . . but a cultural organization, i.e., *a language* [his emphasis].

Thus Whorf would not argue that all things that go on in the mind involve the use of words, but he does hold categorically that one cannot think conceptually, one cannot build a philosophy or a World View silently and to oneself, except by the use of words.

As a heading to one of his papers, there is a quotation from Edward Sapir which reads:[60]

> Human beings do not live in the objective world alone, nor

[58] Whorf, Benjamin Lee, "The Relation of Habitual Thought and Behaviour to Language" in *Language, Culture, and Personality,* Menasha, Wis., 1941, p. 91.

[59] Whorf, Benjamin Lee, *Language, Thought and Reality,* selected writings of B. L. Whorf, The Technology Press of M.I.T., Wiley, N.Y., 1956, p. 66.

[60] Ibid., p. 134.

alone in the world of social activity as ordinarily understood but are very much at the mercy of the particular language which has become the medium of expression for their society. It is quite an illusion to imagine that one adjusts to reality without the use of language and that language is merely an accidental means of solving specific problems of communication or reflection.

The fact of the matter is that the "real world" is to a large extent unconsciously built up on the language habits of the group. . . . We see and hear and otherwise experience very largely as we do because the language habits of our community pre-dispose certain choices of interpretation.

The extent to which a word imposed upon some object can predetermine our whole attitude towards that object is strikingly borne out by a simple experiment conducted by Dr. Samuel Glucksberg of Princeton, who found that by giving a common wrench a nonsense label, in this case calling it a "jod," he could greatly increase the number of novel uses to which a group of students imagined it could be put. In other words, given an ordinary wrench which was just called a "wrench," when the students were invited to imagine themselves isolated somewhere and limited entirely to the use of this one tool and then to list all the things they thought might be done with it, they did fairly well. But when they were handed the same tool and told that it was a "jod" and that they were not to think of it by its old name, they did a great deal better and managed to dream up many more useful applications for it. Glucksberg has also said, "To a certain extent the name determined and limited what the object was and therefore what it could be used for."[61] In the light of this experiment it is a measure of Humboldt's perceptiveness that he could write so long ago:[62]

Man lives with his objects chiefly — one may say exclusively — as language presents them to him. By the same process whereby he spins language out of his own being, he ensnares himself in it; and each language draws a magic circle round the people to which it belongs, a circle from which there is no escape save by stepping out it into another.

It is not hard to see that since language is passed on to each new generation with comparatively small changes in its grammatical structure, though its vocabulary may change, any society will tend to perpetuate its own way of looking at things. And as

[61] Gluckberg, Samuel, "Human Inventiveness," *Science News*, Mar. 4, 1967, p. 216.

[62] Humboldt: quoted by Ernst Cassirer, *Language and Myth*, Dover Pub., N.Y., 1946, p. 9.

there are families of language, so there will be families of peoples who tend to see things in the same way. Since Indo-Europeans have for some reason maintained the evident relationships in their particular family of languages — and the same observation applies within the Semitic languages — it is not surprising that even though they have spread so widely they have continued to share a certain way of looking at things: Indo-Europeans philosophically with an emphasis upon the abstract and the Semites with their emphasis upon behavior from a more transcendental point of view. But what shall we say of the Hamites? From all over the world, wherever they are found and wherever linguists have examined their speech forms and the philosophy of their grammar (to use Jespersen's term), the witness is the same. Their view of the world is an entirely practical one, rooted in the present, wise in a canny sort of way, specific, particular, uninterested in the abstract, inventive, always creating new words or new terms for things, interested in particulars rather than categories, earthy, and very largely disinterested in unlikely possibilities. While we may think of primitive people as being less truthful than ourselves — and most if not all "primitive" people known to us have belonged within the family of Ham — the fact of the matter is quite the reverse. They find it difficult to think hypothetically, to do what every scientist must do, i.e., to tell lies deliberately. If asked a hypothetical question they will not answer it but reject the question as not applicable. Asked how many apples, for example, we would have between us if he had two and I had two, a native would not say "four" but more probably, "Well, I do not have two apples!"

Elie Reclus, an ethnologist, writing some years ago and speaking of certain primitive tribes, notably the Khonds, says of them:[63]

> Veracious and sincere, they disdain to escape a peril to gain an advantage at the price of a lie, or even a voluntary inexactitude. . . . .
> It was one of the rare errors of J. Stuart Mill to assert that uncivilized men take pleasure in lying, and seem incapable of speaking the truth. . . . But the great philosopher would have expressed himself otherwise if a sojourn in the Indies had brought him into contact with Gonds and Khonds, with Malers, Birhors, Donthals, and others, who hold truth sacred, and contract no engagement that they do not fulfill. There is no graver

---

[63] Reclus, Elie, *Primitive Folk: Studies in Comparative Ethnology*, Walter Scott, London, n.d., p. 258.

offence than to suspect their word; it is an insult which they wipe out with blood, and if they cannot slay the offender, they kill themselves.

In a recent communication, Miss Beatrice Myers, a missionary attending the Summer Institute of Linguistics (U.S.A.) said that on one occasion she asked a Cheyenne Indian how he would say, "This is your house." His reply was: "If you owned the house, I wouldn't have to tell you, so I wouldn't say it!"[64] Similarly, the Hopi will speak of ten men because one can actually have ten men: but they would not speak of ten days because one cannot have ten days. Such a concept as a negative number is quite absurd, unless it is seen as a practical indebtedness in economic, or some other such terms. We shall have occasion shortly to document these observations extensively. In the meantime it may be observed that while the family of Indo-European languages is readily identifiable as a family, and the Semitic as a family, this does not apply at all to the third group of languages, the Hamitic. The fact is that Hamites have been so inventive that they invent terms with equal facility, and their languages are in such a constant state of flux that within a few generations even tribes living just across a river from each other will find themselves scarcely able to converse any longer.[65] It is the same strange proliferating tendency which prevented the Egyptians, Hittites, Sumerians, Chinese, and Central American Indians from developing an alphabetical script, even though the numbers of signs they were creating multiplied almost astronomically.

It appears to me that this very fact may have been part of God's providential economy in order to guarantee the quick dispersal of the family of Ham all over the world, to open it up for their brethren who were to follow. A community of language

---

[64] In a letter to her supporters in America and Canada, 1968.

[65] Rapid change of native languages: there seem to be several contributing factors at work here. One, which is cultural, is the practice of giving new names to things which for one reason or another have become "dangerous" to speak about because of some circumstance in their "history," or association with the dead. Another is the tendency to see what is specifically *different* rather than similar in a series of situations. Thus while we strike various kinds of "blows" with the hand (a tap, a pat, a push, a press, a stroke, etc.), we would retain the common word "hand" in each case. Natives do not. A "tap with the hand" would be one word, "pat with the hand" an entirely different one. There are hundreds of words for some particular animal seen in various lights, but no single word for the animal genus. People also adopt names of items as personal names and these then become taboo when the person dies, and have to be replaced!

unites people and binds them together. By contrast, when languages proliferate easily to the point of mutual unintelligibility, the tendency to congregate is undermined and dispersion is assisted. It may thus have been God's way not merely of sharpening their inventive genius, but of ensuring that they would spread at the same time. What divided the Hamites in this way was not a difference in language structure, for the philosophy of their languages remained remarkably similar, so that the ways of thinking of the African native, the Chinese peasant, and the American Indian remained for a very long time comparable; it was the vocabularies which changed. This was not nearly so true with Semites or Indo-Europeans.

But even today, with mobility so tremendously increased and means of rapid communication so greatly extended, it is still true in a way that was largely unexpected, that people hold on to their native language with great tenacity. As Kroeber put it, "Speech tends to be one of the most persistent populational characters and 'ethnic' boundaries are most often speech boundaries."[66]

So it is important to note the difference between the grammar of a language and its vocabulary, for the latter changes constantly whereas the former remains. And it is the grammar which really holds the key to the World View. Ernst Cassirer in speaking of the "inward form of language," put it this way:[67]

> The form of observation, which underlies all speech and language development, always expresses a peculiar spiritual character, a special way of conceiving and apprehending. The difference between the several languages, therefore, is not a matter of different sounds and marks [i.e., ideographs], but of different world conceptions.... Language never denotes simply objects, things as such, but always conceptions.... The nature of concepts depends on the way this active viewing is directed.

It is not what we see so much as how we see it, and as we have already said, we do not see how *things* are, but how *we* are. Cassirer put it this way: "It is not a question of what we see in a certain perspective, but of the perspective itself."[68] To revert once more to Whorf in connection with the difference between the word-content of a sentence and the structure of the sentence itself, i.e., the vocabulary as opposed to the grammar, we find this observation:[69]

[66] Kroeber, A. L., op. cit. (ref. 34), p. 221.
[67] Cassirer, Ernst, *Language and Myth*, Dover Pub., N.Y., 1946, p. 30.
[68] Ibid., p. 11.
[69] Whorf, Benjamin Lee, op. cit. (ref. 59), p. 258.

The meanings of specific words are less important than we fondly fancy. Sentences, not words, are the essence of speech, just as equations and functions and not bare numbers are the real meat of mathematics.

By the same token he holds that thinking is not dependent so much upon words *per se* as upon sentences. He spells this out:[70]

Actually, thinking is most mysterious, and by far the greatest light upon it that we have is thrown by the study of language. This study shows that the forms of a person's thoughts are controlled by inexorable laws of pattern of which he is unconscious. These patterns are the unperceived intricate systematization of his own language — shown readily enough by a candid comparison and contrast with other languages, especially those of a different linguistic form. His thinking itself is in a language — in English, in Sanskrit, in Chinese.

And every language is a vast pattern system, different from others, in which are culturally ordained the forms and categories by which the personality not only communicates, but also analyzes nature, notices or neglects types of relationships and phenomena, channels his reasoning, and builds the house of his consciousness. This doctrine is new to Western Science, but it stands on unimpeachable evidence.

The Type of World View Related to Each Language Family

It is clear to me that with three language families capable of sustaining and contributing in three such different ways towards the supply of man's total needs as a spiritual, intellectual and physiological creature, God has made provision for the preservation of the whole man while His purposes are being unfolded. It remains to be seen now whether the course of events supports this threefold division both with respect to the linguistic evidence and the evidence to be derived from the stream of history itself.

The first part of this task requires that we establish the following: First, that Semitic languages favor a World View which is religious and spiritual in color, that the Indo-European or Japhetic languages favor a World View that is reflective and favorable to philosophical thinking rather than religious in its bent, and that the balance of the world's languages, or Hamitic languages, are of such a kind that they do not encourage reflection or abstract, but concrete, specific, particular thinking, leading to a very practical view of things. In other words, that as each of these three families have developed their kinds of lan-

[70] Ibid., p. 252.

guage, in such a way they have tended to think and so they have tended to act or be.

G. A. F. Knight is quoted by Barr as having said, "God chose Israel to be the vehicle of His revelation.... Now, if God chose Israel, then He chose to use the Hebrew language."[71] On this observation Barr comments:[72]

> The argument may be theologically reasonable, but if it is to be extended to mean that God chose the Semitic languages, and the Semitic culture group, and that His chosen group was the children of Shem and not merely the children of Israel, one wonders if theologians are really willing to go so far: and it is hardy to be reconciled with the constant and obvious struggle of the Israelite religion which was not against Hellenism at all until the latest period, but against neighbouring forms expressed in closely allied Semitic language and Culture.

The point that Barr has overlooked here, I believe, is that if God needed a vehicle for religious truth, especially when that truth was revealed truth, He needed a language best suited to the expression of religious ideas rather than philosophical ones. That other members of the family of Shem also found facility in this direction, though they found it in expression of religious *error* rather than truth, does not alter the fact that the family as a whole was the logical one to choose. It was necessary only to separate out one segment of it and to purify that segment from error whenever it was acting as the vehicle of divine revelation. Naturally, thereafter, their most dangerous enemies were bound to be those who shared the same facility but not the same revelation, namely, the Babylonians and the Assyrians, some of the inhabitants of Palestine, and later the Arabs. Shakespeare has said, "The nearer in blood, the nearer bloody," and although he did not have in mind religious conflict, his aphorism is quite applicable. The Arabs today remain Israel's most bitter enemy and Islam, the religious expression of the Arabs, the most recalcitrant opponent of Christianity, the religious extension of Judaism.

A Semitic language evidently lends itself to the formulation of a strong religious conviction that will regulate behavior and can accommodate itself to people with very different cultural backgrounds. The religious beliefs of the Babylonians and the Assyrians came to permeate much of the ancient world, and in due time formed the basis of paganism. Paganism was the first

---

[71] Knight, G. A. F., quoted by James Barr, op. cit. (ref. 51), p. 19.
[72] Barr, James, op. cit. (ref. 51), p. 19.

great religiously oriented opponent of Christianity, as Islam might very well be the last.

Subsequently, Barr quotes with equal disapproval a statement by Pedersen who wrote, "The Semitic languages are as perfect expressions of Semitic thinking as the European languages of European thinking."[73] And Boman similarly wrote, "The unique character of a people or of a family of peoples finds expression in its own language."[74] Again, Gerleman observes that "its conception of reality and its manner of narration have their correlate and their reflection in the structure of the Hebrew language, in the construction of sentences, and in the lexical stock...the affinity of narrative art with syntax, of Old Testament experience of reality with Hebrew grammar...."[75]

In spite of the fact that Barr disagrees with these ideas (his whole book seems to be an expression of disagreement with everybody), he has already admitted previously that "the typical vehicle in Hebrew thinking is the historical narrative or the future prediction, both being forms of literature in which the verb is likely to be of great significance; and that the typical vehicle of Greek thinking is the philosophical discussion in which nouns are more prominent and verbs are less important."[76] Subsequently Barr writes:

> One may however go farther and assert that not only the frequency but the very existence of and facility in forming the "abstract" type of noun is to be correlated with abstract thinking; and conversely that Hebrew, as the language of a people whose thought is not abstract, does not form "abstract" nouns and its words are characteristically "concrete"....
>
> The Hebrew, almost invariably, thought in terms of the concrete. There are few abstract nouns in the Hebrew language.

---

[73] Ibid.

[74] Boman, Thorlief, op. cit. (ref. 50), p. 27.

[75] Gerleman, G., quoted by Barr, op. cit. (ref. 51), p. 33.

[76] Barr, James, op. cit. (ref. 51), pp. 15, 16, 18 and 40. In his able review of Susanne Langer's *Mind: An Essay on Human Feelings,* Robert B. Mac-Leod (*Science* 157 [1967]: 1544) notes the author's view that our society sees "things" as the substance of reality, not "acts." Action is what happens to things according to our philosophy. This is not true of other cultural world-views, where reality is *action* not object. Langer believes that our problem in establishing the relationship between mind and brain comes about because we are separating "activity" from object and should, rather, see the two as aspects of one single reality. See especially pp. 9-11 of Vol. 1 of her book, published by Johns Hopkins Press, Baltimore, 1967. I am not convinced that her proposal really solves the problem, but it is an interesting idea.

Barr agrees with Boman in one thing at least, namely, that "the thought of other Semitic peoples is on the whole of the same formal structure as Israelite thought.... The Hebrew linguistic pattern is not essentially different from the general Semitic." Thus he concludes, "Obviously the question can be put: Is there an Indo-European cast of mind which somehow corresponds to the known linguistic stock of Indo-European?" To which the answer is, I think, "Undoubtedly." Yet curiously, when Boman wrote, "The unique character of a people or a family of peoples, a race, finds expression in its own language," Barr states his disagreement.

This emphasis upon verbs rather than nouns, upon action rather than idea, has been remarked upon by many who have studied the contrast between Hebrew and Greek, and therefore between the Old Testament and the New Testament. While it is so very generally recognized that philosophy is in some unique way a Greek contribution, it is not so generally realized that (1) they were by no means the sole contributors in this respect among Indo-Europeans, for in India there were Schools quite as extensive and flourishing as the Greek Schools — which were in fact prior in time, and (2) the so-called "philosophers" from among non-Indo-European cultures, from China, Egypt, and Central America, were not really philosophers at all, but intelligent men who were able to crystallize the canny and highly practical wisdom of their own society. The writings of Confucius, of Ptah-hotep, and Pachacuta are intensely practical in their object, almost in the form of proverbs and in some cases quite Machiavellian. The Wisdom Literature of the Old Testament as well as extra-biblical wisdom literature of the Jewish people is of the same kind — though not Machiavellian.

It is surprising how wide a recognition has been given to this matter by writers who nevertheless clearly did not have in mind the overall picture which we are presenting. They record their observances without any apparent awareness of the framework which they are helping to establish. For example, Ralph Linton observed:[77]

> All monotheistic faiths of which we have record can be traced to Semitic sources, and all of them are confronted by the same enigma of an all powerful deity in a Universe governed by law.

And Peter Lange in his *Commentary on Genesis* observes that

---

[77] Linton, Ralph, *The Tree of Culture*, Knopf, N.Y., 1956, p. 293.

the language of the Hebrews did not lend itself to philosophy but was more particularly suited to dynamic religious thought.[78]

It has always seemed to me a strange thing that in the university we were told that the Jewish people were not historians, not really interested in history at all. This is strange because *if* they had a philosophy in the abstract sense, it is to be found in their overall view of history. It must be admitted, however, that their philosophy of history, if it can properly be called such, was not a disinterested one but had an end in view, namely, the ordering of man's moral behavior by using the lessons of history viewed as the working out of the judgments of a righteous God. This is disqualified as philosophy in the strict sense because it has a practical objective. But it would not do to accuse the Old Testament writers of being without any philosophy if by this we mean that their thoughts were shallow and without penetration. On this point Kroeber makes some observations which do not bear on the immediate subject of this paper but do show in what way the study of history differs from that kind of philosophy which ultimately led to the development of science. He remarks:[79]

> Historiographic research, almost alone, remains without systematic and "theoretic" results. Some would say that it is knowledge but not science, because it remains on a concrete level and does not abstract.

It is important to distinguish carefully between the canny wisdom which we have attributed to Confucius and others and the philosophy of history that clearly underlies the Old Testament. And it is even more necessary to distinguish both these kinds of "philosophy" from the unique kind which has been the contribution of the family of Japheth. In order to make this clear, we can with profit note a number of observations made by various authorities on the nature of the intellectual adventure undertaken by Indo-Europeans but not by others.

In *Everyman's Encyclopedia* under Philosophy, there is the following observation:[80]

> It was not until man sought wisdom *for its own sake,* and with no religious or other practical motives, that he philoso-

---

[78] Lange, Peter, *Commentary on Genesis,* Zondervan, Grand Rapids, Mich., n.d., pp. 19, 21.

[79] Kroeber, A. L., "Evolution, History, and Culture," in *Evolution After Darwin,* Vol. 2, Univ. of Chicago Press, 1960, p. 3.

[80] "Philosophy," *Everyman's Encyclopedia,* Vol. 10, Dent, London, 1913, pp. 305, 306.

phized in the true sense; and previous theogonies, cosmogonies, etc., cannot strictly claim the title of Philosophy. . . . The beginnings of philosophy are as a rule attributed to the Greeks, but the Indian ideas of the 6th century B.C. and much later, form an interesting parallel philosophic development.

In her contribution to the series *Great Ages of Man,* Schulberg, writing of historic India, says:[81]

> Even before the 6th century B.C. men of India had demonstrated a philosophical bent. Their earliest religious scripture, the Rig Veda, appeared some time in the second millennium B.C. . . . Some of the Vedic hymns expressed a spirit of philosophical enquiry. . . .
>
> After the composition of the Rig Veda, Indian philosophers began to compose commentaries on the hymns, a practice continued for hundreds of years. The final and most significant portion of the resulting literature is a collection of philosophical speculations. This portion, begun about 700 B.C. and called the Upanishads, provided the foundation for Hinduism. The Upanishads . . . speculate, seeking always to find truth.

Ralph Linton noted that the Hindus were always highly receptive to and interested in new philosophic ideas but showed an almost complete indifference, for example, to improved techniques of manufacture.[82] Their interest was in theory not practice, the material world being considered of so little importance that minor advances in its control were not considered worth the trouble of changing established habits. Similarly, A. L. Kroeber observed that "Hindu civilization is not only other worldly, but mystical, rationalizing, and extravagant in its ethos."[83]

It is not surprising to find, as Miriam Chapin has pointed out, that Hindustani has an enormous vocabulary containing all kinds of scientific concepts, and as a development out of the more ancient Sanskrit it became a language well able to give expression to philosophic ideas and "the most abstruse speculations."[84] The reader will notice here that a language which is good for philosophic ideas is also suitable for the development of scientific concepts.

---

[81] Schulberg, Lucille, *Historic India,* Great Ages of Man, Time-Life Pub., N.Y., 1968, p. 52.

[82] Linton, Ralph, *The Study of Man,* student's ed., Appleton, N.Y., 1936, p. 343.

[83] Kroeber, A. L., op. cit. (ref. 34) , p. 294.

[84] Chapin, Miriam, *How People Talk,* Longmans Green, Toronto, 1947, p. 121.

The philosopher Hegel remarked upon the relationship between Sanskrit and philosophy:[85]

> The recent discoveries of the treasures of Indian literature have shown us what a reputation the Hindus have acquired in Geometry, Astronomy, and Algebra, and that they have made great advances in Philosophy, and that among them the Grammar has been so far cultivated that no language can be regarded as more fully developed than the Sanskrit.

Jacques Maritain has beautifully drawn some of these threads together by remarking:[86]

> It is not surprising that all peoples in the primitive stage of history were ignorant of philosophic speculation. But it is more astonishing that even certain civilizations were devoid of philosophy — for example, the *Semite,* and the *Egyptian,* which is, in this respect in the same category as the Semite. Despite the high level of scientific (technical) culture reached by the intellectual aristocracy of these races, the sole philosophic conceptions, it would seem, which the Egyptians and the Chaldeans possessed, were a few very general ideas implicit in their religion concerning the deity, the human soul, its state after death, and the precepts of morality.... These truths... were never made the subject of rational study and speculation.... Religion took the place of philosophy, and from religion these races received certain philosophic truths; philosophy they had none. In this matter the Jews did not differ from their fellow Semites. Scornful of human wisdom and the achievements of pure reason, and indeed without aptitude for such investigation, they produced no philosophers.

By contrast, the opening words of Maritain's *Introduction to Philosophy* are: "All the great Indo-European civilizations manifest an impulse, which no doubt took widely different forms, towards rational and, in the strict sense, philosophic speculation."[87]

Somewhere about the 8th to 6th centuries B.C., deeply speculative attempts to give a rational explanation to the vast problem of evil, undertaken in Persia, filtered down into India where what had been a religious faith slowly became a non-religious philosophy — though it still retained the appearance of being religiously oriented. Speaking of this, Maritain says:[88]

> When the original religion — the primitive religion of the

---

[85] Hegel, G. W. F., "The Philosophy of History" in *The World's Great Classics,* Vol. 20, Colonial Press, N.Y., 1900, pp. 161, 162.

[86] Maritain, Jacques, *An Introduction to Philosophy,* Sheed & Ward, N.Y., 1955, p. 25.

[87] Ibid., p. 26.

[88] Ibid., p. 27.

Vedas — no longer proved sufficient to satisfy the intellectual demands or social needs of a more advanced civilization, philosophical notions, which seemed to have originated as interpretations of sacrifice and other sacred ritual but developed into a spirit hostile to the ancient traditions and the cult of the gods, found a home among the sacredotal class and took possession of the priesthood... The priests... directed their worship no longer to the old gods but to the undefined and secret forces of the Universe.

This resulted after a period of confusion in the formation of a new system, Brahmanism or Hinduism, which is essentially a philosophy or metaphysic, a work of human speculation, invested from the outset with the sanctions and attributes of religion.

When it is realized that the basic religious concepts which formed the substance of Zoroastrianism in Persia had been inherited by the Persians from the Assyrian and Babylonian priests, it will be seen that what began as a Semitic World View was taken by the Persians, who belong within the family of Japheth, and transformed into a theology. This theology passing down into India lost its spiritual content and reverted more specifically to pure philosophy. In due time under the influence of Cakya-Muni, surnamed Buddha, the philosophy became less pure and more applied to life. Its practical emphasis then made it appealing to the Chinese who adopted it. In the initial stages in India, while the philosophy had been purely speculative, it had not actually been agnostic or atheistic. But under the influence of Buddha it became increasingly more and more agnostic. By the time it had been adopted by the Chinese, it had become entirely nonreligious, a practical guide to successful living and nothing more.

When Buddha had made his imprint on Hinduism, in the 6th century B.C., he had taken a very much more practical view, and Schulberg has observed:[89] "In this, Buddha stands alone among the religious leaders of the world, that he refused to engage in metaphysical speculation about the Universe." Thus, in due time, whereas Buddhism appealed to the Chinese it disappeared almost entirely from India. In this connection Alan Watts observed:[90]

Although Buddhism was originally an Indian religion, emerging from the traditions of Hindu philosophy, it did not attain its full vitality until the T'ang Dynasty in China — about

---

[89] Schulberg, Lucille, op. cit. (ref. 81), p. 60.
[90] Watts, Alan, "How Buddhism Came to Life," *Asia,* Oct., 1939, p. 581.

the 8th century A.D. Philosophy, Buddhas, Bodhisattvas, and religious rites are far less significant in China. Chinese Buddhism ceased to be a matter of other worldly mysticism. . . .

When Buddhism first came to China the method used for attaining spiritual illumination followed the lines of Indian Yoga: a profound state of consciousness obtained by sitting for hours, days, months, or even years in solitary meditation. But this did not really appeal to the practical spirit of the Chinese who wanted a Dhyana that could be applied to everyday life.

Of Confucianism, Maritain says that there can be no doubt it was simply a form of enlightened selfishness, and completely indifferent to metaphysical speculation.[91] In writing of Confucius as a religious philosopher, Epiphanius Wilson, a Chinese Classical Scholar, pointed out:[92]

> The strangest figure that meets us in the annals of oriental thought is that of Confucius. To the popular mind he is the founder of a religion, and yet he has nothing in common with the great religious teachers of the East. They *despised* the present life: to them the future was everything in its promised satisfaction. The teachings of Confucius were of a very different sort. Throughout his whole writings he has not even mentioned the name of God. He declined to discuss the question of immortality. When asked about spiritual beings, he remarked, "If we cannot know men how can we know spirits?"
>
> The influence of Confucius springs, first of all, from the narrowness and definitiveness of his doctrine. He was no transcendenalist. His teaching was of the earth, earthy.

Wilson's assessment is quite in accord with that of a recent Chinese scholar, Liu Wu-Chi, who wrote:[93]

> The distinguishing features of Confucianism are many. First of all it is a moral system which is both practical and practicable. Without any trace of the metaphysical (philosophy) and the supernatural (religion), its contents are readily understood by the man in the street; and its ethical teachings, replete with wisdom and common sense, can be applied in daily life.

Edward H. Schafer in his contribution on Ancient China in the *Great Ages of Man* Series has a wonderfully illustrative little bit of Chinese "legalistic advice." It reads:[94]

Make standards clear.

---

91 Maritain, Jacques, op. cit. (ref. 86), p. 39.

92 Wilson, Epiphanius, Introduction to "The Literature of China" in *The World's Great Classics,* Colonial Press, N.Y., 1900, pp. 3, 4.

93 Wu-Chi, L., *A Short History of Confucian Philosophy,* Pelican Books, England, 1955, p. 9.

94 Schafer, Edward H., *Ancient China,* The Great Ages of Man, Time-Life Pub., N.Y., 1967, p. 83.

Give precedence to achievement.
If the "good" are not profitable to the nation, do not supply rewards.
If the "unworthy" are not harmful to good order, do not apply penalties.

More recently, Ilza Veith in a paper on Far Eastern ideology, speaking about the attitude toward the forces of nature, said:[95]

When the fields were scorched and men waited for rain, when winter lingered and sun was needed to thaw the frozen earth, man saw that heaven was the more powerful and therefore made heaven his supreme deity. But Chinese imagination never personalized this higher being or speculated about its intrinsic qualities.

In a similar vein, Edward H. Schafer wrote:[96]

The origin of this physical world does not seem to have concerned the men of Ancient China very much, despite their great interest in its shape. A few creation myths survive, but creator-spirits did not figure significantly in their religion — a striking difference from Judaism and Christianity.

Ralph Linton notes interestingly enough:[97]

China is unique among the great civilizations in that at no time in its long history has it produced a strong priestly group.
The Chinese attitudes towards religion are a mixture of superstition and practicality. Although there were some mystics during the early periods of developing Chinese philosophy, the general approach of the Chinese is a thoroughly practical one. ... They never persecuted on religious grounds, and there have been few Chinese martyrs. ...
In the 1700's many French Jesuits were sent to China with the hope of converting the Emperor Ch'ien Lung to the faith. They were well received at court, but the Emperor was more interested in their scientific, mathematical and military contribution.

One reason for singling China out from among non-Indo-European people is that the Chinese are particularly useful (in the sense that the Greek philosophers are) as a paradigm or stereotype. They are a people who for many centuries had a far higher civilization than was to be found anywhere else in the world, a people whose technology was advanced and refined, and a people who having reached such a highly civilized state, declined dramatically in many respects almost to the level of a

95 Veith, Ilza, "Creation and Evolution in the Far East" in *Evolution After Darwin,* Vol. 3, Univ. of Chicago Press, 1960, p. 3.
96 Schafer, Edward H., op. cit. (ref. 94), p. 101.
97 Linton, Ralph, op. cit. (ref. 77), pp. 566, 569, and 570.

peasant country. Subsequently, in modern times they have begun a revolution which has brought them to a limited extent within the scientific community. It is worthwhile to note just how much progress *has* been made in this direction and on this matter we shall have a word to say later. In the meantime, Robert S. Cohen remarks of this combination of high civilization yet lack of philosophy:[98]

> The only test comparison with a developed civilization is that of non-theological China. As Needham and Northrope have remarked, theology in China has been so depersonalized, law made so ethical, humanistic, and particular, that the idea of a rational creator of all things was not formulated. Hence the idea that we lesser rational beings might, by virtue of that god-like rationality, be able to decipher the laws of nature never was accepted.

He also notes that if such philosophy had developed, scientific activity would have been stimulated, and "if such scientific activity had been stimulated, *theology might have been developed, too*" [my emphasis].

And what of China today? Writing on this subject, Kurt A. G. Mendelssohn observed:[99]

> Science in the Western sense hardly existed in China before 1950 even at Peking University, proper science teaching did not begin until 1920 and made little headway in the following three decades when the country was torn by civil war and had to suffer Japanese invasion....
>
> I have seen near miracles of shrewd inventiveness and manipulative dexterity in some of the small factories attached to agricultural communities where essentially no machine tools were available at the time.

It is not lack of ingenuity that has "held them back." Very similarly H. W. Thompson wrote recently:[100]

> There are said to be 800,000 students at university level in the whole of China. All universities are financed of course by

---

[98] Cohen, Robert S., "Alternative Interpretations of the History of Science," *Sci. Monthly,* Feb., 1955, p. 115.

[99] Mendelssohn, Kurt A. G., "Science and Technology in China." I have unfortunately mislaid the source of this quotation. It appeared in 1960, in the English journal *Nature*. In the same journal a Dr. K. Mendelssohn (who may not be the same individual) under the title "Science in China" (Vol. 215, 1967, pp. 10f.) indicates in his article that progress is being made, though the emphasis is still upon applied science and technology — not unnaturally.

[100] Thompson, H. W., "Science in China," *Internat. Sci. and Technol.,* June, 1963, p. 88.

the state. The four which I visited, three in Peking and the other in Tientsin, presumably rank among the most advanced. It is risky to generalize, but my impression was that they were devoted almost entirely to teaching (i.e., not to experiment) with much emphasis on sociology and politics. As yet they seem to have little contact with scientific research on the frontiers of science.

I think it is worth noting that Needham in Vol. IV of his great work *Science and Civilization in China* is concerned over the question of why the Chinese did not develop scientific theories in spite of the many practical devices they invented. Needham suggests the lack of an alphabetic language as one reason.[101] The Chinese ideograms, though they are symbolic, are too tightly bound to their original primitive meaning to allow them to be the basis of generalization and abstraction.

In spite of this admission, Needham for some reason still titled his work *Science and Civilization in China*. It is strange in view of the fact that he wonders why they never *achieved* science! I think the confusion arises in part from our tendency to equate science with technology, an unwarranted equation which Conant has written eloquently against.[102] Robert Multhauf in reviewing Needham's second volume, remarks:[103]

> That he fails to produce a clear exposition of the relationship of technology to scientific thought is a weakness of the book, but an understandable one — since it remains to be accomplished in the relatively better known area of Western science.

Our own TV commercials are brilliant examples of this confusion. A man has only to invent a mechanical toothbrush of some kind and it is introduced to us as a "scientific" marvel, when of course it really has nothing whatever to do with science. As L. R. Hafstead, vice-president of research of the General Motors Corporation at the time, wrote a few years ago:[104]

> A scientist's work is completed when an item of information is established and recorded. The same man who makes a discovery may choose, or be persuaded, to attempt to apply it to a practical problem. In this case he *ceases to be a scientist* and works essentially as an engineer.

[101] Needham, Joseph, from a review of his work *Science and Civilization in China,* Vol. 4, Physics and Physical Technology, Cambridge, appearing in *Nature,* Dec., 1962, p. 844.

[102] Conant, James: his very widely read book *On Understanding Science,* Mentor Books, N.Y., 1951, is a protest against this equation.

[103] Multhauf, Robert, in *Science,* 124 (1956): 631.

[104] Hafstead, L. R., "The Role of Scientists and Engineers in Society," *The Tool Engineer,* April, 1957, p. 223.

In short, a technical invention is not to be confused with a scientific discovery, and the toothbrush is the former not the latter, as are most commercially advertised products.

In China the prevailing World View is Taoist, which as Needham points out encourages "technology without science."[105] That technology can thrive independently of science is so easily established historically that one wonders how serious papers can be published in such a journal of international fame as *Science* stating categorically that technology owes its existence to scientific endeavor. In point of fact the truth is precisely the reverse, as Needham himself admits. He says: "Technologists, lacking scientific background to their thought, have a habit of doing the right things for the wrong reasons."[106] Kroeber has observed, "It is significant that the Chinese have made many important inventions but not one major scientific discovery. They have sought a way of life but not an understanding or a control of nature beyond what was immediately useful."[107]

Returning to our more general discussion, it is interesting

---

[105] Needham's words are: "The spirit of technology without theoretical science seems to be found within Taoist philosophy itself" (*Science and Civilization in China*, Vol. 2, Cambridge, 1956, p. 85). The word "philosophy" here really means "view of nature" — not philosophy as a special concern with understanding purely for its own sake.

[106] Ibid., p. 84. The assumption that scientific understanding must precede technological advance is a fundamental error which misleads a number of writers today, even such great ones as Claude Levi-Strauss. Lucien Levy-Bruhl held that primitive people do not think "scientifically." He did not mean "logically," but rather that they were highly specific and observed *distinctions* rather than commonalities, concretes rather than abstracts. He used the term prelogical, which was unfortunate, for he did *not* mean they were illogical but rather that they were logical on different premises. One of the most elaborate challenges to Levy-Bruhl has appeared in Levi-Strauss's work *The Savage Mind*. But this writer is not less misguided, I believe, because he fails to distinguish between technology (which all primitive people excelled in) and science (which they lacked). Levi-Strauss argues that the technology of Neolithic Man was sufficiently advanced that his predecessors, Paleolithic Man, must have had a highly developed scientific attitude to lay the basis for the subsequent culture. His reference to "scientific" knowledge (p. 14) is a serious mistake to my mind. And virtually *all* his illustrations are really proofs of the precise opposite, since the whole emphasis is upon discrete knowledge, knowledge of bits and pieces, of particles — not recognition of wholes, of nonexistent but abstracted categories. The very fact that the Greeks equated philosophers and scientists and that Plato himself defined the former as sunopticoi (i.e., "see-ers of things together") really proves the difference in approach.

[107] Kroeber, A. L., *Configurations of Culture Growth*, Univ. of California Press, 1944, p. 184.

to find that H. G. Wells also noted the fundamental difference between the thought patterns of the Chinese and our own:[108]

> The difference between any of these Chinese tongues and the more Western languages is profound.... The relation of words to each other is expressed by quite different methods from the Aryan method. Chinese grammar is a thing different in nature from English grammar; it is a separate and different invention.... Consequently, any such thing as a literal translation from Chinese into English is an impossibility. The very method of the thought is different.

The fact is admitted by Needham, for he says that caution is required in interpreting Chinese philosophy since "in China the word Philosophy did not quite mean what it came to mean in Europe."[109]

Throughout this whole discussion one sees repeatedly recognition of the close bond that exists between language and World View. Harry Hoijer has put it:[110]

> It is quite an illusion to imagine that one adjusts to reality essentially without the use of language, and that language is merely an incidental means of solving specific problems of communication or reflection. The fact of the matter is that the "real" world is to a large extent unconsciously built upon the language habits of the group.... The worlds in which different societies live are distinct worlds, not merely the same world with different labels attached.

Jespersen repeatedly underscores this fact, and in his famous work *The Philosophy of Grammar* he quotes Stuart Mill with approval as having said, "The structure of every sentence is a lesson in logic."[111]

Considering once more the situation in my own country vis-a-vis the French/English language confrontation and the present discussion about bilingualism as the goal for the average citizen, it is doubtful if any one individual can ever be truly bilingual. Possibly a few exceptional people achieve it in a measure, but since, as Susanne Langer put it, one lives in an entire universe when one speaks and thinks in a language and must move into an entirely new one in transferring to another language, it is hard to see how anyone who was not mildly

---

[108] Wells, H. G., *Outline of History*, new enlarged edition, Vol. 1, ed. Raymond Postgate, Doubleday, N.Y., 1949, p. 150.

[109] Needham, Joseph, op. cit., Vol. 2 (ref. 105), p. 1.

[110] Hoijer, Harry, "The Relation of Language to Culture" in *Anthropology Today*, ed. A. L. Kroeber, Univ. of Chicago Press, 1953, p. 558.

[111] Jespersen, Otto, *The Philosophy of Grammar*, Allen & Unwin, 1963, p. 47.

schizophrenic could adopt at one and the same time a shift back and forth completely from one universe to another. Perhaps when the languages are very closely related in the philosophy of grammar it may happen, but it seems likely to me that a man who believes he has complete "facility" in both French and English has in fact *complete* facility in neither. But I may be quite wrong. The French language sustains a rather different World View from the English and one wonders if one can live in two such worlds at one time.

A modern Chinese philosopher, Chang Tung-San, was quoted as having said recently:[112]

> Take Aristotelian logic, for example, which is evidently based on Greek grammar. The differences between Latin, French, English and German grammatical forms do not result in any difference between Aristotelian logic and their respective rules of reasoning, because they belong to the same Indo-European linguistic family. Should this logic be applied to Chinese thought, however, it will prove inappropriate. This fact shows that Aristotelian logic is based on the western system of language. Therefore we should not follow western logicians in taking for granted that their logic is the Universal Rule in human reasoning.

I think it significant that in her latest book, *Mind: An Essay on Human Feeling*, Susanne Langer, in trying to deal with the old problem of the relationship between mind and brain argues that we have our problems in dealing with the origin of consciousness because we have a "thing-oriented" culture.[113] It will be recalled that a fundamental difference between Hebrew and Greek lies in the emphasis in Hebrew upon verbal forms by contrast with the Greek emphasis on nouns. So Susanne Langer says that as long as we look at the problem as though man were essentially a machine with a driver in charge (two "things"), we shall always have difficulty in accounting for the driver since he cannot be allowed to originate from the same source as the machine he drives. So she argues we need a new approach, and the key to this new approach is not "thing" but "act." When we discuss the subject, when we speculate on the problem on the basis of a "thing" view of reality, we have the old classic materialism, a "nothing but" (no-thing but) philosophy, a reduction-

---

[112] Tung-San, Chang, quoted by Warren Weaver, "Science and People," *Science,* 122 (1955): 1258.

[113] Langer, Susanne, *Mind: An Essay on Human Feeling*, Vol. 1, Johns Hopkins Press, Baltimore, 1967, pp. 5-10 especially.

ist philosophy that has not led to any useful advance in our understanding of how the mind works on the body. We see the mind as one thing and the body as another thing, and we have not been able to dream up a useful idea as to how they interact. Langer proposes that we should abandon the old paradigm stated in the form "agent-action-object" which she believes is "rooted in the grammar of our language." We must not divide the agent from the object but bind them inseparably in the single verb "act." I have not done justice at all to her thesis which occupied nearly 500 pages, but one cannot help seeing in this approach a reflection of the Chinese philosopher's complaint that we must not assume that Indo-European languages *per se* automatically give the only true picture of reality. We may have reached a critical point where the philosophy of grammar of some other culture might have to be called into play to complete our understanding. It is with some such thought in mind that Benjamin Lee Whorf wrote:[114]

> I believe that those who envision a future world speaking only one tongue whether English, German, Russian, or any other, hold a misguided ideal and would do the evolution of the human mind a great disservice. Western Culture has made, through language, a provisional analysis of reality and, without correctives, holds resolutely to that analysis as final. The only correctives lie in all these other tongues which by aeons of independent evolution have arrived at different but equally logical provisional analyses.

What has been said of China is also essentially true of primitive people and of all those civilizations of antiquity which were neither Semitic nor Indo-European. At the very foundation of all civilizations in which organized city life plays a significant part were the Sumerians. One of the most informed students of these people at the present time is Samuel N. Kramer. After considering their inventiveness and having referred to them as a gifted and practical people, he says nonetheless that they never apparently made any search after truth for its own sake. The quite advanced subjects (mathematics, and so forth) which they taught in their schools "did not stem out of what may be called the scientific urge."[115] Subsequently, the whole idea of making generalizations seems to have been unknown to the Sumerians,

---

114 Whorf, Benjamin Lee, quoted by Alexander Gode, "The Case for Interlingua," *Sci. Monthly,* Aug., 1953, p. 90.

115 Kramer, Samuel, *The Tablets of Sumer,* Falcon's Wing Press, Indian Hills, Colorado, 1956, pp. 6, 33, 59, and 83.

and thus, although we have quite a number of Sumerian grammatical lists, "no where do you find a single explicit grammatical definition or rule." Similarly, although we have many mathematical tables and illustrations of problems with their solutions, we have "no statement of general principles, axioms, or theories." Once again, although the Sumerians compiled numerous law codes, "no where is there a statement of legal theory." Speaking of the highly practical medical knowledge which they left on record, there is no evidence that a Sumerian physician ever made use of experiment or verification. Their cosmology was set forth in some detail and the deities of their pantheon appear to have been real enough, yet the Sumerians apparently never tried to correct the anomalies and inconsistencies that were involved in them; these anomalies never seem to have struck them. Similarly J. J. Finkelstein observed:[116]

> There probably has never been another civilization so single-mindedly bent on the accumulation of information, and on eschewing any generalization or annunciating of principles. Ultimate understanding of the Universe, they seem to have held, required nothing but the painstaking accumulation of as much detail as possible about literally everything.

This is not the first step toward scientific thinking: indeed, it may actually be a hindrance against taking any further such steps at all. In his book dealing with science in antiquity, Benjamin Farrington in speaking of the mathematics which the Babylonians inherited from the Sumerians and which, incidentally, was remarkably advanced—involving the use of fractions, of quadratic equations, and even of a kind of logarithmic system—remarked:[117]

> We are in the presence of abundant evidence of Babylonian mathematical ability, but their tables of roots, cube roots, squares, and cubes, etc., are offered to us like our own practical tables for calculating interest, *without proof* of theory. So that as far as the evidence goes, Babylonian arithmetic is under the suspicion of being largely empirical.

The same is equally true of Egypt. Martin Engberg has said, "Nowhere is there any indication that the Egyptians were inter-

---

[116] Finkelstein, J. J., "Mesopotamian Historiography," *Proc. of Am. Philosophical Soc.,* 107 (1963): 463, in a series of papers entitled, "Cuneiform Studies and the History of Civilization."

[117] Farrington, B., *Science in Antiquity,* Home University Library, Oxford, 1947, p. 24.

ested in theoretical problems."[118] Similarly, Sir Alan Gardiner in the introduction to his *Egyptian Grammar* put the matter even more forcibly when he said, "No people has ever shown itself more adverse from philosophical speculation or more whole-heartedly devoted to material interest."[119]

It is general to find in articles written for popular consumption references to the highly developed technology of the Egyptians, which is not infrequently equated with or misnamed science. But William Hayes wrote:[120]

> Though intensely devout, the ancient Egyptian had neither the mental nor the spiritual equipment necessary to the creation or even the adaptation of a great religion. An analysis of the Egyptian religion shows that it consisted of at least four un-related cults or phases, no one of which ever passed beyond what we should regard as a primitive stage. Though intelligent and quick to learn, he had a mind of the practical unimaginative type. He was a materialist, not given to deep speculative thought, and was unable either to evolve or express a purely abstract idea.

It is not surprising that for all their advanced technology and skill, the Egyptians should not have moved into a scientific age for the same reason that they did not develop a theology. The reason for this seems once again to be rooted in their World View which, in turn, was predetermined in each generation by language. P. LePage Renouf in his *Lectures on the Origin and Growth of Religion,* noted that certain languages as vehicles of though appear to be inferior to others, and he proposed as an example the Egyptian language as not capable of giving expression to theological thinking.[121]

On another occasion Renouf, quoting Renan, wrote:[122]

> Certain languages as vehicles of (certain kinds of) thought are inferior to others, and as long as men are confined to the

---

[118] Engberg, Martin, *The Dawn of Civilization,* Univ. of Knowledge Series, Cuneo Press, N.Y., 1938, p. 153.

[119] Gardiner, Martin, *Egyptian Grammar,* Oxford, 1927, Section 3, p. 4.

[120] Hayes, William C., "Daily Life in Ancient Egypt," *Nat. Geog. Mag.,* Oct., 1941, pp. 425f. Susanne Langer says: "The Egyptians and Mayans and Aztecs moved enormous stones, but left no theoretical work on dynamics which would indicate that they knew — or even asked — how and why their methods worked just the way they did" (*Mind: An Essay On Human Feeling,* Johns Hopkins Press, Baltimore, 1967, p. 56).

[121] Renouf, P. LePage, *Lectures on the Origin and Growth of Religion,* Hibbert Lectures for 1897, Williams & Norgate, London, p. 60.

[122] Ibid., pp. 60, 61.

inferior vehicle of thought, they are unable to raise themselves to the levels of others who enjoy a more efficient instrument. It is difficult to conceive the Egyptians as otherwise than incapacitated by their language from profound philosophy. It is hardly possible to read a page written in an Indo-European language, from Sanscrit to Keltic, without coming across some kind of dialectic process of which I do not remember a single trace in an Egyptian text.

Although it is far removed from matters Egyptian, it is interesting to note an ethnologist, Elie Reclus, writing many years ago of the Quoit (Eskimo) and remarking: "Their religion, purely 'instructive,' has little resemblance to our abstract theologies, so closely bound up with metaphysics."[123] He concluded:

> Primitive men have some rudimentary ideas, some moral, religious, and philosophic perceptions which after being refined, elucidated, and arranged, would yield a system neither better nor worse than many others, but they have not elaborated this system.

In his four-volume study of mathematics, James Newman, speaking of the Rhind Papyrus, remarked:[124]

> The Egyptians made no great contribution to mathematical knowledge. They were practical men, not given to much speculative or abstract inquiries. Dreamers were rare among them, and mathematics is nourished by dreamers.

And mathematics is basic to the development of science. Newman continued subsequently:[125]

> The Rhind Papyrus, though it demonstrates the inability of the Egyptians to generalize and their penchant for clinging to cumbersome calculating processes, proves that they were remarkably pertinacious in solving everyday problems ... and uncommonly skillful in making do with the awkward methods they employed.

Similarly, in connection with Egyptian medicine, Ileen Stewart observed:[126]

> Much of the medical law of the Egyptian became the heritage of the Greeks as they fashioned their civilization in the last few centuries B.C. ... The knowledge they inherited was essentially factual, the accumulation of Egyptian observations and

[123] Reclus, Elie, op. cit. (ref. 63) , pp. 87, 229.

[124] Newman, James R., "The Rhind Papyrus" in *The World of Mathematics*, Vol. 1, ed. by J. R. Newman, Simon & Schuster, N.Y., 1956, p. 11.

[125] Ibid., p. 11.

[126] Stewart, Ileen, "Helminths in History," *Sci. Monthly*, June, 1951, p. 348.

experience. The Greeks attempted to put these facts together and to derive a systematic pattern in nature. Many of their interpretations are still tinged with mysticism, but they were philosophical and logical — as the Egyptians had never been.

James R. Newman wrote elsewhere in the same connection:[127]

> The Greeks were the pupils of the East, but as the noted historian Michael Rostovtzeff has said, "they refashioned all they received, and stamped a fresh character upon it." They had an endless curiosity, a passion to discover "the rule of law in nature." The Greeks asked not How? but Why?

Precisely the same thing may be said of Chinese medicine, the achievements of which are quite astounding. George E. Wakerling in the journal *Circulation Research* refers to what has come to be known as "the Yellow Emperor's Classic of Internal Medicine," the Emperor himself being dated somewhere around 2600 B.C., points out that Harvey was anticipated. "The blood current flows continuously in a circle and never stops," is one among many acute observations in this very ancient manuscript.[128] He points out further that in the 16th and 17th centuries B.C. several Egyptian papyri not only counselled examination of the pulse but also direct auscultation of the heart as the source of the pulse. Wakerling refers to several other remarkable observations but concludes, "... then followed the period of the Dark Ages." Technology, or purely factual knowledge, has its limitations.

One might suppose that in Egypt some philosophers would have arisen, and it is customary to refer to such people as Ptah-hotep as one of them. But just as we have seen in connection with Confucius, so of this man James Baikie remarked:[129]

> All the evidence goes to show that the Egyptian was one of the most severely practical of men, who sought learning not for any joy in the attainment of truth for its own sake but simply as a means to an end. ... The wisdom of Ptah-hotep and of Kagemni is in general of a canny, practical nature, concerning itself with the ordinary details of life and conduct and inculcat-

127 Newman, James R., reviewing Morris Kline's "Mathematics in Western Culture," *Sci. American*, Feb., 1954, p. 92.

128 Wakerling, George E., "From Bright Towards Light: The Story of Hypertensive Research," *Circulation Research*, II (2) (1962): 131. I think it is worth noting also that the ancient art of feeling the pulse was also known in China from works dated 2500 B.C. See an article on this by D. E. Bedford, *British Heart Jour.*, 13 (1951): 423-47.

129 Baikie, James, *The Story of the Pharaohs*, Black, London, 1908, p. 59.

ing prudence which, how ever praiseworthy, reaches no high ideals but is based mainly on self interest.

The daily lives of their upper classes must have been as comfortable as one can imagine, their physical needs supplied with elegance and good taste in marked contrast with the Greeks who initiated science in Europe but whose lives were evidently lived in rather comfortless austerity. Clive Bell has pointed out that the disinterestedness of the latter in their pursuit of truth has been made a reproach to them. As he put it, "They sought truth for its own sake . . . not as a means to power and comfort. . . . The Athenians wished to live richly rather than to be rich."[130] The life of a well-to-do Greek in classical times, so rich and complete in thought and feeling, was in most material things, as Clive Bell put it, "indecently deficient."

I think the same is still true of Indo-Europeans: that those who are really immersed in deep thought have a tendency to be totally indifferent to practical things and to the ordinary amenities of life. This in itself is not too surprising perhaps, and while it might conceivably be true in any culture that some of the more thoughtful members were impractical and would tend to be considered merely as lazy, what is to be remembered is that Indo-Europeans have had a tendency to look up to such men, not down upon them. Not every Semite is religious, nor every Japhethite an intellectual— by any means. Nevertheless, the Semites have always recognized the preeminence of spiritual life over physical life, they have had what might be called a spiritual aristocracy. I am excluding those Semites who are not strictly culturally Semites any longer, who have been immersed in a culture that is alien to their own. It is true also that Indo-Europeans have tended always to revere an intellectual elite. And I think it worth noting (*apropos* of the Hamite branch) that many primitive cultures demand that a young suitor prove himself in some way to be ingenious before he is acceptable; and the Chinese produced biographies on a national scale dealing with their inventors but not with anyone else. And there is a tendency for Egyptian and Sumerian records to attach more importance to engineers in the broadest sense than to any other class. We do not know the name of one priest as far as I am aware, but we do know the names of some of their architects, builders, and engineers.

Moreover, as Hegel pointed out years ago, Hindu philoso-

[130] Bell, Clive, *Civilization*, Penguin Books, London, 1938, p. 63.

phers achieved great heights, yet because they attached so little importance to the material world they did not produce science. The dependence of science upon the amalgamation of philosophy and technology needs to be underscored, since the Greeks also failed to bring Europe into a scientific age owing to their stated disinterest in practical things, although in both India and Greece the technical base was lacking for the conversion of philosophy into science. The reasons why science did not emerge in either Greece or India seem to have been much the same, in the final analysis: namely, a scorn for things practical and a distaste for manual labor.

Aryan philosophy in India was not applied to Hamitic technology because the caste of technicians was not to be associated with. It was, on the other hand, applied to religion because the priestly caste was a high one. Consequently, while science did not emerge, theology, in the form of Hinduism — did. Lucille Schulberg observed:[131]

> The enormous racial pride of the Aryans, in fact, encouraged the separation of peoples, and non-Aryan craftsmen who banded together to guard the secrets of their craft, apparently came to supervise all the aspects of the behaviour of their groups.

And again, of these technicians who were the descendants of the original inhabitants of India who had founded the Indus Valley civilization, Schulberg wrote, "These conquered peoples were completely segregated, forced to live in clusters outside the Aryan village boundaries and barred from Aryan religious rites."[132] Aryan philosophical interests were dominant:[133]

> Of all the philosophers that India has produced one who graced the 9th century A.D. ranks among the great minds in all history. That was Shankara, a brahman born in Kerala, in South India. In a brief life of 32 years he did for Hinduism what the 13th century Thomas Aquinas did for Christianity: he took his religion apart and examined it in minute detail, then drew the pieces together again in one cohesive whole. He wrote the most famous of all the commentaries on the Upanishads and established himself as chief exponent of the system of philosophy most esteemed by Hindu intellectuals.

It has often been argued that England lags behind some other countries (notably the U.S.A.) in technology because there is a strong feeling that technology is a somewhat less distin-

---

131 Schulberg, Lucille, op. cit. (ref. 81), p. 139.
132 Ibid., p. 37.
133 Ibid., p. 121.

guished occupation. The true gentleman does not do things with his hands. Against this, it has also been pointed out that in the early days the Royal Society was formed by men who were actively engaged in doing experiments and working at their instruments with their hands. Still, it appears that they were not really concerned with applied technology. Lord Raglan said of them, "Scientists of the 17th century were but little interested in utilitarian aspects of their inventions. Their object was to cause wonder and surprise, to produce 'a most incredible thing.' Nothing was farther from their minds than the idea of developing their inventions for the purpose of altering the conditions under which they lived."[134]

I think Lord Raglan has stated only half the truth about them, because they were driven by an even more powerful urge, namely, the urge to explore and define and demonstrate the orderliness of the universe — almost as an act of worship. The basis of this urge is important in the present context. Alfred North Whitehead asserted that "centuries of belief in a God Who combined the personal energy of Jehovah (the Semitic contribution) with the rationality of a Greek philosopher (the Japhethic contribution) first produced that firm expectation of systematic order which rendered possible the birth of modern science."[135] Their concern was in no sense a practical one.

In our culture the scientist in his ivory tower appears generally as something of a heroic figure. But he can also be a ludicrous one. James Conant says, "The scientific attitude is essentially that of the savants who, drinking to their next discovery, coupled with their toast the hope that it might never be of use to anybody."[136] And Robert Clark in a similar vein refers to the great Irish mathematician, William Hamilton, who when he had developed a theory of quarternions in the middle of the 18th century, "was very pleased because it had no practical application."[137]

Susanne Langer has observed that philosophy has traditionally dealt in general terms and that the reason for its "proverbial uselessness" once the sciences have been "born from its mysterious womb" is that it made general propositions not only its im-

[134] Raglan, Lord, *How Came Civilization,* Methuen, London, 1939, p. 176.

[135] Whitehead, Alfred N., quoted by C. S. Lewis, *Miracles,* Macmillan, N.Y., 1947, pp. 127, 128.

[136] Conant, J. B., op. cit. (ref. 102), p. 117.

[137] Clark, Robert A., *Six Talks on Jung's Psychology,* Boxwood Press, Pitts., 1953, p. 22.

mediate aim, but its sole material."[138] The philosopher's aim is, as she has said, "generality" — but it leads to science which can deal with specifics and is increasingly being called upon to do so in terms of "products" of basic research, though "all really basic thinking is philosophical."

In view of the tremendous strides forward which have resulted technologically as a direct outcome of this philosophizing tendency among Europeans, one may wonder why the Industrial Revolution wasn't paralleled in India where thoughtful men were doing much the same thing. It seems to me that if the Aryans had not so completely destroyed the Hamitic cultures of the Indus Valley when they first moved down from the north into their subcontinent, and had not also degraded the survivors of that culture to such an extent that they never had the opportunity to perpetuate their technical know-how even at a much reduced level, these conquered people might have provided the same kind of pabulum which Europeans inherited partly from the great Middle East cultures and partly from the Far East through the Arabs, which has been the basis of their advance. Had the Indian also made more frequent contacts with the Chinese and some other Far Eastern peoples like the Koreans who were equally ingenious, this too might have supplied their lack. It has been said of the Greeks that they did not move forward toward an Industrial Revolution because they did not need labor-saving devices or technological aids of any kind since they

---

[138] Langer, Susanne, op. cit. (ref. 113), Vol. I, pp. xx, xxi. A. N. Whitehead wrote: "All the world over and at all times there have been practical men, absorbed in the irreducible and stubborn facts; all the world over and at all times there have been men of philosophical temperament, who have been absorbed in the meaning of general principles" (*Science and the Modern World*, Macmillan, N.Y., 1925).

Commenting on this quote, Philipp Frank remarks: "In antiquity and the Middle Ages, there was very little co-operation between these two types of men. Whitehead emphasizes the point that Science in the modern sense was born when such co-operation started, and when both interests, in facts and ideas, were combined in one and the same person.... In the society of ancient Greece the philosophers ... who were interested in general principles belonged to a higher social class than those more interested in the hard facts of technological application, the artisans and craftsmen. The latter belonged to a low class and had no understanding of general ideas.... We know that the ancient Greeks and Romans displayed a marvellous art and skill in building and even in some fields of mechanical engineering but the knowledge of these ancient builders and engineers was not 'philosophic' or 'scientific'; it was purely technological" (*Philosophy of Science*, Prentice Hall, N.J., 1957, p. 25).

were so well supplied with slaves. Farrington and others believe that this is not entirely correct. Apparently, what actually happened was that, having a very large slave population, all menial (i.e., manual) tasks were undertaken by them so that any kind of labor was, in a sense, degraded. Hence the Greeks objected to doing anything with their hands, even to drawing diagrams in the sand to illustrate a theorem.

There were exceptions among the Greeks, but they were exceptions only in a manner of speaking, and the "manner of speaking" is interesting. Ralph Linton has pointed this out:[139]

> At the siege of Syracuse by the Romans, Archimedes really upset them by his constant invention of new devices to burn their ships and disorganize them generally. But Plutarch, writing 600 years later, feels it necessary to apologize for Archimedes having made practical use of his mathematical formulae and so on, and he says that the philosopher had made machines not of his own free will but because the King of Syracuse had requested him to build these machines as a demonstration of the clear laws of mathematics and mechanics which, in this way, could be explained to persons of lower minds who could not perceive the truths in the abstract.

If we go back to Plutarch's own words, we find the following:[140]

> Archimedes had such a depth of understanding, such a dignity of sentiment, and so copious a fund of mathematical knowledge, that, though in the invention of these machines he gained the reputation of a man endowed with divine rather than human knowledge, yet he did not vouchsafe to leave any account of them in writing. For he considered all attention to mechanics and every art that ministers to common use as mean and sordid, and placed his whole delight in those intellectual speculations, which, without any relation to the necessities of life, have an intrinsic excellence arising from truth and demonstration only.

Completely in this tradition is the feeling which has still persisted in parts of Europe, particularly in England, that engineering is a less distinguished and honorable profession than philosophy or scientific research.[141] But so completely deceived

---

[139] Archimedes: see Ralph Linton, op. cit. (ref. 77), p. 665.

[140] Plutarch, *Lives*, trans. by John and William Langhorne, Routledge, London, n.d., p. 221.

[141] On this see *The Integration of Technologies*, ed. by Leslie Holliday, Hutchinson, London, 1966, 167 pp., illus., where it is shown clearly how British social attitudes still militate against the exploration of a scientific technology. In an editorial entitled "Does Every Apple Have A Worm?" in the British journal *Nature*, Dec. 30, 1967, p. 1257, a report is given of the

have we been in the New World by the tremendous strides we have made in technology that we assume our high technology to be the result of our own natural inventiveness and interest in mechanics, and the almost direct outcome of our science. Charles V. Kidd, quoting Vannevar Bush, remarked:[142]

> New products and new processes do not appear full grown. They are founded on new principles and new conceptions, which in turn are painstakingly developed by research in the purest realms of Science.

It is hard to think of any statement on this general subject which is so completely and utterly wrong. Vannevar Bush also remarked: "A nation which depends upon others for its new basic knowledge will be slow in industrial progress...."[143] If the writer did but know it, this too is a complete misrepresentation of history, for it can be shown that our "basic knowledge" in the technical sense — and he is speaking of "mechanical skill," etc. — was derived almost entirely from non-Indo-European sources.

Claude Levi-Strauss tends to make precisely the same mistake when he speaks of the emergence of Neolithic culture as being based on a "long *scientific* tradition" [my emphasis] because the developments which preceded it must have involved an extended period of conscious and deliberate experiment.[144] The fact is that almost all we know about primitive people (with a very few notable exceptions) is that they are *conservative in the extreme* and simply do not experiment to evolve new and better techniques. What they do seem to have been able to do is to hit upon remarkably effective solutions without hunting for improvements as we habitually find we must do. He argues, wrongly I believe, that only experiment "could have yielded practical and useful results." Hamitic peoples have advanced technology because they have a genius for invention, not because

Reith Lectures in which Dr. Edmund Leach of Cambridge said: "If you ask a professional scientist ... he will insist that genuine human control of technology is impossible. That being so, the wise man must avoid all involvement in practical affairs.... Only by detachment can he hope to gain true understanding.... (This) summarizes the basic philosophy of our science-laden society.... His concern is to understand the Universe, not to improve it."

[142] Vannevar Bush, quoted by Charles V. Kidd, "Basic Research: Description versus Definition," *Science* 129 (1959): 368.

[143] Ibid.

[144] Levi-Strauss, Claude, *The Savage Mind,* Weidenfeld & Nicolson, London, 1966, pp. 14, 15.

they have been scientific; and Japhethites have advanced technology because they are philosophically minded and *not* because they are inventive. Our "inventions" are basically imports. In this sense we who lacked technology have been completely dependent in the past upon people who never created science, though we have so far outstripped them that they now look to us instead of we to them.

David G. Barry in the same journal had said this:[145]

> As a culture we have prided ourselves on our "practical nature" and on Yankee inventiveness. These ideas are pleasant to contemplate and are seldom questioned. Historians of American Science have not, however, been able to establish any unusual capacity for inventiveness or practicality in the American record.

Barry points out that we have placed tremendous emphasis as a people on the concept of "utility," but he thinks that this is undoubtedly due to the demanding religious views of the Founding Fathers "who left us with the Puritan ethic of useful work." He shows how very different this was from the practical interest of the non-Indo-European peoples who had no such "other world" aims in view. Although he does not do so, he might also have noted that this was the spark which led to the founding of the Royal Society. He wrote:

> It is generally agreed that this concept is a heritage from the upright and demanding religious views of the New England forefathers, who left us with the Puritan ethic of useful work. However, the operational significance of the early Puritan concept of utility differs greatly from that of the concept widely held in this country today. Utility as early Americans viewed it was an integral part of the Puritan religion blended with their theology and the science they used to support it. The Puritans saw nature and the cosmos as the unchanging product of the original creation. All nature had been designed by the Creator, and was operated with providential utility to benefit man. Man himself was part of this orderly scheme and had a moral responsibility to acquire new knowledge of nature and to seek to understand the divine utility of natural phenomena as part of his daily life. Through such knowledge he could better know the Creator. Thus the Puritan concept of utility was part of an open-ended, ever-expanding system which gave highest honour to pursuit of new knowledge.

We revert once more to the statement made above by Bush.

---

[145] Barry, David G., "Research and Purpose," in a letter to the editor, *Science* 147 (1965): 1524.

Melvin Kranzberg in reviewing a work by Bronowski and others entitled, *Technology: Man Remakes His World,* wrote:[146]

> A typical statement (from the book) reads as follows: "All progress in technology depends on a scientific understanding of the way in which nature works. . . ." Nonsense! For most of human history, when technological progress was dependent on craft tradition, no "scientific understanding" was involved in technological advance.

He gives several further similar examples of this kind of faulty reasoning which in the final analysis is really based on national pride — one might almost say, on racial conceit.

In the next chapter we shall examine some of the evidence which students of the history of technology have begun to uncover.

---

[146] Kranzberg, Melvin, under heading, "Our Industrial Society," *Science* 146 (1964): 237.

Chapter 5

THEOLOGY AND SCIENCE

IT IS CUSTOMARY to view Western Man as the most inventive creature who ever lived, and other peoples as unimaginative and backward by comparison. For this reason it has never surprised those who write textbooks of history that our own civilization has advanced so far ahead of all that had preceded it. Obviously we are more inventive, so we have achieved a higher civilization.

Very few people until quite recently were aware of the achievements of other ancient and modern cultures which have not shared our tradition. It had been popularly admitted that their arts and architecture were remarkable enough; but their technology was of little account except for the occasional odd device like the compass or a very inefficient gunpowder. The indebtedness of our own technology to others completely escaped notice, and even now is not widely recognized.

However, with every study in depth of the historical background of technology in the Western World, it becomes more and more apparent, difficult though it may be to believe, that Indo-Europeans are basically uninventive. And the same may be said with equal force of the Semitic people, including the Arabs whose contribution to our civilization in the field of technology can be shown to have been that of "carriers" of the genius of others rather than innovators themselves.

One often hears it said that many notable advances are owed to outstanding Jewish scientists. This is undoubtedly true. But as Jessie Bernard has pointed out, it is not the Jews who remain true to their cultural heritage who contribute in this way; it is those, like Freud and Einstein — and even in a sense the Apostle Paul — who break with that tradition in thought and language, identifying themselves with Japheth.[147]

The inventiveness of Hamitic peoples has been elaborated at considerable length in another Doorway Paper and we shall not unnecessarily repeat what is said there.[148] However, some repetition is desirable to put the picture into focus. But for the most part we will give some further illustrations of a historical circumstance which can be documented so completely that no serious student can any longer doubt the fact either of the un-inventiveness of Japheth and Shem or the genius in this direction of Ham.

What follows must inevitably read rather like a catalog for, after all, that is essentially what it is. To fill out the context of each statement would lengthen the paper undesirably, but the reader will have the documentation in full and can therefore look up the context for himself and judge whether there is any exaggeration.

Consider first a few random quotations from widely separated sources, separated both in time and space. George Sarton has quoted Hudson as having remarked in 1892:[149]

> It is sad to reflect that all our domestic animals have descended to us from those ancient times which we are accustomed to regard as dark and barbarous, while the effect of our modern so-called humane civilization has been purely destructive of animal life.

It is true that there is one animal we may have been responsible for domesticating, though under somewhat amusing circumstances. Sarton commented:[150]

> The only animal domesticated in historic times is the ostrich; this was a poor achievement which was justified only because some women and generals wanted feathers for their hats.

All the archaeological researches and studies of other cultures

---

[147] Bernard, Jessie, "Can Science Transcend Culture?" *Sci. Monthly,* Oct., 1950, p. 271.

[148] Part IV, "The Technology of Hamitic People."

[149] Hudson, W. H., quoted by George Sarton, *A History of Science,* Harvard, 1952, p. 5, footnote 2. The destructiveness of Western Man in this respect is appalling. According to Dr. James M. Dolan, associate curator of the San Diego Zoological Gardens, more than forty kinds of mammals have been exterminated by man since the beginning of the present century (Letter to the Editor, *Time,* Feb. 23, 1968, p. 8).

[150] Sarton, George, op. cit. (ref. 149), p. 5.

since that time have not essentially altered the picture. Carleton S. Coon has stated categorically: "Linguists tell us that Indo-European speakers did not initially domesticate one useful animal or one cultivated plant."[151]

W. J. Perry, whose reconstructions of history are not too well accepted since he believed that every cultural element spread only by diffusion and never by independent invention, was nevertheless essentially correct when he wrote, "The Celts, like the Teutons, never invented anything; the whole of their culture shows signs of derivation from the Mediterranean."[152] And Lord Raglan said the same thing with respect to the Romans, "The old Roman ritual gave little encouragement to inventiveness, and later cults were imported ready-made from the East. As a result, the Romans invented almost nothing."[153] Or to quote Joseph Needham again, "The only Persian invention of first rank was the windmill.... And unless the rotary quern be attributed to them, the ancient Europeans of the Mediterranean Basin launched only one valuable mechanical technique, namely, the pot chain pump."[154]

Speaking of how little Europeans contributed to the know-how of the American Indians within their own environment, J. Grahame Clark observed, "During the four centuries since the Discovery (1492) the White Man had failed to make a single contribution of importance."[155]

What has been said of Indo-Europeans is true of the Semites also. Thus, speaking of the Babylonians and Assyrians (both Semitic) who succeeded the Hamitic Sumerians in Mesopotamia, Vere G. Childe said, "In the next two millennia one can scarcely point to a first class invention or discovery...." Childe mentions two possible exceptions — the alphabet and iron smelting.[156] There is some doubt, however, about the latter. It seems more likely that the credit for this must go to the Hittites,[157] who, al-

---

[151] Coon, Carleton S., *The Races of Europe*, Macmillan, N.Y., 1939, p. 178.

[152] Perry, W. J., *The Growth of Civilization*, Penguin, London, 1937, p. 157.

[153] Raglan, Lord, op. cit. (ref. 134), p. 179.

[154] Needham, Joseph, op. cit., Vol. 1 (ref. 105), 1954, p. 240.

[155] Clark, J. Grahame D., "New World Origins," *Antiquity*, June, 1940, p. 118.

[156] Childe, Vere Gordon, *New Light on the Most Ancient East*, Kegan Paul, London, 1935, p. 203.

[157] Hittites and iron smelting: see Sabatino Moscati, *Ancient Semetic Civilizations*, Elek Books, London, 1957, p. 52.

though their ruling class appears to have been Indo-European (somewhat analogous to the situation in early Indian history) are nevertheless placed within the family of Ham in Genesis 10. Indeed, they may conceivably be related to the Chinese who also made extensive use of cast iron long before the Indo-Europeans had learned to use it. As far as I know, the raw materials did not exist in Mesopotamia. Ralph Linton supported Childe in his contention when he observed categorically, "Not a single item of later technology was introduced by the invading Semites":[158] they were strictly "invaders" coming into possession of Sumerian civilization ready-made. Elsewhere Linton also noted that "the Semitic language triumphed but not a single item of the later technology was introduced by them."[159]

As for the Arabs, who are essentially Semitic, though somewhat mixed because they have always been great traders and travelers, Lord Raglan having discussed the uninventiveness of the Romans, said:[160]

> Much the same can be said for the Moslems. There was a period of mild inventiveness while their religion was settling down into various sects, but since that process was completed about 900 years ago, no Moslem has invented anything.

Yet this is quite contrary to popular opinion. Their role as carriers from the Far East and from Africa has led to the somewhat widespread belief that they originated what we received from them. But on this point Rene Albrecht-Carrie wrote:[161]

> What is really relevant in this context is that the Arabs — or rather the wide variety of peoples whom they brought under their control and who came to pass under their name — were not so much innovators as collectors, organizers, synthesizers, and, most important, carriers of the contributions of other times and peoples. This is not to deny or minimize the crucial importance of their role or to ignore the fact that they made some valuable contributions of their own, but it remains largely true that the initiation of the "Scientific Revolution" was not of their own making. Nevertheless to this making they contributed mightily. . . . But the Arab contribution was, to repeat, mainly in the form of a transfer of ancient learning.

The role of the Arabs has been remarked upon by a number

[158] Linton, Ralph, op. cit. (ref. 77), p. 300.

[159] Ibid.

[160] Raglan, Lord, op. cit. (ref. 134), p. 179.

[161] Albrecht-Carrie, Rene, "Of Science, Its History and the Teaching Thereof," *Sci. Monthly,* July, 1951, p. 19. Even the so-called Arabic numerals are of Indian origin, Ralph Linton, op. cit. (ref. 77), p. 295.

of writers in recent years. Arthur Koestler in his study of man's changing views of the universe and speaking of the dawn of the Renaissance has confirmed Carrie's observations in a way that contributes to my thesis very pointedly. He wrote:[162]

> But the Arabs had merely been go-betweens, preservers and transmitters of the heritage (i.e., of Classical Greek philosophy) up into Europe. They had little scientific originality or creativeness of their own. During the centuries when they were the sole keepers of the (Greek) treasure, they did little to put it to use. They improved on calendrical astronomy and made excellent planetary tables; they elaborated both the Aristotelian and Ptolemaic models of the Universe; they imported into Europe the Indian system of numerals based on the symbol zero, the sine function, and the use of algebraic methods, but they did not advance theoretical science. The majority of the scholars who wrote in Arabic were not Arabs but Persians, Jews, and Nestorians; and by the 15th century, the scientific heritage of Islam had largely been taken over by the Portuguese Jews. But the Jews, too, were no more than go-betweens, a branch of the devious (cultural) "gulf-stream" which brought back to Europe its Greek and Alexandrian heritage, enriched by Indian and Persian additions. It is a curious fact that the Arabic-Judaic tenure of this vast body of knowledge which lasted two or three centuries, remained barren; whilst as soon as it was reincorporated into Latin civilization, it bore immediate and abundant fruit.

Similarly, Desmond Stewart, writing on "Early Islam," observed:[163]

> Although ninth century Muslims had a passionate desire to learn what the Greeks had discovered, they were limited by two factors. First, the only manuscripts accessible to them were those that had been preserved by the late Greek schools; thus Homer and Sophocles were not to enter the Islamic heritage, because these Hellenistic schools had shown no concern for drama and poetry.
>
> Second, the Muslim's own primary interest was in practical matters, and it was mainly the works of Greek physicians, astronomers, mathematicians and geographers that appeared anew in Arabic dress. Although Greek philosophy had no such practical value, it was related to Greek science and was therefore translated along with the other works.

Thus the Arabs were not *really* interested in Greek literature in so far as it was *philosophical* but only in so far as it had practical

---

[162] Koestler, Arthur, *The Sleepwalkers*, Hutchinson, London, 1959, p. 105.

[163] Stewart, Desmond, *Early Islam*, The Great Ages of Man, Time-Life Pub., N.Y., 1967, p. 85.

importance.[164] Although the Greeks themselves were not practically minded, it is noteworthy that they did regard science as a branch of philosophy, and in fact did not discern between the two. We have perpetuated this by calling a scientist a Doctor of Philosophy.

The Arabs *seem* to have contributed to the sum total of the world's philosophical wealth, but it is an appearance only: as Sir Edward S. Creasy wrote some years ago:[165]

> Much of Hindoo science and philosophy, much of the literature of the later Persian kingdom of the Arsacidae, either originated from, or was largely modified by Grecian influences (arising from the conquests of Alexander the Great). So also, the learning and science of the Arabians were in a far less degree the result of original invention and genius, than the reproduction, in an altered form, of the Greek philosophy, and the Greek lore acquired by the Saracenic conquerors, together with their acquisition of the provinces which Alexander had subjugated nearly a thousand years before the armed disciples of Mohammed commenced their career in the East.

St. Chad Boscawan, one of the earlier cuneiform scholars to popularize the findings of archaeology in the Middle East, came to the same conclusion with respect to Babylonians: "There is a powerful element in the Semitic character which has been, and still is, a most important factor in their national life: it is that of adaptability. Inventors they have never shown themselves to be."[166] As an illustration of this adaptability, James Breasted points out some of the borrowings of the Babylonians from the Sumerians. He wrote:[167]

> Some of the Semites now learned to write their Semitic tongue by using Sumerian cuneiform signs for the purpose. The Semites in time, therefore, adopted their script, their weights, their measures, their mathematics, their system of numerals, their business terms, and a large measure of their judiciary systems.

The extent of this borrowing is reminiscent of the borrowings of the Romans from the Etruscans. Authorities are still not

---

[164] Fothergill, Philip C., *Historical Aspects of Organic Evolution*, Hollis & Carter, London, 1952, p. 9.

[165] Creasy, Sir Edward Shepperd, "The Battle of Arbela" in *Decisive Battles of the World, The World's Great Classics*, Vol. 10, Colonial Press, N.Y., 1900, p. 62.

[166] Boscawen, St. Chad, *The Bible and the Monuments*, Eyre & Spottiswoode, London, 1896, p. 18.

[167] Breasted, James, *Ancient Times: A History of the Ancient World*, Ginn, N.Y., 1935, p. 160.

in complete agreement about the origin of the Etruscans, but one thing upon which there is unanimity of opinion is that their language was not Indo-European.[168] Sir Gavin de Beer in a broadcast in England, observed:[169]

> It may seem remote to us (to ask who the Etruscans were) and yet it affects us closely for the following reasons. We regard the Romans as our civilizers, and we look up to them as the inventors of all sorts of things that they taught us. But it is now clear that, in their turn, the Romans learned many of these things from the Etruscans.

George Rawlinson, the great Orientalist and Classical Scholar, says in this regard:[170]

> The Romans themselves notwithstanding their intense national vanity acknowledged this debt to some extent and admitted that they derived from the Etruscans their augery, their religious ritual, their robes and other insignia of office, their games and shows, their earliest architecture, their calendar, their weights and measures, their land surveying systems, and various other elements of their civilization. But there is reason to believe that their acknowledgment fell short of their actual obligations and that Etruria was really the source of their whole early civilization.

To this list D. Randall MacIver adds their military organization, and in all probability, even the name of the city itself.[171]

To return for a moment to the Arabs: R. F. Grau pointed out that the *pure* Arabs developed "no new industry or technique or trade. The only thing they did invent was a new style of architecture."[172] This situation is complicated somewhat by the fact that in the so-called Golden Age of Islam they owed much to Persian influences. J. J. Winter remarks that the language of Iran had at that time assumed a new significance, and those who wrote in this language made the greatest contribution.[173] This, it seems to me, tends to favor my argument, for the language of Iran belongs within the Indo-European family, and some of the

---

[168] The Etruscans not Indo-Europeans: M. Pallottino, *The Etruscans,* Penguin Books, London, 1955, p. 26.

[169] De Beer, Sir Gavin, "Who Were the Etruscans?" reported in *The Listener,* BBC, London, Dec. 8, 1955, p. 989.

[170] Rawlinson, George, *The Origin of Nations,* Scribner, N.Y., 1878, p. 111.

[171] MacIvor, D. Randall, "The Etruscans," *Antiquity* (June, 1927): 171.

[172] Grau, R. F., *The Goal of the Human Race,* Simpkin, Marshall, Hamilton & Kent, London, 1892, pp. 88, 91.

[173] Winter, H. J. J., "Muslim Mechanics and Mechanical Appliances," *Endeavour,* Jan., 1956, pp. 25, 26.

best known Arab writers who used this language, such as Ibn Sina (930-1037), were noted for their "theoretical postulates." Some extracts are given by Winter of Sina's postulates, and these are completely in the tradition of modern scientific observation. Some Islamic treatises dealt with ingenious mechanical contrivances, but the contrivances were elaborate water clocks derived from China.

As we have already noted, Semites have indeed made notable contributions to the technology of civilization, as for example, Weismann in chemistry and Einstein in physics. But as we have also noted, they were Semites who had adopted an alien culture. In this connection Jessie Bernard observes:[174]

> It is not the Jews who remain within their cultural setting who make the greatest contribution.... It is only, as Veblen says, "When the gifted Jew escapes from the cultural environment created and fed by the genius of his own people, and becomes a naturalized, though hyphenate, citizen in the Gentile republic of learning that he comes into his own as a creative leader in the world's intellectual enterprise."

I think this is a significant circumstance, for in a manner of speaking Shem and Japheth are combined in one individual and the amalgam sometimes bears quite exceptional fruit. Perhaps if we knew enough of the background of certain individuals in terms of their genetics as well as their early culture contacts and the influence of other minds upon their own as they matured, we might find that some of the exceptionally outstanding individuals of Renaissance and later times owed their extraordinary ability to a kind of mixed "inheritance" from Shem, Ham and Japheth which came together in them as individuals due to circumstances. It would appear to me that the vitality of the New World, especially for a certain period of its history, may have resulted from a similar mixing, as a result of tremendous immigrational influx of people from all over the world to form a kind of Shem-Ham-Japheth potpourri. Little by little as the patterns of thought and native languages of these immigrants were exchanged for the English of the Americas, the capacity may to some extent have declined, although so long as its culture remains basically Christian there will continue to be an amalgam at least of Shem and Japheth. Perhaps we are making a mistake in not recognizing the capabilities of the native Indian population in the Americas, although as these people also forsake their

---

[174] Bernard, Jessie, op. cit. (ref. 147), p. 271.

native languages their own special capability may be depressed or surrendered altogether.

Sir Flinders Petrie, speaking of the cycles of civilization, which have so intrigued philosophers of history, says in this connection:[175]

> We have represented the wave of Civilization as falling to a minimum, and suddenly rising again. To what is this change due? In every case in which we can examine the history sufficiently we find that there was a fresh wave coming into the country when the earlier wave was at its lowest.
>
> In short, every civilization of a settled population tends to incessant decay from its maximum condition; and this decay continues until it is too weak to initiate anything, when a fresh race comes in and utilizes the old stock to graft on, both in blood and culture.

This has been the case, it seems, in both the Old and the New World. Ernst Kretschmer arrived at the conclusion, in regard to the share that the Nordic race has had in Western Culture, that their most marked contributions were developed only in those regions where this race has been exposed to intensive mixture with other races.[176] And he holds it to be certain that regions inhabited by the purest Nordic breeds are relatively poor in genius and cultural activity. The most advanced European cultures never had their spiritual centers, he argues, in Scandinavia, in the northern coasts of Germany, or in Scotland: but always where racial mixture has taken place.

The sudden emergence of high civilizations in the New World in pre-Columbian times is not so easy to account for. But the sudden upsurge in the New World since the Discovery is surely traceable to this factor of race mixture. Speaking of this, Harry L. Shapiro pointed out that, although the figures are very approximate only, there are some six million people of mixed racial origin in Europe, whereas the relative number of people of mixed racial origin in the New World is vastly greater so that, as he puts it, "we can have little hesitation in recognizing that the latter is the main centre of race mixture in modern times."[177] And in the same way Fenton B. Turck says:[178]

[175] Petrie, Sir Flinders, *Revolutions of Civilization,* Harper, London, 1911, p. 114.

[176] Kretschmer, Ernst, quoted by Franz Weidenreich, *Apes, Giants and Man,* Univ. of Chicago Press, 1948, p. 90.

[177] Shapiro, Harry L., *Race Mixture,* The Race Question in Modern Science, UNESCO, 1953, p. 21.

[178] Turck, Fenton B., "The American Explosion," *Sci. Monthly,* Sept., 1952, p. 191.

Americans have captured the extraordinary vitality which Science has proved is typical of the first few generations of a people with mixed blood strains.

This shows to some extent why ancient high civilizations did not proceed further. Their World View so homogenized their own particular culture that they were not willing or capable of accommodating much in the way of an exchange of values or ideas. Some exchange occurred of course, but not comparable at all to the phenomenon of our own age. And in primitive society the pattern is even more concretely apparent. Such societies are in most cases so homogeneous that any disruption of the pattern practically destroys the whole structure. And this has been the testimony of history ever since the White Man began to explore and exploit the world for himself — from the destruction of the Indus Valley culture by the Aryans to the virtual destruction of American Indian culture. C. G. Seligman has noted the same thing about China:[179]

> The T'ang period — perhaps that of China's greatest brilliance — was marked by the influx and ready acceptance of foreigners and of foreign (Western and Indian) ideas.

E. B. Reuter, of the University of Iowa, published a paper on the consequences of race mixture some years ago in which he gave illustrations of the remarkable results of "mixed blood" both in societies and in individuals so long as the culture does not degrade individuals of mixed blood socially.[180] At the time he made it in 1930 this was quite a bold statement, because much was then being made of the desirability of purity of racial origins. The argument of Kretschmer is given added weight by the observation of Reuter:[181]

> The same general position is supported by a body of negative evidence. The population groups in the modern world with the highest approximation to racial purity are just those groups of most meagre cultural accomplishment. The fragments of primitive groups still living are the purest in blood and the lowest in culture of existing populations....

The thesis of this paper is strongly reinforced by a statement made by J. C. Curry:[182]

---

[179] Seligman, C. G., "The Roman Orient and the Far East," *Antiquity*, Mar., 1937, p. 10.

[180] Reuter, E. B., "Civilization and the Mixture of Races," *Sci. Monthly*, Nov., 1930, pp. 442f.

[181] Ibid., p. 446.

[182] Curry, J. C., "Climate and Migrations," *Antiquity*, No. 7, 1928, p. 301.

After the third migratory period, civilization burst suddenly into full flower along the southern slopes of the mountain chain, in India, in Persia, in Asia Minor, in Greece, and in Italy. In each case it occurred after a fusion of the Aryan, or Indo-European, races with the earlier inhabitants in a climate suitable to agriculture and to a high stage of development of the Indo-European.

Reference to the potential contribution of the American Indians brings us to a counter consideration, namely, the non-philosophical nature of the members of the family of Ham. For we have now considered briefly some of the evidence which shows that (1) Semites have been religiously inclined but not inventive, and (2) Japhethites intellectually inclined but also not inventive. We have now to show that the Hamites are inventive but not philosophically minded — taking the word philosophy to mean something more than merely wisdom in dealing with life situations. Carpenter, in a lecture in the University of Toronto dealing with native ways of handling abnormal individuals within their own community, noted that some research had been done by Indo-Europeans using these abnormal individuals as subjects. Carpenter observed: "The results showed nothing except in several instances a tendency towards abstract thinking." This is an incidental observation, yet it is interesting because it suggests that Levy-Bruhl and others have noted at some length, namely, that native people on the whole look upon abstract thinking as a rather foolish waste of time. Indeed, in so far as it involves dealing with situations which are entirely hypothetical, i.e., which are contrary to present fact, many native people, as we have noted, find themselves quite unable even to contemplate the abstractions.

Levy-Bruhl, because of an unfortunate choice of a descriptive term for this kind of native thinking, which he decided to refer to as "prelogical," but which his readers misunderstood to mean "illogical," brought himself and his ideas into disrepute.[183] This was indeed unfortunate because his researches were based not upon personal judgments, but upon the experiences and conclusions and findings of a very large number of individuals who had personal acquaintance with primitive cultures, as well as non-Indo-European cultures of a higher order — from every part of the world. So he was not really expressing an opinion, but pointing up a conclusion which was logically to be drawn

---

[183] Levy-Bruhl, Lucien, *How Natives Think*, Allen & Unwin, London, 1926.

from the evidence of a great number of different sources all of which were in essential agreement. These other cultures, primitive and civilized, were not illogical but did not readily think in abstract terms or use languages which, as a reflection of this, were highly specific in their vocabulary and in many cases virtually prohibited the formation of generalizations.

Paul Radin, in protest against the above conclusions, has written a book entitled, "Primitive Man As Philosopher." In this he tries to show that the American Indians often thought deeply about philosophical problems that were in no sense directed toward practical ends but constituted pure intellectual exercise. However, again and again in his book he refers to the individuals whom he quotes as having been strongly influenced by the white man and Christian missionaries. He admits this frankly, but in doing so, it appears to me that his subjects cannot be used to demonstrate what he is seeking to show, for they have been de-culturized. In fact, he says at one point:[184]

> It is from instances where we know European and Christian influence to have been definitely present that our best evidence for the existence of thinkers, and for the philosophical quality of their thoughts, can be derived.

Jacques Maritain would not distinguish essentially between modern primitive people and the ancient non-Indo-European cultures:[185]

> Philosophic speculation ... is unknown to all the so-called primitive races. Indeed, even of the civilizations of antiquity the greater part either have possessed no philosophy or have failed to discover its true nature and distinctive character.

H. Frankfort published a valuable collection of papers under the title *The Intellectual Adventure of Ancient Man*. He was not referring to prehistoric man but to the Sumerians and the Egyptians and certain other Middle East cultures. Later he republished this under a new and significant title, *Before Philosophy*. In his introductory remarks he makes the following observation:[186]

> If we look for "speculative thought" in the documents of the ancients, we are forced to admit that there is very little indeed in our written records which deserves the name of

---

[184] Radin, Paul, *Primitive Man as Philosopher,* Dover Pub., N.Y., 1957, p. 387.

[185] Maritain, Jacques, op. cit. (ref. 86), p. 23.

[186] Frankfort, H. and H. A. Frankfort, *The Intellectual Adventure of Ancient Man,* Univ. of Chicago Press, 1946, p. 3.

"thought" in the strictest sense of the term. There are very few passages which show the discipline, the cogency of reasoning, which we associate with thinking.

It is very important to realize that when one speaks of the absence of "thought" in this way, it is not intended for a moment to imply that such people were any less intelligent than ourselves. There is no question of "racial superiority." It is not the ability to think through a problem that has advanced our Western Culture beyond theirs in its technical aspects. James B. Conant wrote recently:[187]

> To be sure the way an experimental scientist proceeds to find a solution to a given problem is not dissimilar to the way the very same person as a householder endeavours to find what is wrong when all the lights go out. . . . The various formulations of the Scientific Method I have read are hardly more than a description of the trial and error procedures which have been employed in the practical arts ever since our distant ancestors became tool makers. *What was new about the time of Galileo was the slow merging of the inventive tinkering of artisans with the abstract reasoning of mathematicians* (my emphasis).

Elsewhere we have reviewed the evidence touching upon the probable intelligence of Paleolithic man[188] and shown with some measure of force that the inventions he was responsible for required just as much intelligence as modern inventions which, after all, are largely built upon theirs. It is not proper to credit the improver with greater intellectual powers than the originator. What Conant is underscoring is the fact that two kinds of activity, perhaps one should rather say of capacity, were merged: the skill of the technician and the intellectual acumen of the philosopher. This is what led to science. And as we have seen already, science does not emerge unless this amalgam takes place. Hamites have not produced science out of their technology, nor Japhethites out of their philosophy. In isolation neither produces what they *can* produce when they cooperate.

The achievements of the Sumerians and the Egyptians never cease to cause amazement even in our technically surfeited age. Farrington has said:[189]

> We have as yet no proof, in all this evidence from technique, of the attempt to organize even a particular *branch* of

---

[187] Conant, James B., "Scientific Principles and Moral Conduct," *Am. Scientist*, 55, 3 (1967): 312.
[188] "Establishing a Palaeolithic IQ" (Part III of Doorway Papers Vol. II).
[189] Farrington, B., op. cit. (ref. 117), p. 15.

knowledge in a scientific way. Technical achievement itself is not proof of the power of conscious abstraction, of the capacity to detect general laws underlying the variety of phenomena and to utilize these general conceptions for the organization of knowledge. To put the point in another way, we have no evidence . . . that they were attempting to classify . . . that they were asking how one thing could apparently change into another, how bread for instance which a man ate could turn into flesh and blood. . . . We have no certain proof . . . of that kind of curiosity and that gift for speculation which are necessary for the creation of Science in the full sense.

And Kramer has noted that the Sumerians did not even try to correct the anomalies of their cosmology, because these anomalies never struck them. Also Butterfield in his *Origins of Modern Science* observed, "There does not seem to be any sign that the ancient world before its heritage had been dispersed was moving towards anything like a scientific revolution."[190]

Some time ago, long after this thesis had been elaborated and published by a government agency, I came across the following keen insight written in 1898 by that great Christian scholar and defender of the Faith, John Urquhart.[191]

The Hamitic race appears to have been more practical, sharp, and wide awake than the others. It lived with its whole energies in the present and for the present. The other two races were more reflective, and, as we say, had more heart. . . . These two have furnished the philosophers and the poets of humanity. This reflective tendency has shown itself in the languages of the two families; the unreflective tendency has equally manifested itself in the Hamitic. The Sumerians, for example, invented the use of signs to indicate words, and thus were the first to enable men to picture their thoughts to the eye as well as to breathe them into the ear. But they never advanced beyond this point. Neither they nor the Chinese have ever had the idea of using signs to represent letters, or even syllables. Spelling is a process that has no existence for the Chinaman. The Semitic, and the Japhethic or Aryan families, took up the invention of their Hamitic brethren and carried it further. By degrees, they made the art of writing the flexible and perfect instrument which it is today.

Because I wish to refer to it again, I think it is worth noting the fact that while the Hebrews did perfect alphabetic writing, which formed the base of all other European alphabets, this is

[190] Butterfield, Herbert, *Origins of Modern Science,* Bell, London, 1949, p. 163.

[191] Urquhart, John, *Modern Discoveries and the Bible,* Marshall, London, 1898, p. 255.

about the sum total of what was contributed by Shem and Japheth to the art of disseminating the written word. The Egyptians produced the first paper, though the Chinese also had superb papers as did the Central American Indians; the Chinese provided us with printer's ink; and the Koreans developed a technique of block-printing which we have simply copied. It seems that there is very little to which we can point, when we pick up a book, and say, "This is our invention." All types of fibers and fabrics originally used for bookbinding were of non-Indo-European origin, the dyes used to color those fabrics and the glues to stick them together — all these were provided for us. As Crawford has said:[192]

> As a matter of fact Europe has never produced a single original natural fibre or any dye except perhaps Woad. She has not contributed a single fundamental or original idea to the basic mechanics of textiles, nor a single original and fundamental process of finishing, dyeing, or printing.

And the techniques of metal-working, wherewith gold was beaten thin enough to use for lettering, originated elsewhere than in Europe.

What we *can* say, if the context has a philosophical subject matter, is that *here* we made our contribution. When we have philosophized about Hamitic technology we have written books on science, and when we have philosophized about Semitic religious insights we have books on theology. I suppose the highest mental exercise occurs when the theologian explores science, or the scientist theology. At any rate, I think it is safe to say that we have here a framework of history, a kind of paintbox with three colors with which God could, by the providential directing of the movements of history, produce any kind of painting He desired whether monochrome or polychrome, depending on the need. In spite of all the mixing that has taken place in human history, there still remain pockets of pure colors. And as we have already noted, since there seems to be some connection between "natural bents" and the particular families of language which are associated, it should not surprise us to find that just when the world seems on the border of adopting some single universal language, circumstances arise, unforeseen, which engender a rebirth of nationalistic feelings and a fresh interest and concern in a native tongue which was in danger of being lost:

---

[192] Crawford, M. D. C., *The Conquest of Culture*, Fairchild, N.Y., 1948, p. 146.

just as Kroeber said, language barriers are among the most persistent of all cultural dividing lines.

P. M. S. Blackett, writing in *The Bulletin of Atomic Scientists,* wrote:[193]

> One of the fascinating unsolved questions of history is why the scientific and industrial revolutions of the 17th and 18th centuries happened in Europe rather than in one of the great ancient civilizations of the Near and Far East. Craft technology may be said to have evolved to a very high level about 5000 years ago in the river valley civilizations of the Near East, and in India and in China. By 2000 B.C. the level of building, woodwork, fine metalworking, ship building, and transport had reached a point which was not surpassed for nearly 3000 years. Then, for one reason or another, the great civilizations of North India, Egypt, and Mesopotamia became static and finally declined. Then China arose and was socially and technologically pre-eminent from 500 B.C. to 1500 A.D. when Europe started the extraordinary movement which produced the scientific and later industrial revolutions, which were, in three centuries, to transform man's life on the earth.
>
> *The essential foundation on which the Revolution was based was the high level of Technology which was largely of North and Far Eastern origin.* What it was that prevented these ancient civilizations from making the scientific breakthrough is not fully understood. There is no evidence to suggest that there are any demonstrable differences of innate ability between different races of world. . . .
>
> The only sound working rule is that the different peoples of the world, even though they are now at very different levels of development, have the same innate capacity for science and technology as do the rich and proud Western Europeans who created the scientific revolution. Thus the vast differences between the material wealth of Europeans, North America and Australia on the one hand, and India, China, the Middle East, Africa, and most of South America on the other hand, cannot be ascribed to racial differences. Almost certainly the differences were of complex social origin.

In the light of the thesis presented here — and it is fundamentally of biblical origin — I think we may be able to provide an answer. It is certainly true that there are no innate deficiencies in other races, because when they completely absorb the language of Western Man they demonstrate their capacity to enter into the spirit of science. But for reasons which we have already explored all too briefly, God has appointed boundaries to the

---

[193] Blackett, P. M. S., "The University's Mission," *Bull. Atomic Scientists,* May, 1962, pp. 14-18.

nations,[194] knit them together into larger families, and appointed to them certain forms of language in order to ensure that each would be dependent upon the other, in order to realize the maximum capacity of man with his tremendous creative potential. This is a protective measure, and any attempt to unify the world's language with the overt intention of making all men share equally in this potential will only serve to defeat its own purposes in the end. It is in a manner of speaking a repetition of the Confusion of Tongues effectively preventing man's wickedness from being armed disastrously to his own terrible hurt.

[194] Boundaries of nations appointed: Acts 17:26, "And hath made of one blood all nations of men for to dwell on all the face of the earth, and hath determined the times before appointed, and the bounds of their habitation."

Chapter 6

THE INVENTIVE GENIUS OF HAM

I T MAY COME as a surprise to find how many, how varied, and how fundamental have been the inventions of Hamitic people, and how great a service they have thus rendered to mankind in the field of technology. Although some of these achievements may be considered slight by those who have never actually invented anything or contributed anything new to the sum total of human achievement, one should not be deceived by simplicity. Hamitic peoples have been peculiarly ingenious in finding simple solutions that are very effective. The curious thing is that they neither know nor care in many cases why their solutions are so completely successful.

The following developments may be added to the above list (details in Part IV), set forth more or less under similar headings. They are described very briefly, the purpose being merely to show something of the range of devices and techniques which are commonly assumed to be of Indo-European origin but which, as the lists show, are not.

In recent years much has been learned about the earliest clocks. It was thought that the mechanical clock was an invention of 14th century craftsmen. However, descriptions and corroded fragments of complicated astronomical "pre-clocks," such as water clocks, planetary models, and mechanical star maps have survived from Greek and Arabic times, which have raised more questions than they answered since their principle of operation was quite different from European clocks of a later period. Moreover, they were designed for computing the motion of heavenly bodies rather than for timekeeping.[195]

---

[195] On these, see Derek J. de Solla Price, "An Ancient Greek Computer," *Sci. American,* June, 1959, p. 60.

320

Recently a manuscript has been translated entitled, "New Design for an Astronomical Clock," written in 1092 by Su Sung, a scholar of the Sung dynasty. It is a description of a clock actually constructed in 1088 and housed in a pagoda-like tower, from thirty to forty feet high. The details of it show that it was very complicated, with many revolving parts and successions of geared trains. It was also fitted with an escapement mechanism, a mechanism hitherto regarded as an exclusively European invention. Some details of this highly sophisticated mechanism appeared in the English journal, *Nature*, reporting the making of a working model.[196] The clock was driven by water power with an extremely ingenious arrangement for tripping the scoops into which the water flowed and for ensuring a uniform pressure in the water system itself. Joseph Needham has published a work dealing specifically with this subject and notes that Su Sung's clockwork was anticipated in China by many previous similar clocks so that refined mechanisms of this kind were well known in China long before knowledge of them was brought into Europe. Escapement clocks are a Hamitic invention.

Under the general heading of Materials, we may note another claim to priority due to Chinese technologists, in iron and steel production. Again we may refer to Joseph Needham for details.[197] China had an ancient and advanced metallurgical industry, and although in Europe it was the end of the 15th century before molten cast iron was produced (except by accident), Needham gives cogent evidence that this was being done in China on a significant scale at least 2000 years before. From the second century B.C., if not earlier, cast iron was used to produce

---

[196] Escapement Clock: *Nature*, Mar. 31, 1956, p. 601 gave a diagram of such a clock with an escapement, designed or at least described by Su Sung. Further details and descriptive information was given by Aubrey F. Burstall, et al., in an article entitled "A Working Model of the Mechanical Escapement in Su Sung's Astronomical Clock Tower," *Nature*, Sept. 28, 1963, pp. 1242-1244. This was further discussed under "The Chinese Water-balance Escapement," *Nature*, Dec. 19, 1964, pp. 1175f. I think it is significant that in reviewing Joseph Needham's Vol. 4, part 2, *Science and Civilization in China*, E. H. Hutton underscores the fact that the technology of China, though in advance of European technology until the time of the Renaissance was nevertheless "prescientific technology," to use his words. See his "Ancient Chinese Technology," *Nature*, April 2 (Supplement), 1966, p. 46. An article of interest on these clocks also appeared in *Endeavour*, Oct., 1960, pp. 234f.

[197] Needham, Joseph, *The Development of Iron and Steel Technology in China*, Dickinson Memorial Lecture to the Newcomen Society for 1956, reported in *Nature*, Dec. 12, 1959, p. 1830.

steel by carefully controlled decarburization in an air blast, a method known as the "hundred refinings." Later on much Chinese steel was made by a co-fusion technique in which wrought and cast iron were heated together in crucibles, the pasty lumps of the former bathed in the high carbon liquid. By a gradual diffusion of carbon, a steel of approximately eutectoid composition was produced. The basic correspondence of these processes with those of Huntsman, Bessemer, and Siemens and Martin is to be noted. Indeed, as Needham observes, immediately before the work of William Kelly in the United States in setting up the Bessemer process, four Chinese workers were imported as experts at his furnaces at Kuttawa!

The Chinese have always been great metalworkers and their bronzes are superb examples of technological virtuosity. Around 1400 B.C. they were producing what Coon has referred to as "the finest examples of bronze casting in the world, from any place or period."[198] This is a judgment held by other experts in the field. The editors of *Life's The Epic of Man* observed that the Chinese Shang bronzes were "the finest objects of metal ever created by the mind and hand of man."[199] In Part IV, already referred to, a number of observations regarding the metalwork of the Sumerians and Egyptians will be found, including the extraordinary range of techniques they had mastered. The Sumerians had also mastered the technique of soldering.[200]

As perhaps another rather surprising example of a "modern invention" anticipated centuries ago, Marco Polo at the end of the 13th century observed the extensive use of asbestos in Ghenghis Khan's domain, in the province of Chingintalas:[201]

> The asbestos fibres are treated to divide and separate them and they look like wool. They are then spun into not very white fibres which are afterwards burned to come out as white as snow. This is how they are then "washed" after becoming soiled.

Some of these fabrics were sent by the Khan to the Pope.

In connection with building techniques, an article appeared in the *Scientific American* dealing with primitive architecture, in which the authors, Fitch and Branch, describe some of the

---

[198] Coon, Carleton S., *The Story of Man*, Knopf, N.Y., 1962, pp. 329, 330.
[199] Editors of *Life, The Epic of Man*, Time-Life Incorp., 1961, p. 199.
[200] Kramer, Samuel, *The Sumerians*, Univ. of Chicago Press, 1964, p. 101.
[201] Asbestos: see *Travels of Marco Polo*, Library Pub., N.Y., n.d., pp. 67, 68. It is probable that this entry was made about A.D. 1298.

buildings erected by "primitive" people of the world, among whom are included the Eskimo, Sudanese, Siberian herdsmen, and Melanesians.[202] The main thrust of the article is to the effect that these people have shown great ingenuity not merely in the way in which they have employed local materials, with maximum effect from the structural point of view, but also that they have with great effectiveness designed their buildings with an eye to providing shelter against the elements (snow load, wind pressure, earthquake shock, heat stress, cold stress, and glare). They say, "Thus Western man, for all his impressive knowledge and technological apparatus, often builds comparably less well." They speak of these people as showing "a precise and detailed knowledge of local climate conditions on the one hand, and on the other, a remarkable understanding of the performance characteristics of the building materials locally available." They say, "These simple shelters often out-perform the structures of present day architects." As means of shelter against temperature and precipitation, they note that "in culture after culture the solutions found show a surprising delicacy and precision." And subsequently, "Limited to what for us would be a pitifully meager choice of materials, the primitive architect often employs them so skillfully as to make them seem ideal." This last observation is about as profound a compliment as they could have offered, and it does in fact sum up a great deal of the technology of non-Indo-European people. It is nearly always characterized by simplicity, economy of materials, and almost complete suitability. They seem to be able to hit at once upon the proper solution. The only trouble is that having done so, they never have thought it necessary to try to improve upon it in any basic way. The authors conclude:

> One could extend this catalogue of human ingenuity indefinitely. But the examples cited are surely adequate to establish the basic point: that primitive man, for all his scanty resources, often builds more wisely than we do, and that in his architecture he establishes principles of design that we often ignore at great cost. . . . Contemporary United States architecture would be greatly enriched, esthetically as well as operationally, by a sober analysis of its primitive traditions.

While we are on the subject of architecture, I feel I must include a quotation dealing with the stone work of the Great

---

[202] Fitch, J. M. and D. P. Branch, "Primitive Architecture and Climate," *Sci. American*, Dec., 1960, pp. 134ff.

Pyramid, even though several similar quotations appear in the previous Doorway Paper. In his Hibbert Lecture (1879), P. LePage Renouf quotes an architect who examined this structure with a critical eye as follows:[203]

> No one can possibly examine the interior of the Great Pyramid without being struck with astonishment at the wonderful mechanical skill displayed in its construction. The immense blocks of granite brought from Syene — a distance of 500 miles — polished like glass, are so fitted that the joints can hardly be detected.

One might continue this quotation at some length, for it is a eulogy indeed not merely of the masons who fashioned the building blocks themselves but of the extraordinary precision in their laying and in the arrangements which were made for the ceilings of the various chambers and ventilating shafts. The same architect is quoted by Renouf as having said in connection with their other buildings, both temples and houses:

> In all the conveniences and elegances of building they seem to have anticipated all that has been . . . to the present day. Indeed, in all probability the ancient Egyptians surpassed the modern in those respects. . . .

In weaving and in the development of textile fibers and dyes much has already been said in Part IV. But I have recently come across a statement to the effect that the Incas were able to weave pieces of cloth of extraordinary dimensions, 13 feet wide x 84 feet long, with as high as 500 threads per inch![204] Very few fabrics of modern times come anywhere near this, and when they do they are usually limited to comparatively small pieces. In prehistoric times in the southwestern part of the United States all kinds of techniques were known at one time,

---

[203] Renouf, P. LePage, op. cit. (ref. 121), pp. 63, 65. In the same connection, Andrew White in his *Warfare of Science With Theology*, Braziller, N.Y., 1955, p. 265, has the following: "For the perfection of Egyptian engineering, I rely not merely upon my own observation but on what is far more important, the testimony of my friend the Hon. J. G. Batterson, probably the largest and most experienced of workers in granite in the United States, who acknowledges from personal observation that the early Egyptian work is, in boldness and perfection, far beyond anything known since, and a source of perpetual wonder to him."

[204] Editors of *Life,* in *The Epic of Man* (ref. 199), pp. 227, 233. Also, Jonathan N. Leonard, *Ancient America,* The Great Ages of Man, Time-Life Pub., N.Y., 1967, pp. 82, 83.

and all kinds of ingenious ways to accomplish edge-finishes and cloth closures.[205]

The present paper has already referred to block printing as an invention originating with the Koreans. In Joseph Needham's great work on Chinese technology, he mentions that while the Chinese used wooden or earthenware type blocks, the Koreans were the first to use cast type blocks made of bronze.[206]

Under the general heading of Foods, we may note that powdered milk was used by Ghengis Khan, every one of his soldiers being provided with a vessel containing 10 pounds of it.[207] Each morning he would take half a pound and put it in his leather bottle with as much water as suited his taste so that the bottle would then be thoroughly churned by the motion of the horse into a kind of porridge which then formed his dinner. I believe that in a pinch, and provided they had water, his whole army could move for three weeks without any further supplies, if they had to.

While we are on the subject of dairy products, a most remarkable practice was reported recently whereby African natives force or trick cows who are withholding their milk into releasing it. The report notes, "It is remarkable how their methods have been confirmed by recent scientific research." They use a dummy calf, a boy suitably dressed, and then when the cow sees the

---

[205] Edge-finishes, etc. See Kate Peck Kent, *The Cultivation and Weaving of Cotton in the Prehistoric Southwestern United States,* reviewed in *Jour. Am. Anthrop.,* 60 (1958): 951. The reviewer, A. H. Gayton, remarks: "It is impossible to mention here all the techniques known in the prehistoric South-West or the ingenious tricks for accomplishing edge-finishes and cloth enclosures." And again he states that some fabrics are braided, and one twine-plaited shirt is as elaborate in design as the best specimens of similar techniques from ancient Egypt or Peru. He mentions looping, netting, braiding, twine plaiting, and twills.

[206] Needham, Joseph, op. cit. (ref. 105), Vol. I, 1954, p. 231, note d.

[207] Powdered Milk: *Travels of Marco Polo,* p. 81. Polo's report reads: "They have dried milk into a kind of paste to carry with them: and when they need food they put this in water and beat it up till it dissolves and then drink it. It is prepared thus: they boil the milk, and when the rich part floats to the top they skim it into another vessel, and of that they make butter: for the milk will not become solid till this is removed. Then they put the milk in the sun to dry. And when they go on an expedition, every man takes some ten pounds of the dried milk with him. And of a morning, he will take a half pound of it and put it in his leather bottle, with as much water as he pleases. So, as he rides along, the milk paste and the water in the bottle get well churned together into a kind of pap, and that makes his dinner."

"model" they blow up the vagina with air by mouth. A reflex is initiated and the milk flows.[208]

And on the subject of dehydrated foods, it should be noted that the Aymara Indians of Bolivia taught the Americans how to prepare dehydrated potatoes. Claude Levi-Strauss wrote recently:[209]

> The Aymara Indians of the Bolivian plateau are able experimenters in the preservation of food stuffs. It was by direct imitation of their technique of dehydration that the American Army was able during the last World War to reduce rations of powdered potatoes sufficient for a hundred meals to the volume of a shoe box.

On travel, taking the word in its broadest sense, we have already listed many items such as plywood wheels, domesticated draft animals, efficient harnesses, aircraft, ships of all kinds, canal systems, etc. Recently in reading *The Travels of Marco Polo*, I came across this statement of his which must have been written about A.D. 1298, speaking of Far Eastern ships:[210]

> Moreover, the larger of their vessels have some thirteen compartments or "divisions" in the interior, made with planking strongly framed in case perhaps the ship should spring a leak either by running on a rock or by the blow of a hungry whale. . . . The planking is so well fitted that the water will not pass from one compartment to another. They can then remove the cargo to another compartment and stop the leak.

No European vessel was ever built in this compartmentalized way until comparatively recent times, a form of construction hailed by our own shipbuilders as one of the latest examples of progress in shipbuilding, making them "unsinkable."

The Chinese, of course, had a highly organized canal system and developed locks to extend their canals through hill country. The Sumerians also had canal systems, which, according to Coon,[211] were absolutely superb. Although it is not strictly a matter of transport or travel, the drainage systems of some of these most ancient cities were highly developed and Coon spoke of those existing in the Indus Valley cities as being "the most advanced in the world."[212] When we bear in mind the picture

---

[208] Milk-letting: on this see a report by John Hammond, "Man and Cattle," *Nature,* Jan. 11, 1964, p. 121.

[209] Levi-Strauss, Claude, op. cit. (ref. 144), p. 43.

[210] Compartmentalized ships: *Travels of Marco Polo* (ref. 201), p. 237.

[211] Coon, Carleton S., op. cit. (ref. 198), p. 242.

[212] Ibid., p. 324.

that we have of Middle Eastern cities under Indo-European, Jewish, or Arab domination with their virtual absence of provision for keeping them clean, it is clear that the Hamitic people were far more conscious of the importance of these things. The Cretan civilization which was a derivative of the basic Hamitic culture, bears equally striking testimony to their engineering skill in this regard as seen in such cities as Knossos.

Plywood wheels were developed by the Sumerians, and it is well known that these wheels were fitted to carts drawn by oxen.[213] However, the Hamitic Hittites domesticated the horse but found that oxcarts were too cumbersome for these more spirited animals. Accordingly they lightened the structure and by a stroke of genius, which we may find it difficult now to appreciate, they invented wheels with spokes.

The invention of hairpins is to be credited to the Chinese.[214] These items were apparently mass-produced, since skeletons have been found in which the head was surrounded by hundreds of them.

Even more surprising, I think, is the finding — once more through reading Marco Polo — that in the Empire of Kublai Khan beauty contests were held regularly, judging based on a "point system." Points were given for hair, complexion, eyebrows, lips, mouth, and — believe it or not — body and limb proportions. According to Marco Polo, these were set down by rule under some 16 to 20 headings.[215]

Although mathematics would seem to involve the most profound forms of abstraction, we know that the study itself may be developed to a high degree of sophistication and designed only to serve practical needs. We have already noted in a previous paper the use of fractions, square roots and cube roots, squares and cubes, quadratic equations, all kinds of multiplication tables, and even a simple form of logarithms, by the Sumerians and (to a slightly lesser extent) by the Egyptians. The numerous tables have clearly resulted not as an extension of theory but empirically. The Hamitic people as a whole seem to have anticipated the Indo-Europeans in a number of mathematical devices, or if not anticipating them at least developed them quite independently. Thus, the Chinese early developed the place system

---

[213] Ibid., p. 248.
[214] Hairpins: noted by editors of *Life* (ref. 199), p. 200.
[215] Beauty Contest: Marco Polo, op. cit. (ref. 201), p. 108.

328 • A CHRISTIAN WORLD VIEW

as well as the concept of zero.[216] There is evidence that the Indus Valley people at Mohenjo Daru, somewhere around 2000 B.C., were using the zero symbol. Perhaps we have a case of independent development in Central America for long before Europe had "discovered" either the concept of zero or the place system for numbers, the Central Americans were already using both of these in the formulation of their most advanced Calendar.[217]

I have also learned recently that the so-called camera obscura, the principle of using a small hole in a baffle between a well-lighted object and a dark screen in order to get a perfect though inverted image, goes back to Alhazen who died in 1039.[218] I suspect that when the whole story is known it will be found that this Arab had gotten the idea from some Chinese trader.

Although the previous paper has dealt extensively with the medical achievements of non-Indo-European people, it seems that every new History of Medicine brings to light fresh examples of their inventiveness and ingenuity and keen perception in this field of human endeavor. In the first volume of Henry E. Sigerist's *History of Medicine,* there is the following quotation from a work by Sumner which is apropos of my thesis:[219]

> The savages were too near to the raw struggle for existence to hold in light esteem that which they thought contributed strongly to their insurance against ill; it has been reserved for civilized man, *secure behind the bulwarks of which the savage laid the foundations,* to play the wanton fool, as no nature-man could or would, with fanciful and perverse floutings of the knowledge he ought to reverence. Only civilized man is secure enough, *by virtue of the work and thought and suffering of those who gained knowledge for mankind, and for him, to affect contempt and condescension for their indispensable labors* (my emphasis).

This is an important statement, I think, because it is an admission that the basis of so much of our medical knowledge is to be found in the lore of people of non-Indo-European origin,

---

[216] Zero and place value: see J. Needham (ref. 105), Vol. 3, 1959, p. 146, where 14 Chinese "firsts" in mathematics are listed.

[217] Coon, Carleton S., mentions that the early Mexican civilization used the place system as well as zero concept in their calculations. See *The Story of Man,* op. cit. (ref. 198), p. 346.

[218] Referred to by Tertius Chandler, "Duplicate Inventions," *Am. Anthrop.,* June, 1960, pp. 496, 497.

[219] Sigerist, Henry C., *Primitive and Archaic Medicine,* Oxford Univ. Press, 1967, p. 170. Vaccines: see p. 150.

whose views in this direction we have habitually considered to be either pure superstition or outright charlatanism. Moreover, Sumner has noted an important point, namely, that the maintenance of health was not of theoretical interest, but great practical importance, and for this reason was an undertaking for which these Hamitic people as a whole were peculiarly well fitted. At the same time, it is noted quite properly that the margin of survival of such people is just narrow enough that they do not have any excess energy available to do more than merely invent an immediate solution to an immediate problem. It is indeed surprising how little we have actually contributed. We think of modern operative techniques and the use of wonder drugs and imagine that until recently the sum total of the world's medical knowledge and skill was almost infantile. But as we have said, every year brings to light further examples of advanced medical technique that had been practiced by people of non-Western culture almost since the beginning of history.

Jurgen Thorwald has recently listed among such early developments the following: plastic surgery on the face to correct disfigurements resulting from war or disease, bladder-stone removal, the use of mercury for ulcers, pork liver for anemia, anti-diarrhea remedies, contraceptives, the use of incense as an antiseptic in public places, antifungal and antibacterial salves, catheters, enemas and suppositories, kidney-stone dissolvents, and diagnostic techniques for hernias and for intestinal tuberculosis.[220–221]

Livingstone refers to vaccines being used quite extensively

---

[220] Thorwald, Jurgen, *Science and Secrets of Early Medicine,* Harcourt, Brace, & World, N.Y., 1962, pages as follows: plastic surgery, 206; bladder stone removal, 211; use of mercury for ulcers, 242; pork liver for anemia, 244; anti-diarrhea remedies 293; contraceptives, 100; use of incense as an antiseptic for public buildings, 95; anti-fungal and anti-bacterial skin salves, 85; catheters, 166; enemas and suppositories, 173; kidney stone dissolvents, 172; and diagnostic techniques for hernias, 81, and for intestinal tuberculosis, 141.

[221] Contraceptives were known to the American Indians. The Shoshone of Nevada have been using contraceptives for centuries according to an article in *Chatelaine Magazine* (June, 1964, p. 10). They drink an extract of the roots of the lithospermum plant to suppress ovulation. Recent study shows that it contains a previously unknown substance called polyphenotic acid. Under study, it effectively inactivated the sex glands of rats and prevented ovulation in laying hens. Continued use apparently causes no side effects among Shoshone women.

in Africa,[222] and Sigerist writes at some length on vaccination techniques used by primitive people both in Africa and other parts of the world, and in China. As early as 1716 Cotton Mather in Boston learned how inoculation of smallpox was practiced in Africa from one of his Negro slaves. These people protected themselves against certain common snake bite venoms by allowing themselves to be bitten for the first time by a baby snake and then progressively by more mature snakes.[223] It is usual to rationalize their procedures for other diseases by assuming that they had noticed that if a man recovered from smallpox, for example, he was not again infected when the disease recurred in the community. This looks reasonable enough, but if it is just a case of observing the obvious, it is strange that nobody in Europe thought of doing it until the middle of the 18th century.

We have already mentioned that the Chinese had discovered the circulation of the blood, according to one work on Internal Medicine traditionally dated 2600 B.C.; and it is worth noting that they had also discovered the importance of feeling the pulse. Having no watches, they had mastered the technique of comparing the patient's pulse with their own.

In Part IV of this volume we have also referred to that extraordinary operation performed on the skull called trephination, an operation perhaps intended to reduce pressure on the brain due to some head injury. We know that at least some of these operations were entirely successful since the edges of the bone have grown smooth. Several hundred skulls are known from antiquity in which this operation was performed.[224] The operation was exceedingly widespread, found in every part of the world. Even more remarkable in some respects is the fact that Caesarean sections were performed in Africa, long before any European physician had attempted it. One such operation has been described from Uganda in 1879 by a British physician, Robert Felkin.[225]

The Spaniards were amazed at the medical skill and knowledge of the Mexicans. They, too, like the natives of India, performed plastic surgery even to the extent of providing people

[222] Livingstone, *Travels and Researches in South Africa*, Harper Bros., N.Y., 1858, p. 142.

[223] See Elizabeth A. Ferguson, "Primitive Medicine," *Sci. American*, Sept., 1948, p. 25.

[224] Trephination: as reported by Sigerist, op. cit. (ref. 219), p. 111.

[225] Caesarean sections: reported in detail by Sigerist, op. cit. (ref. 221), p. 207.

with artificial noses.[226] They were able to treat gangrene and internal hemorrhage, using for the latter not merely one substance but a choice of several. Similarly, when the French first came into contact with the American Indians, they too were equally astonished that "the savages" successfully used expectorants, emetics, purgatives, astringents, diuretics, and emmenagogues. Jacques Cartier noted in his log (1534) that most of his men had come down with "a deadly pestilence." This pestilence he described in some detail:[227]

> Some lost their very substance and their legs became swollen and puffed up while the sinews contracted and turned coal black, and in some cases, all blotched with dips of purplish blood. Then the disease crept up to the hips, thighs, shoulders, arms and neck. And all the sick had their mouths so tainted and their gums so decayed that the flesh peeled off down to the roots of their teeth while the latter almost fell out in turn.

The Indians told him what to do and provided him with an infusion of the bark and leaves of what they called a "magic tree." His men drank this and he reports, "In six days the miraculous tree worked more wonders than all the physicians of Louvain and Montpellier using all the drugs of Alexandria could have done in a year." And yet so bright are we as Japhethites that we never even took the trouble to find out what tree it was.

Some of the early Sumerian Cuneiform tablets reveal a surprising knowledge of the medicinal properties of common herbs, although they can hardly have had any knowledge of why these

---

[226] Plastic surgery: Jurgen Thorwald, op. cit. (ref. 220), p. 208, with illustration. Also see Irene Nicholson, "Science and Technology in Ancient Mexico," *Discovery*, Sept., 1960, p. 391.

[227] Reported in "Canada and Medicine," an editorial survey in *MD of Canada*, 8 (1967): 62ff. An article on Fray Bartolome which appeared in *MD of Canada* (9: 1968, p. 120) as an editorial item entitled "Apostles of India," quotes Bartolome on the matter of venereal disease as follows: "On several occasions I asked the Indians of this Island (Hispaniola) if this illness (syphilis) was very ancient among them, and they said, Yes, that it existed among them before the Christians arrived, and they had no memory of its origin, and no one should doubt this: and it seems proper also, because Divine Providence gave them the medicine for this disease, which is the guaguacan tree. It is a well known fact that all the incontinent Spaniards, who on this island did not have the virtue of chastity, were contaminated with this disease, and from a hundred hardly one would escape from it. Of the Indians, the men or women who contracted it were afflicted with it to a very small degree, and almost no more than if they had had smallpox, but the Spaniards were in great pain and constant torment from it particularly during the period when the buboes had not yet come out."

substances had the beneficial effects they did. Recently an article on headaches in *The Laboratory* has remarked upon the finding of such a tablet:[228]

> One of the curious by-ways of the migraine story is how the research has come full circle. The earliest statements on headache therapy is a Sumerian clay tablet of about 3000 B.C. that suggests: "Whenever pains attack the head...give kibtu and marru." Now these are substances obtained, respectively, from decayed maize and rye infected with the fungus that is the source of ergot. Today, 5000 years later, ergotic alkaloids are among the most significant drugs in migraine therapy.

And just as a matter of interest, Samuel Kramer notes that the Sumerians had discovered the art of artificial insemination, at least as applied to plants.[229]

Under the general heading of Household Furnishings, one may note a few items from China to be added to the previous list. But just in passing, it will be noticed that in the Time-Life series, "The Great Ages of Man," there is a volume by Schafer on ancient China in which a whole chapter is devoted to discoveries and inventions in that country. Among those listed are four technological inventions of Han and Medieval Times which as the author notes "laid the whole basis for the European exploration and colonization of the world: the compass became the tool of the pioneering seafarers of Portugal, Holland and England; gunpowder enabled Europeans to subdue the lands they found; and paper and printing made possible the wide dissemination of their idealogies and decrees."[230]

The invention of paper is, of course, characteristically, invariably credited in school books to an Indo-European. It is curious how this idea has persisted, but perhaps since we are now so completely dependent upon paper we are unwilling to admit precedence in its development to anyone else. In point of fact, as we have already seen, excellent papers were known centuries before both in China and Central America.[231] It is only very recently that paper has been used tentatively for disposable clothing, but the Aztecs were using paper for clothing as well as

---

[228] Headache treatment: "A headache is a headache is a headache," lead article (unsigned) in *The Laboratory* (Fisher Scientific Co.) 35, 1 (1967): 7.

[229] Artificial insemination: reported by Samuel Kramer, op. cit. (ref. 200), p. 109.

[230] Schafer, Edward H., op. cit. (ref. 94), pp. 125ff.

[231] Papers used in China and Central America: for details see Part IV, "The Technology of Hamitic People."

for other articles besides books before the Spaniards destroyed their civilization.[232] Carleton Coon notes that the Chinese provided their toilets with toilet seats which have a very modern appearance, and these — with characteristic practicality — they placed over their pig pens.[233] Lewis Mumford, speaking of this subject, remarked:[234]

> Before the invention of the trap and ventilatory stack for the toilet, the backing up of sewer gas into the dwelling house almost counterbalanced the advantages of the new improvement. With the water closet came another practice directly derived from the Chinese: the use of toilet paper: more important for domestic hygiene than the wallpaper that came in almost simultaneously.

As a matter of fact, in antiquity much greater concern was expressed over sanitation than was shown in Medieval Europe and England. Lavatory facilities were most elaborate (for example, in Knossos), and some of the installations from the Palace around 1500 B.C. are completely sound from the engineering point of view. From Tel el Amarna in the 14th century B.C. we have wooden toilet seats which in their construction were actually ahead of the toilet seats that were to be found in our own cities fifty years ago, or even twenty-five years ago. It is only in quite recent times that we have learned the advantages of making the toilet seat in the form of a horseshoe with the gap at the front edge. The Egyptians were doing this over 3000 years ahead of us.[235]

In the same general area of household furnishings, we may note that the Chinese developed home air conditioning,[236] the Phoenicians invented the wax candle,[237] and in addition to the use of Naphtha gas piped with bamboo to cast iron stoves (already mentioned in Part IV) the Chinese and the Mongols in Marco Polo's time were using coal for central heating, a material which Marco Polo refers to as being "cheaper than

---

[232] Disposable clothing: in an article by Irene Nicholson, op. cit. (ref. 226), p. 389.

[233] Toilets: C. S. Coon, op. cit. (ref. 198), p. 148.

[234] Mumford, Lewis, *The Culture of Cities*, Harcourt, Brace, N.Y., 1938, p. 119.

[235] Toilet seats: a photograph of one appears in an article (unsigned) entitled "Sanitation in Antiquity," *Image*, Montreal, Mar., 1964, p. 12.

[236] Air Conditioning: see *Ancient China*, Great Ages of Man, Time-Life Pub., N.Y., 1967, p. 40.

[237] Candles: reported in *MD of Canada*, Dec., 1967, p. 5.

wood and burning all night." He speaks of it as a "capital fuel."[238]

Marco Polo also speaks of the practice of gold capping faulty teeth, a practice he says was adopted for both lower and upper teeth by the men, but not by the women.[239] And while we are on the subject of dentistry, we may mention that the world's first toothbrush, looking precisely like a modern one, came from China, and is dated about A.D. 1498.[240]

In addition to the many other games, cards may be mentioned. In an article on this subject which appeared in *The Laboratory* recently, the following statement was made:[241]

> The earliest Chinese playing cards, introduced to Europe via the Holy Land Crusaders, imitated Chinese paper money — "bank notes" that bore pictorial symbols of their value. These pictures furnished the Suit marks of the Chinese pack, and copied in Europe (probably without knowledge of their oriental significance), gave rise to the four Suits of the European game.

It is an interesting reflection of how history cycles upon itself. In the first settlements in French Canada, when money in the form of coinage became scarce, playing cards bearing the governor's signature came to serve as paper currency.

Now consider the Aztec and Maya technique for getting rain. Here we have a case of what seems to be pure superstition. It has been customary to say that the priests were merely fooling the people, that they had sharp-eyed and experienced meteorologists who, perceiving signs of coming rain which the common people were not supposed to have been able to see, put on a fine display of hocus-pocus at the appropriate moment so that when the rain came everybody automatically credited them with having induced it. Ruth Benedict thinks that this is how the Hopi rain dance originated, though not as hocus-pocus. Rather, detecting the approach of rain, people assembled by mutual consent to perform a dance which was intended "to wake up the earth" by much stamping of the feet so as to make sure that none of the rain which fell would go to waste. This does not seem altogether illogical. But it appears now that the Aztecs and Maya were able not merely to predict rain but actually to bring it. In an article dealing with the technology of these people, Irene Nicholson

---

[238] Coal for central heating: Marco Polo, op. cit. (ref. 201), p. 147.

[239] Gold plating of teeth: Marco Polo, op. cit. (ref. 201), p. 177.

[240] Toothbrush: referred by Curt Proskauer, "Oral Hygiene in the Medieval Occident," *Ciba Symposia*, 8 (1946): 468.

[241] Cards: "It's in the Cards," *The Laboratory* (Fisher Scientific Co.), 35 (1967): 35 .

points out how the native ceremony involved the burning of copal and rubber. Carbon soot has the property of accumulating radiant heat. When particles of soot are sprinkled unto a cloud, any drops of moisture that happen to capture one or more soot particles will be warmed by the absorption of sunlight and will lose their humidity by evaporation whereas the drops that remain unsullied will maintain their cold temperature and will fall through the cloud until they join other drops and thus grow to a sufficient size to precipitate. The writer says that experiments were conducted in order to test out whether this reconstruction of the ancient practice was valid, and she notes that "in each of the seven experiments, about two pounds of soot were dropped from an airplane unto a cloud. Taking from two and a half to twenty minutes, the cloud precipitated." She then went on:[242]

> If soot is dropped in a humid atmosphere but without cloud, the effect is just the opposite. The black particles capture sunlight and warm the air. The air rises, expands, and cools. One part of the moisture condenses, and a new white cloud appears in the sky.

> Let us turn again to the ancient Mexicans, and imagine the priests on mountain peaks, burning magic balls of rubber latex on copal to bring rain to their crops. They used a brazier modelled — comically, it seems to us — with the head of the god. In the midst of the incense is placed a jade bead to represent the idea of divinity combined with the greenness of the earth. Above the brazier is a clay hood, formed like the inverted bowl of the sky, which captures the soot and disperses it.

> How much of the theory of their actions the priests knew, we can only conjecture; but they must have known from experience that the ritual was effective.

A number of small items: the ball and socket joint was invented in Crete,[243] the lathe was invented by the Etruscans,[244] bird-banding to identify ownership was used by the Mongols,[245] dactyloscopy — i.e., fingerprinting — was used 2000 years ago in China to identify important sealed documents.[246] Marco Polo mentions that Kublai Khan had a "Lost and Found Department"

---

[242] Rain making: this interesting discovery is reported in the article by Irene Nicholson, op. cit. (ref. 226), p. 389.

[243] Ball and socket joint: Ralph Linton, op. cit. (ref. 77), p. 328.

[244] Lathes: according to "The Origins of the Lathe," *Sci. American,* April, 1963, pp. 133f.

[245] Bird banding: referred to by Marco Polo, op. cit. (ref. 201), p. 126.

[246] Finger printing: referred to by Fritz Kahn, *Man in Structure and Function,* Vol. 2, Knopf, N.Y., 1947, fig. 328, p. 570.

attached to his army.[247] At Mohenjo Daru in the Indus Valley, around 2500 B.C., ingenious traps were invented for catching mice and rats.[248] As early as the 9th century B.C. people in the Middle East were using an artificial breathing apparatus for underwater repairs.[249]

Finally, an even more surprising — one might almost say, ironic — anticipation of modern engineering developments came to my attention recently through the journal of one research organization. The leading article in this journal begins with a photograph of a concrete and rock structure designed to check wave forces against a breakwater. The caption is: "The World's First Perforated Breakwater."[250] This development, known as the Jarlan Breakwater, has a central tunnel running the full length of it with a series of circular openings or orifices leading out to the face exposed to the waves. When a wave comes up against the face of the breakwater, it pours into these orifices flooding the interior. As the wave retreats these floodwaters at once begin to pour out again, and as they do so, they strike the next oncoming wave, thus baffle it, and rob it of much of its destructive energy. The system is most ingenious, and it is believed will enormously extend the useful life of the structure itself besides creating an immediately adjacent area of surface water which by its very baffling will be smoother than the water further out from the face of the dock. Larger vessels tied up may consequently be subjected to less damage. But the chief object of the design is to extend the life of the dock itself. The surprising thing is that this is no new development at all. The early Phoenician and Carthaginian military harbors of North Africa which were first built nearly 3000 years ago anticipated this construction. In speaking of these harbors Deacon, apparently quite unaware of the *recent* developments along this line, wrote:[253]

---

[247] Lost and found department: Marco Polo, op. cit. (ref. 201), p. 126. Polo says of this that it was officially supervised by an individual called Bularguchi, "Keeper of lost property," and he was part of the official army staff.

[248] Mouse trap: described under the heading "Man vs Mouse in 2500 B.C.," in a note in *Sci. American,* May, 1967, p. 60.

[249] Underwater breathing apparatus: this device is described by G. E. R. Deacon, *Seas, Maps and Men,* Doubleday, N.Y., 1962, p. 153. Deacon observes: "As early as the 9th century B.C. men were using artificial breathing apparatus for underwater work. This relief (illustrated) shows Assyrian divers with air tanks of inflated skins."

[250] Reported in some detail in "NRC Research News," 16, 4 (1963), lead

The breakwater was ingeniously built with rows of holes leading to a central channel or tunnel which ran within the masonry along the entire length of the breakwater. This elaborate system was most likely devised to reduce the shock of breaking waves. The holes at Thapsus and Hadrummentum are of the same design.

These brief and rather disconnected notes do not begin to show the range of developments and inventions and techniques that must be credited to non-Indo-European peoples. It happens that my own current research has led me to volumes which deal more particularly with Chinese technology or with medical history, and for this reason the above list is a little over-weighted in this direction. But this should not be allowed to mislead the reader into supposing that the debt is primarily to ancient China or that the field is primarily in terms of medicine. I think it is safe to say that there is no people of Hamitic stock, no part of the world, and no period throughout history which has not witnessed extraordinary examples of ingenuity and technical skill among non-Indo-Europeans. And by contrast, at no period have Indo-Europeans proved themselves inventive in a comparable way, nor technically adept except in so far as they have been stimulated by or built upon a Hamitic foundation.

One final observation brings us back to Scripture itself. I suggest that as Noah's family grew up, the old patriarch noted certain tendencies in his three children which seemed to set them apart from each other. Shem had a devout nature. He tended to be more reverent, more God-conscious, more spiritually inclined than either of his brothers. Japheth, on the other hand, was a thinker, a dreamer of dreams, wondering about things and apt to explore his world with a detached interest that set *him* apart, not in a spiritual but in an intellectual way. Ham was perhaps the "fixer" of the family. There is often such a child. He could repair anything, he constantly mended things that had broken, or invented new and better ways of doing things. He became indispensible to his less practical but more reflective brothers. And as Noah reflected upon their natures and saw them grow into families, tribes, and nations he predicted, under inspiration, that their descendants would tend to share these traits. Not all Shemites would be as religious as Shem, nor all Japhethites as exploratory and curious as Japheth, nor all Hamites as practical and down-to-earth as Ham; but this would be their "bent."

article. The Phoenician counterpart is referred to and illustrated by G. E. R. Deacon, op. cit. (ref. 249), p. 153.

When it came to passing judgment on Ham's family because of his disrespect in the case of Noah's drunkenness, the old man said that they should turn their talents to the service of others rather than themselves, that others would benefit by their service and not they. At any rate, in Genesis 9:24-27 we do seem to have in cameo form a kind of precis of history as it has turned out, as though in four simple sentences God predicted the form which the framework of human history was to take.[251] For he said: "Cursed be Canaan; a servant of servants shall he be unto his brethren.... Blessed be the Lord God of Shem; and Canaan shall be his servant. God shall enlarge Japheth and he shall dwell in the tents of Shem; and Canaan shall be his servant."

---

[251] I think it is of some significance that in Gen. 9:27-29 the phrase "And Canaan shall serve his brethren" is repeated after the reference not merely to Shem's descendants but Japheth's also. The usual interpretation is that the Canaanites in Palestine became "water carriers" to Israel and therefore served them. But in what way have Canaanites served Japheth? If by Canaan is meant the descendants of Ham the situation is clearer. That Canaan may have been cursed instead of Ham who was really the culprit, has been explored in Part III, "Why Noah Cursed Canaan Instead of Ham," in a way that rather illuminates not merely this passage but a number of others in Scripture.

Chapter 7

THE WORLD:
A STAGE FOR THE DRAMA

"THE WORLD was made for the body." How true is this? It
is a curious fact that man still makes the best "measure of
all things," to use Dryden's phrase. It may be an outmoded
philosophy to maintain that the universe should have its significance ultimately and only in the light of man, because we are so
repeatedly assured of man's total insignificance. Nevertheless,
virtually every assessment of every natural process or product is
still being made ultimately with reference to man as a measure
of its meaning. Perhaps it is not too surprising to find a Christian
writer saying this kind of thing. For example, William Tinkle
says, "We value plants and animals by the degree to which they
can be exploited by man."[252] But it is quite common also to find
non-Christian writers using the same standard of reference. When
Karpechenko's attempts to cross a radish with a cabbage supposedly produced a mongrel vegetable that was said to be quite
useless,[253] having neither the "useful" leaves of the cabbage nor
the "useful" root of the radish, naturalists were unconsciously
following the same principle of making man the measure, for in
what other way could one define the term "useful" or "useless"
in this context? To say that the leaves were useful to the cabbage

---

[252] Tinkle, William, *Heredity: A Study in Science and the Bible,* St.
Thomas Press, Houston, Texas, 1967, p. 137.

[253] Karpechenko's experiments: on this question see W. J. Tinkle and W.
E. Lammerts, "Biology and Creation" in *Modern Science and Christian
Faith,* ed. Russell Mixter, Van Kampen, Wheaton, 1950, pp. 88, 89, along
with *Sci. Newsletter,* Dec. 22, 1956, p. 339 under "Biology."

would really be meaningless, even though the cabbage could not live without them. But since the cabbage was developed to serve man's needs and not its own, the leaves are only useful in terms of man. So great is the temptation to view everything thus that even Julian Huxley finds it difficult to avoid implying that the whole of evolutionary history has merely been a prelude to the appearance of man.[254] And LeComte du Nouy is quite forthright on this point.[255] In one of the Doorway Papers we have set forth a proposal, a kind of reconstruction of prehistory of the earth before man, which is an attempt to show that the stage upon which the human drama is performed was prepared by a slow, orderly, meaningful process, the evidence for which can be interpreted either as purposeless and evolutionary in the strictly deterministic sense or as purposeful and developmental, involving specific creative acts throughout.[256] How one sees the evidence depends upon the initial bias one has. In itself the evidence is not decisive, although if negatives can prove anything, the existence of many discontinuities would favor the idea of direct creation in the process.

One thing that has emerged from the tremendous amount of research which has been undertaken (more often than not to demonstrate that there was *no* purpose) is that man is quite a unique creature and that his uniqueness — although it is often most easily defined in cultural terms — is nevertheless dependent upon his anatomy and physiology.

This conclusion is a very important one in the context of the present paper because it shows that the world *was* made for the body. Man's body, which I believe constitutes as important a part of his whole person as his spirit does, is what it is because of the total environment in which he lives — an environment which allows him to be active in a certain way, to have certain kinds of energies, to enjoy certain functional capacities, to oper-

---

[254] Huxley, Julian, *Evolution in Action,* Chatto & Windus, London, 1953, p. 144. His conclusion: "A second major concept is the primacy of the human individual, or, to use a better term, the primacy of personality. This primacy of human personality has been in different ways, a *postulate* both of Christianity and of liberal democracy, but it is a *fact* of evolution" (his emphasis).

[255] Du Nouy, LeComte, *Human Destiny,* Longmans, Green, N.Y., 1947, 289 pp.

[256] "The Preparation of the Earth for Man" (Part I of Doorway Papers Vol. IV).

ate chemically and electrically in a certain way — in short, to be a human being. To enable him to do this, he needed a certain kind of central nervous system,[257] posture, hands and feet, vision and hearing and sound emission, life cycle, appetite, thermal regulation, digestive system, manual dexterity and tactile sensitivity, bodily maneuverability, taste and smell — indeed, to be special in virtually every aspect of his physiology and anatomy.

It is tiresome to hear so frequently the statement made that the differences between man and the animals are differences of degree only and slight at that. Those who study in depth some particular aspect of the functioning of the human body quickly discover that although the differences seem slight enough, they are so fundamental that they constitute man as virtually a different *kind* of animal altogether.

Take one single illustration. Apart from domestication, the territories of animals, including the primates, are surprisingly small.[258] Man is ubiquitous, a fact which enables him to have dominion over every part of the earth. What makes the difference possible? The difference is due to a number of factors including man's superior intelligence, which has enabled him to protect himself artifically against extremes of climate. But in addition to this, in the simple matter of maintaining a normal body temperature apart from artificial aids, man is quite uniquely equipped.[259]

---

[257] E. L. Mascall refers to this fact, quoting Julian Huxley as having said, "Conceptual thought on this planet is inevitably associated with a particular type of Primate body and Primate brain." See his *Importance of Being Human*, Columbia Univ. Press, N.Y., 1958, p. 7.

[258] S. L. Washburn and C. S. Lancaster, in a paper entitled "The Evolution of Hunting" in *Human Evolution*, ed. by Korn and Thompson, Holt, Rinehart & Winston, N.Y., 1967, p. 73, wrote: "Social groups of nonhuman primates occupy exceedingly small areas, and the vast majority of animals probably spend their entire lives within less than four or five square miles. . . . Even for gorillas the range is only about 15 square miles, and it is of the same order of magnitude for savanna baboons; they refuse to be driven beyond the end of their range and double back. . . . In marked contrast, human hunters are familiar with very large areas. . . . Interest in a large area is human." The Eskimo family may occupy a strip 250 to 350 miles long and even more. And men make tremendous migrations with a view to permanent settlements.

[259] This is an area of particular interest to the author who has done years of laboratory research into human thermal equilibrium. "Sweat as Part of the Curse" (Part III of Doorway Papers Vol. IX) treats the subject in some detail and in relation to Scripture. A useful basic bibliography will be found there.

This is especially the case for man at high temperatures. Scattered over his body are about two million eccrine sweat glands. Each of these is composed of a little glomerulus deep in the skin which is connected with the surface via a small spiral tube. No animal, not even the horse, is supplied with this mechanism for the maintenance of body temperature. This spiral tube carries the purest watery fluid in the body from the little glomerulus reservoir to the surface where it spills out and evaporates, cooling the skin in the process. The movement of this fluid to the surface is mechanically effected by a peristaltic wave of contraction which moves from the root of the gland to the surface thus pushing the fluid ahead of it. Thousands of muscle fibers are probably involved in this peristalsis and it is likely that their refractory time is about 1/100 of a second, so that the wave can move along the tubule with a very high frequency if necessary. It should be borne in mind also that these fibers must contract in precisely the right order to ensure unidirectional movement of the fluid. The spiral of the tube is a necessary structural feature which serves the purpose of preventing its overstretching and rupture if the skin is moved relative to the tissue beneath it. It is analogous to the cord on the telephone which is coiled for flexibility. One of the differences between human and animal skin is that the former is stretched comparatively tight while the latter tends to be loose. In the wild, an animal wound that causes a tear in the skin does not gape open and will heal without suturing. But this very looseness makes it impossible for a sweat gland system which man has to be workable in animals, even in the primates supposedly nearest to man. For a tubule supplied with muscle could not be constructed to accommodate itself to the tremendous freedom of lateral movement observed in animal skin.

But there is much more involved in this mechanism. Skin with a low fluid content is a remarkably good insulator, having about the value of cork in this respect. Thus the mere chilling of the external surface by evaporation of sweat, while it might give a comfortable *feeling* — since the cold receptors would be stimulated — it would not substantially remove heat from the body. Thus in conjunction with this whole mechanism is another which is so designed that blood which is overheated deep within the body transports its heat load to the surface of the skin where it is then cooled by conduction before the venous system takes it back to the center again. This is known technically as vasodilatation. Animals do not appear to have this mechanism in the way that man does over the whole periphery. They may have it in the ears (rabbits), or in the tail (some rodents), and so forth, but it is not systemic; and as a consequence of its limited effectiveness, animals are restricted to the kind of environment for which they have been designed.

When one considers that man has this vasomotor adjustment over the whole skin surface accompanied by a "tight" skin which allows a duct system for some two million sweat glands enabling him to survive for a limited time temperatures of even 260° F, and when it is realized that this system of sweat outbreak is so sensitively geared to deep body temperature that a rise of 0.1° C is sufficient to trigger a precise and measurable increase in sweat rate within a second or two over the whole body surface, the organization of the central nervous control will be seen as something amazingly complex and sophisticated. The signals going to each of the two million sweat glands at a rate of up to 100 impulses per second involves an organization that is unimaginably complex. Moreover, in man there is the further physiological complication that this system is functionally parasympathetic but anatomically sympathetic in its control. This mechanism makes it possible for man to live in every climate on the earth. Yet very few people are even aware of the significance of the function except in so far as it helps the sale of deodorants, etc. Animals do not have this, for they do not need it. The difference between man and animals, therefore, even in such a mundane thing as thermal regulation is structurally about as great as it is possible to conceive. I am convinced that when we really know enough about the functioning of the human body we shall be appalled at how mistakenly man was equated with the animals, or even for that matter — one animal species with another.

For all this, man *is* an animal in the sense that his body, for the purposes of investigation, can be treated at certain levels as an animal body. In our own laboratories we have had many occasions to observe how remarkably aptly it can be treated simply as a heat engine. Thus for all his uniqueness as a creature poised between the purely spiritual and the wholly material, he does live and move and have his being within the framework of chemistry and physics. He is related structurally to the world in which he lives and is not able to live unless he takes it with him to some extent—as he does in space. The earth at the present time is his proper home. Huxley states quite simply that man's uniqueness, a uniqueness which he equates not without reason with man's ability for conceptual thought, "is inevitably associated with a particular type of *Primate body and Primate brain.*"[260] In other words, man is not an angelic creature who happens to have the kind of body he does and who might just as easily have been equipped with any other kind of body. He is a creature whose uniqueness from the point of view of his manhood, both in terms of culture and aspiration, *is as much dependent upon the structure of his body as it is upon·the nature of his soul.* It is quite wrong to imagine that man's body is incidental and that he might have been structured like a giraffe, a mouse, or even an ape, and still fulfilled the role for which he was created. The fact is that God's purposes for man required that he have a certain kind of physiological and anatomical structure, and the preservation and maintenance in health of this particular body which he indwells required in turn a certain kind of environment. This environment involved not only the right kind of atmosphere but the right kind of temperature, the right kind of seasonal variations, the right kind of gravitational forces acting upon him, the right kind of materials at hand or extractable for his building a civilized life, the right kind of food, the right kind of shelter, and even the right kind of territory to challenge him and to call forth his wonder, and to allow him to exercise his ability to dominate, to order, to arrange, to govern and to beautify the earth, and to turn it into a garden — and thereby to become a co-worker with God.

The world was "made for the body" indeed, and therefore in the final analysis the world with its time and space co-ordinates and its laws of physics and chemistry, is as essential to God's plan as man himself. The world was created for man, as man was created for God. Was perhaps the universe created for the world?

---

[260] See quote from Mascall on this (ref. 257).

Chapter 8

THE UNIVERSE:
A SETTING FOR THE WORLD

THE TOTAL physical milieu plays an essential part in the development of the whole man. Even a study of the earth's past history contributes in its own way by allowing him through careful enquiry to observe how God prepared the earth as a habitation for him. Recently Bishop Herbert Welch, in looking back over a very long life (a hundred years) set forth some of his thoughts about the meaning of the world around:[261]

> I can see that this world is an unfinished piece of business. It is like the palace of Aladdin, which was built by magic, with one bare plain window while the other eleven were lavishly jewelled — just to give the kind of pleasure of putting the finishing touch upon this marvel of splendour. So God reserves for man the honour and glory of sharing in creative work. God provides the iron; man manufactures it into forms of power and usefulness. God makes the wild rose: God and man together make an American Beauty. Nature, it seems to me, spells challenge and opportunity. . . .
>
> In a word, God has not made a world in which security and ease and happiness are the highest attainment; but rather a world for watchfulness, for work, for struggle, and for suffering as a normal part of a full life. . . .
>
> Life as God planned it is not to be a nursery for the coddling of perpetual infants, but a school for adult education.

The study of the earth's past history does not need to be as prosaic and uninspiring as most textbooks of geology are apt to be today. Hugh Miller's *Testimony of the Rocks*, as one might

---

[261] Bishop Herbert Welch, quoted in an article in *Reader's Digest* (Nov., 1967, pp. 206, 208) entitled, "An Unfinished Piece of Business."

expect from its very title, is filled with paragraphs of great literary beauty because the writer's mind was not merely filled with factual knowledge but with insight into the message which this knowledge conveyed to his devout soul.

I propose to set forth what has appeared to me to be a reasonable interpretation of the data from geology which I see as strongly supporting the view that the earth as a habitation was indeed prepared specifically for the coming of man, and that this preparation took a long time; and that during this long time the living components of it were gradually changed by divine interference in such a way that when man was finally created he could be placed in a total environment that was wholly appropriate for him. This "divine interference" I suggest might be appropriately termed "supernatural selection," which I would then elaborate upon in the following way:[262]

> Among living creatures offspring differ from their parents and this fact provides a means whereby select lines may be encouraged and unwanted lines allowed to disappear.
> If this occurs by accident, it is termed Natural Selection.

[262] This is a passage from "The Preparation of the Earth for Man" (in Doorway Papers Vol. IV) which is an extended study of the question from this point of view, accompanied by 7 pages of documentation.

Many years ago Professor L. B. Walton said: "The supposed progress made in the improvement of domesticated animals and plants is nothing more than the sorting out of pure lines and thus represents no advancement" (*Science*, April 3, 1914), and Sir Alister Hardy speaking of the real limitations of artificial or human selection said: "It was thought that if we selected examples of our animal or plant of, say, larger size than the mean, and bred from them, we should find that their offspring would tend to vary in the same sort of chance way: some being slightly larger, some slightly smaller, with the majority nearer to the *size of their parents*. So it was confidently thought, at this time, that if we went on selecting for larger size, or some other character, generation after generation, we could go on pushing evolution in this or that direction as we liked within, of course, the limits of an efficient working organism. This seemed an obvious deduction because, if variation was really quite a matter of chance, then surely the offspring must continue to range in size more or less equally above and below the size of their parents. It was taken for granted that this indeed was what the stock breeder was doing in producing his different races of domestic animals: sheep with higher wool yield, hens of greater laying capacity, and so on. In the late 90's, when Karl Pearson and others began to put this to the test of experiment they were horrified to find that selection appeared not to work." (*The Living Stream*, Collins, London, 1965, pp. 77, 78). What they did find, apparently, a finding always confirmed since, was that each species has a fixed range of variability and while one may get a higher percentage of offspring at one end of the range, the range itself is never exceeded—except occasionally for pathological reasons.

When it is performed by man, it is termed Human Selection. There is evidence from Palaeontology to support the belief that the progress of forms from simple to complex has not been by chance but by design. The term Supernatural Selection could perhaps serve to define this prehuman process.

It is widely agreed that Natural Selection cannot be creative. Human Selection is "creative" only in the sense that pure lines are sorted out and new varieties are thus produced. Supernatural Selection has something of Natural Selection about it in that by this means less desirable forms (or organs) are discouraged; and the end result may be analogous at times to Human Selection in that the process is purposeful; but it differs positively from either in being a *creative* process whereby are introduced entirely new forms and therefore, presumably, new genes and new gene combinations.

If I am considered as another theistic evolutionist by any one who has read this, the fault will be mine entirely, in not having made clear what the fundamental difference is between my own view and this other currently popular view.

As I understand it, theistic evolutionists are essentially orthodox evolutionists — except that they believe God was behind it all, from the appearance of the first amoeba to the appearance of the first man. The term "evolution" is still taken to mean the gradual transformation of one species into another by natural means and without any genetic discontinuities. These means are explainable in terms of natural processes, the only supernatural element being the initiation of the process and the evidence of purpose throughout. In due course these people hope to be able to demonstrate this in the laboratory. When this happens we shall know "how God did it." The Creator started it all off, and then withdrew from any further interference except on very rare and special occasions when miracles occurred, having assured Himself as it were, that things would end up as He planned.

This is not my view at all, how ever much it may superficially seem to be. I believe God acted creatively, in the most distinct and positive manner conceivable, throughout the whole of geological history, introducing new species as they became appropriate, and removing others when they ceased to be. No laboratory experiment can ever hope to elucidate this creative process, as I understand it. But because God was graciously willing to permit us to see the unfolding of His designs, the geological record can be read as a more or less continuous one, with evidence of the fitness and appropriateness of things throughout the whole process as the earth was prepared for the coming of man.

Because science must, of necessity, reject any appeal to the supernatural, the scientific account must accordingly give only a partial view of the meaning of the earth's past history, and of the universe as a whole. Revelation is essential to make the picture complete.

This appropriateness or "fitness" of the total environment for life and for man has often been remarked upon by non-Christian writers who, while having no sympathy with the idea of plan or purpose behind it, nevertheless forthrightly express their amazement that so many interlocking factors contribute to it. While they categorically deny the *reality* of a "goal," they freely admit the *appearance* of it. We shall look at some of these after we have considered certain other factors in connection with the earth as a heavenly body which contribute to its uniqueness within the solar system. These factors involve (1) its size, (2) its rate of revolution, (3) its mean distance from the sun, (4) the variation in its distance from the sun, (5) the constituents of its surface, and (6) its satellite.

(1) The size of the earth determines the constitution of its atmosphere, and the constitution of its atmosphere determines the nature of the living forms upon it.[263] If it were much larger, it would have retained a large percentage of gases inimical to life. If it were much smaller, its gravitational forces would have been insufficient to retain virtually any atmosphere at all.

The smaller planets with smaller gravitational fields have lost a large proportion of their lighter elements. The larger planets have retained most of their original atmosphere. Actual measurements show that although the weight of Jupiter is only 317 times that of the earth, so great is the amount of atmospheric strata around it that its volume appears to be 1300 times greater than that of the earth.

The planet Mercury, on the other hand, has a weight only approximately one twenty-third of that of the earth and is known to have no appreciable atmosphere surrounding it, its gravitational field being too weak to retain nitrogen, oxygen, and water vapor.

The earth has, therefore, just sufficient mass that it is able to hold around itself a blanket of gases which both supports life and shields it from lethal rays of the sun. Its size is such that certain poisonous gases which formed as the earth cooled were

---

[263] Farmer, F. J., "The Atmosphere: Its Design and Significance in Creation," *Trans. Vict. Inst.*, London, 71, (1939): 39f.

not held in the atmosphere but escaped into space. The carbon dioxide, which *was* held, ultimately supported luxuriant vegetation, which in turn purified it for animal life by setting oxygen free in photosynthesis. Gases, like all other things, have weight, some being heavier than others. It so happens that the gases unsuitable for life were light enough and the earth's gravitational pull small enough that they were lost into space, and thereby eliminated.

An important "natural law," which is otherwise everywhere obeyed, is found to be broken in the atmosphere, which were it not broken would have prevented the introduction of life on the earth. This law is simply the law of gravity. Were it not superceded by the law of the diffusion of gases, the atmosphere would sort itself out so that the heavier gases would be at the bottom and the lighter gases at the top. The consequence of this for the earth would be a layer of carbon dioxide of sufficient depth that all life would soon cease. However, gravity is defied and this heavier gas diffuses through the other gases of the atmosphere so that free oxygen remains available at the earth's surface so that all creatures that breathe are able to obtain energy and sustain life.

(2) The rate of revolution of the earth is just right for the continuous renewal of the atmosphere for animal life. Nothing gets too cold or too hot over most of its area, and plants have just sufficient times of light and of darkness to perform their function of regenerating the air. This is necessary since, according to Laurence Henderson, the unique stability of carbon dioxide depends upon alternating light and darkness.[264]

(3) The distance from the sun determines the mean temperature of the atmosphere and the earth. The pliable materials of which living tissue is composed are made up of molecules which retain their physical characteristics only within a comparatively small range of temperature variation. It appears that apart from the very exceptional properties of carbon in forming these long chainlike molecules, such structures as ourselves and all other pliant forms would not be possible at all. It is only in a very restricted range of temperature that these carbon compounds are stable. If the temperature becomes too cold, these chains become inflexible, and if the temperature becomes too high, they lose

---

[264] Henderson, Lawrence, "The Fitness of the Environment: An Inquiry into the Biological Significance of the Properties of Matter," quoted by K. Walker, in *Meaning and Purpose*, Penguin, London, 1950, p. 102.

their bonds and disintegrate. The range of temperature within which living flesh can continue without artificial protection is quite small relative to the ranges of temperature which may exist on a body in space. Professor Frank Allen of the University of California commented on this:[265]

> If the earth were removed to double its present distance from the sun, the heat received would be reduced to one fourth its present amount, the orbital velocity would be only one half, the winter season would be doubled in length and life would be frozen out. If its solar distance were halved, the heat received would be four times as great, the orbital velocity would be doubled, seasons would be halved in length, if changes could ever be effected, and the planet would be too parched to sustain life. In size and distance from the sun, and in orbital velocity, the earth is able to sustain life, so that mankind can enjoy physical, intellectual, and spiritual life as it now prevails.

(4) The seasonal variations which take place throughout the year are very important for the continuance of human life and probably for the well-being of many other forms of life. Were it not for these changes, microorganisms which cause diseases and which are favored by certain environmental conditions would multiply so extensively that the human race might suffer extinction because of them. Man is not the only animal to suffer on this account. Consider what would happen to the mosquito population if the conditions ideal for their multiplication were to persist throughout the year all over the globe. Surgeon-General C. A. Gordon pointed out that not only does the persistence of a particular temperature and humidity have to be taken into account here, but even the length of the day.[266] The length of day, of course, is governed by the position of the earth with respect to the sun. In his paper, Gordon gives a chart showing the distribution throughout one year of some of the major diseases caused by these microorganisms, thus indicating the benefit resulting from seasonal fluctuations.[267]

(5) The surface of the earth is part water and part dry land, in a ratio of approximately 3 to 1. The uniqueness of water has been pointed out by countless authorities. The existence of water

---

[265] Allen, Frank, "The Origin of the World — By Chance or Design?" in *The Evidence of God in an Expanding Universe,* ed. John C. Monsma, Putnam, N.Y., 1958, pp. 22f.

[266] Gordon, Surgeon-General C. A., "Climate in Relation to Organic Nature," *Trans. Vic. Instit.,* London, 17 (1883): 33f.

[267] Ibid., pp. 51, 52.

in a fluid state is itself fundamental to the continuance of life. Harold Blum has made the following observations:[268]

Water makes up perhaps 80 to 90% of all living organisms, and may be regarded as their principal environmental component, since even forms living in air maintain an aqueous internal environment in one way or another. Most of the water on the earth is in the liquid state, but it is also of importance as an environmental factor when in the vapour state and even as a solid.

Water seems admirably suited for the major role it plays in maintaining a relatively constant temperature for the earth's surface, a matter of paramount importance to living organisms, which can serve only within a very restricted range of temperature. It owes this aspect of its fitness to several properties.

Blum then elaborates upon these properties. His elaboration leaves one filled with wonder at the power and wisdom of God in creating such a medium. But this medium requires a quite specific environment for its continued usefulness. That is to say, it is useful in a unique way — in a unique environment. Blum summed this up by saying:[269]

So fitness partakes of the nature of uniqueness, the uniqueness of the earth as an abode of life is a matter that strikes one more forcibly the more he tries to break out of the circle. Not only is the earth as it is, but it has reached that state through an evolutionary process, each step of which has been dependent upon the one preceding it.

The stage upon which living systems bowed their debut was set by all the preceding events in the history of the earth — or, for that matter, of the Universe. These events placed important restrictions upon the nature of life and its evolution.

Life, it seems, did not arise and evolve as a system free to vary in any direction whatever; but as a system upon which great restrictions were placed, some of them even before the earth came into existence.

He concludes his chapter on the fitness of the environment with these words, "This aspect of fitness is not, then, universal, but exists only in relation to the planet Earth, or to planets that are very nearly like the Earth.[270]

Allen points out that there are four remarkable properties of water, its power to absorb vast amounts of oxygen at low temperatures, its maximum density at 4° C above freezing so

---

[268] Blum, Harold, *Time's Arrow and Evolution*, Princeton Univ. Press, N.J., 1951, p. 62.
[269] Ibid., p. 76.
[270] Ibid., p. 85.

that lakes and rivers remain liquid (and the ice forms a floating protective shield over the water which would otherwise freeze solid from the bottom up and kill all marine life), and its power of releasing great quantities of heat as it freezes thus preserving life in the oceans, lakes, and rivers during long winters.[271]

But the water must also be lifted by evaporation and carried over the land, a cycle which depends upon temperature changes, warmth to raise it, cooling to condense it, and a proper relative surface area of water to land in order that the land may neither be parched through insufficient precipitation nor turned into a swamp through excess. Moreover, topography of the land is important in assisting this process by causing turbulence of the air currents which pass over it thus bringing about a breakup of cloud formations.

(6) The existence of the moon is also of fundamental importance. As far as is known, it is the largest satellite relative to the size of its parent body. From this point of view it is, in fact, huge. There have been some authorities who held that we owe the present distribution of water and land surface to the birth of the moon. The assumption is made that the moon was derived from the earth and at its birth removed from our globe a large segment of its granite crust. What remained of this crust was subsequently fragmented and spread around the earth as the continents. The areas occupied by the missing segments of granite left scars, depressions into which the water which had formerly spread over the globe as a shallow liquid mantle, now collected to form deeper pools, the oceans. The great deeps which now serve to contain those waters did not formerly exist. The irregularities of this once continuous granite shell would then take the form of a large number of comparatively small islands standing in a universal but shallow sea.[272] These islands would permit a high degree of variability by reason of geographic isolation. At any rate, the moon now contributes heavily to the formation of tides, and tides are of great importance in keeping the oceans fresh. Thus, the possession by the earth of such a large satellite as the moon is in more than one way of great importance to life as we know it.

All these "coincidences" add up to an impressive testimony

[271] Allen, Frank, op. cit. (ref. 265), p. 21.
[272] Gamow, George, *Biography of the Earth*, Mentor Books, N.Y., 1948, pp. 42f.

to the uniqueness of the earth as a theater for the unfolding of God's Plan.

So much, then, for the planet itself. What of its inhabitants, the living forms of plants and animals? As living forms have multiplied on the earth and developed patterns of life which render the whole fabric an unbelievably complex network of interdependent organisms, many extraordinary modes of existence and many remarkable patterns of behavior have arisen, as "Nature" solved the problems of cooperative existence on a grand scale. So complex and yet so refined and effective are these adjustments that it is almost impossible not to be forcibly struck by what looks like purpose, indeed one might better say a *striving towards some future goal,* pervading living processes at every level of existence. But the concept of purpose inevitably invites the introduction of a Purposer who, because He must stand outside the physical order, introduces into the situation active forces or agencies which are not subject to scientific analysis.

But, ever since Helmholtz and his two friends issued their manifesto[273] repudiating such forces as vitalism, entelechy, or "goal-seeking" as allowable explanations of observed phenomena, scientists have been increasingly unwilling to admit the *possibility* of plan or purpose in any form whatever. As a consequence, there exists today among scientists a quite extraordinary hostility towards the introduction of any such concept as purpose or creation. Either of these are anathema, and any writer who dares to introduce them is apt to find that everything else he has to say is considered of little consequence — no matter what the evidence is.

Two writers of recent times and of great stature, who were far less hostile to the two concepts of purpose and of vitalism, wrote with what seems to be characteristic eloquence. But their works never achieved the fame that they would undoubtedly have, had they written as Huxley and Simpson wrote, for example, both of whom are *violently* opposed to either. The

---

[273] This was a profoundly important manifesto. The three men were Carl Ludwig (1816-1895), who taught most of the great physiologists of the world active in the latter part of the 19th century; Emil du Boris-Reymand (1818-1896), who was the founder of electro-chemistry; and Hermann von Helmholtz (1812-1894) who needs no introduction. This, in substance, is what they agreed upon: "All the activities of living material, including consciousness, are ultimately to be explained in terms of physics and chemistry." See Chauncey D. Leake, "Perspectives in Adaptation: Historical Background," in *Handbook of Physiology,* Sect. 4, Amer. Physiol. Soc., Washington, 1964, pp. 5, 6.

354 • A CHRISTIAN WORLD VIEW

scientific world has shied away because in the past there was a tendency to allow faith in such metaphysical concepts to serve as an excuse for not persisting in research which did not at once show promise of providing useful insights into otherwise baffling natural processes. People had a tendency to say, "Oh well, the cause is outside of our competence to search out, only God knows what 'life' is and we should not presume to explore what is uniquely in His domain. It is a special expression of divine activity." And so further research tended to be discouraged.

Professor Wood Jones, in his most stimulating and remarkably readable little book *Trends of Life,* repeatedly expressed his regret that those who studied living forms of the past and the present were so adamant in their rejection of the idea of purpose in nature:[274]

> In dealing with questions of vitalism and teleology, we shall find that, although such ideas are today considered as unorthodox and absurd, they are not so considered because science has proved them to be wrong, but rather because some circumstance in the changing phases of opinion has demanded that they be ranked as heresies.

Another writer whose works have received the same kind of unfavorable reviews that Wood Jones' works did, is LeComte du Nouy. I am thinking particularly of his *Human Destiny.* Du Nouy did not question the theory of evolution any more than Wood Jones did, but both men believed that the gradual development throughout geological times of increasingly more complex forms of life was not to be accounted for solely in terms of current evolutionary theory. Present theory holds that purely by chance mutations and natural selection, acting together, have produced the flora and fauna of the world. There was no purpose or plan, and no force outside of nature has ever been necessary. The whole thing can be accounted for without any need for a design or a Designer. Simpson speaks eloquently enough of the *appearance* only of design in nature:[275]

---

[274] Jones, F. Wood, *Trends of Life,* Arnold, London, 1953, p. 129.
[275] Simpson, G. G., "The Problem of Plan and Purpose in Nature," *Sci. Monthly,* June, 1947, pp. 481f. The fitness of things is by no means limited to the environment. There is a wonderful fitness even in the matter of molecular structure. R. E. D. Clark, himself a Ph.D. in Chemistry, has an excellent illustration from his own field of research. He writes: "A good example of recent thinking in this field is afforded by the phosphate group, the unique properties of which (high energy phosphate bonds, etc.) make it irreplacable in the living organism. In addition, phosphate precipitates with

An eye, an ear, or a hand is a complex mechanism serving a particular function. It looks as if it had been made for the purpose. This appearance of purposefulness is pervading in Nature, in the general structure of animals and plants, in the mechanisms of their various organs, and in the give and take of their relationships with each other. Accounting for this apparent purposefulness is a basic problem for any system or Philosophy of Science.

Yet so convinced is he that this is an illusion that he states categorically and repeats almost ad nauseam that "man was certainly not the goal of evolution which evidently had no goal. He was not planned in an operation wholly plan-less."[276]

In his *Human Destiny*, however, du Nouy repeatedly sets forth in no uncertain terms the evidence that such a view is quite inadequate to account for things as they are:[277]

> The evolution of living beings, as a whole, is in absolute contradiction to the science of inert matter. It is in disagreement with the second principle of thermodynamics, the keystone of our science, based on the laws of chance.... No scientist on earth can deny this. To account for what has taken place since the appearance of life, we are obliged to call in an "anti-chance" which orients this immense series of phenomena in a progressive, highly "improbable" direction (incompatible with chance), resulting in the human brain. This amounts to the recognition of the existence of a goal, of an end, for, in at least one line, the same orientation is always observed, on an average and over an extremely long period. Therefore, everything has taken place as if, ever since the birth of the original cell, Man has been willed....

One of the most mysterious aspects of the developing stream

---

calcium to give a complex calcium phosphate, hydroxyapatite, of exceptional strength, crystals of which are formed in the collagen fibres of bone owing to a surprising coincidence in the unit crystal size and repeat lengths of the two materials. This bone ensures a reservoir of phosphate in the body and helps to maintain a steady phosphate concentration in body fluids. The hydroxyapatite has curious electrical properties: it generates a voltage when bone is bent. The potential acts in such a way that the phosphate dissolves where it is not needed and redeposits where the bone needs strengthening...." (*The Christian Stake In Science*, Moody Press, Chicago, 1967, p. 36). So wonderfully pliant is the bone substance and structure that if a fracture occurs in such circumstances that the segments simply cannot fuse together again, a joint, articulate and virtually normal in every way, may form instead. (See Sir Peter Medawar, *The Art of the Soluble*, Methuen, N.Y., 1967, p. 26.)

[276] Simpson, G. G., *The Meaning of Evolution*, Yale, 1951, pp. 292, 344, 345. He felt it necessary to repeat the substance of his faith three times....

[277] Du Nouy, LeComte, op. cit. (ref. 255), p. 224.

of life is the repeated occurrence of what have come to be called "pre-adaptations." These take the form of structures which are of no immediate advantage or use to the organism but after further development prove to be of great importance to it thousands of generations later, as though nature was deliberately making preparations for something yet to be. On this du Nouy said:[278]

> Throughout the development of evolution (whatever that means!) the scientist finds himself facing this unaccountable mystery, the creation of organs destined to improve sketchy solutions so as to increase the freedom of the individual, his independence, with respect to his environment. . . .
> This holds true for the appearance of homoiothermism (constant temperature). This is an immense and unquestionable liberation from servitude to the environment and has, it must be admitted, all the unsatisfactory (sic) characteristics of absolute creation, whereas we feel that such cannot be the case. This stands out today as one of the greatest puzzles of evolution.

And so he concluded:[279]

> Everything always takes place as if a goal had to be attained, and as if this goal was the real reason, the inspiration of Evolution. All the attempts which did not bring the goal nearer were forgotten or eliminated.

In the same connection, Loren Eiseley wrote:[280]

> The reason why a given form of life chooses to launch upon a new adventure is always apt to remain mysterious. One thing however, seems rather plain: animals do not evolve new organs for the specific purpose of intruding into a new environment. Instead they start with what the Biologist calls a "pre-adaptation" — an existing organ, habit or other character which offers the possibility of being used successfully under new environmental circumstances.
> The first vertebrates to leave the water successfully, for example, had already acquired a primitive lung, utilized for

---

[278] Ibid., pp. 70, 72.

[279] Ibid., p. 74. In a similar vein, Konrad Lorenz in his *On Aggression*, Bantam Books, Harcourt Brace, 1967, p. 256, speaking of preadaptations in the human embryo remarks: "All the tremendous neurosensory apparatus of human speech is phylogenetically evolved, but so constructed that its function *presupposes* the existence of a culturally developed language which the infant has to learn."

Likewise, E. S. Russell, in his *Directiveness of Organic Activities*, 1945, pp. 94, 95 remarked in connection with the cell divisions of the growing ovum, "These forms of cleavage are directive towards future goals integrally related to the general process of development, and comprehensive only on this basis, *whatever their causal explanation, if any, may be.*"

[280] Eiseley, Loren, "Fossil Man," *Sci. American*, Dec., 1953, p. 70.

survival in swamp waters of low oxygen content. Other pre-adaptations, such as a muscular fin capable of being transformed into a primitive foot, contributed to the success of the venture. What we cannot so readily clarify in certain of these instances is whether events *forced* the movement across into the new corridor, or whether the restless impetus, the exploring curiosity, the vital drive of the animal promoted the crossing.

To my mind the best explanation of the course of events throughout geological ages until the coming of man is that God worked creatively and in an orderly way towards the world which we now see, by constantly introducing new forms of life, whether plant or animal, as the changing environment permitted them to be introduced. The system is an interacting one in that each new series of forms contributed to this change, in turn starting by their presence directional shifts of the contemporary scene which in due course prepared it to receive another series of forms.[281] Each series of forms was higher than the previous ones and could not be introduced until the previous forms had prepared the way or been removed.

Thus land forms were not possible until there was something for them to feed upon, and since all flesh is grass there had to be vegetation of some sort. The initial sand which resulted naturally from the breakdown of the rocks was capable of supporting certain simple types of plant life which were therefore created first. These in the course of time by their very decay began the building of "soil" which then permitted the introduction — once more by direct creation — of higher forms of plant life, until in due time certain very simple forms of animal life

---

[281] Recently it has become customary in some quarters to attach more importance to the concept proposed by Lamarck that characters which an organism acquires due to environmental "pressures" of one form or another may be inherited by its offspring. The mechanism for this was lacking, and the experimental evidence was entirely against the view. But it is possible that such inheritance of acquired characters could be via the cytoplasm for certain simple forms, as Ephrussi and Sonneborne and others have shown. Now it seems that even higher forms of life may pass on such acquired characters in some way not known but indicated by the great difficulty of accounting for animal "fitness" to the environment in any other way. As Sir Alister Hardy wrote recently: "Again and again Lamarck made the point that changes in the environment can bring about changes in the habits of animals and that it is these *changes of habit* (his emphasis) which can be so important in bringing about evolutionary modifications" (*The Living Stream,* Collins, London, 1965, p. 160). Hardy then elaborates and exemplifies such changes. This is all we need to make my proposal viable: though the word "development" should be substituted for Hardy's "evolution." Such inherited characteristics are now termed dauermodifications.

could be introduced to the land environment, not merely because food was at last available, but also because the plants had "purified" the atmosphere of its excess carbon dioxide and made it respirable.

I do not think that such a process is at all unreasonable since evolutionists themselves would readily agree to the general characteristics of these successive forms, the order in which they would appear, and the reasons for that order. The fundamental difference between their point of view and my own is that I believe each new series of forms was introduced by creative activity, by an activity of which we have no experience in the laboratory. Nor are laboratory experiments ever likely to shed any light on it. Always in view from the very first was the object, namely, a world suited to the requirements of a creature such as man. To this extent the *end,* man, was the cause. To Simpson, this kind of philosophy is complete nonsense. But to the Christian, who is faced with almost overwhelming evidence of a long process of developmental history which he meets in virtually every textbook and which is virtually always attributed to evolution, this alternative view can be very satisfying, since it ignores none of the evidence that has been established as fact. It is only the theory of evolution that must be disallowed. It should be said in fairness to a number of well-informed Christian geologists and biologists that not everyone accepts the evidence for a great antiquity of the earth. There are a number of scientists today who are convinced that modern geology misinterprets the facts, and that a single catastrophe, such as the Flood of Noah's day, could account for stratified rocks.

The overall picture which I have presented above has been shared, and indeed elaborated with keen insight, by a number of informed writers, going back even as far as the Church Fathers, none of whom may be labelled by that rather opprobrious term, theistic evolutionists. The theistic evolutionist, as we have noted, differs from the atheistic evolutionist only in this, that he believes God produced the present world without interfering with it after setting in motion a process which thereafter could take care of itself and could be depended upon by its own powers to produce in the end a creature such as man is. Presumably, the only miracle involved, in the final analysis, would be in the origination of matter: once the elements had been created, the rest would take care of itself.

Because it is sometimes more enlightening to trace the history of an idea backwards rather than forwards, I propose to start with one or two quotations from recent writers and then show how earlier writers viewed the evidence. In his book *The Christian View of Science and Scripture,* Bernard Ramm, whom I feel confident would disagree with a great deal that has been said in this paper, nevertheless gave the following statement with which I find myself in complete agreement:[282]

> Almighty God is creator. . . . In His mind the entire plan of creation was formed with man as the climax. Over the millions of years of geological history the earth is prepared for man's dwelling or as it has been put by others, "the cosmos was pregnant with man." The vast forests grew and decayed for his coal, that coal might appear a natural product and not an artificial insertion in Nature. The millions of sea life were born and perished for his oil. The surface of the earth was weathered for his forests and valleys. From time to time great creative acts, de novo, took place. The complexity of animal forms increased. Finally when every river had cut its intended course, when every mountain was in its purposed place, when every animal was on the earth according to blueprint, then he whom all creation anticipated is made, MAN, in whom alone is the breath of God.

Similarly, Agassiz held that direct creative activity was necessary. He assumed that vast numbers of kinds of animals had become extinct since the beginning of life on this earth. He thought the only possible explanation of these layers was to assume that short catastrophic periods of mountain building would follow long and quiet ages. These catastrophes had occurred possibly a hundred times, absolutely wiping out every plant and animal over vast areas. Then after natural forces had settled down again following each wild crisis, the Creator would again create a new flora and fauna in the desolated area. Agassiz taught more separate, large-scale creative acts than any other man. It was his conviction that the Creator improved and repatterned the successive creations so that more complex forms followed simple ones.[283] Thus, in his *Essay on Classification,* 1859, he wrote:[284]

> Who can look upon such a series coinciding to such an extent, and not read in them the successive manifestations of a thought, expressed at different times in forms ever new and yet tending to the same end, onwards to the coming of Man, whose

[282] Ramm, Bernard, *The Christian View of Science and Scripture,* Eerdmans, Grand Rapids, Mich., 1954, p. 227.

[283] Agassiz: quoted by Henry Marsh, *Studies in Creationism,* Review and Herald Pub. Co., Washington, 1950, p. 34.

[284] Agassiz, Louis, *Essay on Classification,* 1859, pp. 166, 167.

advent is already prophesied in the first appearance of the earliest fishes.

And again, Agassiz wrote:[285]

It is evident that there is a manifest progress in the succession of beings on the surface of the earth. This progress consists in an increasing similarity to the living fauna, and among the vertebrates, especially in their increasing resemblance to man. But this connection is not the consequence of a direct lineage between the faunas of different ages. There is nothing like parental descent connecting them. The fishes of the Palaeozoic Age are in no respect the ancestors of the reptiles of the Secondary Age, nor does man descend from the mammals which preceded him in the Tertiary Age. The link of which they are connected is of a higher and immaterial nature; and their connection is to be sought in the view of the Creator Himself, whose aim in forming the earth, in allowing it to undergo the successive changes which geology has pointed out, and in creating successively all the different types of animals which have passed away, was, to *introduce* man upon the face of our globe. MAN IS THE END TOWARDS WHICH ALL THE ANIMAL CREATION HAS TENDED FROM THE FIRST APPEARANCE OF THE PALAEOZOIC FISHES.

Sir Richard Owen, the great anatomist, had addressed himself also to the same issue. Gillispie set forth Owen's views as follows:[286]

Not less extraordinary but greatly more sound in their application are the views of Professor Owen — supreme in his own special walk as a comparative anatomist. We find him recognizing man as exemplifying in his structure the perfection of that type in which, from the earliest ages, nature had been working with reference to some future development, and therefore a foreordained existence. "The recognition of an ideal example for the vertebrate animals proves," says Owen, "that the knowledge of such a thing as man must have existed before man appeared; for the Divine Mind that planned the archetype also foreknew all its modifications. The archetypal idea was manifested in the flesh, under diverse modifications, upon this planet, long prior to the existence of those animal species that actually exemplify it."

Still earlier, Whewell had expressed himself thus:[287]

---

[285] Agassiz, Louis, in his *Principles of Zoology,* quoted by F. W. H., in *God's History of the World,* Nisbet, London, 1907, p. 149.

[286] Owen: quoted by G. C. Gillispie, in his *Genesis and Geology,* Harper Torchbooks, N.Y., 1951, pp. 204, 205. Owen was writing in 1849.

[287] William Whewell's views, in *The Veracity of Genesis,* Wm. H. Hoare, Longmans, Green, Longmans and Roberts, London, 1860 (p. 165), gives us this passage as from William Whewell's *Indications of the Creator,* Phila., 1845, pp. 161, 162.

We may form various hypotheses with regard to the sudden or gradual manner in which we may suppose the distribution to have taken place. We may assume that at the beginning of the present order of things, a stock of each species was placed in the vegetable or animal province to which it belongs, by some cause outside the common order of nature. . . .

At the beginning of each such cycle, a creative power was exerted of a kind to which there was nothing at all analogous in the succeeding part of the same cycle. . . .

Thus we are led by our reasonings to this view, that the present order of things was commenced by an act of creative power entirely different to any agency which has been exerted since. None of the influences which have modified the present races of animals and plants since they were placed in their habitations on the earth's surface can have had any efficacy in producing them at first.

Sir Humphrey Davy wrote in a similar vein:[288]

There seems, as it were, a gradual approach to the present system of things, and a succession of destructions and creations preparatory to the existence of man.

It is remarkable that centuries before this, Gregory of Nyssa (died c. 395) held a similar opinion:[289]

It was not proper that the chief should make his appearance before his subjects. The king should logically be revealed only after his kingdom has been readied for him, when the Creator of the Universe had, so to speak, prepared a throne for him who was to have dominion. . . . Then God caused man to appear in the world, both to contemplate the marvels of the Universe, and to be its master. . . .

Man was last to be created, not that he should be therefore contemptuously relegated to the last place, but because from his birth it was fitting that he should be king of his domain.

But here is another alternative: Lammerts and Sinclair have held that God needed only to create certain "building blocks" which took the form of mechanisms for the construction of all kinds of eyes, or legs, or internal organs, and that these were brought together in such a way as to interact and produce the different kinds of animals and plants we observe — but as God saw the need.[290]

---

[288] Davy: quoted by Gillispie in his *Genesis and Geology* (p. 131) from Davy's *Consolations in Travel,* 3rd ed., London, 1831, Dialogue iii.

[289] Gregory of Nyssa, quoted by C. Hauret, *Beginnings,* Priory Press, Dubuque, Iowa, 2nd ed., 1964, p. 53.

[290] Lammerts, W. and J. Sinclair, "Creation In Terms of Modern Concepts of Genetics and Physics," *Jour. Am. Sci. Affiliation,* 5, 3 (1953) : 8, 9.

There are quite a few modern writers who hold that it is presumptuous to deny the possibility of there being any divine activity involved, activity which will never be accounted for in terms of simple physics and chemistry. Thus Mascall has written:[291]

> Even if the individual mutations which are so important a factor in biological evolution are random, indeterminate, and "uncaused" from the point of view of physical theory, this does not mean that they have escaped from the primary creative causality of God. . . . To put the matter less technically, what appears from a scientific point of view as chance and indeterminacy is from the theological point of view the area within which God, when laying down the limits within which secondary causes are to operate under the overarching aegis of His primary causality, has left Himself free to act without reference to the patterns of secondary causes at all.

In other words, God can interfere if He wishes to do so without destroying the created order. Geneticists like Patterson and Stone do not deny that such a concept might prove necessary, but they are certainly not prepared to admit it at the present time:[292]

> The only alternative to evolution by selection among random mutations with the majority of the mutations detrimental at the time and place of their occurrence, is directed mutations to fit the needs of the organism, possible only under supernatural guidance, although this is seldom the name applied to the concept.

Weismann simply has reflected this unwillingness to admit metaphysical ideas and has justified himself by saying:[293]

> We accept *natural* selection not because we are able to demonstrate the process in detail . . . but simply because we must. . . . It is inconceivable that there could be yet another explanation capable of explaining the adaptation of organisms without assuming the help of a principle of design.

. . . which allows for a Designer! But not all modern authorities agree that mutations are an entirely satisfactory explanation. Thus Waddington writing on "Evolutionary Adaptation," observed:[294]

> Animals and plants in their innumerable variety present, of course, many odd, striking, and even beautiful features,

[291] Mascall, E. L., op. cit. (ref. 7), p. 16.

[292] Patterson, J. T. and W. S. Stone, *Evolution in the Genus Drosophila,* Macmillan, N.Y., 1952, p. 234.

[293] Weismann, August, quoted by P. Fothergill, *Historical Aspects of Organic Evolution,* Hollis & Carter, London, 1952, p. 118.

[294] Waddington, C. H., "Evolutionary Adaptation" in *Perspectives in Biology and Medicine* (Univ. Chicago) 2 (1959) : 380, 383.

which can raise feelings of surprise and delight in the observer. But over and above this, a very large number of them give the appearance of being astonishingly well tailored to fit precisely into the requirements which will be made of them by their mode of existence. Fish are admirably designed for swimming, birds for flying, horses for running, snakes for creeping, and so on, and the correspondence between what an organism will do and the way it is formed to carry out such tasks often extends into extraordinary detail.

And again:

> Induced mutagenesis as we normally encounter it in the laboratory does not provide any mechanism by which relatively normal environments could induce hereditary changes that would improve the adaptation of the offspring to the inducing conditions.

In short, laboratory experiment sheds no significant light on how this has come about, nor does even the environment (i.e., natural selection) *per se* account for it. He concluded:

> The field of work is clearly one of great inherent interest, but it remains true that the vast majority of changes in the environment do not directly produce any hereditary modifications in the organisms submitted to them, and we are certainly very far from being able to provide a general explanation of evolutionary adaptations in terms of the type of effects which have just been mentioned.

Finally, while "preadaptations" suggest a goal-seeking drive resident in nature, the existence of "gaps" in the great chain of being certainly suggests creative activity. For these gaps do exist between the phyla, orders, classes, etc., and in spite of every attempt to explain them away they still remain as an embarrassment to the evolutionist. The "great chain" is not a chain at all. Discontinuities exist of such magnitude that there is currently no other reasonable explanation of how the stream of life continued except to postulate creative acts to supply the needed bridges.

We are warned against introducing God at these places since they may one day be filled and He would then be "squeezed out." As they (hopefully!) disappear one by one, God is made smaller and smaller. But hitherto the pattern of discovery has not been encouraging to those who expect the gaps to be thus bridged. A useful treatment of these gaps as they currently exist will be found in another Doorway Paper.[295] Meanwhile the ques-

---

[295] Gaps: on this subject see an extended review with full documentation in "The Preparation of the Earth for Man" (in Doorway Papers Vol. IV).
Dr. R. E. D. Clark, in his book *The Christian Stake in Science*, Moody

tion is, Do we need to surrender this evidence of creative activity? If we are careful to remain aware of the fact that God is not merely the God of the gaps but the God of the continuities also, we shall not need to cast away what seems to me a very strong evidence of direct creation.

We do not believe in God simply because gaps exist which seem to demand a God to fill them. We know these gaps exist at present, and there seems every likelihood that they will persist, and so we merely say as Christians, "Such gaps may well be points at which God was at work in Nature by direct means." But those of us who are scientists do not find that such a faith requires of us that we avoid any further search for natural bridges over the gaps on the ground that we already have sufficient explanation. It is true that such a kind of faith may make the search less important, and that it therefore cuts at one of the main spurs to scientific research. But it supplies another compensatory one — the desire to explore God's handiwork in creation simply because *it is His handiwork.*

Thus we are not altogether unjustified in claiming the verdict of "not proven," when faced with the dogmatic assertion so commonly made these days that the concept of plan and purpose is not any longer justified in the light of modern knowledge. There is plenty of evidence in the natural order not only of divine planning and oversight from behind the scenes, as it were, but of direct creative activity. And there is evidence, too, of occasional drastic (one might say dramatic) "corrective" interference for the purpose of removing whole orders of life which no longer contributed towards the Master Plan to form a fit habitation for man. Two passages of Scripture come to mind. The first is in Isaiah 45:18:

Press, Chicago, 1967, pp. 28ff., has some worthwhile comments on the matter of pointing to "gaps" as being reasonable places where God may be presumed to have been at work. In his opinion there is very little danger of anyone losing their faith merely because some of the gaps have in the course of time been filled in. He rightly points out that while certain gaps have indeed been closed by an increase in knowledge, the same increase in knowledge has not narrowed but widened certain other gaps unexpectedly.

Similarly, Arthur Koestler in his new book, *The Ghost in the Machine,* Hutchinson, London, 1967, pp. 1-18, is at pains to show that, in psychology at least, the determination of the behaviorists to eliminate the gap between mind and brain caused that branch of research to become virtually sterile. So did the determination to remove the gap between human and animal behavior by extrapolating for the latter from the behavior of the former, a process which he calls "the ratomorphic view of man."

For thus saith the Lord that created the heavens; God himself that formed the earth and made it; he hath established it, he created it not in vain, he formed it to be inhabited: I am the Lord; and there is none else.

And the second, even more remarkable, occurs in Psalm 139:14-17:

I will praise thee; for I am fearfully and wonderfully made: marvellous are thy works; and that my soul knoweth right well.

My substance was not hid from thee, when I was made in secret, and curiously wrought in the lowest parts of the earth.

Thine eyes did see my substance, yet being unperfect, and in thy book all my members were written, which in continuance were fashioned, when as yet there was none of them.

How precious also are thy thoughts unto me, O God; how great is the sum of them!

EPILOGUE

FOR ME, the World View presented in this paper has been a satisfying one, providing a kind of skeletal framework about which to organize both my faith and my acquired knowledge. A very large proportion of the Doorway Papers contribute to it in one way or another, many of them being essential.

I have, however, passed over without comment one particularly important aspect of the Lord's total work on man's behalf: and this is His Second Coming.

The question that arises is, Why, with the completion of His sacrificial work and having once for all demonstrated unmistakably the love of God towards man, could He not have brought to an end the whole historical process? Of course, His Chosen People had failed to recognize Him as their Messiah. But why must the world still roll on century after century, filled seemingly with an ever growing malaise of fear, hatred, cruelty, sickness and poverty? After all, the refusal of Israel was a *national,* not a personal one. Individuals still believed.

Only one answer comes to me from Scripture, and it is based on Matthew 24:14: "This Gospel of the Kingdom shall be preached in all the world for a witness unto all nations — and *then* shall the end come." Perhaps if Israel had recognized their King, they would have become His messengers to tell the whole world. And who knows how soon all nations might then have heard? It was not enough that the demonstration of God's love be shown to one small fragment of the world's population. The news of it must go to every corner of the globe. Only *then* would the witness to the living be complete.

But Israel having failed, Japheth was called upon to take over their responsibility, dwelling for a season "in the tents of Shem" as Noah expressed it, to become the witnesses to the end of the world, for a period thenceforth to be known as "the times of the Gentiles." When that task is done, *then* the end will come. So far, it seems, in no single generation have all nations been reached with this testimony, for otherwise the end would have come already according to the Lord's own testimony.

Certainly the end will come. But it will really be more of a beginning than an end, for it will see the creation in due course of a new heaven and a new earth wherein dwelleth only righteousness and where sorrow and sighing will be no more — and where God shall wipe away all tears. Then shall we be called upon, in the presence of the only One who will still bear the marks of its cost, to make known to the angels (Eph. 3:10) what was the purpose of it all, that they, too, may comprehend in some measure the wonder of the grace of God....

Thus, by His first creative act, God *through Jesus Christ* (Col. 1:16) brought into being the first order of living creatures, the angels (Ps. 148:2 and 5). While they were dependent for their existence upon Himself, they were independent of time and space; for we know they were already in existence when God created the heavens (Job 38:4-7).

> Col. 1:16: "For by him were all things created, that are in heaven . . . visible and invisible."
> Ps. 148:2, 5: "Praise ye him, all his angels. . . . Let them praise the name of the Lord: for He commanded and they were created."
> Job 38:4, 7: "Where was thou when I laid the foundations of the earth . . . when all the angels [lit. "sons of God"] shouted for joy?"

By His second creative act, God *through Jesus Christ* (John 1:3) laid the foundations for the rule of law in a physical world bound by time and space (Gen. 1:1 and Heb. 1:8, 10). First He created living spirit; now He creates inert matter.

> John 1:3: "All things were made by him: and without him was not any thing made that was made."
> Heb. 1:8, 10: "But unto the Son he saith: . . . Thou, Lord, in the beginning hast laid the foundation of the earth."

By His third creative act, God *through Jesus Christ* brought into being a second order of living creatures, this time embedded in the physical order thus prepared, yet a little above its rigid determinisms, because they were to be guided by the "inspired knowledge" of instinct, a form of involuntary obedience, nevertheless a first step towards freedom (Gen. 1:21 and Col. 1:16).

> Col. 1:16: "For by him were all things created, that are in . . . earth."

By His fourth creative act, God *through Jesus Christ* introduced into this Cosmos an even higher order of living creatures, made at first in His own image, in whom instinct was replaced by a capacity for entirely voluntary obedience to His will (Gen. 1:27 and Isa. 45:12). Thus though, unlike the angels, man was dependent upon the processes of time and space, unlike the animals he was freed from even the compulsion of instinct.

> Gen. 1:27: "So God created man in his own image."
> Isa. 45:12: "I have made the earth, and created man upon it."

By His fifth creative act, God *through Jesus Christ* established a still higher order of creatures (Eph. 2:10) who, by a process of re-creation were not merely able to obey His will, but *earnestly desired to do so* by a new kind of restraint — the law written in their minds and in their hearts (Ps. 102:18; II Cor. 5:17; and Heb. 8:10).

> Eph. 2:10: "For we are his workmanship, created in Christ Jesus."
> Ps. 102:18: "The people which shall be created shall praise the Lord."
> II Cor. 5:17: "If any man be in Christ, he is a new creation."
> Heb. 8:10: "I will put my laws into their *mind,* and write them in their *hearts* . . . and they shall be to me a people."

And by His sixth creative act, God will yet make all things new, the earth and the earth's heavens (Rev. 21:1, 5) wherein perfect obedience to perfect law shall be altogether and everywhere fulfilled by all His subjects who become thereby perfectly free.

> Rev. 21:1, 5: "And I saw a new heaven and a new earth, for the first heaven and the first earth were passed away: . . . and He that sat upon the throne said, Behold, I make all things new."

In short, through JESUS CHRIST:

> The UNIVERSE was created for the WORLD,
> The WORLD for the BODY,
> The BODY for the SPIRIT,
> And, the SPIRIT for GOD.

> "Then cometh the end, when he (Jesus Christ) shall have delivered up the kingdom to God, even the Father. . . . Then shall the Son also himself be subject unto him that put all things under him, that God may be all in all" (I Cor. 15:24, 28).
> "O the depth of the riches both of the wisdom and knowledge of God! How unsearchable are his judgments, and his ways past finding out!" (Rom. 11:33).